Hong Kong Public and Squatter Housing

Royal Asiatic Society Hong Kong Studies Series

Royal Asiatic Society Hong Kong Studies Series is designed to make widely available important contributions on the local history, culture and society of Hong Kong and the surrounding region. Generous support from the Sir Lindsay and Lady May Ride Memorial Fund makes it possible to publish high-quality works that will be of lasting appeal and value to all, both scholars and informed general readers, who share a deeper interest in and enthusiasm for the area.

Recent titles in the series:

A Pattern of Life: Essays on Rural Hong Kong by James Hayes, edited by Hugh D. R. Baker (2020) (City University of Hong Kong Press)

A Stormy Petrel: The life and Times of John Pope Hennessy by P. Kevin MacKeown (2020) (City University of Hong Kong Press)

Grounded at Kai Tak: Chinese Aircraft Impounded in Hong Kong, 1949–1952 by Malcolm Merry (2022) (Hong Kong University Press)

More than 1001 Days and Nights of Hong Kong Internment: A Personal Narrative by Chaloner Grenville Alabaster; edited by David St Maur Sheil, Kwong Chi Man, and Tony Banham (2022) (Hong Kong University Press)

My Dearest Martha: The Life and Letters of Eliza Hillier, edited by Andrew Hillier (2021) (City University of Hong Kong Press)

Settlement, Life, and Politics—Understanding the Traditional New Territories by Patrick H. Hase (2020) (City University of Hong Kong Press)

War and Revolution in South China: The Story of a Transnational Biracial Family, 1936–1951 by Edward J. M. Rhoads (2021) (Hong Kong University Press)

Hong Kong Public and Squatter Housing

Geopolitics and Informality, 1963–1985

Alan Smart and Fung Chi Keung Charles

Hong Kong University Press
The University of Hong Kong
Pok Fu Lam Road
Hong Kong
https://hkupress.hku.hk

© 2023 Hong Kong University Press

ISBN 978-988-8805-64-8 (*Paperback*)

All rights reserved. No portion of this publication may be reproduced or transmitted in any form or by any means, electronic or mechanical, including photocopying, recording, or any information storage or retrieval system, without prior permission in writing from the publisher.

British Library Cataloguing-in-Publication Data
A catalogue record for this book is available from the British Library.

Digitally printed

Contents

List of Illustrations	vi
List of Tables	vii
Preface	viii
Acknowledgments	xiv
Abbreviations	xvii
Map of Hong Kong in 1984	xviii
1. Introduction	1
2. Informality	26
3. Evaluating the Geopolitical Explanation	50
4. The Situation in the Early 1960s	66
5. Riots and Reforms	87
6. The Mangle of Policy Practice	108
7. Supply, Demand, and Failures	128
8. Hong Kong Identity and Squatter Exclusion	153
9. Squatter Area Improvement	183
10. The Squatter Occupancy Survey	209
11. Managing Squatting in Other Asian Cities	228
12. Conclusions	250
Notes	267
Bibliography	290
Index	317

Illustrations

Figures

Figure 1.1:	Squatter area, Yau Tong, Kowloon, 1983	2
Figure 1.2:	Mark II resettlement housing, Kwun Tong, 1982	17
Figure 2.1:	Illegal extensions to private buildings, 1982	45
Figure 2.2:	Pavement squatters in Shek Kip Mei	47
Figure 2.3:	Map of authorized pavement squatting, Cheung Sha Wan	47
Figure 4.1:	Diamond Hill squatters and prewar concrete buildings, 1983	76
Figure 4.2:	Diamond Hill field and houses, 1983	77
Figure 7.1:	Temporary Housing Area, Kwun Tong, 1983	132
Figure 7.2:	Transit Centre, Kowloon, 1999	139
Figure 8.1:	Government publicity materials, "Building Homes for a Hong Kong Million"	155
Figure 8.2:	Public housing flats allocated from 1974–1975 to 1984–1985	166
Figure 8.3:	Demands for temporary housing areas from 1973–1974 to 1978–1979	169
Figure 9.1:	Illegal electrical wiring, Chai Wan	189
Figure 9.2:	Electrification, Sau Mau Ping squatter area, 1983	203
Figure 10.1:	Squatter population registration form	221
Figure 12.1:	Squatter structures, Chuk Yuen Heung, Kowloon, 2019	255
Figure 12.2:	Structure with squatter survey markings, Ngau Chi Wan, Kowloon, 2019	255

Map

Map of Hong Kong in 1984	xviii

Tables

Table 8.1: List of eligible categories for public housing before and after 1973 — 162

Table 10.1: New rehousing arrangement after the SOS in 1984 — 222

Preface

This book resolves questions that emerged from my doctoral and subsequent research and offers a new lens on postwar Hong Kong. After four decades of failing to end new squatting after the Second World War, and with their numbers climbing to over 750,000 in 1982, the colonial Hong Kong government finally succeeded after 1984. A key part of this success was the 1984–1985 Squatter Occupancy Survey (SOS), the first time that the residents of squatter areas had been registered, rather than just their structures. Its importance was that, afterward, only those occupants registered at this time were eligible for resettlement in permanent public housing. It played a crucial role in the turning of the tide against squatting. Similar shifts occurred in the same period against other forms of informality, which reveal a trend toward formalization.

This preface removes from the main narrative of the book autobiographical details of how the research questions it answers were developed. It also addresses theoretical issues of disclosing plausible explanations in the absence of compelling documentary proof.

This book is based on archival research since 2012, supported by more than 26 months of ethnographic and interview research on squatters and squatter clearance in Hong Kong since 1982, a previous major archival project on the origins of the Squatter Resettlement Programme, and MPhil research on colonial governance by Fung Chi Keung Charles. The 30-year rule for access to confidential government documents allowed reading of files that were being generated behind my back while I was conducting anthropological participant observation in the Diamond Hill squatter area in Hong Kong from 1983 to 1985. An important policy change in squatter administration, the Squatter Occupancy Survey, occurred in the middle of my field research, providing an opportunity to challenge and expand my account of the political economy of squatter housing and squatter clearance (Smart 1988). Anomalous squatter property—illegal but bearing socially legitimate value—developed a distinctive informal real estate regime (Smart 1985, 1986), but that system could not persist in its prior form after the new regulatory regime instituted through the SOS.

My funded research proposal to Canada's Social Sciences and Humanities Research Council (SSHRC) asked how and why this Survey was conducted, breaking past bureaucratic precedent. That proposal was supported by a plausible geopolitical explanation of the adoption of that Survey, and more generally the formalization of informality. Prior research had been unable to uncover any smoking guns to support a geopolitical explanation. But I had high hopes for the opening of the files for 1984 and the 1980s more generally. The archival research attempted to evaluate the adequacy of the geopolitical explanation. A key part of this effort was to look for rival explanations not already considered. The archival methodology involved reading or photographing every document that referred to squatter or squatting or other variants, examining every alternative keyword that seemed directly or peripherally connected to my questions and concerns, then pursuing leads that emerged from this reading. I also consulted widely with Hong Kong experts who were willing to offer insight into relevant issues and documents. Josephine Smart was the co-investigator on the project, following up on her doctoral ethnographic research on illegal street vendors in Hong Kong, carried out from 1982 to 1985. While some issues around street vendors will be discussed in this book, the bulk of that analysis and documentation will be the subject of a later book. Their dynamics of formalization took a different trajectory, in part because vendors did not prevent the development of land, only impeding the movement of traffic and pedestrians. Both were seen, however, as posing risks to public safety and public order, while jeopardizing the modernizing look of the rising city.

Charles Fung's involvement in the project began in mid-2020. The outbreak of the COVID-19 pandemic around early 2020 posed a research challenge due to worldwide travel restrictions. Against this backdrop, I asked for his help to access files from the Hong Kong Public Records Office. Previous experience of doing archival research, including the tacit knowledge of locating relevant materials in the Public Records Office, enabled Fung to find unexplored files that I had not been aware of. Before coming aboard the project, he had already done research on colonial governance in Hong Kong. While his MPhil research was about colonial fiscal policy implemented in postwar Hong Kong and Singapore, he continued to explore other relevant topics, including Hong Kong's external relations and the Chinese as an official language movement in the early 1970s.

The collaboration became more ambitious when Fung started to offer ideas about alternative explanations. He suggested that the colonial government's decision to exclude recent Chinese immigrants from obtaining public housing flats was undertaken in the name of being fair to the local people. His earlier research on the changing governing strategy of the colonial government before and after the riots in the 1960s argued that the imperative of promoting loyalty was a crucial factor that made the colonial authority become more responsive to popular demands. In this light, he then wondered if the change of eligibility for permanent public housing, which also exacerbated the problem of housing shortages in the early 1980s, had to do with the local identity/political loyalty that the colonial government tried to foster during the 1970s. Addressing these issues requires tracing the process of how the identity issue entangled with the housing policy, while trying to explicate the role of the colonial government more generally.

Explaining governmental actions and inactions presents large methodological problems. The public explanations given by serving government officers and politicians rarely present more than a portion of the underlying motivations and contexts. Subsequent memoirs can offer useful accounts, but generally are written with self-serving objectives. Even for the most scrupulous and honest of retrospective commentaries, memories shift over time while what is discussed is influenced by priorities, concerns, and issues at the time of writing, including normative bias (the natural tendency to present one's actions as fitting with preferred norms). Interviews with serving officials suffer from the need to support the "party line": no one has an interest in making public that their practices do not fully conform to policy. Interviews with retired officers can be invaluable in getting at more sensitive issues, but details fade over the years. I have had interviews where the original confidential documents were more vibrant, precise, and illuminating than vaguer recollections of what was going on decades earlier. We quote these documents in depth because of this, as well as in acknowledgement that only specialist researchers will ever look at the originals (particularly since they have not yet been digitized). Memoirs can be invaluable, though, in providing crucial context for the discussions. Legal cases also sometimes offer moments of transparency and vantage points on otherwise unmentioned and taken for granted practices (Schneider and Schneider 1999; Chapter 9).

Confidential documents, including transcripts of key meetings, are the most valuable resource for finding insights into the play of debate among representatives of different agencies and viewpoints, particularly into what alternatives were considered to those eventually adopted. In the British Empire in the twentieth century, at least, files on specific issues were circulated, with relevant documents on the right side and a running commentary of minutes added on the left, as the file passed from one desk or office to another. In my previous research on the beginning of Hong Kong's public housing program (one of the largest and most successful in the world, sheltering 45% of Hong Kong's current 8 million population) in the 1950s, these policy files were a treasure trove, full of candid commentary and disagreement in which decisions could go from being considered impracticable and undesirable to becoming essential, sensible solutions. However, the archival rule in the 1950s

Preface

was that confidential documents would only be released after 50 years; most of those involved would be dead or at least retired by the time the material came to light, facilitating very frank and illuminating discussions. Freedom of information rules, and the change from 50 years to 30 years for release in Hong Kong, although in principle desirable, have had the unintended consequence of discouraging officials and politicians from writing down potentially dangerous comments on paper. Even email has become problematic, encouraging face-to-face discussions on sensitive issues, as well as innovations such as the use of removable Post-it®Notes on documents (Sharma 2018).

When I began intensive archival research on the 1980s files released after 2010, the rich materials uncovered in the files for the 1950s and 1960s seemed to be thinner and less thought-provoking. This might have been the result of self-censorship in the corridors of power, but in recent years, another possibility became disturbingly revealed: the extent of "sterilization" of files as part of the decolonization process. I first heard about the sanitizing of the Hong Kong Archive from a senior civil servant, but interpreted it as involving sensitive files being transferred to the National Archives in London to prevent them falling into the hands of the Chinese Communist Party in 1997.[1] It was only with the public scandal generated by the work of Caroline Elkins (2005) that it became clear that there was something more systematically distorting of history going on with the disposition of colonial records. Elkins revealed the preindependence systematic destructions of files about detention centers and pervasive torture during the Mau Mau Rebellion in Kenya. Ian Cobain (2016, loc. cit., 156–162) documented that such actions were common in other British colonies prior to independence. The end of the Empire was "accompanied by an extraordinarily ambitious act of history theft, one that spanned the globe, with countless colonial papers being incinerated or dumped at sea." This was "Operation Legacy . . . intended to erase all trace of the darker deeds of Britain's colonial enterprise."

The Foreign Office's invisible cache of historical records took up 15 miles of floor-to-ceiling shelving, many of which were migrated to a high-security intelligence facility in Hanslope Park, rather than made available through the National Archives. There were 50 meters of Hong Kong papers (Cobain 2016). In 2011, Foreign Secretary William Hague requested Anthony Cary to conduct an internal review into the migrated archives. Cary reported that with the flurry of decolonization—as set out in a Colonial Office guidance telegram of 3 May 1961 on the disposal of classified records—successor governments should not be given papers that might embarrass governments, members of the Police, military forces, public servants or police informers; that might compromise sources of intelligence information; or that might be used unethically by the successor government (Cobain 2016).

The ending of geopolitical constraints on repressive action on squatters may still account for reduced toleration of illegal housing and attendant harsher clearance arrangements, particularly for those who moved into squatter dwellings after the Squatter Occupancy Survey in 1984. The problem might be that the documentation necessary to prove this has been destroyed or is still inaccessible. If so, how could a geopolitical explanation be either supported or rejected?[2] This raises the question of the "plausibility" of explanations. A plausible—as opposed to a demonstrated or proven—explanation is one that is consistent with all available relevant information and makes sense within an adequate theoretical framework but is not definitively supported by strong evidence. Once its plausibility is sufficiently established, the key question becomes whether it is better than all other rival plausible explanations.

Recent developments in abductive methodology, related to the critical realist philosophy underlying structuration theory (Sayer 1992; Bhaskar 2008), have been useful in grounding our search for explanatory plausibility. The idea of abduction derives originally from the work of Charles Sanders Peirce (1839–1914), an American philosopher central to the history of pragmatism and semiotics. Abduction involves the argument that a "surprising fact C is observed; There is reason to suspect that some hypothesis of kind K explains C; Hence, there is reason to suspect that some hypothesis of kind K is true" (Niiniluoto 1999, S440). "Abduction" is used in two different senses. In both senses, the term refers to some form of explanatory reasoning. Historically, it refers to the place of explanatory reasoning in generating hypotheses, while in the sense most frequently used in later literature it refers to the place of explanatory reasoning in justifying hypotheses. In the latter sense, abduction is also often called Inference to the Best Explanation. Hypothetic inference for Peirce "is not only a method of discovery but also a fallible way of justifying an explanation. Thus, in the strong interpretation, abduction is not only an inference to a potential explanation but to the best explanation" (Niiniluoto 1999, S443).

Abductive reasoning—distinguished from both inductive and deductive reasoning but drawing from the strengths of both—is a "form of inference that takes us from descriptions of data patterns, or phenomena, to one or more plausible explanations of those phenomena" (Haig 2008, 1020). Phenomena are uncovered that surprise, since they do not follow from any accepted hypothesis or theory, such as the sudden end to new squatting in Hong Kong in 1984, despite continual failures to achieve this at large expense for three decades. The challenge differed from that in my earlier work on the beginnings of Hong Kong's squatter resettlement program in 1954. These efforts entailed first evaluating, and rejecting, a number of proposed rival explanations. After that, work turned to developing an alternative account that adequately explained the phenomenon while also providing a reasonable

Preface

verification of its veracity to the historical events and processes. In our current effort, there are no extant explanations for the turning of the informal tide after 1984, nor discussions of the role of the SOS in enabling the shift, other than Smart's earlier commentaries (Smart 1988, 1989b).

Once the initial plausibility of an explanation is accomplished, "attempts are made to elaborate on the nature of the causal mechanisms in question. This is done by constructing plausible models of those mechanisms by analogy with relevant ideas in domains that are well understood. When the theories are well developed, they are assessed against their rivals with respect to their explanatory goodness. This assessment involves making judgments of the best of competing explanations" (Haig 2008, 1019–1020). Following these precepts is much less clear-cut than it would be in a laboratory science, but we have attempted comparable procedures. Rather than a formal model, we need to generate a sufficiently robust account of the nature of governmental organization and process in a particular kind of state (colonial) at a particular time and place. From this, we can identify apparently causal mechanisms. Ultimately we needed to combine multiple explanations to adequately account for the outcomes and the paths taken to get there.

The pathway to understanding the pivotal turn of 1984 and its place in the history of modern Hong Kong was complex and winding. Our hope is that our description of it will both convey the reasons for that complexity and try to make the journey as clear and enjoyable as possible. Microhistories (see Chapter 1) and ethnographies alike burrow into the minutiae of everyday life, or everyday policymaking, to shine new lights onto distinctive experiences. In this case, a history of the pathways that led to the end of new squatting reveals how the policy discussions—and the multiple influences on them—moved through multiple waves of "solutions," failures, and gradual awareness of what needed to be done to end what the policymakers called the "squatter problem." Things could have been very different, as we discuss in the penultimate Chapter 11, which uses Hong Kong's experience to consider varying pathways in other Asian cities.

Alan Smart

Acknowledgments

Acknowledging everyone that deserves it for a project that is 10 years old and derives from research done periodically over the last 40 years, is practically impossible. So, we start by thanking most humbly all those we have neglected to mention by name. We turn first to those we acknowledge together, then finish with two final sections, first by Charles and second by Alan. In particular, we are very grateful to the two anonymous readers for Hong Kong University Press—whose meticulous comments have greatly improved the book, even if we could not adopt all of the suggestions—as well as to the advice offered by the staff at the Press. Others who have read and commented on early drafts of chapters or the full manuscript are Rachelle Alterman, Tim Bunnell, Kenneth Cardenas, John Carroll, Richard Harris, Michael Herzfeld, Xyrus Ho, Geerhardt Kornatowski, Martijn Koster, Li Pengfei, Florence Mok, and Sarah Muir. After the first draft of the manuscript was completed, we presented the results and received important feedback at the Hong Kong Studies Annual Conference, Nanyang Technological University, and Osaka City University. Heesup Kim put together the map included in the book. Choi Mei Kei Maggie offered her editing support.

This book would not have been possible without the professionalism and assistance of the staff at the Hong Kong Public Records Office and the National Archives (London). In particular, our sincere gratitude goes to the Hong Kong Public Records Office, Government Records Service for giving us the permission to include images from archival files in this book.

Charles is grateful to many persons and scholars, without which his involvement and output in this project would not be possible. To list them in sequential order might create a false impression that someone's contribution might be greater than others, this is obviously not what Charles meant. Nonetheless, his gratitude must first go to Alan and Lui Tai-lok. Without Lui's introduction and Alan's invitation, he might not be able to work with an excellent scholar whose works are always the source of intellectual inspiration. Doing archival research could be demanding and this is especially the case during a time when the world is under pandemic. Unfortunately, he got infected when

Acknowledgments

Hong Kong experienced the fifth wave of COVID-19. Yet, Alan was patient enough to wait until he fully recovered to continue to work on the project. For this, he is truly grateful.

Charles would also like to thank members of the Hong Kong Studies Study Group, for which the intellectual environment offered by each seminar is always stimulating. He is also thankful to Lee Chun-wing, Florence Mok, and Kent Lee for their encouragement. Bernard Hui provided the most useful suggestions during his visit to the Hong Kong Public Records Office in Kwun Tong. Last but not least, Charles would also like to express his deepest appreciation to his parents, Fung Lai Ping and Lam Siu Hing, for their unconditional support and for Janet Ho Sze Hang's supreme caretaking, as always.

The debts by Alan for the initiation of this research program go back to his doctoral research from 1982 to 1985, as well as to the hospitality, knowledge, and wisdom offered generously by the inhabitants of Diamond Hill and other squatter settlements; workers at the Neighbourhood Advice-Action Council and Society for Community Organization; and various members of the Hong Kong government. It was during this period that he first began to understand the significance of the Squatter Occupancy Survey, as well as the broader context of the ending of new squatting during that period. This initial research was supported by Emergency Planning Canada, while ethnographic research in 1997–1999, archival research in the early 2000s, and the current project were supported by Social Sciences and Humanities Research Council grants and the University of Calgary. The hospitality of his brother-in-law Eric Yau and sister-in-law Eliza Lok, with whom he often stayed during the research, was also of great assistance.

The continuing advice of many scholars in Hong Kong, Canada, and elsewhere have helped to shape this project in diverse and crucial ways. Most important has been Alan's co-researcher, frequent co-author and life partner, Josephine Smart. Filippo Zerilli was a valuable collaborator on the project, and our collaborative publications were key for moving forward the theoretical perspectives deployed here. Ernest Chui helped develop the concept of the ratchet of exclusion, as Thomas Aguilera did with developing the typology of forms of toleration. Those who he received advice and encouragement from in relation to this project specifically include Chris Airriess, Brian Aldrich, Aaron Ansell, Bian Yanjie, Michael Blim, Kate Browne, Carmen Bueno Castellanos, Ken Burns, Ines Calor, Stephen Chiu, Cecilia Chu, David Clayton, Dean Curran, Deborah Davis, Denis Dwyer, Matthew Erie, Ray Forrest, Leo Goodstadt, Udo Grashoff, Tiana Hayden, James Hayes, Joe Heyman, Huang Gengzhi, Huang Shumei, Jiang Wen, Graham Johnson, Lawrence Lai, George Lin, Walter Little, Loh Kah Seng, Setha Low, Lui Tai-lok, Jeff Martin, Gordon Matthews, Lynne Milgram, Byron Miller, Art Murphy, Chris Panella, Martha Rees, Ian Scott, Hyun Banh Shin, Alvin So, Jesook Song, Tang Wing-Shing,

Alina Tanasescu, Eliot Tretter, Anne Varley, Vesna Vucinic, Woody Watson, Tammy Wong, Wu Weiping, Biao Xiang, Ray Yep, and Yip Ngai-ming.

Early results of the project were presented in a variety of venues, at which participants and audience members provided important feedback and suggestions. These include the Innovation Harbour Lecture Series at Xi'an Jiaotong University, Nanjing University, University of Macau, Urban China Research Network conference at Wuhan University, University of North Carolina Greensboro, University of Manchester, Oxford University, City University of Hong Kong, University of Hong Kong, Chinese University of Hong Kong, the workshop on "Comparative Approaches to Informal Housing around the World" in London, the Canadian Anthropology Society, the University of Toronto, the Wenner-Gren Foundation workshop on the Anthropology of Corruption at Sintra, Portugal, the European Association of Social Anthropology, the American Anthropological Association, the workshop on "Illegality Regimes—Mapping the Law of Irregular Migration" at Amsterdam, the World Customs Organization Research Conference on "Informality, International Trade and Customs" at Brussels, the City University of New York Graduate Center, the "Norms in the Margins of the State" conference at Brussels, the workshop on "Colonial Governance in Hong Kong, 1960–1984," York University, UK, and the Society for Economic Anthropology conference. Alan's publications in a variety of journals and books substantially moved the project forward. Since the influence of those publications is rarely direct, and substantial portions are not included without substantial modifications, they are not individually acknowledged here, but rather through the traditional academic practice of citing or quoting them where needed.

Abbreviations

CDO	City District Officer
CO	Colonial Office
CS	Colonial Secretary
ExCo	Executive Council
FCO	Foreign and Commonwealth Office
GCO	Geotechnical Control Office
GLCH	Government low-cost housing
HA	Housing Authority
HD	Housing Department
HDB	Housing & Development Board (Singapore)
HK	Hong Kong
HKPRO	Hong Kong Public Records Office
IPA	Intensive patrol area
JJ	*Jhuggi jhopri* (Hindi)
LDC	Least Developed Countries
LegCo	Legislative Council
NHA	National Housing Authority (Philippines)
NT	New Territories
PH	Public housing
PPH	Permanent public housing
PRC	People's Republic of China
SAI	Squatter Area Improvement Program
SOS	Squatter Occupancy Survey
TH	Temporary housing
THA	Temporary housing area

[Note: $ refers to Hong Kong dollars, which were trading at HK$7.70 to USD$1 on 3 January 1984]

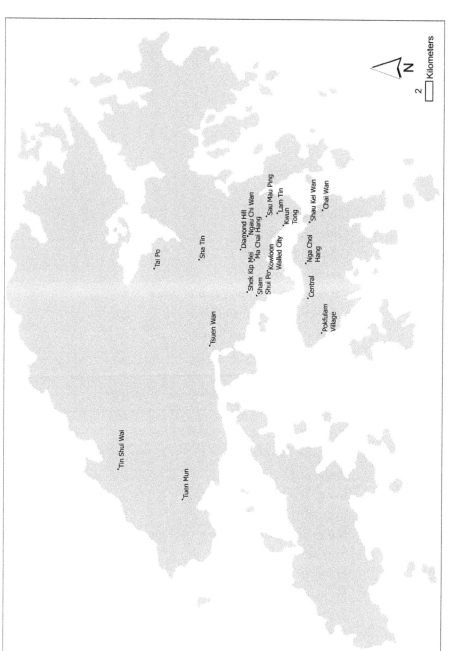

Map of Hong Kong in 1984 with places mentioned in the book

1
Introduction

> Change can never be disentangled from continuity because it is constitutive
> of it: the two together define the experience of historical process.
>
> —Alice Yao, *The Ancient Highlands of Southwest China* (2016, 36)

This book reveals how Hong Kong, after decades of failing to resolve the
"squatter problem," finally succeeded in ending new squatting after 1984.[1] It
has also gradually decreased the numbers of squatters from a peak of about
750,000 in 1982 (Figure 1.1), although there are still over 200,000.[2] This
might seem to some a marginal topic, but that would neglect the global and
local consequences of squatting. Globally, there are over 1 billion squatters
(Neuwirth 2005), and the numbers may be continuing to rise, with immense
consequences in diverse policy domains. Locally, we will demonstrate how
the management of Hong Kong's squatters and squatter areas has played a
major role in structuring the kind of landscape, government, and society that
emerged in the four decades after 1949.

Informality was central to Hong Kong experience and development prior
to 1984, and to a considerable extent afterwards as well. Despite government
opposition, it made major contributions to Hong Kong's economic and social
miracles in the period after the Second World War. It was also of great importance in other colonial and postcolonial cities, with vast attention to it for
the latter overshadowing considerable neglect for the former.[3] Informality
involves practices that do not conform to the prevailing rules and regulations,
but where goods, services or other practices are not inherently illegal, such
as producing informal housing rather than contraband drugs. Up to 80% of
paid work in the Global South is informal (Jütting and Laiglesia 2009, 13),
but if we expand the scope to include unpaid work such as domestic labor,
then more than half of all work globally might be informal. While there are
strong forces and reasons for the expansion of informality, national governments and supranational agencies are strongly promoting the formalization of
informality, either through making informal practices legal (regularization),
or through eradication and eviction, which was the dominant route in Hong

Figure 1.1: Squatter area, Yau Tong, Kowloon, 1983. Copyright and provided by Alan Smart.

Kong (Smart and Smart 2017a). Hernando de Soto (2000) has convinced many international development policymakers and think tanks that the key to poverty reduction is turning informal assets into formal capital, which can be leveraged through loans and other benefits.

Research on informality began with the idea of the informal sector, as opposed to the formal sector of firms included in government statistics and conforming to regulations. Keith Hart (1973) introduced the term "informal sector" in 1971. He used the concept to demonstrate, counter to then-current development ideas, that the urban poor were not unemployed, but instead working in ways that were unregulated by law and invisible to bureaucracy. The International Labor Office presented the informal sector as an opportunity for development, but conceived it as a separate sector of small-scale, low-productivity, low-income activities without benefit of advanced machines. Later research demonstrates that it is not a distinct sector of the economy (Hart 2010; Roy 2005). It is more useful to see informality as a different way of doing things. It is to varying degrees ubiquitous, but often mostly invisible and deniable. The dominant debates on informality and what to do about it were for too long based on dichotomous formal/informal, regular/irregular, or legal/illegal lines, where government/law equates to formality. This echoes the Global North/Global South divide in which the North stands for formality

Introduction

and the South represents informality (Harris 2017). Formality and informality, in such views, are considered domains that oppose and often exclude each other, often to the extent of being defined as polar opposites on a composite range of characteristics.

Ethnographic studies have demonstrated how formality and informality coexist, portraying their entanglement with each other in their formation and transformation (Heyman 1999; Lomnitz 1988; Smart 2001; Smart and Zerilli 2014). Keith Hart (2010, 148) describes formality and informality as inevitably intertwined, but usually in conflict. James Scott (1998, 310) emphasized the inseparability of the formal and the informal: "the formal order . . . is always and to some considerable degree parasitic on informal processes, which the formal scheme does not recognize, without which it could not exist and which it alone cannot create or maintain." Analytically, it is better to think in terms of a duality, with a spectrum of degrees of formality and informality, rather than a dichotomy (Guha-Khasnobis, Kanbur, and Ostrom 2006; Koster and Smart 2019). The position of any particular practice or situation on this spectrum depends on context and the ability of people to legitimize their actions as conforming to prevailing rules.

Many dualistic approaches suffered from using multifactor definitions of the informal sector, lumping together such features as labor-intensity, unsophisticated technology, and failure to follow regulations. These do not necessarily covary. For example, insider trading can use extremely sophisticated forms of financial engineering and large amounts of capital yet adopt informal, if not illegal, practices. It also operates in the gray areas between clearly legal and illegal (Smart 2021a). One result of the dichotomy was to generally equate the informal sector with the poor and marginal, and by implication assume that it did not exist among the rich and powerful. As a result, we know much less about informality among the middle classes and the elite (Browne 2004; Calor and Alterman 2017; Morris and Polese 2015). A single factor definition of the informal economy is much more useful than one that assumes multiple factors uniformly covary. One of the most viable single factor definitions is to see informality as including practices where the goods and services transacted are legal, but the ways in which they are transacted are not (Portes, Castells, and Benton 1989). This approach distinguishes informality from both formality and from the illegal economy, which consists of those fields in which the goods or services themselves are illegal, such as contraband drugs, fencing stolen goods, and so on.

Even the most formal institutions have informal practices (Smart 2018a). The Western judiciary is perhaps the most formal of all, with its efforts to have all rules and their interpretation procedures clearly specified and uniformly applied, providing alleged equality before the law. Yet it still has important and pervasive informal practices and conventions, taken for granted in the daily practices of courts, such as the plea bargaining that keeps the system from being completely overwhelmed by the volume of cases. In other domains and places, informal work-arounds to cope with red tape and bureaucratic inflexibility are ubiquitous—and arguably indispensable. Practices of squatter control in Hong Kong have repeatedly been criticized by people like the Attorney General as lacking in legal foundation (see Chapters 4 and 10). Reforms of the overall policy making process in the 1970s attempted to regularize decision-making (see Chapter 5). While our focus is principally on squatter control, the effort to make sense of how and when key decisions were made requires us to also consider formalization within government itself.

While our project here focuses on the formalization of squatting, a similar process occurred with the "hawker problem"—street vendors illegally selling in the crowded streets of hyper-dense Hong Kong. Informal practices—such as squatter factories, manufacturing in domestic premises, and informal labor management through outwork (Lui 1994)—were a key part of Hong Kong's manufacturing miracle of the 1950s and 1960s, as well as its contribution to the economic miracle of China's Pearl River Delta after 1978 (Smart and Smart 2012). These dynamics, as well as those for other forms of informality that were important in colonial Hong Kong, are considered in Chapter 2.

We next provide a relatively brief discussion of the pathway to the ending of new squatting in Hong Kong, and more generally attempts by government to deal with the "squatter problem." Following that, we introduce the theoretical ideas that underpin our analysis. We end this chapter with an outline of the book as a whole.

Ending New Squatting

The tide turned against Hong Kong's informal housing in 1984. We argue that the registration of squatter occupants—and not just the structures in which they lived, which occurred then for the first time ever—was a big part of making this tipping point possible. This book describes how that event happened and why it happened then, in the way that it did. The path to formalization could have taken other routes, or even never been followed at all.

Hong Kong tried four approaches to formalize squatter areas. One kind of eradication was simply to demolish the structures and evict the residents. This was the only approach used before 1952, but it continued in some circumstances thereafter. The second kind of eradication, dominant after 1954, was demolition plus resettlement. This made the clearance of squatter areas much easier but did not end new squatting. The first approach that involved regularization was tenure change, providing some kind of title or formal security to squatter structures without their having to meet conventional regulations. This was discussed periodically from 1970 but never implemented in

Introduction

the urban areas.[4] The second type of regularization was improvement, which in Hong Kong not only kept the structures themselves illegal but prohibited the private improvement of existing, tolerated structures. Instead, it focused on improving the infrastructure in the area, attempting to reduce the visual squalor that attracted outside criticism, while reducing the risk of fire, landslides, and public health problems.

The core of our book examines the rationales behind the promotion, adoption, and rejection of each of these approaches, and how their consequences constrained and channeled the pathway to ending the squatter problem. These decisions had massive consequences for the landscape, political economy, and society that developed in postwar Hong Kong.

Hong Kong's pathway is perhaps unique, though most comparable to Singapore's (see Chapter 11), but it still has lessons for the continuing global situation of more than 1 billion squatters (Neuwirth 2005). Our main goal, though, is to unravel how the end of new squatting and formalization was achieved. A sustained methodological and theoretical focus on that question is used to draw conclusions about why it happened the way that it did. The consequences of this shifting tide will also be considered. We begin with what we have discovered to be a pivotal decision, and which has not previously been addressed by historians or other scholars of Hong Kong.

The clearest line to the 1984 Squatter Occupancy Survey (hereafter SOS)[5] and the end of the growth of squatter areas, takes us back to 1970, when the Governor of Hong Kong, David Trench, raised concerns over the conditions in squatter areas, specifically in areas not required for development.[6] This issue was prompted by high-level questions from the United Kingdom. In a memo to Hong Kong's Colonial Secretary (Hugh Norman-Walker), the second highest official in the Hong Kong bureaucracy, he reported that:

> You will recollect Mr. Heath's [Edward Heath, Prime Minister of the UK June 1970 – March 1974] concern over squatters, mentioned while here and conveyed to us recently by the Secretary of State [Sir Alec Douglas-Home]. Mr. Royle [Anthony Royle, Parliamentary Under-Secretary of State for Foreign and Commonwealth Affairs] has raised this with me again and has asked if we could not do something more about them: in spite of the fact that our whole corpus of argument on this general problem is accepted as valid.[7]

These were surprisingly high-level interventions into the "squatter problem." In addition to Prime Minister Heath's original concern, Douglas-Home was not only the Secretary of State for Foreign and Commonwealth Affairs but had been Prime Minister himself from 19 October 1963 to 16 October 1964, and leader of the Opposition for the following year, in which post he was succeeded by Edward Heath. Hong Kong had generally operated with a high degree of autonomy, in part because it characteristically operated with budget surpluses and did not require financial support from Britain. Economic success in a colony increased its autonomy, from both imperial oversight and local economic elites (Scott 1989). The exceptions to colonial autonomy tended to be when issues became public concerns or scandals within Britain itself or in Parliament (Ure 2012; Faure 2003a). Even in such cases, the Hong Kong government was usually able to deflect such metropolitan interventions with more modest reforms than those suggested, by explaining the local conditions that made more radical reforms impractical.

By the 1970s, however, London's[8] interventions had become more forceful and consequential. They were more successful at prompting action, but we will show that the kind of action undertaken was largely the outcome of local processes, constraints, and preferences. Hong Kong's massive public housing program, initially a squatter resettlement program, resulted not from pressure from the Colonial Office, but instead was the outcome of a learning process after other efforts failed to solve the squatter problem. Resettlement of squatters was an undesired and reluctantly adopted solution, conditioned by the way in which the geopolitical situation—a precarious colony on the edge of Communist China during the Cold War—made squatter clearance without resettlement impractical and risky (Smart 2006; Smart and Lam 2009).

It seemed reasonable that geopolitics might also offer an explanation for the turning point for the squatter problem that is the focus of this book: the effective ending of new squatting. The timing of the SOS made this explanation even more plausible, since it coincided with the negotiations for the Sino-British Joint Declaration on the Question of Hong Kong, signed on 19 December 1984. The UK transferred sovereignty over Hong Kong to the People's Republic of China (PRC) on 1 July 1997. The constraints posed by the threat of Chinese intervention in support of "oppressed" squatters disappeared in a context where Beijing, Guangzhou, London, and Hong Kong all shared interests in social and political stability in the transition to 1997. Research had located substantial documentary evidence, including several smoking guns, in support of the geopolitical explanation of the multistorey squatter resettlement beginning in 1954 (Chapter 3, Smart 2006).

In the research reported in this book, we have intensively looked for smoking guns and other evidence supporting a geopolitical explanation for the end to new squatting and the SOS, but without success. While it seems reasonable that more forceful options might have become available for dealing with the squatter problem because of geopolitical change, we have not found statements to demonstrate that this directly affected the decisions we are concerned with. While absence of evidence is not evidence of absence, it does complicate any argument that relies on a change in constraints on governmental actors. Instead, we broadened our search of the formerly confidential documents from the period, trying to make sense of how and why the crucial decisions were made. We reconstruct the path of choices and motivations that

Introduction 7

eventually lead to the SOS and more generally the policy choices that made possible the end of new squatting from 1984. From this research, we have generated a number of alternative explanations for the turning of the tide against informality, all of which seem plausible in one way or another. We develop and evaluate a range of explanations looking for the best possible one; that is, one that is both logically and empirically strong. Ultimately, we found that a combination of several explanations could be put together into a better account, with each contributing a different dimension of what was going on that led to the turning point.

Governor Trench's 1970 proposals sparked one of several pivotal policy discussions that we focus on in this book. These discussions and debates often result in formal reviews or new organizations through which problems are processed, squeezed into acceptable frames, and mixed up with other issues that are either connected or just hot at the same time. These discussions, decisions, and new procedures create the context in which new problems—or resurgences of old problems—generate, in turn, additional novel issues. The result is ramifying threads that link debates and decisions and that threaten to spin out of control, leading us into what Tim Ingold (2008) calls "meshworks"—widely interconnected tissues of entangled materials, problems, and causal chains. Our method is to find issues that promise to shed light on our basic question, try to make sense of those that appear to contribute to one of the four pathways to formalization, and follow them onward and outward through their consequences.

The discussions that Trench sparked in 1970 had major impacts on housing policy, most of which took place during the term of Governor Murray MacLehose. We chart the squatter problem's progress through bureaucratic circles, as documented in the many minutes and documents in the files, but also through how the actions and responses of squatters (as well as profit-oriented builders of squatter structures, "racketeers" in the official framing) troubled and often undermined governmental actions and objectives. Making conclusions about these questions from the various documents is a challenge; as Steiner (1969, x) says, "[e]ven when abundantly available, documents are only stones in a complex mosaic." This statement does not go far enough. Because the mosaic metaphor is static, it neglects the likelihood that the stones are sometimes more mirage than steppingstone, and that the patterns only emerge through time.[9] We prefer a different metaphor developed by science scholar Andrew Pickering (1995): the old-fashioned washing machine mangle, which helps dry laundry by squeezing out the water. For Pickering, scientific work is mangled through the resistance of the material world which must be worked with. We consider how certain kinds of policy deliberations, particularly investigative commissions and working parties, act as policy mangles, squeezing together distinct agendas and problems, sometimes leading to significant transformations. The path to the SOS involves a passage through a variety of different policy mangles, each of which refocuses the situation while creating new challenges and risks (see, especially, Chapter 6).

Our key empirical puzzle of the SOS might seem a technical issue, but it played a key role, and led to a complicated and productive search for evidence (e.g., Smart and Smart 2017a; Smart and Aguilera 2020). In this way, it fits the description of a microhistory as research that focuses on small units of research—such as an event, community, individual or a settlement—but which addresses larger issues through doing so, seeking to answer large questions in small places or issues (Magnússon and Szijártó 2013). In this case, we focus on a policy (requiring the registration of squatters for them to be eligible for resettlement) and an event (the carrying out of the SOS).

Applying the ideas of microhistory to policies is rare in the field (an exception is Brewer et al. 2011). This is likely because of the emphasis of microhistory on the mentalities and lifeways of groups left out of mainstream histories and criticism of emphasis on the history of battles, kings and policy-making elites (Magnússon 2003; Sahlins 2004). Microhistory struggles to retrieve the lives and thoughts of those who (for the most part) do not write documents and are distorted or unrepresented in official historical archives. If we were to attempt a more conventional microhistory, we would use the confidential documents we explore here as part of the process of giving voice to the voiceless—the squatters who were the target of governmental interventions. While we do this in part, it is not the main focus, since the book is building on intensive ethnographic research conducted with the squatters during the 1980s and, more briefly, in 1999. Rather, what we are concerned with is the official mentalities or culture that formed and transformed understanding of the squatter problem and offered contending suggestions about how that problem might be solved. The course of decision-making cannot be read from the official statements and reports, although they have value for our project. Like the preindustrial worldviews of Italian peasants, these official ways of making policy must be read through the tangled obscurity of multiple policy discussions and reactions to unexpected events such as landslides, fires, protest movements, and the unexpected resilience of the squatter problem in the face of intensive squatter control efforts. Robert Darnton (1985) advised that we should try to enter the cultures of the past at points where we do not understand something.

The attempt to comprehend how and why new squatting was ended after 1984 has driven this research project. Although the usual approach to microhistory would involve the attempt to reconstruct the ways of life and thought in the squatter areas through the distorted lens of the statements and reports produced by colonial officials, this is not necessary here, because of the prior ethnographic work.[10] Rather, it is the way in which the policies and decisions

Introduction

9

are transformed by the recalcitrance of the squatter problem that is crucial. This distortion is produced in part through the official (mis)understanding of who the squatters are and how they will react, as well as the risks posed by both excessively aggressive and encouraging policies and how they were implemented.

Reconstructing how the Survey might have come about parallels the challenges faced in *The Shek Kip Mei Myth* (Smart 2006), but the materials for the current reconstruction are less rich. The SOS's significance first became clear during ethnographic research in Hong Kong in 1985. Little was documented about it, and at that time research was restricted to the impact of the policy change, with no information about the source of the policy changes. At that time, Smart assumed the relevant confidential documents would eventually become available; getting the answers would simply require patience. In this expectation we have been disappointed, apparently victims of the "history thieves" who sterilized archives during decolonization (Cobain 2016). For example, Smart has copies of multiple reports collected from government departments during fieldwork from 1983 to 1985 (some used in this study), which have never emerged in an extensive study of relevant files. However, Fung's archival search skills located a wide variety of relevant materials, often in files with unpromising titles and descriptions.

A brief explanation of why the SOS made a difference is needed here, although a fuller appreciation of its importance requires the context and background provided in subsequent chapters. In April 1985, the Housing Department completed this territory-wide registration of all occupants of registered urban squatter dwellings. The new policy was that only these registered occupants would be eligible for resettlement in clearances, and any other occupants would have no rights of resettlement (see Chapter 10). Such a policy destroyed, in theory at least, the foundation of the widespread squatter property market which had evolved up to that point (Smart 1985, 1986), since buying a squatter dwelling would no longer entitle the new occupier to resettlement. In as much as the squatter property market was intimately involved with hopes of getting into public housing, or at least some form of compensation for clearance, the system of squatter dwelling exchange would necessarily be transformed. What was less clear at the time was what would be the result. The government's intention, unfulfilled, was to freeze the population of squatters as a step toward the long-term plan of eliminating all squatter structures in Hong Kong by 1995 (Hong Kong Housing Authority Annual Report, 1985–86, 84). With the new policy, even if more people moved into squatter areas, they would not thereby be eligible for permanent public housing (other than by possible increase in demand for temporary housing or space in transit centres, since they would be resettled if these were to be demolished for redevelopment). In addition, they would not prove an obstacle to the objective of eradicating squatter areas (except in terms of any possible physical or political resistance which they might undertake) by increasing the rehousing obligation. We show that this was a primary constraint on squatter clearance actions. Smart and Ernest Chui (2006) described this as a ratchet of exclusion, because the numbers of those eligible for resettlement in permanent public housing could only go down, except through births to registered occupants. Previously, political and geopolitical pressures and constraints had often increased the numbers of those eligible, despite various and frequent exclusionary efforts (see Chapter 7). We describe the conditioning geopolitics in Chapter 3, which evaluates the explanation based on geopolitics, particularly the removal of constraints that had inhibited prior solution of the squatter problem.

The Survey was important because it provided a key set of tools for the capping and eradication of the urban squatter settlements, freed up a large amount of extremely valuable land for development, and helped enable the creation of an urban landscape compatible with the promotion of Hong Kong as "Asia's global city" and as a showcase for modernity and efficient urbanity. Exactly how it contributed to ending the growth of squatting will become clearer once we explain why previous efforts to solve the squatter problem had been, at best, temporary. In addition, given its efficacy, we will also ask not only why it was adopted in 1984 but also why it was not used earlier.

While the core of this book is devoted to what happened and why it happened that way in colonial Hong Kong, the results are relevant for understanding experiences elsewhere, and for discussions of effective policy strategies for managing informality. Most postcolonial cities have failed to end new squatting, with Singapore an important exception. But most have also attempted to control it, while some have adopted ambitious formalization strategies of squatter titling. Some of the varying patterns will be described in Chapter 2, while Chapter 11 takes the findings of our research on Hong Kong and develops a model for comparing other approaches to squatting, focusing particularly on Asian cities.

Theoretical Approaches to Plausible Historical Explanations

For Michael Ball (1983, 17), housing provision is "the product of particular, historically determined social relations associated with the physical processes of land development, building production, the transfer of the completed dwelling to its final user and its subsequent use." The same can be said of informal or illegal housing, although the state of our knowledge about it is much less complete than it is for conventional housing in the developed countries (Smart 2020). In both domains, the historical structuration of the patterns of housing provision is crucial: interventions occur based on what has happened previously, and act upon the situation to create new outcomes

Introduction

and new problems (often referred to as *path dependency*). Analyses of squatting need to deal with the complexities of interactions between the occupants and producers of informal housing, considering them in the context of governmental interventions, including attempts to maintain or expand control over these areas. Such analyses require theoretical frameworks attentive to both the agency of the residents and the constraints imposed on their choices and actions by the dynamics of the social context. Contexts enable, as well as constrain, certain kinds of action, including illegal actions and governmental interventions that would not be possible if undertaken against holders of fully legal private property. To understand 1984's shift of the tide toward eradication of informal spatial use, we need to consider how structure and agency interact in a late colonial context. Historically, the dramatic changes during the 1960s and 1970s, particularly in reaction to the crises of the 1966 and 1967 riots, are the most important regulatory context for the issues addressed in this book, although the negotiations and agreements of the 1980s also had an impact on the final phases (see Chapters 4 and 5).

When Smart first conceived of the geopolitical explanation of formalization in Hong Kong (discussed in Chapter 3), he was working at the intersection of structuration and Marxian theories, both of which incorporate insightful historical perspectives. His doctoral and postdoctoral research concentrated on understanding the political economy of squatting and squatter clearance, not just to show how colonial states and capitalist modes of production structured the built environment of Hong Kong, but also to reveal the impact of the responses of squatters on governmental interventions and regulations. Anthony Giddens offered one way of bringing agency into the structuring and restructuring of the regime, although such ideas can be seen earlier in the work of Edmund Leach (1964). Our review of relevant scholarship is short and selective, because this is not primarily a theoretically driven book, but rather one that uses theory as a set of tools for understanding problems and puzzles.

Structuration theory argues that ideas of action and structure presuppose each other. Action is both enabled and constrained by structures, which consist of rules and resources that must be reproduced through social practices. Dualisms of individual/society or micro/macro need to be supplanted by the duality of agency and structure. Analytic and theoretical progress required the dethroning of rival imperialisms of the subject and the social object. Giddens argued that we could transcend these opposed positions by refocusing on social practices ordered across space and time, rather than prioritizing either individual experience or social totalities. Prior social theories had usually neglected space and had inadequate conceptualizations of time, so that both had to be elaborated as the contexts within which structuration linked action and structure. Social life occurs in and through intersections of presence and absence in the flow of time-spaces implicated with daily routines, which are part of the unfolding of daily life in serial and repetitive ways (Giddens 1984; Low 1996; Smart 2018).

Giddens has often been critiqued for ending up with a chicken and egg problem: Which comes first? The structures that enable practices? Or the practices that bring structures into being? Yet, in evolutionary terms, which came first is hardly unanswerable: an ancestor of the chicken laid an egg that was sufficiently different to be classifiable as a chicken. By incorporating history into structuration, we take a circle and stretch it out into an undulating wave, where structures enable practices and practices reproduce and transform structures in sequences extending back into the past and forward into the future. The study of societies becomes predominantly the theorization of history—particularly appropriate for the investigations in this book.

William Sewell (2005) notes that much of the best social history of the previous 40 years implicitly adopted approaches consistent with Giddens's structuration theory. Sewell is critical, though, of the conceptualization of structure in structuration theory. He believes the "rules" that are paired with resources in Giddens's definition would be better understood as schemas that can be generalized and transposable from one context to another. Resources, in turn, are not virtual but can be seen as effects of cultural schemas. Most importantly, he emphasizes the need to acknowledge that structures are multiple and intersecting, so that structures themselves are at risk in the social (and geopolitical) encounters they shape. Agency in turn arises from the actor's knowledge of schemas and ability to apply them to new contexts. Yet, this is not accomplished in any uniform way, and it is crucial to recognize, along with the Marxist critics, that structures empower agents differentially. The pluralization of structure is an essential move in making structuration theory more open and dynamic—indispensable features for our empirical project.

The dialogue between Marshall Sahlins (2004) and William Sewell (2005) provides key insights into classic questions in the theory of history about what makes something an event, and the relationship between structure and event. The dichotomy between event and structure is itself part of the problem (Smart and Smart 2009). In the traditional intellectual division of labor, events are the concern of historians, while social scientists tend to bracket events in the process of analyzing (relatively) enduring structures or systems within which those events occur (Wagner-Pacifici 2017). Events only become particularly relevant for this traditional version of sociology when they result in the transition from one system to another. Similarly, for Slavoj Žižek (2014, 9), the basic feature of an event is "the surprising emergence of something new which undermines every stable scheme." The no-man's-land between event and structure is the limbo in which sequences—such as a series of disasters, disturbances, or crises—tend to disappear from sight.

Introduction

In *Islands of History*, Sahlins (1985) attempted to overcome the dichotomy between event and structure. He argues that the cultural system is inherently historical, while history is inevitably cultural. A happening only becomes an event as it is "appropriated in and through the cultural scheme," and only if it does so will it "acquire an historical significance" (xiv). The "event is a relation between a happening and a structure (or structures): an encompassment of the phenomenon-in-itself as a meaningful value, from which follows its specific historical efficacy" (xiv). Series of events, such as the two visits of Captain Cook to Hawai'i, are culturally ordered according to meaningful schemes of things. Neither the framing of something as an event nor the linkages between them made by narrators can be analyzed without attention to these meaning-making systems.

While seeing Sahlins's work as the "most impressive and systematic theoretical discussion of the event," Sewell (2005, 198) identifies limitations and tries to transcend them. Most fundamentally, he rejects Sahlins's tendency to think about structure in the singular. In particular, "determining which happenings are to be regarded as events would be a far less haunting affair if structures were conceptualized as multiple rather than singular" (211). With a singular structure, the question is whether an incident that has "clearly changed the meaning and relations of categories in some particular corner of social relations is important enough to be called an event from the point of view of the cultural structure as a whole" (211). With a multiple conception of structures, that incident can simultaneously be an event from a local point of view and insignificant in a broader cultural formation. A singular conception of structure also makes acts of sense-making more automatic and less contingent (212). If actors commonly negotiate relations between "noncongruent cultural structures, it follows that they should have some intellectual distance on the structural categories themselves; that they should be able to view one set of cultural categories from the point of view of others that are differently organized," facilitating better understanding of human creativity (213).

In *Apologies to Thucydides*, Sahlins (2004) illustrates his theory by reference to two Major League Baseball (MLB) playoff victories: the World Series victory for the New York Yankees in 1939; and the famous triumph of the New York Giants in the 1951 National League Championship Series. Challenging the epistemological flatness of the structure/agency debate, Sahlins argues that people who can make a difference in cultural history are those who are "structurally empowered." It is "the 'position' in a system or a social situation that transmits the acts of certain authorized persons into fateful consequences for the community as a whole" (198). Bobby Thomson won the National League pennant for the underdog Giants with a home run in the last inning of the final game of the series, whereas the 1939 Yankees dominated the season from beginning to end and became the first team ever to win four consecutive

World Series Championships. The Yankees' win is best accounted for by an analysis of the structural development of a powerful team, whereas the Giants win ultimately came down to the performance of an individual. The Yankees' "pennant was developmental, where that of the '51 Giants was evenemential" (128). The latter term is based on Raymond Aron's idea of the history of events in which "[t]he event . . . that is to say the act accomplished by one or several men, localized and dated, is never reducible to the conjuncture, unless we eliminate, by thought, those who have acted and declare that anyone else in their place would have done the same" (quoted, 196). Sahlins is critical of Aron's argument as a "radical . . . brief for the disengagement of event from structure, of intentional action from cultural order—and so, beyond that, of narrative history from historical ethnography" (quoted, 196). What constitutes an event, and who can do something that counts as an historical event, is for Sahlins a property of the cultural structure. It is for this reason that he criticizes the social historical rejection of the history of kings and battles. Where we find a "structure that generalizes the action of the king as the form and destiny of the society," attending to kings and battles is not elitism but analytically necessary (Sahlins 1985, xi). Attending to Hong Kong's governors as well as poor squatter families can be seen in the same terms.

What Sewell calls "eventful temporality" acknowledges the power of events in history. While most human actions reproduce social and cultural structures without significant change, he argues that events are "that relatively rare subclass of happenings that significantly transforms structures" (Sewell 2004, 100). Events generate historical change by transforming "the very cultural categories that shape and constrain human action" (101). Change is possible primarily because of the multiplicity of structures, the transposability of cultural schemas from one context to another, and the unpredictability of accumulation of the resources on which reproduction depends (140–141).

Sewell usefully opens up the black box of events. Events are not instantaneous, their boundaries are uncertain until long after they have occurred, and the successful framing of an event determines its scale and scope. For our concern with pathways toward formalization in this book, his definition of events is useful but creates additional challenges: "sequences of occurrences that transform structures" (261). With this definition, "an occurrence like the assault on the Bastille will be implicated in the transformations of a number of different structures, and each of these transformations will have a different spatial and temporal range" (261). While bringing history, the series and sequence into the foreground, it also makes a "theory of the series" even more difficult, because it becomes necessary to clarify whether two incidents should be seen as part of a series, or components of a single event.

Is Trench's 1970 memo on squatters an event, or simply part of an event that includes the discussions that precipitated from it? For Sewell, "social

Introduction

temporality is extremely complex" because historical events "always combine social processes with very different temporalities" (9). Furthermore, events involve novel conjunctures or ruptures of structures in which actors are "attempting to make structural sense of a highly volatile situation" (223). If Trench's memo is an event, what kind of ruptures did it envision and produce? By a methodical reconstruction of the trajectory of the discussions activated by his memo, we try to understand its contribution to how Hong Kong turned this historical corner toward greater formality.

For Michel Foucault, the state only exists through practices, techniques, and programs. One contribution of the Foucauldian approach for our concerns in this book is its emphasis on the broader stakes and implications involved in what might be seen as mundane details. From street plans to sewage, scientific knowledge of hygiene and planning are applied to normalizing the urban environment in order to promote the welfare of the population (Rabinow 1995, 10). Governments use bureaucracies and new techniques to shape the conduct of members of a population. Pursuing this line of inquiry draws our attention away from abstract theories and toward concrete techniques and tactics. Doing so will be crucial throughout this book. Such ideas provide many useful starting points for the study of colonial administration, but also have limitations. In particular, Foucauldians have usually devoted much greater attention to procedures than to their implementation in difficult, often refractory, or resistant conditions. Colonies in some ways penetrated more intensively into the lives of individual peasants than home governments. Timothy Mitchell (1988, 8) proposes that because Foucault's work concentrated on France and northern Europe:

> this focus has tended to obscure the colonizing nature of disciplinary power. Yet the panopticon, the model institution whose geometric order and generalized surveillance serve as a motif for this kind of power, was a colonial invention. The panoptic principle was devised on Europe's colonial frontier with the Ottoman Empire, and examples of the panopticon were built for the most part not in northern Europe, but in places like colonial India.

As with prisons, the application of the Foucauldian perspective has tended to exaggerate the extent of control exercised by colonial administrations. For example, John and Jean Comaroff (1991, 5) state that colonizers:

> everywhere try to gain control over the practices through which would-be subjects produce and reproduce the bases of their existence. No habit is too humble, no sign too insignificant to be implicated. And colonization always provokes struggles—albeit often tragically uneven ones—over power and meaning on the frontiers of empire.

Colonizers may attempt to gain such all-encompassing control, but whether they succeed in their ambitions is another matter, one too often neglected by those who apply Foucault to colonial governance. Governmental plans often, perhaps usually, go astray. It also does not seem to fit the squatter problem very well, yet extensive squatter areas sprang up in many colonial cities. A fuller development of the promising beginnings of the Foucauldian analysis of colonial governance requires an examination not just of the techniques of control and surveillance, but also of their failure, and of the outcomes deriving from interactions between the two. Our analysis of the genealogy of the SOS emphasizes that the path leading to it was littered with false starts, failures, and uncertainty.

Political economy encourages us to follow the money, and the power of those who control the assets that generate authority as well as wealth, while Foucault considers how government has its own dynamics, potentially but not necessarily synchronized with the "needs" of the dominant mode of production. Structuration theory provides an open-ended methodology for incorporating a non-dogmatic consideration of both political economy and Foucault into our processes of theorizing concrete histories of the development of states, societies, and economies. This line of inquiry also provides techniques for yoking them together in provisional assemblages of temporary fixes and responses to crises and other challenges. Accordingly, this book uses these theoretical insights to help us trace those pathways toward formalization of informality which were thought possible, as well as balancing interests, power, resources, and ideas that made certain decisions and choices appear more desirable and practical in the circumstances. The outcomes and consequences occasionally encouraged the abandonment of plans and their replacement by alternatives, sometimes those that had previously been rejected. The course of our collaborative research has been comparable, as plausible explanations came to be seen as inadequate in the light of issues and discussions we had either been unaware of, or which previously did not appear to connect to our concerns. The minutiae of policy debates are examined in detail, and with considerable attention to the words used to frame and contest them, not simply because of a historical fascination with them, but because they resulted in choices that made Hong Kong the kind of place it became in the last decades of colonial rule. In turn, the colonial territory that they helped form continues to ramify and echo through contemporary Hong Kong, where more informality might make the controls of an increasingly authoritarian government easier to cope with in the second half of Hong Kong's promised 50 years of autonomy under the People's Republic of China.

Outline of the Book

Many of those who are quite familiar with Hong Kong history know relatively little about squatters, governmental concerns about the squatter problem,

Figure 1.2: Mark II resettlement housing, Kwun Tong, 1982. Copyright and provided by Alan Smart.

or the actual responses beyond the public representation of the Squatter Resettlement Programme by the colonial and postcolonial governments (see Figure 1.2). Its successor, the Public Housing Programme, has taken on mythological tones that were deployed to legitimize and celebrate the contribution of British colonialism in the transition to 1997 (Hampton 2015; Smart 2006). The first chapters provide a background and context for the examination of the processes that resulted in the end of new squatting in 1984. They also explain the nature and significance of informality and squatters, both within Hong Kong and globally.

Chapter 2 engages with concepts of informality, more useful than the older dualism between the informal and formal sectors. Rather than being restricted to the poor and marginal, informality is ubiquitous, with informal practices having great importance among the powerful, the middle classes, and within government agencies, such as police forces (as the Black Lives Matter movement is making distressingly clear). We situate economic informality, the subset which has received the most attention, in the broader context of informality in general. To a considerable extent, modernity is the extension of formal rules to a growing number of domains which had previously been treated informally, such as the punishment of children. Economic informality has received the most attention, concerning informal organization and practices in commodified fields such as commerce, lending, manufacturing, and services. It is useful to distinguish between economic informality as involving cases where the good or service is legal, but the way in which it is produced, distributed or reported does not follow extant rules. If the good or service itself is illegal, then we are dealing with illegality rather than informality (although there is certainly a great deal of informality within illegal economies as well). Informality is about squatter housing or unlicensed street vending, not heroin or contract killing. The chapter then turns to the widely discussed and implemented practices of the formalization of informality, such as providing land titles to squatters or changing the rules to legalize food trucks. Finally, the pervasive informality of Hong Kong in the period between 1945 and 1966 is described, focusing on several domains of informality beyond squatting.

Chapter 3 concentrates on the importance of Hong Kong's vulnerable geopolitical situation in explaining the failure for four decades to resolve the squatter problem. It also helps us understand the changing geopolitical situation from 1984, with the signing of the Sino-British Joint Declaration to return Hong Kong to Chinese control in 1997. It explains how the geopolitical situation, and its inhibition of harsh responses to the squatter problem, accounted for squatter resettlement, while most rival explanations accounted only for the clearance and demolition of squatter areas and not for resettlement. Issues like threats to public safety and public health could be dealt with by clearance alone. They did not explain why large resources were devoted to rehousing squatters and hardly anyone else, especially since squatters were very low on the scale of "deserving" recipients of public housing in the minds of officials' minds. It then discusses how the 1984 deal—and its need for stability in the period of transition—offered a plausible explanation for the turning of the tide against squatting, since the prior constraints on harsher treatment of squatters had disappeared and public attention was averted.

Despite the apparent plausibility of a geopolitical explanation, thorough archival research has so far failed to uncover any smoking guns that support a conclusion that it clearly does provide a reason for the end to new squatting, and formalization more generally. That does not mean, of course, that the geopolitical explanation is not indeed correct. In the absence of direct evidence for its accuracy, a conclusion supporting a geopolitical explanation requires not only a demonstration of its analytic adequacy, but also the rejection of other plausible explanations as less powerful or less empirically supported. This would leave the geopolitical context of 1984 as the most plausible reason for the timing of these shifts in Hong Kong's landscape of informality, but we do find other explanations that are at least equally plausible. The second objective of Chapter 3 is to provide some necessary context for understanding the political economy of Hong Kong, and its influence on governmental regulation and intervention into informality and related issues. This context will help ground the following chapters, which offer alternative plausible accounts for the changes leading to 1984.

Chapter 4 provides more context for the remainder of the book by describing Hong Kong in the first half of the 1960s, concentrating on housing, squatting, and immigration from China. It builds on Smart's ethnographic research by providing a case study of the Diamond Hill squatter area, where he conducted his doctoral participant observation research, and interrogating the confidential government documents that help to explain why this large

Introduction

(about 50,000 people) and well-located squatter area (on a large piece of flat land near the old airport and a large industrial zone, bisected by a major arterial road) survived until 2001.

Hong Kong in the first half of the 1960s was largely a straight-line continuation of the 1950s. That decade is described in *The Shek Kip Mei Myth* (2006). Pervasive informality persisted and grew, with hills in Hong Kong Island and Kowloon covered with both resettlement estates and squatter settlements, streets filled with itinerant pedlars and more static street vendors (both ready to flee at any sign of the hawker control squads), and corruption still rampant among governmental agents. The economy included strong representation by both small and medium-sized informal workshops and factories. Their influence was expanded through their associated informal outworkers doing piecework at home (Lui 1994, Smart 1992). The level of prosperity had increased, with wages higher than rivals in the region. Rather than leading to larger factories with greater economies of scale, rapid exploitation of new product niches through networked outsourcing of orders intensified. The established production system sped up even more. Along with soaring numbers of migrants from China, the cost of private housing continued to increase. Redevelopment displaced many people. Demand for public housing soared as well, but most could not access it except through living in a squatter structure demolished for development (see Chapter 8). Absence of significant democratic influence within the governance system fostered more dissatisfaction among the increasingly well-educated population, particularly since the serious undersupply of local university admissions lead many to study overseas.

Chapter 5 continues by presenting the context for the transformation of efforts to deal with the squatter problem. Between 1949 and 1984, the biggest turning point in Hong Kong history was the "riots" of 1966 and 1967. It is widely thought that these disturbances resulted in widespread reforms, which stopped short of any significant democratization due to the geopolitical situation. This chapter discusses the nature of the disturbances and their impact. The 1966 riots were much shorter in duration and smaller in scope and space compared to 1967, which involved the violent spillover of China's Cultural Revolution into Hong Kong. Documentation, though, demonstrates that 1966 did have an important impact and likely would have led to reforms even in the absence of 1967, because it was clearly of Hong Kong origin and represented a long festering set of issues. On top of anger about the housing situation, there was widespread resentment of the high profit margins of monopolies such as the Star Ferry and the power utilities (Goodstadt 2005). Without direct political influence, anger was more likely to emerge in street protests, which could turn violent—as has been occurring in dramatic fashion in contemporary Hong Kong.

One key narrative on the riots stresses how Governor Murray MacLehose (serving 1971 to 1982), instituted a decade of major reforms that created what many have seen as a discontinuity with previous governors. The MacLehose era has been "fondly remembered as a period marking a turning point in colonial rule in Hong Kong and in socioeconomic development in the postwar decades" (Yep and Lui 2010, 2). MacLehose's major achievements included consolidation of the "four pillars" (public housing, education, medical and health services, and social welfare) and establishing the Independent Commission Against Corruption. In particular, since unaffordable and insalubrious housing was at the top of Hong Kong's list of concerns, a massive public housing program was launched in 1972. This set off dynamics that eventually resulted in the ending of new squatting. The chapter also examines the issue of Hong Kong's limited autonomy and the influence of intervention from London, one of the alternative explanations for the end of new squatting. Finally, we engage with the growing literature on crises and how they should be conceptualized. We suggest that series of crises often have a greater impact than a single one, which can foster a trend toward loss of trust in government, or, in other circumstances, a process of learning on the part of leaders.

Chapter 6 examines policy discourse around squatters on land not needed for development, first to generate an alternative explanation for the formalization process in Hong Kong, and second to evaluate the adequacy and plausibility of this explanation. This chapter is limited to the initial commentaries; the consequences of the decisions taken will be explored in subsequent chapters. These discussions emphasize practicality, envisioned possibilities, and constraints. They begin by muddling through, with some possibilities arising only to disappear from sight, while others condense as more suitable alternatives. Initial contingency grows into selected paths, which become easier to follow as they become established, and sometimes retrospectively appear to have been inevitable.

The third plausible explanation points to the contingent collision of distinct policy issues in a political and geopolitical context, which made possible an initially unintended course toward formalization. We call this the mangle of policy practice, based on science and technology scholar Andrew Pickering's (1995, 23) metaphor of the antique washing machine mangle. Material objects frequently lead to the failure of human projects to achieve their goals. Humans must work with and against material resistance to our intentions. This idea can be extended to the unpredictable transformations worked upon whatever gets fed into the mangle of policy debate. Perhaps it can be more relevantly thought of as a sausage grinder, in the spirit of the adage misattributed to Otto von Bismarck: "To retain respect for sausages and laws, one must not watch them in the making." Mangle analysis goes beyond path dependency by considering how multiple policy paths occasionally intersect

Introduction

through the mangles of working parties, commissions or inquiries, resulting in unexpected entanglements and decisions. Ideas get fed through these policy mangles and often end up following paths no one fully anticipated or perhaps even wanted, such as the 1950s transformation of the squatter problem into the Resettlement Programme (Smart 2006). Early choices can have substantial unexpected effects, but can also subsequently turn into dead ends. This chapter addresses some early choices that made formalization possible, while related initiatives will be considered in later chapters.

It is in Chapter 6 that we turn in detail to the key intervention from London in 1970 about the problem of squatters on land not needed for development, which launched the path toward the SOS. This chapter is the first deep dive into the confidential documents, exploring how discussions emerge from the circulation of files, and the outcomes can often be unexpected. In this case, neither of the solutions (resettling all squatters or giving them title) suggested by the governor to the problem raised by London were accepted. Instead, a third alternative of squatter area improvement without formalization or legalization emerged, temporarily successful, but ultimately being rejected in 1984. The chapter also demonstrates that the second possible explanation, intervention from London, is inadequate. London's influence succeeded in insisting that "something" had to be done about squatter areas that were attracting questions in Parliament and the press, but what that "something" was resulted from local deliberations much more than metropolitan influence.

Chapter 7 develops a fourth explanation based on imbalance of supply and demand of both temporary and permanent public housing in the Ten-Year Housing Programme. This was instituted during the term of Trench's successor, Governor Murray MacLehose. It was intended to resolve the housing problems experienced by most of the population, and thereby encourage loyalty and confidence in the colonial government. These and other reforms were in part responses to the riots discussed in Chapter 5. However, the massive housing developments launched in 1972 were undermined by problems in clearing squatter areas to allow new development, and by resulting imbalances between the supply and demand for temporary and permanent public housing. Despite the massive impact of the Ten-Year Programme for Hong Kong, the confidential documents appear as yet underexplored in other studies. The chapter examines how these failures derived in substantial part from failure to make enough land available for development. This failure in turn resulted from delays in clearing squatter areas, impeded by shortage of temporary housing to relocate them. Only the occupants of the squatter dwellings surveyed and tolerated in 1964 huts were eligible for permanent housing, while families occupying those built after 1964 but surveyed in 1976 were eligible only for temporary accommodation. Two-storey temporary housing was lower density than the squatter areas and permanent public housing estates, so in a land-scarce context, the eligibility policies created a major obstacle.

The decision to undertake the SOS in 1984 emerged from a "review of public housing allocation policies," which in turn had been a response to a review of housing objectives and the Ten-Year Housing Programme in 1980. At that point, housing targets were being missed by a large margin. In particular, far from ending the squatter problem (which had been listed as the first target), 1980–1982 saw the largest number of squatters ever, peaking at over 750,000 in 1982. This upsurge was due in part to a large influx of migrants from China, but also to failures in squatter control, which are discussed in this chapter. In 1981, it was acknowledged that to deal with the shortage of temporary housing, it would be necessary to revise the criteria for admission into permanent housing so as to make a greater proportion of cleared squatters eligible for permanent housing. While resolving these problems, policy changes to resolve the imbalance with more generous treatment of squatters and migrants fostered the emergence of localist identities, while squatter improvement failed to remove the dangers of squatter areas on dangerous slopes. The earlier policies had generated an imbalance between the supply and demand for temporary housing and a solution required more generous treatment of squatters. But this leaves the question of why these policy-generated imbalances were created in the first place. The supply and demand imbalances are an important part of explaining the path to the SOS, but it does not account for why the imbalances existed.

Chapter 8 turns to citizenship and identity issues to explain how this imbalance developed. By the mid-1970s, the prominence of squatters and migrants in public housing allocation was fostering public sentiments that people who were born in or were longtime residents of Hong Kong were more deserving of the limited and widely desired public housing. Access through the means-tested Waiting List often required more than seven years, while many cleared squatters could be rehoused immediately and without being subject to the means test. The rise of Hong Kong identity in this period is a complicated process with various causes proposed by different scholars, but the conflict over public housing allocation seems to have accelerated the process and, so far, has not received adequate attention.

The chapter returns to the Ten-Year Housing Programme, offering a broader assessment of its motivations, outcomes, and failures. In particular, the chapter concentrates on the tensions around allocation quotas and explicates the discursive role of the colonial government in managing the tensions that arise from it. Beyond the resentment of squatters and migrants as undeserving of scarce public housing, the review of housing allocation also focused attention on the public housing tenants who had become rich, or at least better-off and benefiting, while poorer people languished on long Waiting List queues. Fairness became a key battleground for the future of Hong Kong's public housing system. However, fairness conflicted with practicality, since imposing income limits on cleared squatters, for example, was recognized as complicating and probably delaying development clearances, and thereby endangering the completion of the housing production targets. Fairness also complicated the management of Chinese migrants, who were not eligible for public housing except through squatter clearance, and who mostly could not afford private housing. As a result, they became more concentrated in squatter areas, particularly in the 1980s, which contributed to their stigmatization.

Chapter 9 investigates the colonial will to improve, which formed one of the alternatives to eradication of squatter structures. This chapter has three objectives. First, it offers a description of this path to formalization in Hong Kong: squatter area improvement, which emphasizes formalizing the infrastructure, while leaving the legal status of the dwellings unchanged. Second, it considers another possible explanation for formalization: the colonial desire to improve problematic spaces and places, or more generally what James Scott (1998) describes as "seeing like a state," making its territory visible and accountable through "rational engineering of all aspects of social life" with an assumption that this would "improve the human condition" (Scott 1998, 88). The problem with this explanation lies in the belatedness with which such desires took hold in Hong Kong, and in squatter areas, and the need to offer further reasons for why it took place when it did. The third objective is to use the case of squatter area improvement to consider the strengths of some of the other plausible explanations posited in previous chapters.

Long before the 1982 launching of the Squatter Area Improvement Programme in Hong Kong, squatter areas (and squatters) were seen as in dire need of improvement, both by London and in Hong Kong's Government House. The most desired way to improve these areas was to demolish them completely and permanently, replacing them with something legally ordered. There were various constraints to this, particularly on land that was difficult to develop. Improvement in the absence, or delay, of demolition became an alternative after other solutions to the squatter problem failed, sometimes repeatedly. At the least, squatter improvement could help avert London's gaze and criticism on the squatter problem. Without a definite timeframe for persistence, infrastructure spending in tolerated squatter areas could not be adequately discounted, making them riskier and less attractive investments. Awareness of the considerable costs for moderate improvements may answer why the program had such a short life—1982–1984—although with a longer gestation and afterlife, since long delays in clearance after 1984 prolonged the need for infrastructure improvements. The collapse of the improvement strategy opened the path to the adoption of the resettling-all-squatters approach, with the SOS serving to limit the future costs involved in doing so.

Chapter 10 has two objectives. The first is to examine the crucial policy changes between 1982, when the Squatter Area Improvement Programme was put into place, and 1984, when it was decided to instead phase it out over five years, to resettle all squatters on vulnerable slopes, and to carry out the SOS. These decisions were influenced by growing awareness of the political and economic costs of managing landslip risks affecting squatters. The second objective is to describe the implementation and consequences of the Survey.

The main rationale for carrying out a survey of squatter occupants was that the survey of squatter structures alone does not prevent them changing hands, either being sold by racketeers or by the squatters themselves. This loophole enabled a number of people to jump the queue into public housing. Nor was there any way of controlling the increase in the numbers of people occupying existing surveyed structures. The importance of the SOS was that people not registered in it would not be eligible for resettlement in public housing. This capped the number of squatters to be rehoused during clearances, other than increases through births to registered occupants. Combined with more effective squatter control, the result would be that every time there was a clearance, or an occupant moved out or died, the number of squatters eligible for resettlement would ratchet downward. This made the decision in 1984 to resettle all squatters, even on land not needed for development, feasible by limiting the commitment to those already in place. It also avoided encouraging additional squatting. It put the final nail in the coffin of new squatting.

Chapter 11 builds on the results of the study of how Hong Kong ended new squatting after 1984 by considering a number of Asian cities with differing experiences. The comparison is focused on the mode of eviction used, and the reasons for tolerating squatting, drawing on typologies that Smart has previously developed for comparison in this field. Singapore is the only other example of a complete ending of new squatting addressed in this chapter. It generally has the most similarities with Hong Kong, particularly its huge public housing provision system. Kuala Lumpur is also close to having ended new squatting, although it is less controlled in other parts of Malaysia. It also shared the legacy of British imperial rule. Indian cities also echo their British heritage but have taken a more political path to the control of squatting, with widespread toleration giving way to a much more repressive regime of control in the last two decades. China, despite its cultural commonality with Hong Kong, has a heavily political mode of control of informal housing, which is generally unauthorized building in urban villages rather than squatting as such. Manila has the strongest and most effective squatter movement and has a legacy of in situ informal settlement upgrading and regularization, although this is currently eroding.

The Conclusion will draw together the argument that has been developed throughout the book, evaluate the six plausible explanations offered for the

Introduction

end to new squatting and the turning of the tide against informality, and consider again the nature of historical explanation. It will sketch the state of informality in the Hong Kong of the 2020s and consider some of the consequences of the decline of informality. It will also draw out the policy implications of the study for the management of informality and consider some of the theoretical issues that have been raised.

2
Informality

Formal codes and regulations were viewed as the means to bring everything into line . . . And yet the authorities were continually frustrated in their attempts to make everyday life conform to the dictates of law.

—William Cunningham Bissell, *Urban Design, Chaos, and Colonial Power in Zanzibar* (2010, 318)

Introduction

Chapter 1 briefly introduced the concept of informality and the importance of it for colonial Hong Kong. The ending of new squatting was pursued through four different general approaches. All of these are variant types of what is known as formalization. Formalization, however, was in certain ways undertaken through rather informal procedures. Most research on informality has concentrated on marginal groups. This chapter will argue that informality is also pervasive among other groups and may be particularly significant among powerful people. Even if its prevalence among them is lesser than among the poor and working class (and this is not certain), the consequences of informal practices among the wealthy and powerful can be much greater.

This chapter has two main goals. The first is to introduce the reader to the key elements of both informality and governmental projects to formalize it. As part of this, we argue for a broad understanding of informality in general, which is ubiquitous in all state-level societies.[1] Most research on informality has concentrated on what we call *economic informality*, where the practices are commercial or are more broadly directed at making money (or a livelihood more generally when we include barter arrangements and mutual aid) through the sale of goods and services. Squatting fits into this category, as does much of the kind of governmental informality that we label as *corruption*. However, a great deal of, probably most, informal governmental practices are instead undertaken in pursuit of achieving their policy or political objectives, or for dealing with problems that arise from these objectives (Lee 2014, Roy 2005). In addition, we consider what is known about governmental projects to formalize informality, with particular attention to informal housing and land use.

The second goal is to apply these ideas to describe informality in Hong Kong from 1950 to 1966. This description will provide a baseline for the subsequent discussion of the reforms adopted in the aftermath of the 1966 and 1967 riots: widespread disturbances. It will also serve to go beyond squatting, the main focus of this book, to sketch a variety of domains in which economic informality flourished, while also offering an initial discussion of governmental informality in colonial Hong Kong. In doing so, we will be providing a more general overview of informality than is usually given in most of the literature, which is particularly true for the historical study of colonies. The chapter will help to highlight what the book contributes to our knowledge of informality as well as to the study of Hong Kong.

Informality in General

On a normative level, the mainstream approach to informality is that it represents the failure or limitations of governance, planning, and development, and that therefore informality needs to be curtailed or transformed (Harris 2017). A contrasting position can be seen in the claim by Peter Evans (1995) that successful developmental states are characterized by the "embedded autonomy" of an internally cohesive state bureaucracy that is also connected with private sector entrepreneurs. A bureaucracy that is too closed off from societal influences, too committed to formal rules and procedures, may be insufficiently responsive to facilitate development, while one that is too closely bound up with societal or business networks ("for my friends, anything, for my enemies, the law") may fail due to nepotism, corruption and rent seeking. Evans uses international comparisons to argue that states that succeeded in developing have fostered institutions that allow them to steer a middle course between excessive societal embeddedness and excessive bureaucratic autonomy (between informality and formality, in the terms we are using here). His position offers a useful corrective to Hernando de Soto's argument for formalization as a solution to global poverty, discussed in the next section.

Both Evans and de Soto are exploring ways in which institutions of property and governance have important consequences for economic development and efficiency. There has been a growing body of research that applies institutional analysis to informality, as well as proposals for formalization (e.g. Bruce 2012; Guha-Khasnobis et al. 2006; Oviedo et al. 2009). Lawrence Lai et al. (2014) provide an exemplary application of such ideas to compare the institutions governing land squatters and marine squatters in Hong Kong. While the emergence of more robust, rather than dualistic, economic analyses of informality is certainly to be welcomed, our concerns in this book are neither to argue what should be done, nor to evaluate the desirability of measures adopted by the colonial government.[2] Rather, we are primarily interested in explaining *how* the Hong Kong government came to make certain decisions about the management of squatting, which are in turn affected by the consequences of their actions. This might in certain contexts spur them to change directions again. And so on.

Formalizing agents themselves rely on informality to get their work done (Gandolfo 2013; Gupta 2012), as do other street-level bureaucrats (Lipsky 2010; Smart 2018). The informal practices of governments generally operate through the medium of what Herdt and Olivier De Sardan (2015) call "practical norms which diverge from formal definitions of corruption, and often involve attempts to 'get the job done'" in difficult or otherwise impossible circumstances. Both for ordinary citizens and civil servants, there are distinctions between legitimate acts—regardless of whether the law might consider them bribes or corruption—and illicit acts that are in no way illegal (van Schendel and Abraham 2005). Anti-corruption campaigns often involve adding new layers of formal rules, and rules about the application of rules, and can lead to high levels of formalization of the informal practices of mundane government. These controls are often stricter at the lower levels of government, leaving much more room for discretion (and perhaps corruption) at the higher levels (Gupta 2012; Scott 2013; Smart 2018a; Wedel 2012).

In civil society and the economy, informality is also everywhere, but often poorly understood. Consider friendship and how it relates to the Chinese practice and discourse of the art of *guanxi* (the simplest gloss of which is as "connections," but which has broader implications). Guanxi, which has received a great deal of attention due to the rapid rise of China to being the second largest economy in the world, is one style or variant of a broader, perhaps universal, pattern of networking (Bian 1997; Smart 1993; Yan 1996; Yang 1994). Informal networks are used by all classes and in every country to find jobs and recruit employees (Granovetter 1973); make deals with reduced risk and increased efficiency; assemble supporters for political campaigns; obtain investment information; get advice and support in applying for graduate programs; and most other activities. However, there are also countervailing trends to formalize such informal activities, which are seen as leading to nepotism, insider trading, corruption, favoritism, inefficiencies due to discrimination, blocked opportunities for immigrants and minorities, and a whole range of other social ills that modern states and legal systems frequently attempt to control or eliminate.

Hernando de Soto (2000) argued that the most effective way to reduce poverty is to make the informal economy formal by turning the assets of informal operators into legal capital. He argued that "most of the poor already possess the assets they need to make a success of capitalism" (5). But the

Informality

problem is that "they hold these resources in defective forms" such as houses on squatted land (5). By legalizing or formalizing the various forms of undocumented and informal wealth, it could be used as collateral for loans and so on, rather than staying as unconvertible "dead capital," and thereby promote successful economic development.

What do we mean by informality when we do not confine it to some distinct informal sector of the economy, but consider it in its most general way? In classic anthropological terms, how broadly applicable is the concept to diverse human situations and ways of livelihood? Instead of beginning with the informal, what if we begin from formality?

Modernity itself can be seen as the rise of formality, progressively displacing the personalism and venial alliances of monarchial courts with rational rules and procedures that theoretically apply to all citizens. The rule of law should constrain the decision-making practices of governments and public corporations alike. The growth of formality, however, is not complete and arguably could never be complete. If formality and informality always coexist, it is also true that the balance between them varies between different kinds of social contexts and different times. In his influential work on the frontier, for example, Frederick Jackson Turner (1920, 344) argued that "America does through informal association and understandings on the part of the people many of the things which in the Old World are and can be done only by governmental intervention and compulsion." Robert Putnam (2000) saw the decline of such informal institutions as the cause of many problems in American society.

An important question is whether there is a zero-sum game between the informal and the formal. Does, for example, the growth of formal systems of social control based on police and the courts displace informal social control based on cultural expectations, gossip, and private sanctions? Or can the two operate in tandem in ways that expand or reduce the total amount of social control? Barbara Misztal (2000) argues that only societies that reach an optimal balance between informality and formality can create conditions for cooperation, cohesion, and innovation.

Max Weber and Norbert Elias could be seen as diagnosing a long historical shift toward formality at the expense of informality. In *The Civilizing Process*, Elias says that "[i]n all differentiated societies . . . there are categories of social situation in which the social code demands . . . that they behave in formal ways . . . and there are other categories of social situation where . . . a more or less high degree of informality is appropriate" (Elias 2000, 28). One interpretation of Elias's idea of the civilizing process is that formality grows at the expense of informality. For example, the growing importance of social media magnifies the potential for informal communications with the public by police officers, but also creates pressures for new formal regulations to control the risks involved in such informality. Police forces historically have gone from tolerated illegality (thieves operating as "thief-takers" for bounties) to heavily informal in how they manage violence to being much more formally regulated. Still, even today, there are informal practices among police—intensely contested by movements such as Black Lives Matter—determining how force should be managed and how much is too much.

Max Weber's "iron cage of bureaucracy" is something that perhaps most of us at universities (and other institutions) can clearly recognize, as things once handled informally are increasingly subjected to formal procedures and regulations covering everything from receipts for research expenses to catering departmental events. This has often been described as *audit society* (Power 1997) or *audit culture* (Strathern 2000). Does formalistic bureaucracy inevitably reduce dynamism and creativity, as many suggest? Is informality in dealing with the rules a necessary corrective to avoid these problems? Or, as during a pandemic like COVID-19, do informal practices (such as underground barbers and stylists) undermine public safety?

Interpersonal interactions in society raise other kinds of questions about formality. How much formality is desirable in particular kinds of relationships? A British Victorian bourgeois husband and father would be appalled at the informality at contemporary dining tables and other domestic contexts, not to mention being addressed by his first name by cashiers and waiters. A contemporary teenager, though, would find the demands for manners, respect, and obedience oppressive and unacceptable. Harold Garfinkel, one of the pioneers of ethnomethodology, revealed how seriously such practices and idioms of in/formality can be taken. For one of his infamous "breaching experiments," which he assigned to his classes to demonstrate the unacknowledged rules and procedures of everyday life, he asked students who lived at home to interact with their family as if they were lodgers in a boarding house (Garfinkel 1967). Their exaggerated politeness was in a number of cases treated as mockery, resulting in serious fights within the family. It is worth noting that incidents like these contributed to the imposition of formal rules restricting research on human subjects without ethical oversight and informed consent (which would clearly have made the breaching exercises nonviable). Public discussions of civility—usually bemoaning its decline and blaming younger generations, or culturally distinct others, for not conforming to socially desirable forms of interaction or behavior in public—raise fascinating issues around the relative desirability of in/formality (Koster and Smart 2019). Is being too casual in language, dress, or comportment a problem, or does it contribute to breaking down inflexible hierarchies and oppressive demands that less powerful individuals "stay in their place," and may thereby facilitate innovations?

A very large and important question presents itself: Which historic force—formalization or informalization—is stronger? Is it a zero-sum game? Or are

Informality

31

there certain optimal mixes between quantities and qualities of informality and formality (Misztal 2000)? These questions would be very hard to answer without a serious quantitative effort based on solid conceptualization and operationalization, which is not possible here.

The most fundamental challenge to the utility of informality as an analytic concept has recently been posed by Michael Herzfeld (2021). He suggests abandoning the "methodological legalism" pretense that "the formal-informal dichotomy serves any useful purpose other than as a term of abuse" (39). The ability of the nation-state to "relegate already marginalized citizens to the bleak exile of informality parades as the rule of law, common sense, hygiene, and security" (40). The key argument he makes is that there is nothing informal about the rules that operate to influence practices in sectors like informal settlements, which demand and enforce "adherence to a clearly codified set of rules. That these rules are not always written down [does] not make them less formal" (42). He uses examples from a variety of contexts to persuasively demonstrate that such rules involve little that is informal, "if by informal we mean an absence of procedure" (49). Following this, he demonstrates that formality is "not an objective quality; it is an attributed one" (50). Labeling something as informal is a performative action; it makes a settlement evictable, for example. Thus, he argues for a rejection of "the language of formality" because it "merely cedes conceptual authority to the state" (49). Adopting this language obscures the agency of bureaucrats who create vulnerability to intervention by such labelling. Herzfeld (personal communication, 2021) suggests that we could usefully undermine methodological legalism by focusing on the process of informalization as well as formalization.

This is a coherent and convincing argument for the incoherence of the formal/informal distinction and the desirability of rejecting an attributed claim that intensifies the marginality of those who rely on practices more susceptible to being labeled as illegal or informal. It would be a completely reasonable methodological decision to avoid any discussion of informality, or formality, due to its deficiencies. Yet, there are still reasons for attempting to make informality more useful as an analytic category and less of an arbitrary stigma. If we rigorously pursue a single factor definition of informality as practices that do not follow prevailing authoritative rules (usually but not necessarily legal in origin), then it becomes clear that the rich and powerful partake of informality, as do those who live in precarious circumstances. The problem is not the invidious distinction in itself, but the unwillingness to recognize informality anywhere and everywhere it exists. We would argue that a study of informality in general that is not biased from the beginning, but instead agnostic about how and where it operates, is equally valid to a rejection of it based on the demonstration of its problematic methodological legalism.

There is a second reason for persisting in trying to make sense of informality, however. That is because, even if we were to accept that its procedures of identification and control were methodologically invalid and unjust, they still have real-world consequences. Just as witchcraft operates with life-and-death results, even if there are no "real" witches with supernatural powers, the attribution of informality has consequences for billions of people. And counter to Herzfeld's claim that this is to the disadvantage of the marginalized, the distinction between the informal and the illegal has facilitated substantial (although inadequate to the task) interventions by governments and supranational agencies to upgrade squatter areas and regularize other informal practices, such as street vending and sex work. His general point on the importance of denaturalizing the specious concreteness of informality, though, is very important.

Economic Informality

Most research on informality focuses on economic informality. It is easier to define informality in the commercialized realm than it is to characterize its more general nature, and it is more subject to policy interventions than informality in the private realm. When complete suppression fails, governments attempt to confine informal practices and economies by space, time, and the scope of what is allowed. Selling things, for example, can be confined to particular spaces (privately owned stores or official public markets, or areas not subject to lockdown), scope (various goods cannot be sold, or specific licenses are required to sell them, as with pharmaceuticals), or times (Sunday closing laws or bar closing times). Informality goes beyond one or more types of confinement (Smart and Smart 2017a). We can describe something as informal in situations where the goods and services transacted are legal, but the ways in which they are transacted are not. In the illegal economy, by contrast, the goods or services themselves are illegal: contraband drugs, fenced stolen goods, and so on (Beckert and Dewey 2017). What makes an economic practice informal is its transgression of one or more of the types of confinement. For instance, profit-seeking activities in public space are informal when practiced in such a way as to break the rules, prohibited items are sold (cooked food or pirate DVDs), or resources are moved in illegitimate ways from one domain to another (moonlighting, smuggling), etc.

Fernandes and Varley (1998) estimated that about 40% of the population of cities in Global South cities live in illegal housing or work in illegal ways. Without considering that scope, you really cannot understand those cities (Neuwirth 2012). If the formal economy—the measured economy (where you have economic statistics to be used by government decision-makers)—is only half or less of the whole economy (Jütting and Laiglesia 2009), and the informal economy moves in a different rhythm than the formal economy, interventions may be seriously mistaken. You may think the economy is slowing, but the informal economy might be going in the other direction. If so, you may end up doing the wrong things, with damaging unintended consequences resulting from inappropriate economic management interventions (de Soto 1989; Feige 2007; Hart 2010).

When the formal economy declines, there is often a substantial increase in informal, or underground, economic activities to fill the gap in people's budgets and to allow them to preserve what they value. These activities may buffer, to a lesser or greater degree, declines in formal economic transactions. Informal survival strategies include bartering, informal childcare, tutoring, sex work, casual work, working off the books, commercial discounts, informal renting of rooms or suites in houses (Tanasescu and Smart 2010), and moving back in with family members.

The nature of informal economies is structured by conflict between two forces. First, governmental strategies of control and co-optation attempt either to eradicate informal economies or to restrict them to delimited places, times, and ways of doing things. Second, the transgression of these forms of regulation by informal actors in pursuit of survival or advantage. The result can be a series of cat and mouse games, where tactics and responses of both sides evolve through their interaction, changing the practices of informality and its controls interactively. The general public has an impact as well—as consumers that prefer the convenience and lower prices of the street to the permanent marketplace or the supermarket, or as members of a public that declaims the mess, disorder, and congestion produced (Hansen, Little, and Milgram 2013).

Informality operates in the spectrum between repression/eradication and legalization. There are varying degrees of repression and encouragement between the two poles. On one extreme, there is complete suppression of informal housing (non-existent in the Global South and increasingly rare in the Global North due to soaring unaffordability of housing). On the other extreme of the spectrum is complete erasure of any distinction between housing that was initially built or occupied illegally, and those units developed legally. Both extremes are rare. They share the absence of any toleration of informality. Most real-world cases operate somewhere on the spectrum between them. As a result, to make sense of economic informality, we have to consider the specific nature of the tolerations that allow informal practices to persist and continue (Smart and Aguilera 2020). Some circumstances fit with what John Cross calls *semi-formality*: situations where "the government actively negotiates the implementation of regulatory norms without, however, changing the actual regulations" (Cross 1998, 35). When informality is accorded semiformal recognition, the government allows it to exist under a system of extralegal norms that emerge from conflict, negotiation, and compromise, and often corruption as well (Cross 1998). An administrative system is established that provides partial regulation without legalization. This applies well to the toleration of Hong Kong's squatter areas. The key distinction between the semiformal and the legal, however, is that toleration and regulation are concessions rather than rights. Semiformal regulation may quickly change when the government or state agents feel that the system no longer meets their interests, or new strategies for control of informal activities emerge.

One useful way of thinking about tolerated informality is that it creates gray zones where formally illegal practices can take place. Gray zones can be spatially delimited areas, such as red-light districts. They can also be domains of practices accepted only while within certain regulatory boundaries; for example, illegal street markets that are raided heavily whenever they too blatantly sell pirated DVDs or designer goods, which might cause difficulties in international relations due to concerns about intellectual property rights (Smart 2021a). Oren Yiftachel (2009) uses the term *gray spaces* to refer to the spatial dimensions of grayness—territories that only partially incorporate people into the urban community. As a result, they are excluded from full, or any, urban citizenship. Gray spaces are "positioned between the 'whiteness' of legality/approval/safety, and the 'blackness' of eviction/destruction/death. They are neither integrated nor eliminated, forming pseudo-permanent margins of today's urban regions" (89). His approach recognizes that there is *gray space from above*, where those with power break the rules, or have the rules changed to fit the non-conforming uses of their mansions, golf courses or development projects, as well as the more usually recognized *gray space from below* of proletarian informality and illegality. These two distinct sets of processes result in gray spaces being subject to either *whitening* or *blackening*. The first refers to "the tendency of the system to 'launder' gray spaces created from above," while the latter entails resolving "the problem of marginalized gray space by destruction, expulsion or elimination" (92). Informality is thus not only a tactic of the marginalized. It may even be more often tolerated when undertaken by the powerful.

Toleration can be explicit and bound by clear rules, even if those rules conflict with formal laws. Or it can be implicit and problematic to the extent that no one wants to make the practice public or open. Such variations produce different forms, or types, of toleration. Toleration is poorly studied in the relevant literatures, certainly in comparison to its extent and practical importance (Smart and Aguilera 2020). Lacorne (2019) distinguishes between *toleration*—derived from the Latin verb *tolerare*, which means to endure, to put up with—and *tolerance*. His focus is on non-majority religions, which throughout early modern history have either been repressed or tolerated—suffered "for the sake of keeping peace" (1). The contemporary meaning of tolerance is "more often understood as the welcoming acceptance of a wide variety of

Informality

beliefs and viewpoints where diverse communities respect one another and act collectively for the common good" (1). This kind of tolerance began to emerge during the Enlightenment, whereas reluctant toleration of heterodox religious belief was common in multiethnic empires such as the Ottoman dynasties. In this sense, governments deal with informality through toleration rather than tolerance, although social movements and activists are more likely to advocate tolerance of economic informality because of its contributions not just to the livelihoods of the marginalized, but also to the color and vitality of the urban landscapes (Chalana and Hou 2016).

Urban informality has had a massive influence on the political economy of cities, structuring them in pervasive but often poorly understood ways (Fairbanks 2009; Hart 1973, 2010; Roy 2005). Its influence and effects are the result of both the activities themselves and the governmental responses. Some projections suggest that informality will be of even greater importance in coming decades, with the informal sector growing faster than the formal sector on a global basis (Oviedo, Thomas, and Karakurum-Ozdemir 2009). Whether that occurs, however, is affected by a variety of factors, including governmental responses and technological changes. New web-based applications such as ride-sharing and home-booking tend to be more informal than the taxis and hotels they are competing with, but more formal than long-standing informal systems such as motorcycle taxis and boarding houses. The COVID-19 pandemic may increase informality due to the economic downturns and lockdowns of formal businesses, or undermine it through intensified controls over informal business activity and sanitation. The outcomes are likely to vary sharply from jurisdiction to jurisdiction, and the overall impact remains to be seen.

Formalization

Many governments have tried to put informality "in its place" through formalization. Such efforts attempt to make informal practices conform to formal rules or to close them down. For Keith Hart (2010, 148), forms are "necessarily abstract and a lot of social life is left out as a result," so the official spheres cannot just be abstract forms and procedures but "consists also of the people who staff bureaucracies and their informal practices." Bureaucratic attempts to incorporate the informal into their projects and plans create new abstractions and routinized procedures. Formalizing the informal requires reporting procedures, benchmarking, formal evaluation of outcomes, and so on, which may destroy the sources of informality's strengths. As a result, there has tended to be oscillation between trends to decrease the bureaucratic barriers to innovation of excessive formality and, contrarily, to act against the risks and problems created by informality. Sometimes, formalization dominates while at other times there is a resurgence of informalization.

Under Reagan, Thatcher, and International Monetary Fund structural adjustment programs, informality was widely seen as representing competitive entrepreneurialism and self-help, a free commerce from which the "over-regulated" developed economies could learn (de Soto 1989; Peck 2021; Roy 2010; Smart and Smart 2005). Informality became seen as a solution rather than a problem—poor people entrepreneurially "pulling themselves up by their bootstraps" in ways consistent with the economic doctrines of the Thatcher and Reagan administrations. Critiques of public housing and slum demolition by John Turner (1976) and others criticized public housing and slum clearance while arguing that facilitating self-help through informal housing could more effectively provide affordable housing for the poor. These ideas were adopted as policy recommendations by the World Bank, which reduced support for public housing (Harris 1998; Smart 2020). A more recent policy shift since the 2008 financial crisis sees the growth of informal economies as "unfair competition" to formal sector businesses that (allegedly) follow rules and pay taxes. This more anti-informal perspective is helping to promote formalization with different approaches, such as using value-added taxes. These penalize those who do not register their businesses and pay taxes since they cannot claim as deductions the valued-added taxes they pay.

Institutional support for formalization was substantially increased through the influence of Hernando de Soto (2000). He has had a great deal of impact on development strategies through his argument that converting into real capital the vast amounts of "dead capital" frozen in the extralegal property of the informal sector would result in the rapid development of the developing world. This would further the interests of the poor by allowing them to take advantage of the equity otherwise frozen within their informally acquired and protected homes and businesses. He estimates the total value of "real estate held but not legally owned by the poor of the Third World and former communist nations" to be at least $9.3 trillion (de Soto 2000, 35). Effective development requires secure tenure and other forms of documented ownership. Ray Bromley (2004, 275) summarizes the argument as being that by "removing the legal barriers which exclude the poor from effective participation in the economy . . . formalizing the informal sector" will allow the whole population to "participate fully in the national economy" Formalization strategies have been promoted by several supranational agencies, including the World Bank. UN-Habitat established the Global Campaign for Secure Tenure to pursue the Millennium Development Goal (MDG) target on slums (Durand-Lasserve 2006).

The consequences of formalizing informality are intensely debated. Disagreement revolves around multiple issues, including whether formalization

Informality

has the positive outcomes claimed; whether the unintended consequences might undermine any positive outcomes; if de facto tenure security without the heavy expenditure required for de jure security is sufficient to obtain the positive outcomes; and who benefits most from formalization (Obeng-Odoom and Stilwell 2013; Soliman 2010). Easing the formal registering of a business was the most popular policy in business regulations from 2003 to 2012 (368 reforms in 149 economies), but the results have been at best modest. Most informal firms have no net benefit from formalizing. Easing the transition will not induce them to do so and increased enforcement of rules are needed to promote adoption (Bruhn and McKenzie 2014).

Programs to provide title for informal property, for example, have been shown to frequently disadvantage women, who may lose existing customary claims on land and property (Varley 2007). Rural land policy had "for too long been informed by two contradictory paradigms, namely the 'install full private policy paradigm' and the 'leave customary law undisturbed' paradigm" (Otto and Hoekema 2012, 7). Local conditions determine the relative utility of these approaches, and often hybrid forms are more appropriate. De Soto has also exaggerated the novelty of his argument by ignoring prior efforts at formalization, particularly of land and housing, although usually in other words (Bruce 2012; Harris 1998). His call for formalization is distinct not in its novelty but rather in the grandness of the claim to end global poverty and in the breadth of his audience reception.

Roy (2005, 150) stresses that formalization of informal property is "not simply a bureaucratic or technical problem but rather a complex political struggle." A great deal of research has focused on debating and prescribing policy, with a smaller but growing amount evaluating the outcomes of formalization programs in particular places, or more generally (Obeng-Odoom 2013). Much of this evaluation does not support de Soto's strong claims. For example, Krul and Ho (2020) found that while forest lands had been widely titled under central government encouragement in southwest China, these titles mapped at best loosely onto the situation on the ground so that forest registration has emerged as an "empty institution." Benjaminsen et al. (2009) found that land formalization may benefit the powerful and result in increased conflicts. Even less empirical work has been done on how and why such programs have been adopted and implemented (Durand-Lasserve 2006; Li 2007; Mukhija 2003). Sometimes there are incentives and pressures from supranational agencies such as the World Bank or other donors (Roy 2010; Harris 1998). In other cases, such as for illegal ridesharing companies like Uber Technologies Inc. in Estonia, influences come from "techno-optimistic discourses" (Lanamäki and Tuvikene 2021, 2). By contrast, squatter areas are generally seen as vestiges of the past that need to be modernized to better fit with images of improvement and progress (Curran and Smart 2021; Ghertner 2010). Titling informal property has been undertaken in 23 countries in Africa alone, but none have proceeded past pilot projects and demand for titles has been weak (Panman and Lozano Gracia 2021). President Fujimori of Peru created a massive property titling project in 1996. De Soto's influence was clear here, but Newman (2020) found that a major motivation was to increase the president's power. Leaders in squatter areas had accumulated considerable power acting as brokers for the provision of services. Formalization could sharply reduce local politicians' influence by centralizing tenure security and services. Procedures attempted to minimize the discretion of street-level bureaucrats. The result, however, was that bureaucratic resistance slowed implementation where local leaders were strong, so that titling occurred disproportionately in more marginal areas where leaders were weaker.

Precisely how formalization is undertaken has large stakes for cities and their affected populations. Since the World Bank put its weight behind regularization, it has become rhetorically the dominant strategy, although forced evictions remain common in most countries, particularly China. Mario Huchzermeyer (2011) claims that the translation of the Millennium Development Goal into the slogan "Cities without Slums" has helped in many countries to legitimate slum eradication rather than upgrading and titling (see Chapter 11).

We can see formalizing projects in the West as a component of neoliberal efforts to extend (formal) markets into arenas where they have been restricted or constrained by social, political, or legal circumstances, while those in China are driven more by the logics and interests of the party-state. *Formalization* can be achieved either by converting the informal into the formal (*regularization*) or by ending the informal practices (*eradication*), or both. Regularization can be achieved by changing the rules to make it easier for informal sector actors to conform. Or it can be produced by forcing informal actors to comply with more or less unchanged rules (Smart and Smart 2017a). Hong Kong is unusual in its consistent emphasis on eradication and its unwillingness to engage with regularization, particularly for squatter settlements, although the possibility was mulled at various times. Part of the distinctiveness of the Colonial Secretary's initial response to Trench's memo about squatters on land not needed for development was its raising of the possibility of regularization, although this alternative ended up not being adopted even after it was occasionally discussed for more than a decade (see Chapter 6).

One area where more work would be valuable is the provision of better knowledge of why and how governments attempt to formalize economic informality. There have been remarkable shifts in dominant governmental attitudes toward informal activities, from failure to notice it except as "eyesores," blight, and "traditional native markets" before the 1970s, to attempts to facilitate it as entrepreneurial "bootstrapping" consistent with new neoliberal ideas, and

Informality

most recently to a concern about unfair competition and negative impacts on the overall economy and the competitiveness of formal sector firms. While there are broad international discourses that have influence through the policies of agencies such as the International Labour Organization, the World Bank, the International Monetary Fund, and the Organization for Economic Cooperation and Development, there have also been important local influences on national and subnational attitudes toward informality, often influenced by politics, such as by the utility of informal sector populations as groups easily mobilized through patron-client relations (Cross and Morales 2007).

Other than explicit programs to formalize informality, there are a myriad of other governmental and corporate projects that have the same outcome, such as the requirement of global standards, particularly the International Organization for Standardization in supply chains. Smart city projects offer a useful contemporary example. Proponents of smart cities beg the question of what makes a city smart, and in doing so neglect forms of intelligence that do not involve sophisticated technology controlled by technical and corporate elites. For example, making traffic flow more smoothly in a sprawling, auto-dependent urban region is a very limited conceptualization of smartness. Cities can be "smarter" (if we mean anything other than the quantity of information and communication technology) in a variety of ways, including (1) citizen engagement, (2) low-tech but effective architectural and urban design, and (3) high-tech (distributed cognition through studding cities with sensors used with big data analytics). Eradicating or formalizing informal practices with higher technology alternatives may not make a city smarter in this broader sense (Smart 2023).

In many smart city projects in the Global South, urban informality is treated as an obstacle to modernizing (Smart and Curran 2023). Yet, many studies show that informal practices are better than formal institutions at meeting many real needs of citizens. Cities are frequently not effective at meeting the needs of low-income people. Urban policies often make things worse.

If informality can make it possible for people to achieve desirable goals (e.g., employment, adequate food or shelter) not met by existing institutions, this seems to have the effect of increasing the responsiveness and intelligence of urban arrangements. Informal governance makes some things better (Morris and Polese 2015). If smart cities are to be more than islands of privilege and connectivity, we need to consider their impact on people involved in informal activities, which is most (if not all) of the world's population. More than simply acknowledging a need to mitigate negative consequences due to the displacement of informality, more intelligent cities require thoughtful consideration of how to work effectively with informality, to harness its capacities rather than struggle to extinguish them.

Smart city projects in the postcolonial world are part of a long genealogy of urban policies that see slums, street markets, and informal transport as eyesores and threats to public safety, security, and morality. Modernist urban planning in all its forms has usually been directed at replacing such inefficient and destructive "traditional" urban forms. Going back further, to a great extent the forms of urban planning that developed in the industrializing Global North and its colonies in the late nineteenth and early twentieth centuries were responses to risks that threatened to spread from the slums to the elite districts: fires, riots, and epidemics (Smart and Tretter 2023).

An issue that emerged as we began to write this book was the global disruption of the COVID-19 pandemic, which apparently created a new set of pressures toward formalization. Lockdowns are having a disproportionately harmful impact on informal economic enterprises and practices. Even the economic assistance offered to those suffering economically may miss out those engaged in informal livelihoods because their activity is not measured and even sympathetic governments may struggle to get payments to them (*The Economist* 2020a). In Canada, a spokesperson for the federal tax agency describes the underground economy as the biggest challenge in managing help to struggling small businesses and warns that those submitting applications may get the money at first but may expose themselves to punishing audits in the future. Migrant remittances are in aggregate a much larger international cash flow than foreign aid for many countries in the Global South, worth US$46 billion in sub-Saharan Africa in 2018 compared to $32 billion for foreign aid. Remittances can be crucial to many households as well as countries: in Lesotho they account for nearly 16% of GDP. The COVID-19 responses impact on remittances in multiple ways: migrants lose their livelihoods; their family members have increased needs; and the often informal institutions that move money between countries are also affected, often locked down. One payments company found that transfers from Britain to East Africa fell by 80%; from Italy to Africa by 90% (*The Economist* 2020b). Lockdown measures have had serious consequences for residents of squatter areas and others involved with informality. In Brazil, for example, such "measures to contain the virus have already had a drastic impact on the livelihoods of communities composed mainly of black people, with limited access formal employment and getting by through work the service industry—which is generally precarious, intermittent and informal. One example is access to public transport. Using trains and travelling between cities now requires proof of formal employment" (FASE Rio de Janeiro 2020).

Informality in Hong Kong, 1945–1966

This section will provide an account of informality in Hong Kong prior to the twin disturbances of 1966 and 1967 (and the reforms that they prompted; see Chapter 5), focusing on economic informality and governmental informality. It is intended to describe the broad spectrum of informal activity before shifting to a focus on squatting only in the remainder of this book. The second objective is to focus on the informal aspects of colonial governance in Hong Kong and its impact on efforts to control economic informality. The section also provides a concrete illustration of the concepts of informality in operation together in a particular time and place. Context is of particular importance to informal practices, while formality attempts to apply more generally to control what Sally Falk Moore (1978) described as "situational adjustment" of rules to fit local or individual preferences.

In the early 1980s, informality in Hong Kong was ubiquitous, despite decades of efforts to control or eradicate it (Jones and Vagg 2007). Informality took on manifold forms and penetrated almost every form of human endeavor. In a city with the highest population densities in the world, those varieties that competed for public space or encroached on government land were most subjected to government intervention. Illegal street vending (McGee and Yeung 1977; McGee 1983; Josephine Smart 1983; Josephine Smart 1988), whether fixed or itinerant, and squatting (Kehl 1981) were the highest profile categories. Both received a great deal of attention and many interventions throughout colonial history, although squatting was less common until after the Second World War. Despite such attention and the visibility that such informal activities possessed (in comparison, for example, to informal finance, sex work, or corruption, which can operate more covertly), eradication efforts consistently failed, while regulation had limited, often perverse, results. Various varieties of cat and mouse games between informal agents and regulators persisted throughout the postwar period until 1984, at which point momentum shifted in favor of a widespread, if still incomplete, formalization of the Hong Kong cityscape and economy. The interaction between informal practices and governmental responses—particularly toleration, repression, and resettlement—has had a major impact on the kind of place Hong Kong became in the second half of the twentieth century. We return to the post-1967 situation in subsequent chapters; here we focus on the two decades after the Second World War.

Before the 1941 Japanese invasion, Hong Kong's population was estimated at 1.64 million up from 850,000 in 1931, swollen by a half-million people fleeing war in China. The population quadrupled from 600,000 to 2.4 million between 1945 and 1950. A United Nations report estimated that 1,285,000 people entered Hong Kong between September 1945 and

December 1949 (Podmore 1971). This influx, in a mountainous territory of 1,000 km²—with the vast majority of people concentrated in less than 100 km² around the harbor—overwhelmed the formal housing and economic systems. In 1950, the Korean War resulted in an international blockade placed on trade with China. This attempt at spatially confining Communist China destroyed Hong Kong's livelihood, which had been most dependent on servicing the China trade since the colony's establishment in 1841. Hong Kong's exports to China dropped from HK$234.8 million in January 1951 to HK$88.9 million in September 1951. By early 1955, official trade with China was only 15% of Hong Kong's total (Zhang 2001). Hong Kong, though, was the People's Republic's most important trading partner in Asia and was particularly crucial as a place where the embargo could be circumvented through smuggling. Chinese trade officials felt that so long as the Western embargo continued, Hong Kong would be a "primary base" to offset the pressure of economic sanctions (Zhang 2001). During this period, smuggling was one of China's key ways to obtain foreign currency and scarce goods, but it continued afterward for other purposes. Without Hong Kong's unofficial and illegal (but often tolerated by the Hong Kong government) role in these difficult early years for China, Chinese policies might have taken quite different paths out of necessity (Smart and Smart 2012). Subsequently, Hong Kong's role in smuggling goods in and out of China has not always been seen so positively by China, however, such as its central role in facilitating illegal art exports (Vagg 1992, 312). Other economic contributions of informality during this period include the South Sea trade in dried seafood and birds' nests, still vital in Hong Kong today, and which has long been organized through a cluster of family businesses on Hong Kong Island. Hong Kong firms have also been and continue to be heavily involved in the facilitation of remittances and exports of speciality goods to Chinese communities in the Americas and elsewhere (Hsu 2000; Mathews and Yang 2012; Sinn 1997).

A vast array of informal practices of livelihood and commerce helped the poor cope with the very hard years of the 1950s. Ultimately, though, an economy relies on production or external trade, particularly when one is dependent on imports of basics such as food. The colony survived the economic crisis of the early 1950s and created a "Hong Kong miracle" primarily through manufacturing (Hsia and Chau 1978). The initial growth of manufacturing has been attributed to the outflow of industrialists from China, particularly Shanghai, fleeing the anti-capitalist policies of the Chinese Communist Party in the early 1950s (Hamilton 1999; Wong 1988). In 1946, there had been only 30,000 factory workers out of a population of 1.6 million. Between 1948 and 1965, employment in registered factories increased sixfold, and by 1966 included two-fifths of the total labor force (Brown 1971). However, these official numbers obscure a longer history of industrialism in Hong Kong.

Government reports in the prewar period treated manufacturing as negligible, but Chinese sources revealed 600 to 800 factories in 1931, employing 100,000 workers. This vibrant sector was undermined, however, by the Depression and by lack of support by the colonial government, which was under pressure from the United Kingdom due to its success in various sectors like footwear (Ngo 1999). Local Chinese manufacturing in the early 1950s was also underappreciated, partly due to the minimal effort given to collecting statistics (Goodstadt 2006).

Fast economic growth enabled a 110% increase in real wages between 1960 and 1967 (figures that largely left out informal workers), but productivity rose even faster. Labor's share of manufacturing income fell from 64.1% in 1960 to 30.3% in 1970, while the gross rate of return on capital soared from 19.5% to 47.4% in the same period (Lin et al. 1980). The relatively slow growth of wages helped manufacturing to remain competitive despite high costs of living, especially for housing. It also created incentives for workers to become self-employed.

Manufacturing relied to a great extent on informally operated small and medium enterprises, often run out of already overcrowded homes or in squatter areas, many of which did outwork for the larger factories (Chiu et al. 1997). In 1977, 92.1% of the total manufacturing establishments and 40.2% of the employment in manufacturing were in enterprises employing less than 50 workers, although they generated a much smaller proportion of measured Gross Domestic Product. The average number of employees per manufacturing enterprise dropped from 30.04 in 1959 to 27.65 in 1973 (Lin et al. 1980, 94) and again to 18.5 by 1984 (Hong Kong Government 1985, 323). Victor Sit et al. (1979) found that 80% of small manufacturing enterprises were informally housed in domestic buildings, often or usually with the entrepreneur's family sharing living quarters with production. Family businesses, often with unpaid workers, were a large part of Hong Kong's successes (Salaff 1995). There were also many factories located in squatter settlements, with large as well as small ones in Diamond Hill, such as a workshop where all the world's stone-washed denim was once produced. Such small and medium enterprises were a key factor enabling the export success of the elite economic networks that became a key part of the twentieth century rise of the Pacific economy (Hamilton 2021). The competitiveness made possible by "self-exploitation" of informal outworkers and small businesses in turn created concern among British industrialists (Clayton 2007; Smart and Smart 2005; see also Chapter 5).

Small business practices were predominantly informal, particularly in finance (where bank loans were generally unobtainable) and work relations (Chiu 1998). A common pattern was that a partner in a firm—or an engineer, supervisor, or skilled worker—broke away to set up his or her own production enterprise, taking along numerous workers. This occurred mostly in expanding markets; when the market for a product contracts, the smallest businesses fold or move into new products (Sit et al. 1979, 309). The smallest businesses were usually either subcontractors or dependent upon orders from import-export firms. These small fry acted as buffers between volatile market demands and the large, well-established businesses (Chiu et al. 1997; Chu 1992; Lui 1994). Pragmatic attitudes on the part of firms who endorsed this fissioning process helped to generate a highly networked industrial landscape, since they are described as characteristically not "holding a grudge," accepting the situation by recruiting the new firm as a subcontractor during high market demand periods (Yeung 1998). The continual reproduction of the entrepreneurial stock and the preservation of an economy based on informally operated firms is encouraged in a context where employees had few protections (Clayton 2007). Immigrants from China were more likely to become proprietors in manufacturing than in commerce, partly because their backgrounds put them at a linguistic disadvantage in service sectors. Making the transition from employee to employer, however, requires access to assets such as capital and connections; thus the effective utilization of social networks for informal finance was crucial in the process for those with small amounts of their own capital (Chiu 1998; Topley 1964), just as networks have been argued to be central to the operation of the larger capitalist sector among overseas Chinese (Hamilton 2001; Yeung 1998). The types of products manufactured in Hong Kong helped make possible this pattern of enterprise fission and the reproduction of the small-scale character of industry. When little capital and much skilled labor is required, economies of scale have slight significance so that large and small manufacturers can operate side by side (Lin, Ho, and Mok 1980). Low capital-intensiveness eases product changes responding to market conditions. This is especially critical in fields where fashions change quickly. This was of greater importance for Hong Kong in the 1960s and 1970s than were low wages, since other countries could provide cheaper labor. During a period of Fordism and vertical industrial integration—when few had heard of the "Toyota model," "just-in-time production," or flexible production—Hong Kong's ability to switch products quickly and make profits on short production runs provided a great competitive advantage on new niche products, such as wigs in the 1950s and quartz watches in the 1980s (Chiu, Ho, and Lui 1997; Enright et al. 1997).

Workers, though, needed places to live and doing so legally in the 1950s was too expensive for the large majority of people in Hong Kong. High rents left less money for other needs, so that the lower prices of street vendors, as well as other kinds of informal commerce, helped make ends meet.[3] Official concerns focused heavily on squatting and hawking illegally in the streets, although informal practices were found throughout Hong Kong in the 1950s and 1960s, including within government in the forms of widespread corruption, perks, and interested use of discretionary powers (Ng 2020; Scott 2017). The numbers of those making a living by selling things in the streets grew from perhaps 13,000–16,000 before the Second World War to about 70,000 in 1947, only 10,524 of whom were licensed (McGee 1973, 43). In 1981, there were 63,000 full-time hawkers (40,000 unlicensed), with many more involved part-time or as assisting family members. In 1983, street hawking contributed an estimated HK$1 billion to the economy, accounting for 11% of retail sales (Josephine Smart 1989). Informal provisioning of consumer necessities and housing made it possible to keep wages down and industry competitive, which public housing also supported after 1954 (Castells 1986, Chiu, Ho, and Lui 1997)

In 1948, there were only 30,000 squatters, despite population growth and housing shortages. The government controlled all provision of land by leasehold, but failed to make enough land available for development. With the failure of the formal private sector and government to provide anywhere near enough housing, which was badly needed, squatting offered informal solutions to housing shortages (Hopkins 1972). By the end of 1949, the number of squatters had risen to 300,000 from an estimated 45,430 in June 1949 (Smart 2006).

High rents and low wages resulted in some of the highest population densities recorded anywhere (Shelton et al. 2011), leading to pervasive efforts to gain control over a little more space for living or working (see Figure 2.1). Control over public space required eternal vigilance against encroachment in many different ways, including illegal additions to legal private buildings (Leeming 1977). The capacity for control in Hong Kong was limited. Inability of the legal built environment to incorporate enough new housing encouraged squatting, particularly once people discovered that they were likely to get

Figure 2.1: Illegal extensions to private buildings, 1982. Copyright and provided by Alan Smart.

away it. The larger the numbers attempting to build on unoccupied land, the harder it was for the authorities to stop it. The number of squatters soared in the 1970s until 1982, peaking at over 750,000 (Smart 1992).

The government wanted to control these informal transgressions on public space but failed for the first three postwar decades. The government owns all land: real estate is leasehold and the revenues generated have always been central to government revenues, often accounting for a third or more of the total (Smart and Lee 2003). The beginning of squatter resettlement in the 1950s (which led to one of the world's largest public housing systems) offered a viable way to regain control of encroached space at a time when geopolitics constrained repressive clearance without rehousing (Smart 2006). However, despite massive squatter resettlement, new squatting continued. Certain forms of informal housing were explicitly tolerated (but without an official legal basis) by the government in this period, the most prominent being Licensed Areas (a kind of regulated self-built housing in specified lots, later transformed into Temporary Housing Areas (see Chapter 7). However, after fires in squatter areas, victims were often authorized to sleep in the streets, although this in fact involved allowing them to build temporary structures on the streets and sidewalks, as well as providing some toilets and bathhouses for them (Figure 2.1).[4] In part because many of the large squatter fires occurred near it, the already crowded New Kowloon neighborhoods of Sham Shui Po and Cheung Sha Wan became host to the majority of these authorized street squatters (see Figure 2.2; for more details, see Smart and Tang 2014).

This last example highlights the importance of not neglecting governmental informality, although the vast majority of informality research does. The most public form of it is mercenary corruption, but there is a continuum from clear cases of this through "practical norms" underlying everyday practices, which may be tolerated by superiors without approval of them (De Herdt and Olivier de Sardan 2015).

Hong Kong has gone from being seen as deeply and corrosively corrupt before 1974 to being a poster child for effective anti-corruption programs (Manion 2004). More recently, there are concerns about a fall from grace after a series of corruption charges and convictions at the very top of the government (Smart 2018). Such shifts in the prevalence of corruption can be better understood through attention to the informal processes operating within government, influencing how the consequences of policies may end up very different from those intended. To be effective, corruption control depends on fundamental change in the operation of the informal norms of governmental routine, and more generally in the rules of the game. Changes in governmental informality also reverberate in the more marginal forms of informality within the economy, influencing not only the extent of informal practices but also how they are organized.

Figure 2.2: Pavement squatters in Shek Kip Mei. Source: HKRS306/1/120.

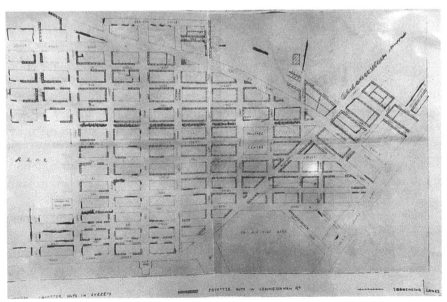

Figure 2.3: Map of authorized pavement squatting, Cheung Sha Wan. Source: HKRS163/1/1743.

Anything that is regulated creates opportunities for profits by those with discretion over control of the activity. One scandal concerned testing for driving licenses (Goodstadt 2011). Domains where government tolerated informal and illegal practices, such as squatting, were particularly prone to corruption. Unlicensed street vendors "were perhaps the most vulnerable" (Hampton 2012, 228). A senior official in the Resettlement Department wrote that he regularly rotated his junior officers out of squatter control to limit the temptations they faced (Hayes 1996). In 1960, Governor Robert Black wrote to the Colonial Secretary in response to some corruption scandals that "the exercise of discretionary power by junior officers is inevitably open to abuse. When we begin a revision of the laws in November, it is intended to pay particular attention to those laws which give discretion to junior officers."[5]

In 1964, the Advisory Committee on Corruption reported on reforms intended to reduce the problem. They included the simplification of procedures in the Building Ordinance, while other departmental licensing procedures were "simplified, accelerated and clarified." Heads of Department were reminded of the need to do this "whenever it appears that procedural delays would cause corruption in some form or other."[6] Early efforts to control corruption were limited because the Anti-Corruption Branch was a unit within the Police Force. As late as 1970, new anti-corruption legislation depended on enforcement by the police (Scott 2010, 8), so that solidarities among police officers and shared expectations undermined its effectiveness. Only the establishment of the powerful and well-funded Independent Commission Against Corruption in 1974 created the conditions for a widespread diminution of corruption. Ian Scott (2013, 78) notes that until recently, Hong Kong's approach had been to formulate stronger and clearer rules to control corruption. The trend elsewhere to emphasize the promotion of values for anti-corruption has been adopted in Hong Kong since 1997, but this "has not led to more personal discretion in decision-making but rather has resulted in the development of informal rules to deal with new ethical concerns and the tendency to push issues, where discretion might be exercised, to higher levels in the organization for resolution" (Scott 2013, 78). Widespread governmental informality was greatly reduced after 1974, but recent corruption convictions at high levels of the Hong Kong government have revealed considerable informality at the top (Smart 2018).

Governmental informalities other than corruption were widely seen as legitimate, even when not in conformity to law, by officials at all levels due to the need to get things done despite inadequate resources and conflicting demands. We will consider numerous examples of this extralegal action, from operating extralegal licensed areas to the fundamentals of the act of tolerating surveyed squatter structures (see especially Chapter 10), but it extended far beyond the management of the squatter situation. For example, Kenny Ng

Informality

(2020) reveals how the colonial film censorship system operated without legal authority.

Policymaking in the 1945–1967 period was very personalized among small numbers of administrative officers and members of the Executive Council. That situation was subjected to formalization processes that reduced discretion and expanded the scope of rules to be followed by Hong Kong government officials (Scott 2013; Smart 2018a). In 1972, Governor MacLehose appointed the consultancy McKinsey to review the colonial system of governance. We return to those reforms in Chapter 5; here we only stress how the review portrayed the weaknesses of the existing system. The small group of elite administrative officers (called *cadets* in the 1950s) were overwhelmed. Responding to urgent demands overwhelmed capacity to address continuing or prospective future important issues. Senior administrative officers "had long been part of the policymaking process but they were not strictly speaking policymakers," which officially should have been the prerogative of the Governor-in-Council; that is, the Governor with the Executive Council (Tsang 2007, 145). The reforms "emphasized the development of formal plans" (Tsang 2007, 143), and their influence continues to the current administration (Scott 2010). A key "achievement of McKinsey's review was to start modernizing and upgrading the government machinery to enable it to take on new social and developmental dimensions of government, for which planning ahead and additional resources were essential" (Tsang 2007, 147). While adding new administrative procedures and formalizing policy decision-making in various ways, some McKinsey reforms "resulted in staff officers being given line responsibilities on dubious constitutional grounds" (Tsang 2007, 145). The modernization of policymaking processes thus fostered a new kind of informality.

The next chapter considers the initial working hypothesis that began this research project; that the 1984 beginning of the end of the squatter problem, and specifically the adoption of the Squatter Occupancy Survey as a means to make that possible, can be explained by geopolitics and how they were transformed by the reaching of an agreement to return Hong Kong to Chinese sovereignty.

3

Evaluating the Geopolitical Explanation

Hong Kong cannot be studied in isolation. Constantly subject to the repercussions from the changing political and socioeconomic conditions outside the colony, all major events in Hong Kong have been the results of interactions between local and external forces.

—Tsai Jung-fang, *Hong Kong in Chinese History: Community and Social Unrest in the British Colony, 1842–1913* (1993, 8)

Introduction

The first explanation we considered for the end of new squatting in 1984 was based on geopolitics, proposing that changes in the geopolitical context made possible an end to the squatter problem (Smart and Smart 2017a). Despite the apparent plausibility of this explanation (see Preface), thorough archival research failed to uncover smoking guns to prove or strongly support any conclusion that change in geopolitical constraints was the primary reason for formalization's successes at that time. That does not mean, of course, that a geopolitical explanation is wrong, only that it cannot be shown to be right. In the absence of direct evidence for its accuracy, a conclusion in its favor requires not only a demonstration of its analytic adequacy, but also the rejection of other plausible explanations as less powerful or less empirically supported.

Successful exclusions of all rivals would leave the geopolitical context of 1984 as the most plausible reason for the timing of these shifts in Hong Kong's landscape of informality. As the remainder of this book demonstrates, though, there are indeed other explanations better supported by empirical evidence. However, the greater strength of other explanations still allows that a geopolitical explanation might be part of the circumstances supporting an answer that combines several explanations. The second objective of this chapter is to provide some context for understanding the political economy of Hong Kong, which has been constantly influenced by the geopolitics related to its position on the edge of two former empires (Carroll 2005). This will help ground

Evaluating the Geopolitical Explanation

the following chapters, which provide alternative plausible accounts for the changes leading to 1984.

Approaches to Hong Kong in a Geopolitical Context

Geopolitics and its attendant competition between states are a central part of historical understandings of imperialism. The dynamics of political competition between metropolitan countries are given substantial attention in studies of geopolitics. Less consideration is paid to the interaction between geopolitics and the domestic politics within colonies. This inattention may be due to expectations that international and diplomatic politics are under the control of the imperial homeland, with governors primarily offering information and following instructions. Expecting the colonial government to serve as simply an organizational arm of the imperial homeland is problematic; it overlooks the autonomy that governors had when dealing with the instructions coming from London. To account for the variations of colonial native policy in the German Empire, Steinmetz (2007, 29–31) contended that the colonial government had to be considered in its own rights since it possessed "dual autonomy," with profound impacts on colonial governance as well as specific colonial policies. As he argued, this "dual autonomy" entailed the relative independence of the colonial government vis-à-vis the metropolitan state and local interest groups. Retaining room for manoeuvre on both sides enabled the local officials to have bounded agency to shape the policy trajectory when instructions from the imperial homeland came. The underlying logic of his argument is that the metropolitan government neither attempted nor had the capacity to "micromanage the daily activities in the colonies." The result was that effective imperial sovereignty "resided with the legendary 'men on the spot' . . . who were in direct contact with indigenous leaders and communities" (29). Yet, the impact of geopolitics, considered as interstate relations, could profoundly shape the outcome of colonial governance by acting as an overarching framework that sets the scope of how far the colonial government could maneuver.

Although Steinmetz's research focuses on the German Empire, his insights appear applicable to the case of Hong Kong. With respect to the agency of the "men on the spot," Bickers (2013) argued that the relationship between London (Whitehall and the Colonial Office) and the Hong Kong colonial governors involved "loose ties": the imperial homeland could invigilate and issue instructions, but colonial governors "could always buy time by turning back on the Colonial Office . . . or less overtly they could always simply be obstructively tardy in their responses . . . London would generally eventually notice, but there was much room for procedural manoeuvre" (49). Yet, autonomy of the colonial governors was not given but emerged through a series of negotiations. Yep (2013) identified at least five factors that shaped the degree of colonial autonomy: trust within the circle of elites; reciprocity in terms of fulfilling the interests of the imperial homeland, so that non-compliance by the colonial governors could be tolerated; agendas of the sovereign power; whether conflict resolution mechanisms were in place; and finally the capability of the local leadership to pursue effective governance.

As Yep (2018, 247) argued elsewhere, if the colonial governors saw metropolitan intervention in colonial domestic affairs as undesirable, they could "take pre-emptive measures in containing the prospective intrusion from London." An exemplar case of this sort of preemptive move is the establishment of an independent body (later, the Independent Commission Against Corruption) in 1974 to combat corruption (Yep 2013). On some rare occasions, the colonial officials within the local administration could even take a proactive move to intrude into the imperial domain to force the metropolitan state to accept the deal. This could be seen in the (least likely) case of the development of Hong Kong's unusual degree of "external autonomy." For example, despite London warning Hong Kong's Financial Secretary to "stay his hand" in their Asian Development Bank membership application—as the Financial Secretary had no formal role to play in the foreign relations of the colony—the Financial Secretary made a unilateral public announcement that "the parliamentary bill on Hong Kong's admission would be scheduled in the coming summer" (Fung and Fong 2019, 179). After that, London had no choice but to bitterly accept the deal and support Hong Kong's application to become a member of the Asian Development Bank. The Financial Secretary simply responded to London's inquiry by writing that "there can be no going back now" (Fung and Fong 2019, 180). The point here is to register that the understanding of colonial governance and policymaking in Hong Kong could not be reduced to London's initiatives. This preemptive and proactive move showed that the colonial governors exhibited a certain degree of autonomy, similar to what Steinmetz found within the German Empire. The question, therefore, is not whether colonial autonomy existed but under which condition(s) Hong Kong's remarkable degree of autonomy emerged?

It is for this question that geopolitics is relevant. The literature about geopolitical impact on Hong Kong could be roughly divided into two waves of scholarship. Most scholars of the first wave were interested in topics such as Hong Kong's political-economic development. This could be seen as a response to the mainstream explanations and discourses that failed to account for the remarkable yet anomalous case of Hong Kong. For example, in response to the limitations of the modernization and developmental state literature, So and Chiu (1995) used world-systems analysis to shed light on how global interstate dynamics created by the Cold War enabled Hong Kong to undertake rapid industrial growth during the 1950s under the laissez-faire policy of the colonial government. World-systems analysis offered many

Evaluating the Geopolitical Explanation

important insights, including its emphasis that Hong Kong's unique economic trajectory had to be understood at the regional and global level. In So's (1986, 246) words, a "favorable world-market situation" created by the US government's containment policy against China; "the lack of domestic class struggle" due to Beijing's nonconfrontational approach in Hong Kong, so as to retain and utilize the capitalist enclave to circumvent containment policy; and the capital brought by Shanghai entrepreneurs as a result of their fleeing from communist rule "help to explain the liberal and the non-intervention policy of the Hong Kong state" and the colony's economic success. In short, what the world-systems analysis achieved is to put Hong Kong's geopolitical context up front, so that "the effects of history [regarding the decisions shaping the institutional logic of industrialism] are [to be shown] geographically embedded" (Chiu, Ho, and Lui 1997, 158). The distinctive location of Hong Kong allowed the colony to have more influence on London than usual, as well as within the global political economy.

The world-systems analysis could be seen as an exemplar case for illustrating how geopolitics matters, but it is not the only approach that finds the geopolitical form of explanation useful. Kuan (1991, 774; see also Lau 1987) used the concept of "power dependence" to describe the evolutionary nature of political change in Hong Kong, where "the choice of the rulers of the hegemonic country who set the rules of the game is crucial for political change in the dominated polity." As the power dependence thesis implied, decisions regarding Hong Kong's political change were made outside the colony, as determined by the existing (and incoming) sovereign after Hong Kong formally entered the transition phase in 1984. Seen in this light, geopolitics is understood as a constraint. In this vein, it is unsurprising to see that existing scholarship on geopolitical impact on Hong Kong's political development would consider the 1984 Sino-British Joint Declaration as a historical juncture because it clarified China's policy over Hong Kong. Even though London had already begun to prepare to decolonize Hong Kong, due to the 1969 long-term study that concluded Hong Kong's future "must eventually lie in China" (Mark 2017, 259), political change was still perceived as a risky choice that the British should strive to avoid (Lui 2017). The Joint Declaration served as a signal that not only put an end to the uncertainty surrounding the colony's future, but also indicated that Hong Kong would "be run by the people of Hong Kong" after retrocession (Tang and Ching 1994, 161), and that the incoming sovereign "appeared to have passively endorsed Hong Kong's democratisation scheme" (Tsang 2004, 232). The geopolitical change brought by the Sino-British Joint Declaration was thus an easing of preexisting structural constraints, whereby the British recalibrated interests and statecraft. Previous risky choices, such as real estate investments, would become possible and help maintain confidence.

A limitation of the first wave of scholarship is that it tends to conceive the British colonial power as a unitary actor and thus overlooks the different interests between London and Hong Kong. It also tends to conceive the geopolitical effects as if it worked similarly at the local as well as the international level. The second wave of scholarship could be seen as a remedy to these limitations. It tries to overcome the limitations through revisiting the local dynamics of the Cold War in Hong Kong, interrogating how the geopolitical process unfolds in the colony and how it shaped colonial policy making. Tsang's (1997) study of the neutrality policy of the colonial government and Mark's (2004) *Hong Kong and the Cold War* are often regarded as the important texts of this second wave of scholarship. These works, and the subsequent studies (e.g., Wong 2002; Airriess 2005; Lee and Choi 2020; Roberts and Carroll 2016) that drew insights from them, paid attention to circumstances of the military indefensibility of Hong Kong and how Hong Kong–China relations complicated the process of colonial governance after the Second World War.

It should be noted that most of these works are attentive to the Cold War period, but they are not Cold War studies per se. Rather, they are treating the Cold War circumstances as a manifestation of, to appropriate Krasner (2001), "contested [colonial] sovereignty," where the presence of the unified communist China produced various pressures on the colonial government and posed challenges to colonial rule (Roberts 2016). The origin of such "contestability" of the colony could be traced back to Sino-British relations before the Second World War and the Hong Kong question (e.g., Lane 1990; Wesley-Smith 1980; Chan 1973; Tsang 2004, Chapter 8; Fung 1991). A crucial factor that contributed to the persistence of contestability was Britain's postwar geostrategy of retaining the colony to "keep a foot in the door" of China (Ashton 2004). In a nutshell, it entailed keeping Hong Kong under British control, since it was seen as too valuable to abandon in peace, but without "committing scarce resources" for its survival at war, as it was seen as too peripheral to merit them (Mark 2004, 1). It was under this circumstance that the colonial government improvised its policies to meet the challenges created by such a peculiar geopolitical situation. The task was to leverage the nonmilitary measures to hold the indefensible colony, so that China would not perceive the capitalist enclave to be a security threat and, in so doing, deter China's aggressive actions (Mark 2004, 121).

These studies suggest that the colonial government had to explore unconventional strategies to tackle the geopolitical challenges of a bipolar world. Matching such exploration and "impressive juggling" between the global powers (Roberts 2016, 23), at the local level, the viewpoints of the colonial government and London diverged. One indication of these disparate viewpoints was the observation of the UK Minister of Defence, Albert Alexander, in June 1949 that Governor Alexander Grantham complained about the military measures proposed by Lieutenant General Francis Festing (Kwong and Tsoi 2014, 239). To Grantham, these military measures were "harmful to the development of the colony." He even threated to resign so that he could—and eventually did—retain the "right to protest to the Colonial Office" when there was "a clash of opinion" (Kwong and Tsoi 2014, 239). The occasion of having conflicting viewpoints brings us back to the question concerning the conditions for the emergence of Hong Kong's autonomy. It was clear that the peculiar geopolitical situation mattered but, at the local level, it served more to motivate the colonial governors to explore unconventional strategies and, in doing so, to sometimes clash with the imperial homeland's viewpoints.

To be sure, there is no reason to believe that the viewpoints of the "men on the spot" must prevail, nor do we imply here that London would offer concessions when the colonial governors remained disinterested in the instructions made by London. Instead, what the second wave literature suggested is that, when London's instructions came to the colony, the degree to which the colonial government had to comply was negotiable (see Ure 2012) so long as it did not jeopardize broader diplomatic relations (see Fung and Fong 2019, 96–98). It was such negotiations that profoundly shaped the colonial policy trajectory, and the implementation of these policies could have payoffs at the level of high politics. As Maurice Yip (2020, 374) concludes, when he dissected a New Town development plan lead by mainland Chinese capital investment in the Northwest New Territories in the years before the 1984 Joint Declaration, "Diplomatic negotiations are not only high-level interactions between state powers about territorial disputes, political agenda, or ideological conflicts but could also have impacts on, and being influenced by, the ongoing urban transformation within the territory."

Plausible Explanations of Squatter Resettlement

The geopolitical hypothesis considered in this book emerged from Smart's efforts to explain the origins of Hong Kong's Squatter Resettlement Programme. The importance of Hong Kong's public housing program, once housing half of the population (now 45%), resulted in various efforts to explain how it started. Scholarly attention was also prompted by Hong Kong's reputation for committing to laissez-faire economic policies (locally reframed as "positive non-intervention"). Today, Hong Kong is still routinely listed near the top of global indices of economic freedom, with luminaries of neoclassical economics such as Milton Friedman seeing it as an exemplar of free markets (Peck 2021). The question naturally arose of how to reconcile the vast government housing sector with laissez-faire policies. The problem was to explain squatter resettlement, rather than just squatter clearance. Why not simply clear them off needed land? If public housing seems advisable for other reasons than regaining control over land, why not house those perceived to be most worthy rather than those who have broken rules and created problems of public order and public safety? An adequate explanation of squatter resettlement must account for why clearance would not have been enough, or even better.

There are five different kinds of explanations for the origins of public housing in Hong Kong, which sometimes overlap in the work of individual scholars. These focus on, respectively: (1) governmental intervention to improve public welfare in a situation where the private sector was incapable of producing affordable housing (e.g., Hopkins 1971); (2) the need for intervention in order to free up scarce land for private sector development that was otherwise obstructed by illegal squatting (Drakakis-Smith 1979); (3) state intervention to reproduce labor power at a cost low enough to support development through export-oriented manufacturing (Castells et al. 1990; Lui 1984); (4) pressures from Britain to change squatter and housing policy (MacKay 2000); and (5) sanitary concerns (Ip 2004, Jones 2003).

The Shek Kip Mei fire on Christmas Eve 1953, which destroyed the homes of an estimated 53,000 people, was a key part of later governmental explanations for the starting of squatter resettlement. The Shek Kip Mei myth they fostered ignores a whole series of qualifiers (e.g., not the first, was not a program but just a one-off project until later, etc.). The Shek Kip Mei story condenses, simplifies, and intensifies a much more complicated history, as do all good myths. The antagonist that had to be responded to by the colonial culture hero was not a single fire, but a whole series of large squatter fires that plagued Hong Kong throughout the 1950s (and continuing into the 1980s).

While innovations, particularly governmental construction of multistory buildings, are present in the responses to Shek Kip Mei, earlier massive squatter area fires, such as the 1950 Kowloon City and 1951 Tung Tau fires, left tens of thousands without shelter. The minimum number of people who lost their homes to squatter fires during the 1950s totals 190,047. Scholarly accounts rarely point to Shek Kip Mei as more than a catalyst—perhaps determining the timing of large-scale intervention but not the cause in of itself. The cause was instead located in broader dynamics or motivations. This perspective is most central in the welfare explanation: the idea that the Hong Kong government began to directly provide housing to meet massive housing needs that the private sector was unable to satisfy. While the current official account, the founding myth, stresses the needs of the Shek Kip Mei fire victims themselves, academic proponents of the welfare explanation have focused more on the needs of the general public (Pryor 1973). However, the welfare position seems to be clearly contradicted by government statements at the time and later.

David Faure (2003a) offers an intriguing alternative argument. He proposes that public statements saying intervention was not done out of consideration for the welfare of squatters should be seen as subterfuge, rather than prima facie evidence of what the Hong Kong government was thinking. Contrary to academics' usual biases, which lead us to be sceptical of claims that government is simply acting for the public good, we may be too ready to accept governmental disclaimers of welfare as a motivation. Faure suggests that while the colonial government, along with influential figures in the Hong Kong community, were not interested in intervening on the behalf of welfare, the UK government was. Playing up the emergency of Shek Kip Mei allowed them to succumb to Colonial Office pressure to do more about the housing and squatter problems (Faure 2003b). This argument that welfare concerns truly were important but were hidden by government officials would account for resettlement, not just clearance, but is not supported by the archival record. It is also belied by the implementation of resettlement, which does not appear to be driven by a concern for the welfare of squatters. In his critique of the welfare position, David Drakakis-Smith (1979, 34) demonstrated that the 1 million squatters resettled by 1971 were relocated onto land equivalent to only 34% of the space previously occupied. Moreover, squatters were generally resettled on land more peripheral and less valuable than where they previously resided. The central motive appears to be to displace squatters from land badly needed for development, but that only accounts for clearance, not for resettlement. Note that this focus also implicitly sets up the unmentioned category of squatters on land not needed for development. The needs to be met by welfare provision were those of the government more than those of the displaced.

While the welfare explanation fails—both for inadequacy and by being undermined by the best available evidence—it subsequently became part of the official narrative. Given the low level of development of public participation and social welfare in colonial Hong Kong, public housing came to be both a key governmental strategy for building a sense of citizenship and commitment from Hong Kong residents, and a symbol for the positive dimensions of the colonial legacy. Both became extremely important after the 1966 and 1967 riots and in the transition to 1997. They can be seen clearly in the housing reforms of the 1970s initiated by Governor MacLehose. Welfare concerns were certainly much more important by then and will be examined in close detail in this book, particularly in Chapter 8. But they cannot account for the beginning of multistory public housing projects, nor for why the beneficiaries were squatters rather than law-abiding members of the working poor, or low-level employees of the government. Squatters were not sympathetically represented in the minutes and memos of the time; even when sympathy was expressed, there was a much greater concern about the risk of encouraging additional squatting.

David Faure's critique is important in that he identifies significant shifts in British Colonial Office policy toward welfare and development in the Empire. But understanding the impact of these London-based pressures on housing policy requires a careful look at how Hong Kong responded, and at the strengths of the sticks and carrots that London could use to promote reforms. Faure's argument applies more appropriately to the 1970s than to the 1950s, where he deploys it to explain the beginning of squatter resettlement.

We turn, then, to explanation (2) providing support to property development and property developers. David Drakakis-Smith identified the reason for squatter resettlement as the desire by government to make land available for development by private enterprise and for public works. Although state intervention to encourage private building seems paradoxical, he argues that the bottleneck created by illegal usurpation of land could only be overcome through government action. While consistent with some of the outcomes, and better supported by evidence, the assistance for private developers' approach fails to explain why squatters should be rehoused and not simply cleared, making even more land available for private development. It also neglects criticism of resettlement by developers and private property interests during that period.

If the government had truly been committed to maximizing the freedom of action of private property developers, squatter clearance without resettlement would have been a more optimal approach. This would also have been consistent with the strongly expressed desire of officials to regain control over potentially valuable space. What is missing is an explanation of why clearance without resettlement was either not desired or not seen as achievable. What is also underplayed are the conditions that prevented the private sector from providing legal housing. It was not simply the poverty of the refugees; rents per square foot were as high or higher for cubicles in squatter structures as they were in legal private housing. Rather, governmental restrictions were a major factor. Despite Hong Kong's fame as a place where capitalism is largely unfettered, a major exception is land, ownership of which is monopolized by the state. Furthermore, obtaining rights and permissions to develop land has been a complex and time-consuming process; one that largely excluded indigenous villagers in the peri-urban areas from undertaking it by themselves. The centrality of the state in land administration, combined with a colonial government in considerable disarray after the Japanese occupation, generated a near deadlock in making land available for building. The inability of the private sector to cope with housing the rapid influx of refugees was, in part, a product of state intervention. Richard Wong (2015) has stressed the importance of the imposition of rent control in 1945 as a major contributor to the housing problem. The five rival explanations tend to take private sector failure for

Evaluating the Geopolitical Explanation

granted, so that the question was not whether the government would intervene in direct low-income housing provision, but only when, how, and why.

The problem of explaining squatter *resettlement* and not just squatter *clearance* also undermines (5) the sanitation/public hygiene approaches offered by Jones and Ip. Both provide compelling evidence that the government saw squatter areas as problematic because of threats they posed to public health. But it is hardly at issue that the government wanted to wipe illegal settlements off the map. Although health and sanitation concerns were central to the official colonial worldview, even without this, the government would have wanted to eradicate squatter colonies for the sake of public order, to free up land for development, and for general aesthetics. What none of these desires explains is why clearance without resettlement was not viable. A similar objection applies to Richard Wong's (2015, 1) argument that public housing was a "response to the devastating consequences of rent control," since he only accounts for one of the conditions that fostered the growth of the squatter problem, without addressing why these groups had to be rehoused at government expense rather than simply displaced.

The third explanation concentrates on the impact of public housing on the Hong Kong economy. The argument is that public housing reduced the cost of labor and thereby facilitated the rapid growth of export-oriented manufacturing (Castells 1986; Lui 1984), which was the basis of Hong Kong's rapid economic expansion from the 1950s until the opening of mainland China after 1978. What Castells (1986, 97) referred to as the "Hong Kong model of economic development" emphasized how the social wage, particularly public housing, facilitated lower wages and enabled Hong Kong to compete successfully in manufacturing exports. Similarly, Schiffer (1983) argued that low wages threaten the reproduction of labor, and that the state reacts by providing resources such as housing to subsidize workers and to promote peaceful labor-management relations This can be seen as a functionalist argument from effects to causes. While there are clear methodological problems with functionalist explanations, they can serve as an effective way to identify plausible explanations (Cohen 2000). However, in the process of evaluating such an explanation, we should identify mechanisms through which the effects can generate their cause, such as a desire by decision-makers to achieve such effects. Again, at most, it seems that the desire to keep the cost of labor down might explain the development of a low-income housing program, but it does not account for its establishment as a squatter resettlement program. The focus on keeping labor costs down is largely without empirical evidence. The merit of the explanation for my questions, though, is that, like the welfare explanation, it would account for resettlement as opposed to squatter clearance alone. However, a focus on subsidizing the cost of reproducing labor power does not by itself explain why for 16 years it was squatters, rather than simply low-income workers, who were provided with subsidized housing. Keeping wages competitive, though, was probably a contextual factor that helped make the expansion of low-cost housing feasible and attractive, particularly in the period from the 1970s on, when Hong Kong wages were higher than other competitors such as Taiwan and South Korea (Chiu et al. 1997). That it may have had the effect of allowing lower wages does not in itself provide a mechanism for the initiation of the program. In any case, low-wage manufacturing is consistent with the extensive toleration of illegal squatter settlements, where labor power can also be cheaply reproduced.

We are left with only the fourth explanation: pressures from Britain for changes in squatter and housing policy. While this is clearly a factor by the 1970s, whether it could account for squatter resettlement in the 1950s is much more dubious. The strongest argument in favor is that by David Faure, who presents Governor Grantham as being caught between pressure exerted by the British government to toe their social policy line, and the need to accommodate Hong Kong's Legislative Council (LegCo), which was suspicious of extension of social services or welfare (Faure 2003a, 665). But his evidence is quite weak for housing, since *social services* seems to have been focused on juvenile delinquency for the Colonial Office. Hong Kong was also asked to consider establishing a Department of Social Welfare, but the Social Welfare Advisory Committee in London had only in 1942 changed its name from the juvenile delinquency subcommittee of the Committee on Penal Administration. In any case, delay and deflection was easily accomplished, unlike the confrontations in the 1970s described by Yep and Lui (2010) and discussed in Chapter 5. The action in the week immediately after the Shek Kip Mei fire, in which a decision to build emergency housing was taken, seems to have been entirely locally generated.

All five of these explanations for squatter resettlement fail for one reason or another. They are inadequate as an explanation because, at most, they account for squatter clearance but not for resettlement (2, 3, 5), or they account for public housing but not for priority being given to squatters (3). Or, if the explanation is adequate as an explanation, there is good evidence that the claims are undermined or unsupported by the archival evidence (1, 4). Applying the same criteria to the geopolitical explanation, does it hold up?

The Geopolitical Explanation of Resettlement

In 1989, in response to the empirical and theoretical inadequacies of the three explanations current at the time (1, 2 and 3), and based on archival research of files opened to about the year 1957 (but with the key policy files around the Shek Kip Mei fire still unavailable), Smart proposed an alternative approach. It emphasized the ways in which the eviction of squatters without permanent

Evaluating the Geopolitical Explanation

resettlement ran the risk of destabilizing the diplomatic and geopolitical situation. In the absence of resettlement, squatters were also likely to resquat, so that the squatter problem was at best removed to more peripheral areas.

During the period of clearance without resettlement, resistance, often violent, was common enough that numerous minutes and memos commented on the risks involved. Housing officers expected the possibility of serious resistance, so they came in large numbers with police support. It was the provision of resettlement housing that quieted squatters, who were for the most part willing if not eager to be rehoused by the government. Resistance continued, however, particularly for squatters in categories not eligible for permanent public housing (such as those living in unsurveyed buildings, recent migrants, or fire victims). The efficacy of this resistance shifted with public sentiment and media coverage.

Violent responses from displaced squatters occasioned political responses from China (Grantham 1965). Anger, and the likelihood of violence resulting from displacement, achieved influence that they would not have had if not for the context: an "indefensible" British colony was precariously perched on the edge of a country where the anti-imperialist Chinese Communist Party (CCP) had recently come to power in Beijing (Tsang 1997; Mark 2000). Research on Hong Kong in the aftermath of the rise to power of the CCP in 1949 has emphasized the importance of geopolitics for Hong Kong in the postwar period, as well as the concern about the potential for internal disorder. Mark (2000, 838) concluded that the "likelihood of a direct Communist military attack on Hong Kong worried the British less . . . than the internal unrest caused by the influx of refugees and Communist-inspired strikes." A key argument of *The Shek Kip Mei Myth* was that the impact of large squatter fires prior to Shek Kip Mei reveals a close relationship between what was happening at a very local level among disgruntled squatter fire victims and the geopolitics of the early Cold War era. The capacity for resistance was a neglected cause of resettling squatters rather than just clearing them from needed land. By itself, resistance would have been insufficient. Its impact had to be amplified by the constraints generated by the difficult diplomatic and geopolitical situation. Documentation of these claims is available in Smart (1989, 1992, 2006).

What makes this geopolitical explanation of resettlement better than the other five is that it provides a mechanism to convert the desire to end the squatter problem (and thereby to make land available for development and to end the threats to public order, public safety, public security, etc.) into resettlement, not just clearance. In addition, the government had tried multiple other approaches in pursuit of an end to the squatter problem, all of which failed in one way or another. Officials eventually learned that the most effective and cheapest way to solve the problem was to provide public housing of minimal amenities and maximal density. This lesson was learned despite great resistance within the government, but it was eventually accepted as the only viable solution (Smart 2006; Smart and Lam 2009). The argument of geopolitics can account for the phenomenon of resettlement rather than just clearance. As well, its impact is well documented in the archival information, and it is more effective in offering empirical evidence than any of its rivals. It met all the requirements for a provisional acceptance of a plausible explanation—provisionally, of course, unless or until a better alternative emerges, which has not yet occurred.

Does this kind of geopolitical explanation continue to be plausible and adequate for the period after the 1966 and 1967 riots, when reform became more central to the agenda for both Hong Kong and London? Did geopolitics still constrain the colonial government from undertaking excessively regressive actions against squatters, which could have perhaps finally ended the squatter problem by another path? How long did this situation last? The hypothesis that underlay this research project was that the Sino-British Declaration in 1984 changed the geopolitical situation in ways that finally made solving the squatter problem possible, even if only for new squatting. It also facilitated transforming the regulation of existing squatter structures by registering their occupants during a snapshot of time. After that moment, any new occupants would have a very different relationship with the government and its housing systems, creating a situation where the numbers gradually decreased (see Chapter 12).

However, coincidence is certainly not proof of causation. The timing could be accidental, in which case some other cause was operating to produce the regulatory changes. Was the end to new squatting really only possible because of the disappearance of constraints derived from the expectations of Beijing and Guangzhou regarding the disposition of the colony? Or was something else going on? The counterfactual question to be asked is whether it is plausible that the policy changes still would have happened at the same time and in the same way if the negotiations had not started or were still incomplete. To maintain this position, it would seem necessary to identify alternative mechanism(s) that would work at around the same period, and which would support a different plausible argument or explanation.

To think counterfactually in another direction, what if the same intervention to register occupants and not just squatter structures had taken place in the 1970s? To address this, we must consider why it was not considered desirable to register squatter occupants earlier. Between 1954 and 1984, the Hong Kong government followed a policy of formal toleration of surveyed squatter structures combined with the refusal to accept the legitimacy of ownership rights in irregularly developed structures. At the same time, those living in registered squatter dwellings when they were scheduled for demolition were eligible for rehousing according to their household characteristics and current rehousing policies. Toleration allows illegal conditions to persist, but without modifying the official situation. In other words, letting the structures and the occupants stay is a concession, rather than an acknowledgement of rights. To avoid giving the appearance of providing property rights to squatters, until 1984 it was officially the structures that were registered and tolerated, not the specific occupants.

The government's avoidance of anything that would give the appearance of providing property rights to squatter dwellings, or any entitlements that were not clearly identified as being ex gratia privileges rather than legal rights, greatly influenced its regulatory practices. Compensation for clearance was based on policies which could be changed as needed. To allow residents to expand their dwellings would have increased the number of people who could live in a structure and thus increase the rehousing commitment in the event of a clearance. It is less clear why the government did not—and still does not—allow the replacement of temporary with more permanent materials, so long as this did not increase the dimensions of the structure. One possibility is that it was easier for squatter control officials to identify any rebuilding activities without having to distinguish whether they were to improve the quality or to increase the size (Smart 2003b). An alternative explanation is that the policy was due to the desire to avoid attribution of property rights and entitlements to the squatters, who might have been able to claim they deserved compensation for improvements made to the property, a standard rationale for compensation in land-resumption procedures. The denial of any implication of ownership of squatter structures also resulted in a distinctive feature of resettlement, that it was those residing in a structure, rather than those "owning" it, who were resettled. This produced a distinctive squatter property market in which squatter structure sales were open and common, yet renting was generally not practiced except through a large key money payment that could be seen as compensation for the possibility of resettlement, which would benefit the renter rather than the "owner" (Smart 1986). In particular, it was thought to be a bad idea to generate any kind of form or document that included both the details of the dwelling and the occupant because of its similarities to a title deed.

In addition to the concern about potentially conveying the message that squatters had rights to their dwelling, protests and public support might have prevented an earlier successful implementation of the SOS and its attendant reduction of "rights." Even if "owners" could still sell their property after the Survey, ineligibility of the buyer for permanent public housing resettlement would certainly reduce the value and sale price (Smart 1988). For whatever reason, this direction was not taken, and squatter settlements remained in the liminal state of tolerated illegality.

However, in 1984, little or no public attention was being paid to squatter issues. Attention was focused on the negotiations and what would become of Hong Kong after 1997 and in the transition period. Just as Beijing is alleged to currently be taking advantage of global inattention during the COVID-19 pandemic to crack down on protests and media and take a hard line on political controversies in Hong Kong, governmental actions could have been possible during the unusual year of 1984 that might have been harder to accomplish prior to the onset of the negotiations. Did the negotiations enable the policies, if only by providing a large and obscuring distraction? That would certainly seem to have been the case. However, more was involved. Once an agreement seemed likely, both sides developed an interest in post-agreement stability. Actions taken by Guangzhou or Beijing to support squatters as the oppressed subjects of British colonialism, which could destabilize the situation, would have become less likely. Perhaps the clearest indication of this changed atmosphere was the demolition of Kowloon Walled City in 1993, which had persisted as a high-rise illegal settlement since 1898 due to disagreements between Hong Kong and Beijing (Lai 2016).

The geopolitical explanation—that more repressive measures to deal with the squatter problem were encouraged by the convergence of London, Beijing, and Hong Kong because of successful negotiations and their shared interests in social stability—initially seems quite plausible. The preoccupation of the public and the media would strengthen that possibility by providing cover for any controversial actions in the squatter settlements. But, as indicated in the Introduction, the problem for this explanation is that a thorough search of the archives has failed to uncover any documents saying something like "we can do this now, because of the Joint Declaration." In other words, we have not found a smoking gun confidential document to support the plausibility by offering some indication that it did indeed affect their decision-making. It seems very possible that the changed context may have created a situation where it was no longer necessary to raise the possibility that disgruntled squatters might cause problems, as had happened so often in the past. The new situation may have allowed new directions without anyone saying so or perhaps even recognizing that it was affecting their choices. Alternatively, given the pre-decolonization sterilization of files, such documents might have existed but are no longer available. Perhaps they were destroyed or are located in Hanslope Park, yet to be opened to the light of day. But, for whatever reason, we have been unable to find evidence to support the geopolitical explanation beyond plausibility, its adequacy relying on the absence of strong rival explanations.

Given this situation, much of the remainder of this book is devoted to developing another explanation, one that is much less elegant, involving multiple steps and convoluted routes through a variety of official debates and issues, ultimately leading to the adoption of the Squatter Occupancy Survey.

Evaluating the Geopolitical Explanation

This, in turn, was finally the effective solution to the squatter problem after so many decades of efforts. The alternative explanation would seem to fail on the grounds of Occam's razor; that when presented with competing hypotheses making the same predictions, one should select the solution with the fewest assumptions. However, if the evidence is solid and the argument adequate, a complicated solution is of course preferable to a simpler one that lacks solid, or any, evidence in its support.

Because of the complexity of the genesis of the formalization of informal housing, some background is needed to situate the complex unfolding of policy paths and debates. The next two chapters address this need: Chapter 4 describes the situation in the 1960s up until the 1966–1967 riots, and Chapter 5 considers the reforms under Governors Trench and MacLehose.

4

The Situation in the Early 1960s

Introduction

The United Nations declared 1959–1960 World Refugee Year. As part of the campaign publicity, Trafalgar Square in London became home to an installation of 40 huts, "such as would be found in the squatter settlements in Hong Kong," in order to demonstrate "how refugees lived on a daily basis" and left the British public "with an absolutely desperate picture of life in the colony" (Madokoro 2016, 89). The 1960s thus began for Hong Kong with unusual publicity for the difficult conditions of its squatters. Not all, though, were refugees. Many were born in Hong Kong. This chapter attempts to sketch the situation in the 1960s before the 1966 disturbances, with particular attention to migration and housing. The broad squatter situation is described through the discussions and decisions of a 1963 Working Party on Housing report that resulted in the White Paper entitled *Review of Policies for Squatter Control, Resettlement and Government Low-Cost Housing*, published in 1964. It was a turning point for policy on the squatter problem and was still influential in the mid-1970s. The adoption of the Squatter Occupant Survey (SOS) in 1984 can be traced in important ways to this Review. Subsequent policy interventions attempted to address the problems that eventually resulted from measures adopted in its wake. A local perspective on squatters prior to the 1964 Review is provided through an examination of squatter clearances planned in Diamond Hill in the early 1960s. The following chapter picks up from there, exploring the consequences of the twin riots of the Star Ferry (1966) and the Cultural Revolution (1967).

In many ways, Hong Kong in the first half of the 1960s was largely a straight-line continuation of the 1950s. Pervasive informality persisted and grew. The economy buzzed with small and medium manufacturing operations. The level of prosperity had increased, with wages higher than rivals in the region. Rather than simply leading to larger factories with greater economies of scale, rapid exploitation of new product niches through networked outsourcing of orders intensified. Along with soaring numbers of migrants from China, the cost of private housing continued to increase, and redevelopment displaced many people. Demand for public housing soared as well, but most could not access it except through living in a squatter structure demolished for development. Absence of significant democratic influence within the governance system fostered more dissatisfaction among the increasingly well-educated population.

Housing and Squatting

It was a "sudden upsurge in illegal squatting" that led to the appointment of a Working Party "*to advise* what changes in policy, if any, might be required".[1] From 1957 on, the problems with the policy of squatter containment became more and more apparent. Since the main route into public housing before the 1970s was squatter resettlement, redevelopment of prewar tenements and migration were placing unmanageable pressures on housing for low-income people. Intensified use of the surviving tolerated squatter structures was one result, new squatting another. The Commissioner for Resettlement's Annual Report for 1961–1962 stated that "[v]irtually all Crown Land in the Urban Area that is not impossibly steep is occupied to a greater or lesser extent by residential squatters or illegal cultivators" and mentions cases where 1,500–2,000 people were living in a single acre of one-story wooden structures.

One indication of the attractions of squatter areas—not just as a solution to housing problems but as a path to public housing—can be seen in income statistics. The expectation of many would be that squatters would be the most marginal and poorest segment of the population, but this was not always true. The possibility of getting into public housing more quickly through resettlement meant that there was a strong attraction for even middle-class households to take up residence in irregular settlements. The result, combined with the substantial level of social mobility for the working classes during this period, was that many squatter areas had substantial numbers of middle-class households and average incomes that were fairly close to the Hong Kong average. The median monthly income of private temporary housing (squatters in structures of temporary materials) households in 1981 was 76.12% of the Hong Kong median; by 1996, however, it had dropped to 54.9% (Census and Statistics 1981, 1996). The drop seems to have been due at least in part to the rule that only those registered as occupants of squatter dwellings in 1984 could be eligible for permanent public housing in a clearance (Smart 2001).

What we think of as *implicit principles* emerge from consistent trends in discussions and practices but are not clearly codified. Implicit principles are more about practice, supported by commentary in confidential contexts, than about public and published policies—what we might also call the hidden transcripts (Scott 1990) of rule.[2] Two implicit principles that continued or intensified until at least 1984 are particularly significant. The first was that resettlement was a means to the end of facilitating land development stymied by the encroachment of squatters on public land. Only land needed for development received resettlement clearance.[3] Other squatter structures would be either formally tolerated (usually by conducting a physical survey of them and declaring by government gazette that only occupants of those surveyed structures would be eligible for resettlement) or informally tolerated (until another "final" survey took place once the pressure and problems of unsurveyed structures became too great). There was generally an attempt to limit the extent of resettlement obligations, in part because land supply in the steep landscape of urban Hong Kong was difficult. The Hong Kong government has particularly tried to limit and reduce its housing commitment to squatters. Various categories of squatters, recent migrants and fire victims were made ineligible for permanent public housing. They were shifted into licensed areas and later into temporary and interim housing with much lower amenities. The anomalous situation of the early 1970s, when a shortage of temporary housing (TH) spurred efforts to make more squatters eligible for permanent public housing, was a result of this general principle resulting in too much exclusion, creating imbalance problems. It will be addressed in Chapter 7.

The second principle was to prevent any appearance of squatters' rights, or more generally any sense by squatters of having any kind of property rights in their homes (Smart 2001). Squatters' rights in the common law tradition are more technically referred to as adverse possession, which in turn is defined as a method of acquisition of title to real property by possession for a statutory period under certain conditions (De Biasi 2019). In the Report on Adverse Possession published by the Law Reform Commission of Hong Kong, adverse possession refers to how title can be acquired to someone else's land by continuously occupying it. The adverse possessor's claim needs to show three elements: he has been in actual possession of the land; the possession has been adverse (that is, he intended to possess the land against the wishes of the owner); and that such possession has lasted for a period of time stipulated by law. In Hong Kong law, this is 60 years for government land and 12 years for private land (Yang et al. 2017). In Hong Kong, most cases of adverse possession that have gone to court have been on agricultural land in the New Territories (Merry 2020). It is unclear why squatter areas that have persisted for more than 60 years—and there are some—have not used this legal mechanism, but at the time of most intense squatter political activity, the 60-year period would not have been surpassed.

This principle of avoiding actions that legally or informally create the impression of ownership by squatters helps to account for the practice that even tolerated structures could be demolished without eligibility of the occupants for resettlement in permanent public housing if they were found to have expanded the building envelope or rebuilt in permanent materials. It also created the administrative gap where squatter structures but not squatter residents were registered, until the SOS in 1984, since before that, officials worried that having the dwelling and its occupants listed on the same register might look too much like a title registry (Smart 2003b). In the early 1960s, it accounts for the difficulties discovered in the Working Party proposals for "permitted areas."

The terms of reference for the Working Party on Housing were "[t]o advise what changes in policy, if any, are required with regard to the provision of and eligibility for resettlement or low-cost housing and with regard to the clearance of squatters and the provision of temporary resites for squatting." The Secretary for Chinese Affairs, McDouall, was Chairman and the other members were the Director of Public Works, the Commissioner for Resettlement, the Deputy Economic Secretary, a Police representative and four Urban Council representatives. The Working Party followed on from the Special Committee on Housing, which argued in its 1958 Final Report that "the provision of low-rent public housing on this scale [an estimated 700,000 living in public housing by 1957] will itself tend to constitute an attraction to immigration, to deter the production of housing by private enterprise in the same field, and to create a large privileged class of public housing tenants; to this extent, therefore, public measures for the improvement of the situation will themselves tend to create further difficult problems for the future."[4] In 1959, targets were set to double resettlement building to 100,000 new units a year, but an average of only 65,000 was achieved in the four succeeding years. The delay was not due to lack of funds "but site formation on rough hillsides, the provision of roads, sewers, water supplies etc., and difficulties over the clearance of cultivated plots and factories in New Kowloon all contributed to delays in implementation. Only now, with a number of sites becoming available together, is it possible to clear off the backlog in the original programme."[5]

The Working Party found only two possible ways to control new squatting. The first was "the present (1954) policy of demolishing at sight all new squatter structures." While failing by the 1960s, when formulated it had appeared to be "realistic" and "for some years it worked despite the warnings which the then Deputy Commissioner of Police unavailingly uttered about certain of the very abuses and difficulties which have since arisen." The alternative would be "the containment of old and new squatter structures within certain areas."[6] The 1954 policy of containment and discouragement had led to "(1) Failure, on an increasing scale, to stop new squatters; (2) Exploitation of squatters by criminals and opportunists; (3) Constant sources of misunderstanding between the Resettlement Department, the Urban Council, the police, and squatters; (4) Disaffection, which has shown signs of more serious discontent, among squatters; (5) Nine years' tacit acceptance by Government of large numbers of 'tolerated' squatters openly, and necessarily, flouting the law by squatting undisturbed on Crown land." While natural increase within the squatter areas was about 50,000 between 1959 and 1963, movement from tenement buildings was more than 85,000 people in 1962 alone, with perhaps half moving into illegal structures. Illegal migration from China also increased sharply in 1962 with about 60% of that cohort moving into squatter colonies.[7] There were a total of 142,000 migrants, legal and illegal, from China between 1959 and 1962.[8]

The Working Party recommended a pragmatic approach, acknowledging that in the circumstances, "[n]othing can be done to bring a complete halt to new squatting," while private "building interests by themselves cannot solve the housing problem for existing or for potential new squatters." A better policy would be "containment based in part on the selection and demarcation of certain Permitted Areas of Crown Land, on which squatters will by law be permitted to erect their temporary structures" subject to conditions, along with increased squatter control patrols.[9]

The 1964 White Paper followed the Working Party to propose policies that largely continued until 1976. The White Paper set out the problem in clear terms: "Today's 600,000 squatters are not simply a bigger problem than the 260,000 of 10 years before, and the solution does not simply lie in accelerating the building rate. New factors have appeared and the problem is different in kind as well as in size. Clearly any solution to today's problem must take into account the increasing incentive to squat on Crown land resulting from the accelerated redevelopment of old property, the greater number of danger-ous buildings closed, and the expansion of the population caused by recent influxes and natural increase." The growing difficulties of implementing the 1954 policy "gave rise to anxiety during 1963 and emphasized the need to make squatter control more obviously an integral part of the positive and con-structive programme of squatter clearance and resettlement."[10]

With one major exception, the 1964 White Paper followed the recommen-dations of the Working Party. Newly erected domestic structures on rooftops or private land should be demolished, "the occupants being eligible for entry to Licensed Areas only if they can satisfy the Resettlement authorities that they have nowhere else to go." The Resettlement Ordinance would be amended so that after warning, the erection of new structures would "render the landlord liable to prosecution." New pavement dwelling (see Smart and Tang 2014) was to be "contained as far as possible by the police, but no attempt will be made to move those already living in tolerated structures on pavements until they can be offered resettlement. Existing clusters of boat squatters on foreshores will be treated as tolerated structures and strictly contained. The prevention of new squatting on Crown land will continue. New squatter huts will be demolished,

The Situation in the Early 1960s

but if the occupants can satisfy the Commissioner for Resettlement that they are homeless they will be admitted to a Licensed Area."

It was in the conception of Licensed Areas that the White Paper made a significant "departure from their recommendation on the choice of sites and the basis of legality. The Working Party proposed to establish new 'permitted areas' based initially on existing clusters of 'tolerated structures.' This proposal suffered from the fundamental defect of legalizing squatting on Crown land. It also established a right to squat by any who wished to do so, thereby intensifying rather than diminishing the difficulties of control and clearance, and delaying redevelopment. This fundamental objection does not apply to the granting of a conditional right to erect a structure on a designated site by a licence under the Resettlement Ordinance." This fits with our claim that the attempt to avoid the provision, real or apparent, of "rights" rather than revocable concessions was a consistent thread of official thinking about the squatter problem.

There were "equally strong practical objections" to setting up the kind of permitted areas suggested by the Working Party. Existing clusters of tolerated structures were not thought able to house many more people, and were "often in places likely to be needed for development in the next few years." Setting up new areas "based on existing haphazard clusters of squatter huts" would lessen the "chances of maintaining proper and effective control." The Review proposed instead to ensure that existing collections of tolerated structures would be frozen. Existing huts "will not be cleared but their present size and numbers will be strictly contained until such time as they are cleared in the course of the many development schemes now in progress" (4). This hope, of course, was at most temporarily and partially met, and the squatter problem eventually grew even greater, until 1984.

Instead, the proposed Licensed Areas were to be in outlying areas, which should make them "less attractive than the Working Party's 'permitted areas' based on existing clusters of 'tolerated structures' [and] eliminate the possibility of large numbers of people leaving their present accommodation in favour of them. Those living in Licensed Areas will have no prospect of early resettlement and this fact . . . will also have the effect, recommended by the Working Party, of making Licensed Areas unattractive" (4). The cost of the program would be "considerable and it is regarded as fair that they should not be simply a subsidy." A license fee of $3 a month would be charged for domestic structures, plus $10 per month for every 120 square feet of non-domestic structure. For each group of 60,000 people the capital costs would be about $1.4 million, with recurrent costs of $180,000.

On the broader housing issues, the Working Party recommended building at the rate of 130,000 resettlement units per year at least until 1970. The White Paper Plan was to build 900,000 units in the six years to March 1970

72   *Hong Kong Public and Squatter Housing*

at an estimated cost of $766 million. A "Technical Planning Target" of 1.9 million units was adopted for the 10-year period to April 1974 at an estimated cost of $1.691 million. The numbers of units are strikingly similar to the Ten-Year Plan target of 1.8 million units adopted under Governor MacLehose but intended to run from 1973 to 1982 (see Chapters 7 and 8). The need for such a massive housing program derives in substantial part from the high levels of migration from China in the early 1960s, which we turn to in the next section of this chapter.

Immigration from China

Influxes from China had intensified the housing problem in Hong Kong since war with Japan began, and particularly after the end of the Second World War, although at first a substantial proportion were Hong Kong people who had fled to China during the Japanese occupation of Hong Kong (Snow 2003). The population quadrupled from 600,000 to 2.4 million between 1945 and 1950 (Hopkins 1971). A United Nations report estimated that 1,285,000 people entered Hong Kong between September 1945 and December 1949 (Podmore 1971). With a devastated housing stock and incapacity of the government to make land available for development, housing shortages were intense and growing before 1954.

For the first time, in March 1950, entry permits were required of all Chinese coming from China, except for natives of Guangdong, "because of sheer population saturation." Other than a "short lived series of protests inspired by sentimental, commercial or political motives, these restrictions were accepted by the general public as an inevitable outcome of overcrowding." In December 1951, China also imposed a system of entry and reentry permits.[11] In 1959, Governor Black argued for stronger controls on refugees and legal migrants from China for fear that Hong Kong "might be so swamped with Chinese that it would be an easy and ripe plum for China to eat" within a decade. Black felt the threat was particularly intense while Hong Kong failed to meet the basic needs of its population (quoted in Tsang 2010, 18).

Government pronouncements insisted on "the impossibility of distinguishing between the needs of refugees and those of the Hong Kong squatters."[12] This link between squatters and *refugees* (a contested term later ejected from official discourse; see Madokoro 2016, Peterson 2008) from China and squatting in the official mind (if not always in reality) is clear from a secret level file planning for the danger of mass migration in 1967.[13] The prevailing plans were based on "the experience of 1962," when an influx of illegal migrants peaked at 5,000 a day; along with legal migrants under quotas of 50 per day, the total may have been 115,000 (Lin and Tse 2005). Illegal migration from China increased sharply in 1962 (provoking an internal crisis), due to

The Situation in the Early 1960s 73

relaxation on the Chinese side related to the famine caused by Great Leap Forward policies; it was estimated that about 60% of the unknown number of illegal migrants moved into squatter colonies.[14] An estimated total of 142,000 people entered Hong Kong from China between 1959 and 1962 (Ku 2004).

The large influx in 1962 resulted from the Great Leap Forward-induced famine, which resulted in over 30 million excess deaths (Dikötter 2010) and a temporary reduction of border controls on the Chinese side, which initiated a diplomatic crisis (Vogel 1969). Already in 1959, illegal immigration was estimated at 30,000, but in May 1962, China relaxed its border controls so "a steady flow became a flood . . . Overnight, Hong Kong became the free Berlin of the East. The great exodus was well planned . . . Speculators in Guangzhou even sold improvised compasses called Paradise Pointers" (Dikötter 2010, 240). By June, "China had closed its border again and the influx ceased as suddenly as it had started" (241). The government was concerned by the "great local sympathy aroused by the refugees and the large number of local residents who had gone to the Border areas where they had considerably hindered operations." It was agreed that, in the future, the Army would "backstop lines along the main road/river boundary of the enlarged Closed Area [which] would have to operate to keep the sympathisers from going north as well as refugees from going south."[15]

The Hong Kong government worried that the disruptions of China's Cultural Revolution—which were splashing across the border to produce the disruptions of 1967 (see Chapter 5)—might result in an even larger influx, perhaps one intended to help destabilize the colony. Planning was based on up to 10,000 refugees a day, adding up to as much as half a million. It was "thought that the increase in squatting which occurred during 1963 resulted from the extra pressure on accommodation caused by the influx" of 1962. It was stated in a secret memo from the Colonial Secretary that the "essential elements of any plan to deal with refugees are . . . the use of every available means to prevent entry into Hong Kong by land or sea" and the "rounding up of those who contrive to enter the Colony." It was debated whether illegal immigrants should be absorbed into the general population, as it had been "suggested that the mingling of a large number of refugees among the population would create such severe internal security problems that they should be segregated in a refugee camp on an island." This presented various problems, particularly the costs, so it was concluded that "the policy aim should be that once refugees are accepted as Hong Kong residents they should, so far as possible, be treated as such and be entitled to no more and no less than other Hong Kong residents in similar circumstances i.e., the aim of the policy should be to absorb the refugees and not segregate them."[16] The question, though, was how to do so. For migrants without:

relatives to go to, the following possibilities exist . . . to transport refugees to the urban areas and to release them there; . . . to transport refugees to sites where they will be allowed to erect their own huts; . . . to transport refugees to sites where completed huts would be offered to them. The more attractive the reception in town, the fewer will foist themselves on relatives and probably the slower will be the absorption of refugees. Even the provision of sites will mean that some of the refugees will form an identifiable physical concentration of refugees and possibly create an air of helplessness and despondency which will make it difficult to absorb them. The more they can be interspersed among the Hong Kong residents the easier it will be to follow the policy of equal social benefits for all residents – new or old.

Against this consideration was balanced another: "the bleaker the reception given to refugees when they arrive in the urban areas the greater would be the criticism on humanitarian grounds from both local and world opinion. Some middle course of action will have to be followed. If the government were to build huts it would have to build for all refugees—and if for refugees why not for the Hong Kong homeless who are now entitled only to a site in a re-site area? If really large numbers arrive it might quickly become physically impossible to build fast enough." Out of this decision calculus, it was "considered that when the decision is taken to move refugees into the urban areas they should be transported either to dispersal points where they will make their way to relatives or friends, or to sites in re-site areas where they will be treated as homeless Hong Kong residents and allowed to erect their own huts."[17] The association between refugees and squatters is starkly displayed here, as is the concern not to accord illegal migrants better treatment than Hong Kong residents (see Chapter 8), and the feeling that in the absence of government provision some kind of self-help housing would be the default. The question was how government should regulate it.

The equation of squatter with refugee or migrant worked to the disadvantage of both squatters and refugees. Although consequential, it was far from accurate, although it would become more so because of exclusionary housing policies adopted after the 1960s. Screening of cleared squatters in 1952 found that almost half of the squatters were families born in Hong Kong or resident there since 1946 or earlier. The first postwar census conducted in 1961 found that 46% of squatters were born in Hong Kong, compared to only marginally more (48%) of the total population (Smart 2006, 54). Agnes Ku (2004, 340) writes that the problem of illegal immigration "was never simply about excessive population; it was often associated with different sorts of social and political concerns and fears. Such concerns and worries were encapsulated in a discourse of the problem of people, which, by the mid-1960s, was elaborated more proactively as a matter of resource control as well as of long-term state economic planning." The "thesis that Hong Kong, with a shortage of

The Situation in the Early 1960s   75

land, was threatened by immigration from Mainland China thus became one of the most prominent features of public discourses in Hong Kong" (Leung 2004, 101). While the influxes provided an abundant supply of cheap labor, even this presented some difficulties for government, as industrialists in Britain worried about resulting unfair competition. The Colonial Secretary suggested responses to a complaint from the National Association of Glove Manufacturers that would stress that "[s]tringent efforts are made to keep the number of immigrants as low as possible."[18]

The idea of the problem of people continued well past the 1960s. High rates of illegal immigration periodically resulted in loss of effective control over new squatting (see Chapters 7 and 8). Another illustration of its continuance can be seen in a discussion of policy options for controlling Hong Kong's population, which toyed with using housing eligibility rules to discourage large families. The Secretary for Housing mused about the Housing Authority announcing that:

> families now with (say) 3 or more children will not be eligible for public housing if any further child is born between (say) end-1976 and the date when a tenancy would otherwise have been offered. This could apply to development and other categories as well as to Waiting List applicants—in clearance cases however we could perhaps offer LA [Licensed Area] space on the basis that they could not expect to be offered proper public housing at a later date. A more extreme step would be to refuse to give public housing to families with more than, say four children.

It was decided not to use public housing as a policy control lever, with the Director of Housing stating that "draconian measures were not planned for the draft Memo for ExCo [Executive Council]."[19]

The next section uses a case study of the Diamond Hill squatter area to illustrate the dynamics and difficulties of squatter clearance in the 1960s, even before the politicization of the 1966 and 1967 disturbances.

Diamond Hill Clearance and Politicization

In researching this book, it was of great interest to discover that there was quite extensive discussion specifically of Diamond Hill and difficulties over clearance in 1963, right up to the level of the Secretary of State for Colonies. This makes it a good example of the situation for squatter control in the early 1960s. A number of important issues appear in the files. In addition, it is the squatter area that Smart knows best, both ethnographically and historically.

It was his ethnographic research focused on Diamond Hill that first convinced Smart of the need to do archival research. His research in the Public Records Office, then in the inauspicious setting of the Car Park Building in

Central, began in 1984 because he could not make sense of the built environment of Diamond Hill, which contrasted greatly with the squatter settlements described in the literature of the period. It was an extremely heterogeneous built environment. The typical ramshackle corrugated galvanized steel roof and plywood constructions were common, particularly on the fringes of Diamond Hill. But in the central areas, anomalous forms of construction were more common. There were old village stone houses. There were dilapidated three- and four-story apartment buildings built of reinforced concrete. There were larger buildings subdivided into a warren of cubicles, which residents told me "used to be lived in by rich people." The high quality of these residences was attested to by the survival of a garden gazebo with a Chinese-style tiled roof, now subdivided and with additions to form several separate dwellings. An unusual lane with ceramic tiles turned out to have been the deck of a swimming pool, now filled in and covered over with temporary structures. Rather than a homogeneous shanty town occupied by the poor, there was a sedimentation of very different types of structures, varying greatly in size and quality of constructions, and undermining expectations of what a squatter settlement should look like (see Figure 4.1). Attempts to make sense of Diamond Hill's landscape through interviews did not adequately resolve this confusion, and Smart first turned to the archives to learn how the area came to look like it did (for details, see Smart 1992).

Figure 4.1: Diamond Hill squatters and prewar concrete buildings, 1983. Copyright and provided by Alan Smart.

The Situation in the Early 1960s

The area that is now Diamond Hill (now visible mostly as a Mass Transit Railway station) became part of Hong Kong in the 1898 Lease of the New Territories (Smart and Tang 2014). Until the Second World War, it was a sparsely populated village area, gradually becoming more urbanized through the building of villas by wealthy outsiders through converting agricultural lots into a building lot. There were also a few low-rise apartment buildings. Squatting began after the end of the Japanese occupation, sometimes with permission of the agricultural landowners, sometimes without. A substantial number of high-quality houses were built of permanent materials for more affluent refugees from China; they were illegal because they were constructed on agricultural land without conversion to building land (see Figure 4.2 and images in Smart 2006). A 1950 guidebook said that people visited Diamond Hill for its scenic beauty and "like to wash their feet in the river and listen to the tinkling echo of the crystal-clear water" (Tong, quoted in Wong Tai Sin District Board n.d., 6). This would not be recommended after the establishment of squatter factories in the late 1950s. A major expansion of squatting took place in the late 1950s, at which time most of the affluent residents left, as well as most descendants of the pre-1898 villagers,[20] due to deteriorating conditions.

The population was an estimated 55,000 in 1968, along with 320 squatter factories (Fung 1968). This may have been the peak population for Diamond

Figure 4.2: Diamond Hill field and houses, 1983. Copyright and provided by Alan Smart.

Hill, which dropped to 28,600 after some major clearances, although the number of factories increased to 800, some licensed rather than illegal (Wong Tai Sin District Board 1984). There were minimal government services in the 1960s, but 94% of residents had illegal electricity, 32% their own toilet, and 14% water taps inside their house; 42% of households had an income over $600 per month, compared to 27% for the colony as a whole and 8.4% of families in all squatter areas, making it a significantly wealthier squatter area (Fung 1968).

Diamond Hill was a physically attractive area for development, including an area of flat land, where squatting emerged around the old villages, below the steeper and more rugged upper sections, where new squatters concentrated after 1962. Already in 1958, the Special Committee on Housing (1958, Appendix A, 5) proposed a clearance of the whole area, highlighting it as "an area which lends itself to comparatively rapid development or redevelopment because of proximity to the existing urban area." The Kowloon town plan completed in May 1960 had left the area south of Diamond Hill for private development or redevelopment, possibly because of the resistance of other old villages in New Kowloon in the 1950s.[21] Objections to the plan came from four village organizations in Yuen Ling and Tai Hom.[22] These objections, including reference to their forefathers and ancestral halls, received only modest concessions of narrowing what became Lung Cheung Road from 120 feet to 100 feet, as well as two smaller roads.

Commissioner for Resettlement Morrison felt that "all possible sites in the urban area should be fully exploited . . . I have no desire to bulldoze three old villages and in particular the settlement of film stars, but consider that the land to the west and elsewhere around these villages is sufficiently extensive to warrant the construction of a sizeable estate."[23] The Superintendent, Crown Lands & Survey, encouraged early redevelopment of the area, stressing that "the only way that development can take place at all expeditiously is by means of a large public housing project and it seems likely that whatever the difficulties with local opinion, the creation of a resettlement estate covering the larger part of this area is more or less inevitable."[24] By 1962, though, the plan for a Resettlement Estate would "start such redevelopment on the comparatively little built on western part of the area and not take in the more densely built area to the east embracing Sheung Un Ling, Hau Un Ling and Tai Hom Villages until later, in the hope that many of the land owners in these villages would eventually surrender their land in exchange for new building lots which they could not only develop more intensively but which would front made-up roads and be connected with services."[25] By June 1962, it was decided not to proceed with a new estate in the area, in response to a memo from the Secretary of Chinese Affairs that pointed out that the 1960 plan's explanatory statement stated that "the speed of redevelopment will depend very largely on

The Situation in the Early 1960s 79

the initiative of people owning land within the planning area. Nobody will be obliged to redevelop his land, but those who wish to do so must do it in accordance with the final approved Town Plan."[26] The Superintendent, Crown Lands & Survey, agreed that "to attempt to go back on the assurances given to the villagers recently would be politically dangerous and morally indefensible." He expressed concern about the "insanitary and inflammable nature of these semi-squatter villages," the solutions to which would require redevelopment which, "in turn, is dependent upon the surrender of existing lots on a fairly large scale." He "hoped that surrenders of private lots in exchange for land elsewhere will proceed apace so as to allow redevelopment to take place but I am not very optimistic in this respect."[27] The District Commissioner, New Territories, responded that he felt that the full potential of development in North Kowloon should be used before contemplating high-density development in the New Territories. He thought it "worthwhile considering whether any of the new techniques which I have recently adopted in the NT [New Territories] for encouraging the voluntary surrender of land required for a public purpose could be adapted for use in the urban areas to assuage particularly the feelings of owners of Old Schedule agricultural land in New Kowloon; that is that OS [Old Schedule] building land could be largely dealt with by the creation of enclaves."[28]

As discussed above, 1962 and its high levels of migration put an end to the relative control of squatting ushered in by the Resettlement Programme in 1954. Until 1962 and a major typhoon, squatter control "was able to deal with all new illegal structures in accordance with the present policy. But thereafter the number of new huts involved, the persistent and speedy rebuilding by the would-be squatters after repeated demolitions and the employment of Control Staff on other work created by the Typhoon made the task of effective control very difficult for them. During this time . . . the number of new huts which have withstood repeated demolition action or so far avoided it has gradually increased."[29]

In 1963, outbreaks of "mass squatting" occurred in numerous districts of Hong Kong. Diamond Hill became the one with the highest political profile. Governor Robert Black sent a telegraph to the Secretary of State for Colonies on 16 September 1963 on the issue, addressing a letter from Urban Councillor Elsie Elliott to Prime Minister "Harold Wilson about the clearance of squatters at Diamond Hill, Kowloon . . . I am telegraphing immediately in the hope that you may be able to forestall a reply to Mrs. Elliott on the lines given." The clearance operations "were directed against persistent new squatters trespassing on Crown Land and who are not, repeat not, eligible for resettlement. The site in question . . . is not itself required for any immediate development, and it was in pursuance of normal policy of preventing fresh squatting and because, in addition, the area affected is unsuited for habitation due to proximity of a quarry and for other reasons that these huts had to be removed." About 600 affected persons were permitted to "rebuild their huts on a resite area. It aroused considerable press comment ... and this attention, stimulated by Mrs. Elliott and the Standard papers, attracted far greater numbers to Diamond Hill than were involved in the original clearance operation."[30] By 1 November, three Members of Parliament had made statements including comments by Elliott on Diamond Hill, and the Secretary of State for Colonies asked the Governor to respond to the claims.

The governor responded at length, noting that attempts at "clearance had been made since January 1963 and the squatters were never under any illusion that they were being tolerated in that location ... Not unreasonably during the course of the Diamond Hill events, which attracted considerable publicity and involved racketeers and newcomers trying to find means to enter a resite area, Police were in attendance and Squatter Control staff made surprise night visits under a standard technique to try to find out more accurately the number of regular occupants of the huts." Resite Areas became a central concern of squatter management in 1963. Elliott and many others offered stark criticisms of the conditions in them, but Governor Black commented that "[a]lthough it is obviously necessary, under the official policy of deterring fresh squatting, to avoid making resite areas, which have no legal existence, into areas where living conditions are sufficiently attractive to induce fresh squatting, the government through the Resettlement Department has provided minimum sanitation facilities and water supplies where this could be done economically." After defending against multiple other charges, the governor ended by requesting that "[i]n these circumstances and in the light of this report and earlier correspondence I trust that you will feel able to assist me by reassuring the individual Members of Parliament concerned that their correspondents' complaints are biased and unfounded and that their very dissemination, however well intentioned, does more positive harm and damage than the official policies and actions which they criticise."[31]

While C. G. M. Morrison (Commissioner for Resettlement) was confident that the situation in Diamond Hill in August had been "well under control and was not a potential source of serious trouble" patrols had been trying "to prevent squatting on this site since the early part of the year, but have never been completely successful." In August "the position deteriorated rapidly. This, according to Mr. Morrison, has been due principally to the activities of Chiu Chow racketeers building huts on the site and attempting to sell them to potential squatters." Because of "the element of racketeering which has entered in, we cannot allow the position to deteriorate ... the Police took active measures yesterday against the racketeers, warning people through loud hailers not to be taken in by people who purport to be able to sell them a hut which will not be demolished ... Action is going ahead to clear the

The Situation in the Early 1960s

site completely and to identify, and provide for, some 26 families who have genuinely built their own huts." He stressed that the "site at Diamond Hill is dangerous for the squatters because of the presence of large boulders on a steep hillside and is also close to, or part of, a quarry area."[32]

By the end of August 1963, the Commissioner for Resettlement concluded that "the lesson learnt from the recent occurrences is as follows. Where there is mass squatting exploited by irresponsible elements, the Resettlement Department has not the strength to withstand, even when it is well known that many of the squatters are already suitably housed elsewhere. Urban Councillors are either irresponsible such as Elsie Elliott or fence sitters such as Cheong-Leen." Support by Urban Councillors added to other reasons for the weakness of squatter control, including "the regrettable decision taken in 1959 to withdraw patrol labourers from the individual control of the Area Officers and to place them in a central pool," and because squatter control "can be dangerous work and there have been a number of assaults, including chopper attacks on members of the staff. Despite this fact, Police escorts are not readily available and it is customary to give at least 48 hours' notice."[33]

Morrison presented possible responses: to allow "indiscriminate squatting which will lead to a situation such as that which applied throughout the Colony in 1953," or "to quadruple the existing Squatter Control staff." Doing the latter would be challenging without policy changes because "Area Officers cannot be recruited except with extreme difficulty and many prospective candidates refuse to accept an appointment involving unpopular Squatter Control duties." Another option would be "to increase the number of resite areas and offer a site to virtually anyone with any excuse. Inasmuch as 2 million people are underhoused, the potential number of applicants is vast and their bona fides cannot possibly be checked." He concluded that "despite the press campaign, the best solution is still to carry on as at present and for me to offer resites at my discretion. The price is the provision of more sites by the PWD [Public Works Department] and the expenditure of funds on basic amenities. It will then be possible to deal with small pockets of squatting by normal demolition action and the larger pockets by ad hoc measures, generally involving resite."[34]

Responding to this memo, the Secretary for Chinese Affairs described the recommendation as offering only "one of two choices—(1) To disappear. (2) To go to a Resite Area." The first "would not now seem to be very realistic. The vast majority of these or of any other squatters have nowhere else to go: therefore faced, as it would seem to them and to the public, by Pontius Pilate and his basin, they could in fact do only one of two things . . . Create as big a furore as possible (they would have plenty of potential and vociferous allies)." Or "squat somewhere else illegally, knowing that their shacks will be pulled

82 *Hong Kong Public and Squatter Housing*

down again and again, until they have learned how to win a respite through corruption, 'protection' or other means." The second option, resiting:

> would be still more undesirable. Admission to a Resite Area, apart from a long list of other objections, would mean that these illegal squatters, including imposters, exploiters and recent immigrants, would thereby be officially and gratuitously guaranteed permanent and undisturbed occupancy until they were resettled. Similar action over Diamond Hill squatters, who were also evicted from barren land not wanted for development, has resulted in their having been provided in addition with special water tanks by Government and with a great deal of flattering attention. They and those who stand to make political, news or financial capital out of the situation not unnaturally agitate for a good deal more in the way of amenities.[35]

The Secretary for Chinese Affairs believed that "[t]hese troubles are only symptoms, though symptoms which may well soon grow more serious, of a deeper malaise and ad hoc decisions on individual bits of action may well turn out to be even more undesirable than the symptoms to which they are directed. In addition, it would be unwise to authorise or initiate any marked departures from present practices in a way that would be interpreted as prejudging if not committing the Working Party."[36] In this message, he supported continuation of the status quo until the report was completed.

A police response was also skeptical, agreeing "whole heartedly" with the Secretary for Chinese Affairs; but it also suggested that to avoid "snowballing" (the stimulation of more squatting by earlier successes) and "to prevent the population getting any ideas of a relaxation on the part of Government in respect of the erection of squatter huts, that the Squatter Control of the Resettlement Department carry on with their patrols preventing the construction of the huts before they become occupied. Most of our troubles arise through allowing the huts to be built and then Resettlement Department parties coming along and pulling the huts down over the heads of the occupants who have set up house with all their belongings."[37] The Police Special Branch dismissed the idea of

> political influence in the squatter issue. Neither the C.P.G. [Chinese People's Government] nor Taiwan has shown any interest and although MA Man Fai as Chairman of the United Nations Association of Hong Kong showed some interest in the squatters' complaints at Diamond Hill in the early stages . . . he soon lost his enthusiasm when he found that the majority of the squatters were looking to Mrs. Elsie Elliott for help. Mrs. Elsie Elliott, an elected member of the Urban Council, was first approached for assistance by the Diamond Hill squatters on the 25 August 1963 and since then she has openly criticized the Resettlement Department's handling of this particular squatter issue . . . Her interest is believed to be motivated entirely by personal feelings

The Situation in the Early 1960s

of pity for the squatters and there is no information that she is being directed by outside influences.[38]

The policy of relocating some squatters to resite areas was at the heart of these discussions. Resite areas were designated sites where squatters—but also some people affected by fire, typhoons, and evictions for redevelopment—were "individually permitted to build, within a specified period of time, on a marked site in an assigned area, a temporary structure (technically an unlawful structure but tolerated by the Squatter Control Authority) of specific dimensions with approved materials at the squatter's own expense." Sometimes this applied to people eligible for compassionate resettlement when resettlement spaces were not available. In July 1963 there were over 34,000 persons living in 22 resite areas. While useful for management purposes, their legality became an issue in 1963: "There is the question as to whether the department can lawfully treat these people as squatters and exercise at will its powers as provided in Section 9 of Ordinance 16/58 when it becomes necessary to clear and resettle them. There is also the question as to whether the department has any legal power to enforce the conditions set forth in the 'written undertaking.'"[39]

The Legal Department was very disturbed by the situation presented by the resite areas, protesting that:

> at no time during all the lengthy discussions with your department during the draft of the [Resettlement Ordinance 1958] was mention ever made to me of the fact that there are, under your control, not two types of accommodation, Resettlement Estates and Cottage Resettlement Areas, but three, these two and Resite Areas, because it must be conceded that Resite Areas do constitute a third type of resettlement . . . If my attention had been drawn to this third type of resettlement, I would have pressed strongly for its validation by legislation. I am prepared to concede that it may be necessary to 'turn a blind eye' to existing Resite Areas. I would, however, suggest that it is not a practicable proposition to continue the practice of creating Resite Areas under the present scheme.

In legal terms, "each and every so-called 'lawful occupant' of a Resite Area is guilty of a criminal offence . . . I realize that a blind eye has to be turned to numerous offences against this section by the continued occupation of Crown Land, outside Resite Areas, by squatters, but I would suggest that this is a very different matter to Resite Areas where Government officers, under your direction, procure the commission of offences against the section by directing the occupation, without permit, of Crown Land." He regarded the "present system as unsupportable" for legal reasons as well as due to "practical difficulties which must inevitably lead to endless trouble. Since the occupation is itself unlawful . . . any conditions imposed upon the occupation are invalid and unenforceable as conditions imposed upon the carrying out of an unlawful act. On the other hand, the fact that the Crown not only connived, but, indeed, encouraged, the commission of the unlawful act, must necessarily inhibit the Crown from seeking to take advantage of the fact that the act was unlawful." The imposition of conditions, such as accepting demolition when land becomes needed, would be arbitrary since "although an occupant of a Resite Area is always a squatter within the meaning of s. [section] 2 of the above Ordinance, he is to be treated as a squatter only when you decide that he is to be so treated." They recommended that no new Areas be created and that "every effort should be made either to end or to legalize the present Resite Areas."[40] A police memo described the implications of this legal advice as suggesting that "the fact these people are forced to break the law . . . will breed further lawlessness. I do not consider this argument is in any way acceptable. I am quite sure none of the occupants of Resite Areas know the legal background to their position or are in the least interested. They have a home for the present and the promise of eventual resettlement in a multi-storied estate in the future. It would appear more reasonable to suggest this will help to discourage lawlessness, not encourage."[41]

This legal problem became a key issue addressed by the 1963 Working Party, which suggested establishing Permitted Areas, which the 1964 White Paper relabeled as Licensed Areas. Later, they were transformed into Temporary Housing Areas (THAs) and finally interim housing (see Chapter 7). While this discussion of how to make them legal was ongoing, another investigation on how to deal with squatter control in the interim was delegated to P. B. Williams, who was appointed by the Colonial Secretary "(a) to make an urgent assessment of the situation arising from the recent marked increase in squatting on Crown Land in Hong Kong, Kowloon and New Kowloon, (b) to examine the present organization, duties and methods of the Squatter Control section of the Resettlement Department . . . and (c) to make a report to the Colonial Secretary, through the Commissioner for Resettlement, of your findings, including proposals for such measures as appear to you necessary to keep control of the situation and prevent fresh squatting."[42]

Williams concluded that "[n]ew squatting is likely to spread quickly outside the present five areas and get out of control unless the Squatter Control Section is reinforced as a matter of urgency." Even with more financial support, recruiting new officers was difficult as "[t]he events of recent months, the adverse publicity, lack of support from certain unofficial members of the Urban Council and the general unpleasantness of the task of squatter control have lowered the morale of a number of officers." Low morale brings a "consequential drop in efficiency." Williams ascribed this to "[t]he Diamond Hill Clearance and subsequent publicity" and "the persistent and increasing defiance of squatters who are encouraged by the aftermath of Diamond Hill and the interest of Mrs. Elliott."

The Situation in the Early 1960s   85

Despite the "undoubted increasing pressure to squat on Crown Land," Williams did not "consider that the stage has yet arrived where new squatting cannot be contained." While "there is so far no sign of general active hostility to Squatter Control staff" several Area Officers described "the new squatters as fierce and fear that they would be attacked if they carried out demolitions without adequate support in the new areas of squatting." He recommended adding staff, reorganizing work, patrolling on evenings, and better liaison with police. Although necessary, "[t]he presentation of Government's case for the present policy of squatter control and prevention is one of the most difficult, because demolition of huts and evictions immediately attract the sympathy of the public to the new squatter families irrespective of the prevention process and government's policy."[43]

Once staff was available, "the areas of new squatting should be dispersed gradually and not by major clearance operations. The grounds for the operation should be safety, fire prevention and public health. Some huts, in the more inaccessible areas could remain on site but the majority should be moved gradually to selected sites either on the remoter fringes . . . or to selected sites on the fringes of other tolerated areas." The Finance Committee approved new staff, and the Colonial Secretary directed the Commissioner of Resettlement to implement Williams's proposals, emphasizing that "[r]esiting to be avoided where possible, dispersal of new squatting areas to be gradual, and a distinction between huts completed and occupied by squatters for any length of time and unoccupied huts or those not lived in for any length of time."[44] The 1964 White Paper ushered in a new legal and governance regime for the squatter problem and resite areas.

The contested clearance of 1963 had involved only new squatters in the upper slopes, leaving the area around the old villages unaffected. By 10 August 1964, the Secretary for Chinese Affairs argued that for Diamond Hill the "pace of clearance should be stepped up." This was because earlier there "was justification for worries over the local opposition similar to those we met during the Wong Tai Sin clearance in 1957. I now think that with the improved understanding of the people, the more effective system of resettlement and the more favourable terms of compensation and land exchange, the political climate is now ripe to take a different attitude. I expect that there will be little unsurmountable difficulties."[45] The Resettlement Department, however, replied that there were no plans for redevelopment of Diamond Hill at that time, suggesting that the previous discussion of a Resettlement Estate for the area had been shelved. A planning study by consultants completed in 1983 was not implemented and had only brief mentions of squatters and villagers (Mott, Hay and Anderson 1983). By 1985, however, the only redevelopment other than constructing fire breaks had been on the Tai Hom Wor area, which had been affected by a major fire. By that time, there was a general intention to clear all remaining squatters by 1992, which did not happen. Some clearance took place for construction of the Tate's Cairn Tunnel, and more fires had broken out. The final clearance of remaining squatters was only concluded in 2000. Of the 6,251 remaining residents living in 2,528 structures (which also included 170 businesses), only 24.72% qualified for permanent public rental housing, and 75.28% were to be assigned Interim housing (Smart 2001).

5
Riots and Reforms

Understanding the legacy of colonialism requires a thorough understanding of its complexities: its uncertainty, accident and serendipity; its deep engagement with various forms of moral reform, including temperance and abolitionism; and the complex responses of mimicry, appropriation, and warfare by the objects of colonial transformation.

—Sally Engle Merry, *Colonizing Hawai'i: The Cultural Power of Law* (2000, 12)

Introduction

The disturbances and riots of 1966 and 1967 were perhaps the most important event[1] in Hong Kong's postwar history between the 1953 Christmas Eve fire in Shek Kip Mei and the 1984 signing of the Sino-British Joint Declaration on the Question of Hong Kong, the agreement to return Hong Kong to Chinese sovereignty. However, just as Shek Kip Mei retrospectively came to represent the birth of public housing while in historical practice it is better seen as simply the largest of a series of consequential squatter fires, the nature of the riots is anomalous. Leaving aside whether *riot* is the appropriate label for a variety of disturbances, ranging from peaceful protest forcibly suppressed by police to terrorist bombings injuring innocent bystanders, what does it mean to merge rather different sets of disturbances in two years into a single event?[2]

The 1970s was a decade in which many social reforms were first enacted in Hong Kong, although important precursors were discussed and sometimes implemented in moderate forms before 1966. The 1970s reforms substantially changed the nature of the political economy; society was transformed in parallel. The catalyst for these changes has been repeatedly described as the riots of 1966 and 1967 (Scott 1989). But there is disturbing ambiguity about the precise causation. Most commonly, both years are mentioned, sometimes only 1967 is singled out, and occasionally 1967 is omitted. The two sets of disturbances were very different in their duration and intensity, the immediate responses to them, their causes, and the kinds of societal problems that they were perceived by decision-makers as reflecting. Thus, while it is possible that 1966 and 1967 were lumped together as a cause for concern and social response among those who promoted the reforms of the 1970s, it is also possible that the consequences of the two were quite distinct (Smart and Lui 2009). The 1966 riots might have prompted the same or similar initiatives even without 1967. Steve Tsang (1995, 248) argued that after 1966, political culture shifted among the young and led them to reflect on "their life and their role in the local society, and voice their views in a significant way for the first time." On the other hand, the smaller scale of the events of 1966 might have resulted in the concerns fading away without reinforcement from other incidents. Even if the reforms were likely to have occurred after the 1966 Star Ferry Riots without reinforcement, the distinct nature of 1967 resulted in significant differences in the character of those reforms. These reforms in turn created many of the institutions and practices that ultimately lead to the end of new squatting in 1984, and the subsequent general decline of the number of squatters in Hong Kong.

The Events of 1966 and 1967

On 4 April 1966, a 27-year-old male translator, So Sau-chung, began a hunger strike at the Star Ferry Terminal in Central District to protest the government's decision to increase the Star Ferry fare by 25%. Hours after he was arrested for obstructing the passageway, over 1,000 people gathered to protest. After So was sentenced to two months in jail, a larger crowd gathered and violence broke out, including attacks on a police station, fire stations, and power stations, along with the looting of shops. Riot police fired 772 tear gas canisters, 62 wooden shells, and 62 carbine rounds. The disturbances lasted two more nights; 1,465 persons were arrested, 905 were convicted, and 323 were sentenced to imprisonment—50 to girls' or boys' homes and seven to a training center. There were 10 recorded police casualties, one civilian death and 16 people injured. The incident disclosed long-standing social problems and discontent with the colonial administration (Cheung 2009).

The report on the disturbances mildly criticized the administration, although it praised the restraint of the police, noting a "gap" between the government and the people and that a colonial government "tends to be at a disadvantage in evoking or securing the support of its people" (quoted in Cheung 2009, 12). This gap, a short term to express a large distance (Scott 2017), is an outcome of what Lau Siu-kai (1984) termed a minimally integrated sociopolitical system, which at most "administratively absorbed" the Chinese elite into deliberative institutions but left the mass of the population politically disconnected and lacking channels of influence (King 1973). From the other side, the gap represented considerable ignorance and misunderstanding of the life of ordinary Hong Kong people. Peter Harris (1988) described the politically unreformed colonial government as an "administrative state" where, domestically, power was centralized on the top of the colonial bureaucracy and the civil service was insulated from social and political forces. Such insulation enabled the colonial government to make relatively autonomous decisions, but it was also easy for it to become "too remote to grasp the impact on ordinary lives" (Goodstadt 2009, 28). Hong Kong thus risked what Peter Evans (1995) called excessive "bureaucratic autonomy," which could undermine effective development in a less imperialistic era.

"Bridging the gap" became a slogan in many subsequent programs, such as the City District Officer system (Mok 2019a; Scott 2017). Senior civil servants subsequently acknowledged the existing system was unsustainable and new forms of legitimation were needed. The question was whether the earlier system of anti-communist measures, little social policy spending, and minimal contact with the masses of the population could be preserved, or whether a new path should be followed; and if the latter, should it involve more democracy in the Urban Council (Scott 2017). Ian Scott (2017) asks why such a relatively small disturbance should have created such intense deliberation within the government. He concludes that unlike previous riots or 1967, 1966 pivoted on local conditions and concerns. As well, senior officials recognized that they were "bereft of ideas about future political development" (132) despite being under pressure from Urban Councilors to adopt more democratic reforms. The Commission of Inquiry also exposed administrative shortcomings. Finally, some senior civil servants agreed with the Commission and "saw the gap as a potential means of bringing about reform" (132). These factors combined to create a sense that there was a serious problem that could have grown without significant attention.

In 1967, demonstrations broke out in May after labor disputes in shipping, taxi, textile, cement, and artificial flower companies. Pro-Beijing trade unions were involved. Demonstrations turned into violent riots between pro-Beijing leftists and the Hong Kong government. Bombs were placed in various locations, continuing until October. Fifty-one people were killed and 832 were injured. Almost 4,500 people were arrested, and 2,077 convicted. A strike at an artificial flower factory "became a major anti-colonial movement led by local leftists . . . countered by a full range of emergency and security measures" (Bickers and Yep 2009, 1). A specific conflict escalated when the Chinese Ministry of Foreign Affairs protested to the British, and the All Circle Struggle Committee in Hong Kong was formed. Draconian emergency powers were enacted, and the Police Commissioner was pressured to retire due to "reluctance to commit his forces to firm action" (Yep 2012, 1010). Daily life was disrupted for months by 253 bomb explosions, the discovery of 1,525 "true bombs" and the planting of 4,917 hoax bombs. Geopolitics showed its face

90   *Hong Kong Public and Squatter Housing*

locally, in the spillover of China's Cultural Revolution, and in the subsequent pressure from London to release those imprisoned to improve relations with Beijing (Yep 2012).

Comparing 1966 and 1967

The Star Ferry riots were much smaller in time, scope, and space compared to 1967. Documentation, though, demonstrates that 1966 did have an important impact and would likely have led to reforms even in the absence of 1967 because it was clearly of Hong Kong origin and represented a long festering set of issues. The official Report on the 1966 disturbances noted that "the pressures due to overcrowding . . . combined with the hard struggle for a living . . . and the underlying insecurity of life in the colony, resulting from international political and economic conditions, create tensions which elsewhere would be more than sufficient cause for frequent disturbances" (quoted in Young 1994, 138). In addition, there was widespread resentment of the high profit margins of monopolies such as the Star Ferry and the power utilities (Goodstadt 2005). Without direct political influence, anger was more likely to emerge in street protests, which could turn violent, as has occurred repeatedly in the history of Hong Kong (Lam 2004).

The official report on the 1966 disturbance diagnosed the event as a "communication gap between the government and the people" (Commission of Inquiry 1967; Scott 2017). The disturbance also indicates the colonial government's failure to cultivate trust and win the support of the Hong Kong Chinese (Fung 2022). The need for trust and support from the colonized were not new during the terms of Trench or MacLehose. Rather, they can be seen in the geopolitical needs of the Grantham administration to fortify the precarious colony in the 1950s against United Front strategies and patriotic propaganda from the Kuomintang and the Chinese Communist Party. These constraints fostered the program of integrating the transient population of Chinese into the local colonial society (Mark 2007). Governor Grantham called it a "practical form of social defence" that aimed to "turn potential little hooligans into responsible citizens."[3] In that sense, the geopolitical factor served as a source of motivation that encouraged the colonial government to adopt new strategies of colonial governance. The concurrence of the 1966 disturbance and the 1967 riots thus paved the way for an adjustment of governing strategies.

The character of reforms arising from 1966 without 1967 would presumably have diverged from what actually transpired. Counter to most comparisons, a plausible case can be made that the reforms were more of a response to 1966 than to 1967; the disturbances of 1967 could be dismissed as external provocation, while the Ferry rate riots seemed to reflect local problems needing attention. John Young suggests that the 1967 disturbances "eventually removed some of the heat generated by the riot the year before, and as it became more and more Communist controlled, the Hong Kong population lent its support" to the government (Young 1994, 139). On the other hand, David Faure suggests that the government would have been less impelled by the 1966 disturbances to "re-think its relationship with Hong Kong society had it not been for the need to organize support for itself when its authority was challenged by the riots of 1967" (Faure 1997, 287). For Ian Scott (2017, 140), 1967 convinced remaining doubters that the gap was a crucial problem, and that "the existing legitimation of political authority was no longer adequate and that new justifications had to be found for colonial rule." The Police Special Branch concluded in 1968 that the Hong Kong government had to "counter this new phase of communist activity not only by maintaining law and order and its own authority, but also by continuing carefully considered policies to effect genuine and lasting improvements in standard of living, endeavouring to avoid genuine grievances where possible and by gearing the public relations machinery to meet the communist propaganda challenge" (quoted in Chu 2017, 69). Pressure from the governing Labour Party in the UK reinforced the sense that reforms were needed.

But the kind of reform needed was still up for grabs, with greater efforts at communication and social services eventually winning out over even modest efforts at democratization. The failure to implement significant policy reforms was the result of major administrative flaws, which slowed decision making and needed additional impetus (Scott 2017). This came from 1967 but also from a more demanding Foreign and Commonwealth Office (FCO, see Chapter 6). In a nutshell, initiatives of reform could emerge in the colony and metropole, and these initiatives could be reinforced by factors found in both arenas. However, the trajectory of reform and content of the policy were more the outcome of a complex web of factors in the colonies, including but not limited to colonial state capacity, bureaucratic ethos, availability of resources, and the instances of unrest. As Stoler and Cooper (1997, 29) remarked, "imperial elites may have *viewed* their domains from a metro-politan center, but their actions, let alone their consequences, were not necessarily *determined* there." Here, we see both sets of disturbances as important, but with different qualities, influenced by the distinct ways in which the impact of each was magnified by their sequential occurrence.

Situations like this can be thought about with concepts derived from the dynamics of contention literature. Particularly relevant to our account here is a description of its basic approach, which requires the analyst to:

> Identify its recurrent causal mechanisms, the ways they combine, in what sequences they recur, and why different combinations and sequences, starting from different initial conditions, produce varying effects on the large scale. (McAdam et al. 2004, 13)

92   *Hong Kong Public and Squatter Housing*

Focusing on a series of events, rather than single events or issues, exposes processes, such as escalation, gradual shifts in cultural approaches to the situation, and the production of unintended consequences. Considering outcomes may help promote learning from mistakes (Smart and Smart 2009). The emergence of social conflicts and the formation of government policies both follow patterns where temporal sequencing is of great importance but receives insufficient attention.

An incident of protest will be affected by the participants' knowledge or perceptions of past protests and their outcomes. As well, protests may lead to modified government policies and programs. Some modifications may resolve the problems that prompted the protests, but more commonly they fail to do so, or displace, even magnify, the problem. Even when the problem is apparently resolved, the response may create new related problems as a result of unintended consequences. At the same time, government interventions to resolve the situation or to meet the state's own requirements may fail to meet these objectives but result in a learning process where future interventions benefit from the lessons of prior unsuccessful efforts (Smart and Lam 2009).

There has been a great deal of work done on the policy learning process, but very little from nondemocratic states. The approach has generally been seen as an alternative to seeing states as arenas for social conflict, in which the balance of power between contending social forces and their ideologies determine the direction of governmental actions (Bennett and Howlett 1992). By integrating the analysis of sequences of conflicts and policy learning, it may be possible to obtain some of the advantages of both society-centered and state-centered analyses of governance. Yet sometimes it is very hard for states to learn, even when the lessons are simple (Smart 2006). The remainder of this book uncovers how the lessons that made possible the end of the (new) squatter problem resulted from tensions, imbalances, and needs. These needs in turn responded to domestic, geopolitical, and global economic pressures and opportunities.

Crises and Consequences

A succession of crises affecting the same group of people generally has much greater consequences than a single incident (Smart and Smart 2009). It is also more likely to result in policy learning and perhaps even more effective policy (Smart and Lam 2009). However, decisions about what fits into the series of crises are not innocent or some kind of objective reality. They are socially constructed and contested. Decisions about the appropriate series in which an event or situation should be positioned can have immense political and social consequences.

What then is a crisis? Its conceptual history is fascinating. For the ancient Greeks, the source word indicated "choices between stark alternatives—right or wrong, salvation or damnation, life or death" (Koselleck and Richter 2006, 358). In the field of strategy, it referred to decisive battles determining the outcome of war. Generally, the concept "registered all the decision situations of inner and outer life, of individual humans and their communities. It was always a question of definite alternatives over which an appropriate judgment had to be passed" (Koselleck 2002, 237). While these meanings remain to a degree intact, its usage has expanded since the eighteenth century to the extent that "there is virtually no area of life that has not been examined and interpreted through this concept with its inherent demand for decisions and choices" (Koselleck and Richter 2006, 358). Beyond the individual level, a negative situation becomes a crisis when it can be seen as an event that has consequences for some dimension of the social structure. Even when this is the case, the outcome often involves little more than finding new ways to return to the status quo. This ultimately seems to have been the case for the 2008 financial crisis.

Robin Wagner-Pacifici (2010, 1358) lays out a useful analytical toolbox for "political semiosis." She sees political semiosis as a superior "method for capturing the restless conveyance of power and meaning in the eventful constitution of history." As social actors "struggle over the right interpretations of events (and thus simultaneously struggle over the event trajectories), they assert diverse relevant scenes" (1356). That is, the raw materials of sequences of social action are constituted in a particular temporal order for specific reasons, but this is only achieved after multiple sets of actors propose distinct framings (1372). Once again, individual actors, usually in ambivalent positions (Leach 1964, 352; Sewell 2005), become linked to these framing projects. Is this a riot or a revolution or a legitimate challenge to electoral fraud? Is it aggression or humanitarian intervention? Is it a natural disaster or government bungling? Is it too many episodes of bungling in a row to be forgiven? Claiming that a particular frame is the right one and struggling to have it accepted are at the heart of politics.

Wagner-Pacifici identifies three main elements of any act of political semiosis. The first element involves performatives in the sense used by Austin: statements and acts such as marriage vows, peace treaties, surrender, or imposition of states of emergency that create reality (Wagner-Pacifici 2005). The second is particularly relevant for considering series of crises or events more generally. Demonstrative features "operate to highlight possible and necessary orientations within and toward situations." Actors must "get their bearings . . . they must determine what is ahead and what is behind, what is close up and what is far away, what is central and what is marginal" (Wagner-Pacifici 2010, 1360). While demonstratives are not limited to linking with past similar events, it seems to be a particularly important form of orientation, because the sequence helps to make stronger assertions about trajectories outward from the event under discussion. Are riots a sign of future problems, related to desires for decolonization, or simply a sign of a "gap" of communication between rulers and ruled that can be resolved with modest reforms? The third central feature of political semiosis is representation. Narratives are analytical constructs "that unify a number of past or contemporaneous actions and happenings . . . into a coherent relational whole . . . made up of the raw materials of sequences of social action . . . in a particular temporal order for a particular purpose" (Larry Griffin, quoted in Wagner-Pacifici 2010, 1372). The meaning of an event, and its consequences, are open until the various contenders attempting to frame and fix the event have completed their contest, often only for the time being, since subsequent events may reopen the question. Are riots a result of juvenile delinquents, outside agitation, frustrated political expression, or desperate need? At the beginning of a crisis, interpretations seem up for grabs, but usually after a relatively short period of time only a few rival narratives remain in contention, limiting the likely paths of outcomes and consequences.

Interpreting the Reforms after the Riots

One key narrative on the riots stresses how the Governor from 1971 to 1982, Murray MacLehose, instituted a decade of major reforms that created what many have seen as a discontinuity with previous governors. The MacLehose era has been "fondly remembered as a period marking a turning point in colonial rule in Hong Kong and in socioeconomic development in the postwar decades" (Yep and Lui 2010, 2). MacLehose's major achievements included consolidation of the "four pillars" (public housing, education, medical and health services, and social welfare), and establishment of the Independent Commission Against Corruption, as well as:

> reorganization and reform in the civil service, and community building by launching various campaigns at the grass-roots level and the creation of mutual aid committees. His ambitious Ten-Year Housing Program . . . the introduction of nine-year, free, universal education, the building of partnerships with the voluntary sector in providing welfare services, and the massive success in combating corruption were perceived as the foundation of a new social order for Hong Kong society. (Yep and Lui 2010, 251)

However, research on released confidential documents by a number of scholars have argued that there is much more continuity with David Trench's term than popularly thought (Smart and Lui 2009; Yep and Lui 2010). Ray Yep (2013) argues that many of the key initiatives that resulted in the successes of the anti-corruption campaign were initially proposed by Trench but objected to by the Foreign and Commonwealth Office and the Hong Kong Police Force. Despite resistance, Trench passed legislation in 1970 that included a reversal of the onus of proof of assets or a standard of living incommensurate with present or past official pay, considered too draconian to be attempted in Britain itself.

In a document on the Aims and Policies of the Hong Kong government, written in September 1970, Hong Kong's Defence Secretary wrote that their policies had three aspects, each "contributing to the maintenance of confidence, which is as much the key of our future as it has always been." These three were the framework of law and order, the maintenance of sound economic and financial policies, and "a soundly based programme of social development, using in term in a wide sense to embrace not merely such as housing, education, health and welfare, but also the development of a sound sense of community." They "interlock . . . All three are vital and all three are receiving the attention of the Hong Kong Government . . . We have to expect that subversive elements will seize on opportunities for exploiting real or imaginary grievance."[4]

In his dispatch to London in April 1970, six months before the end of his term, Trench wrote:

> the Government is pressing on with a wide range of programmes in the social service area, as well as in the more concrete field of improvements in the general environment. We are aiming at a steady improvement in the Government's performance at the level at which it has direct impact upon ordinary people, and as close a correlation between public policy and public opinion as sound administration permits . . . Indeed, while 1967 was a year in which many plans had to be delayed and 1968 was a year in which these plans had to be dusted off and momentum regained, 1969 has seen many of them brought to fruition or far along the road towards it.[5]

Both Trench and MacLehose emphasized the need to enhance public confidence in Hong Kong's government and its future, and many programs and reforms were premised on this need.

While Trench saw the need for confidence as requiring "effective governance after two major disturbances," MacLehose saw it as requiring a "longer-term development of a new kind of state/society relationship" (Yep and Lui 2010, 5). Rather than seeing MacLehose as a reformer in principle, it is better to see him as concerned to strengthen colonial rule in a difficult time. In the context of the disturbances and the looming 1997 issue, both of which threatened confidence in very fundamental ways, reforms were a powerful tool to achieve it. This is very apparent in the ways in which he responded to demands for reforms from London. Fittingly, since 1967 started with a labor dispute in a factory, these demands asked for substantial improvements in labor policies and social security for workers. This remained an area of contention throughout the 1970s, with London arguing that not enough had been done, influenced by concerns that Hong Kong was unfairly competing with British exports due to low wages and social welfare (Clayton 2009).

Trench "represented in form and in spirit the colonial service tradition, seeing Hong Kong's best prospects in terms of a constitutional status quo" (Harris 1974, 260). One area where Trench was very conservative was in terms of voting of any kind. Even modest efforts to democratize the Urban Council came to nothing during his term, and on this issue Trench and London seemed to concur against local proponents of reform (Faure 2003a). MacLehose would also concur with the consensus renewed between Trench and London surrounding the political prospect of Hong Kong, though he eventually gave in to a proposal that led to district administrative reforms in 1980–1981 after local social movement groups built a coalition with British Parliamentary Ministers to exert pressure on the colonial government (Lui 2017). Our point is that one must beware of the received wisdom and tendency to see the 1967 riots as the rupture point between the Trench and MacLehose administrations (e.g., Cheung 2009). This is not to deny the credits of the MacLehose administration, but to recognize some continuities without which social reforms might not be possible.

One continuity was the bureaucratic reform that was often regarded as crucial for the success of the MacLehose administration. In his seminal work, Ian Scott (1989) remarked that the colonial government was able to institute structural reforms including but not limited to the reorganization of administrative structure, the introduction of the use of Chinese language, and the establishment of the Ombudsman to redress grievances that were crucial for the colonial government to gain political legitimacy. By the departure of Governor Trench in October 1971, the colonial government had developed a more sophisticated colonial bureaucracy. The colonial government expanded tremendously its numbers from 23,867 in 1954–1955 to 117,495 in 1977–1978 (Lau 1984, 49–50). By 1982–1983, the figure further rose to 168,298, making it seven times greater than the figure in 1954–1955 (Scott 1989, 139).

Having more manpower contributed to various ramifications (see Tsang 2007, Chapter 6) but two are relevant here. On the one hand, there was an increase of the administrative strength that gave the colonial bureaucrats necessary state capacity to accomplish tasks such as drafting plans of social policies. This trend of strengthening state capacity was further reinforced by the MacLehose administration through the McKinsey reforms (see Chapter 2) so that government machinery could be modernized to "take on new social and developmental dimensions of government, for which planning ahead and additional resources were essential" (Tsang 2007, 145; Scott 1989, 133). Goodstadt (2006, 23) argued that the colonial government suffered from the

Riots and Reforms 97

unavailability of statistical information, which led to the weakening of the colonial government's capacity for formulating effective social and housing policy, not to mention market intervention. While Goodstadt insisted that, in the case of financial regulation, the colonial government still suffered from unavailability of statistical information in the 1970s, we found that the colonial bureaucrats were able to collect statistical information, calculate to match housing demand and supply, and use these numbers in the process of housing policymaking (see Chapter 7). Without the bureaucratic expansion, the tasks of planning to house squatters in the course of resettlement and building sufficient housing for Hong Kong society in a difficult time would not be possible.

On the other hand, the bureaucratic expansion also enabled the colonial government to extend administrative penetration to the local level through the frontline bureaucrats of the City District Officer (CDO) Scheme (Scott 1989, 140). The Home Affairs Department's CDO Scheme began to function in 1968, but its development had to be understood in a longer temporal context. Former colonial bureaucrat Trevor Clark (1998, 6) recounted that an administrative reform process already began inside the colonial bureaucracy in April 1966, after Governor Trench found that there was an "insufficient effort to affect the outward manners of a society." The insufficiency was an indication where the senior colonial bureaucrats realized that there was a need to innovate their approach toward a rapidly changing Hong Kong society when the established mechanism of soliciting political support through the Chinese economic elites and the Kaifong leaders was no longer effective (Mok 2022). Thus, the state-society communication gap exposed by the 1966 riots was already apparent to the senior colonial bureaucrats even before the two riots. However, efforts in modifying colonial governance came with little success. One reason was that, as Scott (2017, 140) argued, the colonial bureaucracy was internally divided by the "reformers" and "conservatives, who sought to retain the [political] status quo." The internal division between reformers and conservatives was best seen in the case of the Report of the Working Party on Local Administration (also known as the Dickinson Report; see Clark 1998). Although reform-minded official Bill Dickinson considered that prudent electoral reform was one of the possible ways to bridge the gap "so long as external interference was avoidable" (Clark 1998, 17), it was the conservatives' decisions and rationales that prevailed (see Bray 2001, 37).

Yet conservative-minded officials such as Denis Bray were able to make use of some suggestions of the Dickinson Report where "District Officers (DOs) should be appointed in the urban areas" (Clark 1998, 4). It was in this way that the CDO scheme was put in place to bridge the gap without the expansion of political franchise, but rather extension of administrative reach. In Mok's (2022, 12–13) terms, the CDO plan was an organizational device that enhanced the "eyes and ears of the colonial state" so that the colonial bureaucrats became sensitive to the changing public opinion. Such enhanced sensitivity was apparent and could be seen in the MacLehose administration's Executive Council papers, where a standard "Public Relations" section could be found. Both Trench and Bray were what Ure (2012, 7) called the "bureaucratic entrepreneur," able to "define a distinctive policy, to develop the capacity to implement it and to build a coalition in support of it" (12). Like entrepreneurs, colonial bureaucrats were able to explore and exploit the opportunities offered by the unspecified areas of the Letter Patent and Royal Instructions that stipulated the constitutional and administrative scope of the colonial government. This is evident in former District Officer Patrick Hase's (2001a, 427) account of how Denis Bray attempted not to "play it by the book" and, elsewhere, he also recounted how senior colonial officials during the MacLehose era were "willing and able to adapt their [policy] proposals to achieve a consensus position" (Hase 2001b, 134).

Thus, when Governor Trench passed on the "the torch of reform" to his successor (Tsang 2007, 192), he was also passing a more competent and adaptative colonial bureaucracy—with deeper administrative penetration into the local society—to Murray MacLehose. The MacLehose administration was still structurally autocratic. Lau (1984, 38) called it "bureaucratic centralism." Yet the colonial administration was more sensitive to popular demands and changing public opinion. This could be seen in the formalization of the decision-making practices inside and during the MacLehose administration, where assessment of the policy impact on public relations (i.e., how the people would think of the colonial policy) through the suggestions mainly offered by the Home Affairs Department became a standard practice. Senior colonial bureaucrats in the post-riots era were able to hold the reins within the colonial administration, but they were also capable of dealing with administrative procedures skillfully. These features, resulting from bureaucratic reforms, enabled the colonial government to be more capable to deal with the squatter problem, as subsequent chapters will show.

The Reforms under MacLehose

One of the eventual outcomes of the 1967 riots was Governor MacLehose's decision in the 1970s to replace the Resettlement Department with the new Housing Authority. In 1972, MacLehose announced a Ten-Year Housing Programme to address the problems of slum and squatter areas, and redevelop the first type of resettlement estates. The target was to "house 1.8 million people over the next ten years in permanent self-contained homes with good amenities and a decent environment at a standard of 3.3 m^2 per person. A new Housing Authority was set up to consolidate government efforts in attaining this goal" (Yeh 1990, 442). The program was perhaps overambitious: few of its targets were achieved by the end of the 10-year period (see Chapters 7 and 8). To phase out house sharing, 400,000 public housing units would have been needed within the 10 years. However, only 220,577 units were completed between 1973 and 1982. Yeh (1990, 442) argued that this was a "result of bureaucratic restructuring problems and the constraints of finance, manpower, and land resources in the early implementation stages of the programme." In Chapter 7, we address these problems by pointing to another explanation: imbalances in supply and demand for both temporary housing and public housing.

The sporadic occurrence of unrest ironically and eventually undermined the fatalistic attitude that the Hong Kong Chinese were unreliable and ultimately loyal to China rather than Hong Kong. At the same time, changing international politics (such as China joining the United Nations and its new diplomatic relations with Western countries) contributed to a change in the perspective of the colonial administration, alerting it to the need to build a new kind of state-society relations in the aftermath of the two major disturbances in the 1960s. More efforts were attempted to promote a Hong Kong identity and sense of commitment to the territory, in part through the expansion of social citizenship in the form of housing and the expansion of free education (Chapter 8; Smart 2008). Cold War geopolitics played a crucial role in forming the governing strategy, with multifaceted effects. Constraining, the Sino-British relationship made the colonial government put democratic reform into cold storage, since the British considered that any attempt to alter Hong Kong's colonial status would provoke the CCP's aggression and thus was "too risky." The 1967 riots alerted London and reaffirmed the preexisting belief that "Hong Kong's future must eventually lie in China." The objective of the British officials—in both London and Hong Kong—was to prepare to negotiate Hong Kong's return to China when there was a "favourable opportunity."[6] This made Hong Kong undergo the pathway of "decolonization without independence" (Lau 1987). The regime remained authoritarian with a strong pro-business character (e.g., Goodstadt 2005; Ngo 2000; Jones 1990) until 1997, and arguably afterward.[7]

While the main thrust of the adjusted governing strategy was to preserve the undemocratic political structure due to the so-called China factor (Lui 2017, 79), it entailed that the colonial government had to be reformist and responsive (Fung 2022). As the Colonial Secretary wrote in 1969, "the objective of the Hong Kong Government is the promotion of the best interests of all inhabitants of Hong Kong" where "the legitimate grievances of individuals can be rectified."[8] Through this learning from episodes and series of unrests, MacLehose became conscious of the need for an "autocratic form of [colonial] government" to cultivate trust and win the support of the populace. As MacLehose's report to London stated, "[p]romotion of cohesion and loyalty amongst the population of Hong Kong is vital." The Hong Kong government "must manage things so that the population feel that the Government is *theirs*, and identify themselves with it." One approach to attempt to achieve this is to "aim at civic pride through drawing up and dramatizing adequate social programmes."[9] These social programs and the promotion of loyalty were not the ends in themselves, however. They were the means aimed to strengthen Britain's diplomatic position vis-à-vis China when the negotiation over Hong Kong's future finally came. In his "Hong Kong Objectives" dispatch, MacLehose declared his goal to "make Hong Kong a model city of international standing" so that "China might be reluctant to try to absorb." Meanwhile the colonial government could retain the loyalty of the local population.[10] These thoughts implied that the "[traditional social] problems should be faced and solved now . . . at whatever cost" before Hong Kong's "vulnerability in the '80s and '90s" had to be faced.

Governor MacLehose (quoted in Faure 1997, 308) stated that the creation of 1,500 mutual aid committees was "not only a considerable administrative achievement, but indicates the great need that these organizations fill."[11] He acknowledged that there was "indeed, a void: a void which was as dangerous for the Government as it was unwelcome to the ordinary citizen, who was left without means of influencing conditions outside his own door."[12] While democracy was seen as too risky because of the precarious situation of the colony in relation to the People's Republic of China, other forms of bridging the void were increasingly explored in the years after 1967. These efforts included but were not limited to the use of public opinion polling devices (e.g., Movement of Opinion Direction, Flash Points, and Talking Points) conducted by the Home Affairs Department through the CDO Scheme so that the colonial government could be more responsive (Mok 2019a). The Home Affairs Department also conducted covert surveillance (i.e., Standing Committee on Pressure Groups) that targeted pressure groups' activities when the local social movement phenomenon began to take root in Hong Kong (Lui, Kuan, Chan, and Chan 2005, 65; Lo 1997, 41). These sorts of surveillance enabled the colonial government to be cautious of an increasingly vibrant civil society. It also helped to channel political pressures generated by protest actions to the consultative system, so that government policies could be improved (Lui, Kuan, Chan, and Chan 2005, 65; see also Fung 2022, 64–66). Last but not least, the colonial government also mobilized the Hong Kong Chinese community through state-sponsored campaigns such as "Keep Hong Kong Clean" and "Fight Violent Crime" to build a more benevolent image of the colonial government to mitigate its legitimacy problem (Lui, Kuan, Chan, and Chan 2005, 64; Ku and Pun 2004, 4).

MacLehose's final dispatch to the FCO on 17 April 1982 stated that "[m]y 10-and-a-half years here have been dominated, for me, by the prospect of negotiation about Hong Kong's future in the early or mid-80s" (quoted in Chu 2017, 2). Reforms were intended, if not always stated, to stabilize the situation, increase loyalty in the population, improve livelihoods to provide a strong contrast to China, and create a stronger negotiating position for the inevitable negotiations. Reforms such as the Mutual Aid Committees, the localization of the civil service, and the acceptance of demands for the use of Chinese as a second language (Fung 2022) were adopted to build a stronger relationship between the population and the government. Lui (2017, 95) points out that MacLehose's emphasis was "on the building of a sense of civic pride and *not* on the notion of citizenship and/or public participation." As a result, these projects of community building were "almost necessarily self-contradictory" as the leaders recruited from more diverse backgrounds "were not expected to assume the political role of local representatives" (95). It was hoped that they would more effectively transmit messages from the government to the people but tried to avoid influence in the opposite direction.

Pressure from London

The pressures on the Governor from London intensified in the 1970s. As Lui Tai-lok (2017, 77) said, "there was enormous pressure from the United Kingdom on the colonial administration to initiate social reforms and political changes." This counters David Faure's (2003a) claim that there was a growing degree of autonomy for the Hong Kong government from the time of Governor Grantham's term in the 1950s until the term of MacLehose. He suggests that Governor Trench's sidelining of proposals to make the Urban Council more democratic might be seen as "the first open declaration of this virtual autonomy" (Faure 2003a, 200). He might be correct about an increase in autonomy if we limit it to a comparison of the Trench era with the first postwar years. There was a "rule that a colony in debt to London would not be freed from British Treasury supervision of its spending before it had proved its fiscal solvency with three years of balanced budgets after its borrowings had been paid off" (Goodstadt 2013, 93). Hong Kong, wanting to avoid pressures from London to institute a progressive tax system and establish a democratic legislature, claimed a budget surplus in 1948—though with some slippery accounting tactics. The colonial government not only avoided borrowing from London but also consistently endeavored to limit the defense contribution and to scale down social services in the early 1950s.

In so doing, Hong Kong accumulated a sufficient amount of fiscal surplus, which served as a ground for it to request financial autonomy and, with that autonomy, to deflect—and sometimes fend off—the policy instructions from the metropole, such as fiscal reform (Ure 2012; see also Littlewood 2010). By the mid-1950s, London's approval of the annual budget had become "almost a complete formality" so that in effect the "colonial administration had ousted London from the budgetary process, which was an astonishing achievement in the absence of representative government" (Goodstadt 2013, 93). In Ure's (2012, 215) terms, "Hong Kong had the capacity to manage its finances effectively, the Secretary of State was left with little room for manoeuvre." In 1958, London finally granted Hong Kong financial autonomy, to which Ure (2012, 215) argued that it was a "belated *de jure* recognition." More generally, the extent of Hong Kong's autonomy from London's control "was probably unique in colonial history," particularly regarding relations with China (Goodstadt 2013, 84). There was a significant ideological difference between London and Hong Kong, with the colony opposing any kind of welfarism and associated fiscal policies to "advance economic and social progress." This opposition was bolstered by a Malthusian response to the influx of refugees, whom it hoped would be convinced to return to China (Goodstadt 2013, 88; Madokoro 2016).

There is little evidence of an expectation of acquiescence to London's commands before the 1970s. Instead, there seems to have been a more pro forma need to *respond* without necessarily following the suggestions from the Colonial or Foreign and Commonwealth Offices—so long as plausible reasons for why complying would not be practical or desirable could be mobilized. Repeated questions from London about the housing situation illustrate this clearly. For example, the Secretary of State for the Colonies sent a message on 12 December 1949 requesting information on "progress made with housing in Hong Kong since the end of the war, with details of any schemes or plans that are projected" (quoted in Faure 2003b, 90). The reply offered details of minimal government schemes and a reliance on private building. The Undersecretary of State responsible for Hong Kong and the Pacific at the Colonial Office sent another message on 3 January 1950, noting that "it is fully recognized in the department that housing conditions in Hong Kong are shocking" and that "[i]t looks very much as though the prewar reliance on private enterprise to provide housing for the poorer sections of the population will have to go." He then reminded Hong Kong that they were waiting for their response to the Abercrombie Report (Lai 1999)[13] and that "we cannot allow the matter to drift much longer" (quoted in Faure 2003b, 93). However, it was also acknowledged that government involvement with housing on a large scale would require very large sums of public money.

In the absence of substantial money from London for low-income housing, or the willingness of the Hong Kong government to undertake it, concerns and questions from the United Kingdom prior to the 1970s did little more than prompt replies, reports, and subcommittees (Smart 2006). The subsequent history of public housing in Hong Kong shows very little direct influence from outside the colony (indirect influence is another matter, as the geopolitical explanation suggests), whether from London or supranational agencies like the World Bank, which has had so much influence elsewhere in the Global South (Harris 1998; Smart 2020). Public scandals such as the Trafalgar Square World Refugee Day in 1959–1960 (see Chapter 4) or the Shek Kip Mei fire might generate calls to "do something," but what was done seems to have been very much dependent on Hong Kong itself. While questions from London about housing conditions continued periodically, it does not seem that it created commitments for Hong Kong to act in any particular way. Housing was to have another form of impact, however, as part of a British debate about whether Hong Kong was an "industrial slum" whose "poor social welfare and inadequate labor protection were seen as factors contributing to Hong Kong manufacturers underselling British producers" (Yep and Lui 2010, 6). While mentioned in Parliament in 1967, the issue gained much higher profile in 1975, during a period of British economic crisis, and the Labour government of Harold Wilson from 1974 to 1976.

This episode of reform in the aftermath of the riots, though, was structured in a different situation under the FCO than under the Colonial Office. Both British manufacturers' lobbies and trade unions criticized Hong Kong's industrial situation, demanding protection from exports they claimed were produced by sweated labor and child workers (Goodstadt 2013). Political criticism was intensified by a 1976 Fabian Society publication entitled *Hong Kong – Britain's Responsibility* (England 1976). The author also cowrote an influential critique of Hong Kong's labor relations with John Rear (England and Rear 1975). Prime Minister Wilson and Governor MacLehose agreed on a public pledge in 1975 that Hong Kong would "achieve broad comparability of labour legislation and social welfare with other Asian countries, excluding Japan" by 1980 (quoted in Goodstadt 2013, 96).

In response, the FCO produced the *Hong Kong Planning Paper* in 1976.[14] The Paper argued that rapid reforms were needed in labor rights and social security. Besides reaching labor conditions at least equal to its Asian competitors, Hong Kong would be expected to achieve speedier progress in applying International Labor Organization Conventions. Specific targets were set for more rest days and holidays (1977), annual paid leave (1978), and banning employment of minors under 14 (1979). It also urged consideration of a minimum wage and unemployment benefits. These reform demands exceeded MacLehose's intentions (Yep and Lui 2010). A more radical reform plan was being expected of the Governor "and it was the duty of the Governor to find the ways and means to translate this grand scheme of reform into reality" (Yep and Lui 2010, 9). The intention to move toward these reforms was signaled in his 1977 policy address.

Confidential documents, however, revealed that beneath a cordial surface—what Lui (2017, 77) calls the "political opacity" of a colonial situation—there were serious tensions between Hong Kong and the FCO. While

MacLehose acknowledged the powers of London, he argued that there was an informal "tradition of respecting the man on the spot as enjoying the last word on how his jurisdiction should be governed" and claimed there was no precedent for the Colonial Office "imposing a comprehensive program of reforms" on a colony through such a planning paper (Yep and Lui 2010, 10). In his efforts to divert the more concerning elements of the plan, MacLehose went so far as reminding London that as a last resort, a governor could be dismissed if his service was not seen as consistent with Her Majesty's government. As implementation in Hong Kong failed to follow the plan, the Minister of State for Foreign and Commonwealth Affairs wrote in a 1976 telegram that:

> I am rather anxious therefore lest some of the qualifications and reservations you include may endanger the precise time-scale we envisaged for the implementation of agreed measures. And here and there the emphasis on the various stages which will have to be completed before decisions are taken and action initiated do seem to me to blunt the sense of urgency which we would like to see (quoted in Yep and Lui 2010, 259).

To achieve some of the reforms that the FCO envisaged, Hong Kong needed to change its fiscal arrangements, which produced an even stronger response from MacLehose. London felt that the reforms should have priority over fiscal discipline and argued that public expenditure could be increased to about 25% of GDP to facilitate them. However, the 1976 budget speech argued that the maximum should be 20% and that with a strong economy it should fall lower. These conflicting visions generated a flurry of tense communications, but ultimately there was no major change in the tax system at that time. Yep and Lui (2010, 18) conclude in their detailed account of this history that "[d]riven by domestic pressure from the Left and strategic calculation over the future of Hong Kong, the FCO showed no mercy in imposing a grand scheme of social reforms on the colonial administration" and were indifferent to local concerns. Yet the outcome of reforms, while considerable, was more modest than desired by the FCO. The reforms were being steered in a more locally acceptable direction by MacLehose's persuasion; by reference to convention and local opinion; by a threat to resign; and by direct confrontation. Even in a context much less sensitive to Hong Kong's autonomy, pressures for reform could be diverted and softened (Yep and Lui 2010, 18–19).

In addition to pressure from London and the FCO, MacLehose's reforms were influenced by a motivation that is very relevant to the squatter problem: "my object in Hong Kong must be to ensure that conditions in Hong Kong are so superior in every way to those in China that the CPG [Chinese People's Government] will hesitate before facing the problems of absorption. These objects coincide with what we, as the administrative power, would wish for the Colony in any case" (MacLehose 29 November 1971, quoted in Lui 2017, 78).

Riots and Reforms 105

The geopolitics of the increasingly unignorable factor of 1997 and the expiry of the lease thus created a context in which reforms of the potentially scandalous conditions of the colony became seen as more desirable.

Conclusions

The main message to stress from this account is that the 1970s were a period when London became more activist and demanding of reforms from Hong Kong than had been the case in the past. Despite this situation, it was possible for the local administration to deflect and modify these demands. In comparison with the 1950s, however, the situation had become one where it would be very hard not to concede in some way to metropolitan concerns for reforms, particularly those that were tied to Britain's own interests such as its perceptions of unfair and damaging industrial competition. Unlike the housing question in the 1950s, when there was only a general sense from London and the Colonial Office that the squatting and housing situation was appalling so that "something had to be done," very specific targets were being set out for MacLehose, and foot-dragging could only reduce or redefine these targets; British influence on social and economic policy in Hong Kong had certainly increased.

In another way, however, 1967 and the merger of the Colonial Office into the FCO expanded Hong Kong's autonomy. Fung and Fong (2020) argue that in the post-1967 context, the FCO encouraged Hong Kong to expand its "external autonomy" in order to rebuild confidence in Hong Kong's future, becoming an "independent actor in the international arena," beginning with membership in the Asian Development Bank in 1969, and "ultimately participating in more than 50 international organizations at the end of the colonial period," winning three medals, the most ever, in the 2021 Tokyo Olympics as a contemporary example. The following chapters address how these multiple influences might have played out, first in the policy environment that resulted in the question of what to do about squatters on land not needed for development, and second in the more general process of dealing with the squatter problem.

Returning to the question of the impact of the Riots on reform, the conclusion is less clear-cut than often presented. Firstly, reforms were beginning, if modestly, prior to 1966, and many of the MacLehose reforms are better seen as continuity than sharp divergence. This was acknowledged in his "valedictory dispatch" of April 1982: "Many of these programmes were little more than extensions of previous trends of Government" (quoted in Chu 2017, 2). For example, Governor Trench "took charge of this meeting," about housing issues on 10 June 1971, "from the start. He had obviously worked hard on the papers and voiced his thoughts clearly. He suggested . . . a body similar to the current Housing Board to act as a general advisor to Government on housing including public and private. . . . It should be chaired by an unofficial and be responsible for advising Executive Council on rents, income groups, requirements for aided housing etc. It must have an effective secretariat." The second key proposal was that

> the Resettlement Department should gradually work itself out. No more Resettlement Estates as such should be built. Instead, new L.C.H. [Low-Cost Housing] and mixed estates should be managed by the authority referred to below. At present the Department should retain squatter control and clearance. (c) that a new authority be created with Colony-wide responsibilities to take the place of the existing Housing Authority. This should be much smaller and consist of officials, some unofficials elected by the U.C. [Urban Council], N.T. representatives and unofficial specialists. It should be chaired by the head of the department serving it. (d) that the new authority be served by a new department based on the U.S.D. [Urban Services Department] Housing Division.

These prescriptions sound very much like the new Housing Branch and Housing Authority created under MacLehose. And as we saw in Chapter 4, in 1964 a ten-year program public housing construction target of 1.9 million units was proposed, even more than the 1.8 million in MacLehose's Ten-Year Programme.

The disturbances intensified the perception of the necessity and urgency of reform. Together, 1966 and 1967 seem to have had more impact than either would have separately. However, strong claims that the multiple reforms of the 1970s derived from the Riots, growing perception of the dangers of the gap between the government and the population, and the activist efforts of Governor MacLehose are only partially supported by archival evidence. Crucial parts of the story include an increasingly activist bureaucratic overseer, the new FCO, which operated in new ways compared to the old CO, and changes in the global political economy that made Hong Kong seem an unfair economic competitor. David Faure's argument about the role of London's demand for more social welfare and social services seems to be correct, but inaccurately dated from the time of the origins of the Resettlement Estates. Rather, changes in the United Kingdom, both administrative and political economic, are crucial. Decolonization, as David Faure asserted, is part of this, but only part.

The riots were events—or perhaps a unitary, double-head event—that had impact, but becoming an event was not a natural consequence; rather, it was the product of political processes that latched onto the opportunities the crises presented. Žižek (2014, 8) asks, "Does everything that exists have to be grounded in sufficient reasons? Or are there things that somehow happen out of nowhere? How, then, can philosophy help us to determine what an event – an occurrence not grounded in sufficient reasons – is and how it is possible?" The riots were clearly an event, or events, underdetermined by the solutions preferred respectively by Hong Kong and London, but constructed out of the understanding of the situation, the options thought to be practical and not excessively repugnant, and the course of discussion and debate about what should be done. Subsequent chapters will consider other episodes of decision-making that, while not emerging as a public event, had comparable consequences within the corridors of power in Hong Kong. The next chapter returns to the issue of squatters on land not needed for development to consider how changes of government in London and Hong Kong might have conditioned the situation and outcomes.

6

The Mangle of Policy Practice

[Policy is] assembled from multiple resources (intentions, ambitions, discourses of legitimation, anticipated 'delivery agents', political and organisational alliances, and more). These may not fit comfortably together; indeed, here, the streamlined and integrated model of the assembly line gives way to more handicraft images of things being cut and pasted, or bodged together, in processes of what Levi-Strauss (1966), in his studies of totems, called 'bricolage'.

—John Clarke, Dave Bainton, Noémi Lendvai, and Paul Stubbs, *Making Policy Move: Towards a Politics of Translation and Assemblage* (2015, 31)

This chapter considers debates about what to do about squatters on land not needed for development—the toughest part of the squatter problem. Beyond shedding light on a key section of the path toward formalizing squatter areas, we also use this rich material to generate an alternative explanation, the policy mangle approach, for the formalization process in Hong Kong, and then to evaluate the adequacy and plausibility of this explanation. This chapter is limited to the initial discussions, concentrating on 1970–1972. The consequences of the decisions taken will be explored in the remainder of the book. These discussions emphasize practicality and envisioned possibilities and constraints. They reveal a process of muddling through, with some possibilities arising only to disappear, while others condense as more suitable alternatives. Initial contingency grows into selected paths. Such paths become easier to follow as they become established, and sometimes retrospectively appear to have been inevitable.

A useful way of thinking about this process involves what can be called the *mangle of policy practice.* Andrew Pickering (1995, 23) analyzes laboratory science by using the metaphor of the washing machine mangle, which mechanically squeezes out water, to invoke the way "material and social agency are mangled in practice." Human actions and projects are transformed through a "dialectic of resistance and accommodation" where human endeavors must use non-humans as partners in a "dance of agency" where outcomes diverge from those initially expected due to these material resistances (17). In addition to obstacles placed by humans, material objects, as well as life-forms such as COVID-19, frequently contribute to the failure of human projects to achieve their goals. This kind of failure resulting from the material characteristics of squatter areas, such as the difficulty of developing them and their susceptibility to catastrophic landslides and fires, punctuate and channel the housing policy endeavors in the decade after 1972 (see Chapter 7). Failure subsequently requires accommodation by humans in response to the resistance of the situation to our intentions, demanding tweaking or replacement of our practices and projects. This idea can be extended from Pickering's focus on laboratory science to the unpredictable transformations worked upon whatever gets fed into the mangle of policy debate. Perhaps the mangle can be more relevantly thought of as a sausage grinder, in the spirit of the adage that has been misattributed to Otto von Bismarck: "To retain respect for sausages and laws, one must not watch them in the making."[1]

The mangle perspective is particularly relevant to discussions like those about squatters, where the responses of other humans with divergent agendas and interests are accompanied by the resistance of the material landscape. Steep slopes were made even more dangerous by their geological features as well as by existing road and other infrastructure, or their absence. All of this created the problem of land that is not easily developed. The landscape is the silent dance partner in this categorization of informal settlements: it makes some areas easily developed and thus valuable, and others harder to develop and less valuable. Classification of the geography in turn creates the problem of squatters on such land since the standard solution of development clearance cannot be applied to resolving it. Material resistance of the geography of Hong Kong, and of a landslide-prone geology, will be further discussed in Chapter 9.

When other policy issues, accidents, and events put the safety and welfare of this residual population on the agenda, the material substrate and built environment of the squatter areas squeezed and transformed proposals. They did this through procedures put in place to evaluate alternate possibilities to deal with recalcitrant spaces (Ascensão 2016). Ideas and proposals get fed through these policy mangles and often end up following paths no one fully anticipated or perhaps even wanted, such as the 1950s transformation of the squatter problem into the Resettlement Programme (Smart 2006). Early choices can have substantial unexpected effects but can also subsequently turn into dead ends. This chapter addresses some of the early choices that made formalization possible, with their subsequent developments considered in later chapters.

Policy mangles often involve constituted commissions or working parties, such as the 1963 Working Party discussed in Chapter 4. For Pierre Bourdieu (2014, 27), a commission brings together people to "elaborate a new legitimate definition of a public problem." The establishment and operation of a commission involves complex calculations of who needs to be included, and those choices are intended to generate decisions that strengthen or undermine a "certain state of the balance of forces" (111). What we would like to add is our observation that for most policy mangles, the inputs are not simply those that concern the apparent policy issues, but also other kinds of issues that are tangled up with the problem contexts of the decision makers at that point in time.

Commissions can be seen as policy mangles, but they are only one type of this broader category of bureaucratic deliberation on problems. Commissions are public, while some policy mangles are kept confidential and internal to government, such as the ones analyzed in this chapter. Commissions often include experts who are not part of government, particularly those about something that has been done scandalously (inquiries), as opposed to those more concerned with how policies could be improved.

An Informal Policy Mangle about the Squatter Problem

Governor Trench's letter to the Colonial Secretary about Prime Minister Heath's expression of concern over the squatter problem initially resulted in a more informal and confidential mangle of policy debate. Heath's concern had been reiterated by the Secretary of State for Foreign and Commonwealth Affairs Douglas-Home and again by Parliamentary Undersecretary of State for Foreign and Commonwealth Affairs Anthony Royle. Douglas-Home was not only the Secretary of State for Foreign and Commonwealth Affairs but had been Prime Minister himself from 19 October 1963 to 16 October 1964, and leader of the Opposition for the following year, in which post he was succeeded by Edward Heath.

Royle informed the Secretary of State that he "spoke privately to the Governor while I was in Hong Kong about his reply of 17 September to your letter of 3 August [1970]." He indicated to the Governor "that you could not leave matters as the Governor's letter had left them. The new Government recognised how much had been done up to date: we did not necessarily want a radical acceleration, but we did want the momentum to be maintained and be seen to be maintained. This would help the F.C.O. to help Hong Kong." On housing, Royle acknowledged the Governor's warning against devoting scarce resources to eradicating squatter areas:

The Mangle of Policy Practice   111

but, on the other hand, these areas were frequently the cause of damaging criticism by tourists and other outside visitors and you could not be expected in view of the Prime Minister's personal interest in this matter to let matters rest. . . . The Governor said that consideration of these matters could not be taken out of the hands of the Housing Board. I agreed, and the Governor agreed to put the problem again to the Board, for reconsideration of their previous advice and a further study of the problem of squatters on Crown Land not needed for development: since it was here the remaining problem lay – those on land needed for development would be resettled in the normal course. Whilst he was not hopeful that they would find it possible to eliminate the squatter problem early and entirely, it might conceivably be possible by undertaking a change or extension of policy to find some acceptable way of rehousing the (very much estimated) 50,000 squatters on land not needed for development if geographical and other physical problems could be overcome.[2]

This message has been quoted at length to document a number of key issues. First, Governor Trench appears to have been following the venerable course of slowness in responding while providing information designed to indicate why what was being done was what should be done, and why what had been suggested would be impractical (see Chapter 1). Second, that the FCO was less tolerant toward this kind of response than had been the CO. Third, that waiting for an agency to report was an acceptable reason for delay but increased the significance of that report. The Housing Board was a kind of policy mangle, but one with little authority. Fourth, that possibly poorly informed comments by visitors about disturbing or unsightly elements of everyday life like squatter areas could contribute to a desire by the FCO to ensure that "something" would be done, and that that "something" would be sufficient to address questions in the media or Parliament.

Pressure from the FCO on squatters and housing continued in the following months. The Secretary of State asked Trench for a progress report on 20 November 1970 because of a debate in the House of Lords on Dependent Territories. The debate was originated by Lord Shepherd, who called attention to the problems of British Colonial Territories and the need for a "full review of policy to improve the economic and social conditions of their peoples."[3] Trench's response, which did not arrive until 5 December 1970, said that the Housing Board Annual Report was expected in about two months, and provided some details. There were about 410,000 squatters then in the urban areas. Against this had to be weighed the existing resettlement commitment of 528,000 people from the existing categories of eligibility in the next six years. These categories were: squatters cleared from land for development; victims of fires, natural disasters, and compassionate cases; families displaced from dangerous buildings; clearance of squatter resite areas (see Chapter 9); and relief of overcrowding in resettlement estates. Because the commitments effectively balanced the building plans, any "major resettlement of squatters on Crown land not needed for development can therefore only be done at the expense of clearances of those included in the present categories."

The Housing Board was "examining the question of housing priorities to see whether any higher priority can be given" to non-development squatters, or "whether there can be any in situ improvement in the squatter areas themselves, and further to see whether it is possible to accelerate the housing programme by finding more suitable sites." Additionally, the Board was thought likely to recommend that 30,000 squatters living in the worst areas not required for development and not included in those categories should be resettled. He downplayed suggestions of adopting a crash program to resolve the problem, arguing that "the Hong Kong housing programme has in fact been a crash programme extending over a period of 18 years," during which the Colony had devoted resources to it needed for "other problems of equal urgency."[4]

The strength of Douglas-Home's concerns was amplified by a telegram on 8 December 1970 reminding Trench of their "clear understanding" that Trench would "aim at a special report by the Housing Board within a couple of months."[5] The Colonial Secretary, as Acting Governor since Trench was travelling to London, replied the next day that it was a "matter of regret if there has been a misunderstanding but if the intention was that the Board should delay the preparation of its general report (which is urgently needed) in order to attempt to deal in isolation with one aspect of a problem which has to be looked at in its totality I should have felt bound to advise against this. Also I must emphasize that there has not been and will not be any loss of momentum in this exercise."[6] The implication here is that while the FCO was reacting to minor embarrassments and questions, the Hong Kong colonial administration was juggling difficult and interconnected problems to which they would prefer not to add. The pressure did not end at this point: on 7 January 1971, in the first sentence of a nine-page letter, Trench stated that "Mr. Royle was anxious that I should, on my return [to Hong Kong from London] look again into the position as regards the re-housing of squatters, about which Mr. Heath had expressed concern." The Deputy Undersecretary Leslie Monson responded on 29 January with further inquiries, including about the number of boat squatters, following on from a question by Baroness Summerskill in the House of Lords debate on Dependent Territories (on boat squatters, see Airriess 2014; Smart 2018).

On 6 April 1971, Monson forwarded a long letter to the FCO by the Worker-Student Political Action Committee, which was very critical of the housing situation in Hong Kong.[7] It was forwarded because "It has been sent to the Press and Baroness Summerskill, and in case we are tackled by them it would be most helpful if you could let us have your comments as soon as

The Mangle of Policy Practice

possible." In a draft reply to a later request, after providing more information for a reply to a Parliamentary question, an assistant to the Colonial Secretary added that "I must protest about the very short notice given for reply to this question . . . Typhoon Freda passed the Colony this morning and Government offices are still under-manned. It is most unreasonable, in my view, to expect a detailed reply within 12 hours of receipt of any Parliamentary Question under normal circumstances, still less in typhoon conditions," although this comment was not included in the transmitted reply. Comparable requests for information and action to forestall public criticism continued throughout 1971 and afterward, although perhaps not as frequently as during this period.

The Colonial Secretary's letter of 11 November, circulated widely within the colonial administration, opened up a wide-ranging discussion of the concerns and issues it raised. The Governor was quoted as being concerned particularly with the "clearance and resettlement of squatters and the improvement of squatter areas. The problem of squatters on land not required for development is primarily in question since other squatters will be resettled eventually."[8] The Colonial Secretary quoted two alternative approaches outlined by Governor Trench. The first was to "accept as a very major change of policy that all squatters would be resettled." The second was to "give the squatters some form of title to lots on this unwanted land, and allow them to build (with their own money if they have it) NT [New Territories] 'village type' houses on patterns approved by the Building Authority."[9]

Both of these would represent considerable transformations of prevalent policy, which in practice appears to have been based on two implicit principles: limiting rehousing commitments and avoiding giving any appearance of property rights to squatters (see Chapter 5). These principles help to explain why these proposals from the Governor ended up not being adopted, but instead were channeled through more conventional approaches to squatting, approaches seen as more consistent with practical concerns, particularly the pursuit of enhanced control and the need to contain demands on limited administrative resources.

The concerns expressed by the Governor himself about his two alternative solutions to the problem of squatters on Crown land not needed for development (sometimes summarized as non-developable squatter areas) are enlightening about the nature of colonial governance at the time. On the first, accepting the resettlement of all squatters, three difficulties were identified. Clearance and resettlement is "compulsory, and it is distasteful to use such powers for other than a public purpose." Development, thus, is a public purpose, but without development, resettlement does not automatically serve a public purpose. If, perhaps, all squatters were eager to be resettled, it might not be a problem, but that did not appear to be the case. Based on surveys, Leung (1983, 77) found that 30% of squatters preferred to remain rather than be rehoused, and the Kwun Tong City District Office (1983) discovered that 48% of residents of four squatter areas also preferred not to be cleared. A survey in 1967 by Golger (1972) revealed that 40.6% of squatters did not want to be resettled, even if nearby. Smart's survey of 156 households in Diamond Hill squatter area in 1984 took a different approach. The other surveys asked about preferences based on existing policy at that time, which meant that recent migrants and others would only qualify for Temporary Housing areas or would have to resettle in the distant New Territories, while singles would receive no rehousing. He wanted to know whether they would prefer to remain even if they were given their most preferred resettlement options. For this hypothetical question, 12.7% would still prefer to remain, while for distant options, 77.5% would opt not to be resettled. Those who were most resistant to resettlement were more likely to be retired, self-employed, or clerical/managerial/professional workers. They were also more likely to work in Diamond Hill, to have lived in their residence for a longer period, and to have larger dwellings (an average of 382 square feet compared to 220 square feet for the whole sample). They were also more likely to be involved with local political or voluntary organizations (Smart 1992). Thus, voluntary resettlement might have reduced the problem but would not have eliminated it without making the offers very attractive.

More problematically for Trench, "experience tells us that other squatters would take over the area in a flash in the absence of development. We could not keep them off without the danger of a degree of violence."[10] Here again we see an acknowledgement of the risks of physical resistance, which in turn might create security concerns, which the Special Branch of the Hong Kong Police Force often warned against in relation to clearances (Smart 2006). As well, the issue of resquatting was a perennial one, particularly prior to the beginning of the Resettlement Programme in 1954. Non-developed sites required considerable efforts to prevent new squatting, including weekly or more frequent patrols by squatter control agents (Smart 2002). The risks of resquatting expanded after 1984 when new squatting ended, reducing options for those desperately needing housing; control intensified. A Housing Department official interviewed in October 1999 said that "[w]hen residents of a squatter area are allocated spaces in either permanent public rental housing or in interim housing, their dwellings are demolished. In some cases, however, because their dwelling is only part of a larger unit, or because it shares a structural support with another unit, we cannot tear down the dwelling. Then, we will endeavor to make the unit uninhabitable, by pouring lumps of concrete on the floor or spraying large amounts of insecticide everywhere. Still we sometimes find other individuals illegally moving into these spaces" (Smart 2001, 37). More generally, solving the squatter problem had repeatedly bumped up against the

The Mangle of Policy Practice   115

difficulty that resettlement or toleration encouraged new squatting, necessitating continual expenditure on squatter control (Smart 2013).

The final liability mentioned by Governor Trench was that non-development squatters would "have to be assigned a resettlement priority which could only be at the bottom of the list. It would be a long time (if ever) before we got around to resettling them."[11] This would mean that without reducing the numbers of those to be housed from categories considered more worthy than those wrongfully occupying scarce land, most of the non-development squatters would remain in the interim in their squatter areas. The problem of criticism and questions in Parliament and media would remain. Accepting the principle of resettling non-development squatters would complicate the effort to limit rehousing commitments without fully resolving the visible "squalor" that prompted the interventions from London. The first approach, resettling all squatters, was therefore "impractical" and only possible in the long term, prior to which the problem of alleviating conditions in squatter areas would remain.

The problems of the second approach—titling squatters and allowing them to improve their homes (a very common response to squatter problems in the twenty first century, see Chapter 2)—were framed by Trench as practical: finance for improvements, provision of services such as water and electricity, and the risk that many squatters given title "would simply sell the house and land for a quick capital gain and squat somewhere else."[12] Practicality was a key concern for any administrative innovation; what made a proposal practical or impractical was often discussed in minute technical detail, but in other cases was presented as simply common sense or learned experience, such as the risk of profiteering from governmental programs.

The idea of giving the squatters "some kind of title to lots on this unwanted land" and allowing them to build New Territories "village type" houses in ways approved by the Building Authority (licensing rather than titling) was described as "following the NT pattern." This description highlights a key dualism in government land and development policy: treating the NT in a completely different manner than the urban areas. But *New Territories* is an ambiguous category in Hong Kong's colonial administration. The 99-year treaty signed in 1898 included what became called New Kowloon, lying between the ceded part of the Kowloon Peninsula and the Kowloon mountains chain. In administrative and popular speech, though, the New Territories is applied only to the parts of the leased area north of the Kowloon mountains chain, as well as the islands. New Kowloon was neither ceded colony nor treated as part of the leased NT. Until the 1970s, the areas beyond the Kowloon mountains were expected to stay mostly rural, while it was thought desirable that those parts adjacent to Old Kowloon should urbanize as quickly as possible. The indigenous residents were treated in very different ways, with New Kowloon villagers getting a much poorer deal (Smart 1992). The former villages of New Kowloon have been dissipated, unlike beyond the Kowloon mountains, where they are largely intact and their associations, such as the Heung Yee Kuk, politically influential. When development has displaced NT villages, they have often been resited as a group in ways that helped maintain intact communities (Hayes 2012). For New Kowloon, by contrast, displacement and rapid development was assumed to be necessary and desirable (Smart and Tang 2014).

The Governor's discussion of the titling and improvement option raised a variety of issues. The difficulty of squatters finding money to build in accordance with the Building Ordinance (which had rather demanding requirements) might "possibly be overcome through the Hong Kong Building and Loan Agency." This private company was born through a government initiative in 1964 to make affordable mortgage finance available to the middle class. The four biggest local banks and the Commonwealth Development Corporation were shareholders (Nthenda 2017). It went public in 1972 and had a current market capitalization of HK$178 million in 2020. Since titling did not take place, this point ended up moot. Of more lasting significance was the observation that "services (water, electricity, etc.) would have to be provided to some agreed extent," which ended up, along with slope stabilization, being the core objectives of the Squatter Area Improvement Programme (see Chapter 9).

The next comment was that "allocation would virtually have to be by grant; to which there are obvious objections."[13] The standard form of allocation of Crown land to private lessees is by auction; however, exceptions are made for purposes promoting the public good, such as subsidized housing provided by voluntary associations like the Housing Society. Finally, on this option, it was noted that "many would simply sell the house and land for a quick capital gain and squat somewhere else." Thus, titling and improvement might resolve the issues in particular squatter areas, but without effective overall control, would displace the squatter problem to other locations.

The Governor's suggestions and observations were first directed to the Housing Board. It had been established in 1965 after a recommendation in the 1964 White Paper on the *Review of Policies for Squatter Control, Resettlement and Government Low-Cost Housing* discussed in Chapter 5. The Housing Board was an advisory body that "reviewed and monitored housing and related policies, assessed present and future housing needs, and advised the government on the balancing and coordinating of various programmes," bringing the various agencies into the view of a single planning body for the first time (Cheung 2003, 210). However, the Housing Board "lacked the political base to formulate long-term policies" and had only a small administrative staff, so it lacked the resources to implement its recommendations (Yip 2003, 364). Along with the merging of the Resettlement Department and the old Housing Authority, the Housing Board became part of the new Housing Authority created as part

The Mangle of Policy Practice

117

of MacLehose's Ten-Year Housing Programme in 1973 (MacKay 2000, see Chapter 8).

The first Housing Board paper that resulted from these discussions in 1970 set the questions in the context of the broader housing program.[14] The Board recommended that "squatter areas where housing conditions are very bad indeed should be cleared." It came to preliminary identifications of such areas in Hong Kong Island and Kowloon, but left recommendations on the NT to their District Commissioner. They did suggest proposals "on similar lines to those already agreed for the urban areas." The 20 January 1971 and 1 February 1971 meetings of the Housing Board discussed another letter from the Colonial Secretariat, dated 15 December 1970, and drafted by D. Aker-Jones, Principal Assistant Colonial Secretary.[15] The letter asked the Board to consider and make recommendations on the "principle of making use of future government low-cost housing for resettlement purposes" by Waiting List based on eligibility by income (see Chapter 8). This possibility arose "as a result of the recommendation made by the Housing Board in its last report, which has been accepted by Government, that the same standard be employed in building Resettlement and Low-cost Housing." The letter also asked the Board to consider using some portion of newly constructed low-cost housing for resettlement accommodation to achieve "more flexible use of public housing resources in solving our various housing problems."[16] A merger of these two types of public housing did in fact take place in 1973 as part of the Ten-Year Housing Programme under Governor MacLehose, which will be discussed in Chapters 7 and 8. More immediately, however, the timing and other discussions suggests that the proposal was prompted by the pressure to respond to the problem of squatters on land not needed for development. These various issues were becoming mangled together in consequential ways.

The first meeting resulted in the Commissioner for Resettlement saying he would produce a general paper on the topic in "hope of obtaining agreement on the general approach to the problem." Some Board members asked for a detailed paper on the problems of clearing specific squatter areas. The Commissioner for Resettlement agreed to "produce as much detail as possible in his paper but that this would mean a delay in presenting the paper to the Board." While discussing the forecast of public housing available in the next six years, the Director of Public Works J. J. Robson noted it was the "lack of suitable sites and not any shortfall in building capacity which was preventing higher targets being set. Another aspect was the difficulty in finding sites in areas to which people were prepared to move." Development clearances ended up posing a major obstacle for the goals of the Ten-Year Housing Programme and the resistance to moving to the NT (see Chapter 7). Both the Commissioners for Housing and Resettlement had no "objections in principle." A second paper covering eligibility for accommodation and the long-term building requirements would be drafted with the departments concerned and the coordination of Akers-Jones.[17]

The Resettlement Department's paper, circulated on 8 February 1971, responded more fully to the Governor's proposals. It presented the first approach, resettlement of all squatters, as "not a completely satisfactory solution to the problem, at least in the short term. Even if this were regarded as the long-term solution to the problem (and whether this is practicable is itself open to question), there remains the question of what should be done to alleviate conditions in squatter areas during the very long period it would take to carry out such a policy."[18]

More consideration was given to the second approach, "to give the squatters some form of title and allow them to build 'village type houses.'" The Resettlement Department "sounded out the reactions of the squatters themselves to this proposal," and allegedly found them to be "unanimously opposed to the idea" of titling. Objections raised by the squatters included the belief that the scheme would reduce fire risk, but not the danger of landslides. The predominance of steep hillsides as the location of remaining squatter areas (particularly in urban areas) meant that reconfiguring them would require tricky site formation. This, in turn, would "mean heavy expenditure for the squatters and technical approval of site formation plans will be essential on safety grounds. The squatters see this as involving red tape at best and possibly corruption. Many existing huts are on stilts over other huts or on sites too small for village type houses."[19] It should be noted that these "reactions of the squatters themselves" are reported mixed in between points like "technical approval of site formation plans" unlikely to have been raised by squatters in that form at least, and so were probably fed to the squatters consulted, or simply added to the interpretation. Furthermore, the Report continued, since some squatter huts were "owned by up to half a dozen families" this would make redevelopment "very complicated and the existing squatters fear they would lose out to outside speculators." The squatters also worried that the scheme "would benefit only rich squatters and racketeers, who would exert pressure on them to sell out their huts." Others saw the plan as a "Government device to extract money from them, since they already have a high degree of security of tenure."[20]

The Resettlement Department "tentatively favours a 'third approach', less ambitious but, perhaps, more realistic than the first two." This would involve "enlarging both the volume and scope of our present scheme, introduced in 1968, by which minor improvements are introduced in squatter areas by means of a Local Public Works vote, similar to that of the New Territories." This "scheme was introduced on a modest scale as an experiment and at present its scope is severely limited by the rules . . . and by the size of the vote, which is now only $100,000 a year." In this pilot project, "improvements are

The Mangle of Policy Practice 119

only carried out where the squatters can perform the job themselves or can contribute towards payment for labour and supervision charges";[21] government contribution is limited to providing construction materials.

In 1970, and during the drafting of these key Housing Board reports, Paul Ka-cheung Tsui was the Commissioner for Resettlement. After serving in the British Army Aid Group (a paramilitary organization for British and Allied forces in southern China during the Second World War) he became the first local ethnic Chinese Cadet Officer of the Overseas Civil Service and an Administrative Officer of the Hong Kong government (Lo 1995). He remained the top local administrative officer throughout his career.

He wrote a memo on 15 February 1971 to the Secretary for Home Affairs, Ronald Holmes, who was the first Commissioner for Resettlement from 1953 to 1955. Paul Tsui wrote that he was "taken aback by the supposition in your memorandum . . . that our draft paper was intended as our last word on this subject, since this would imply that we had entirely disregarded His Excellency's suggestions. We are in fact working on them and, although we are not yet ready to give you our conclusions, we can give you the results of an informal survey of squatter opinion, which we did as a first step."[22] This is perhaps the clearest acknowledgement of the ironic situation that within a couple of months, the two alternatives suggested by Governor Trench had become largely if not completely (or permanently) sidelined. In addition, Tsui clarified that the draft under consideration, from 20 January 1971, "was not in fact intended to be our response to last year's intervention but had the much more limited objective of explaining in more detail the specific problems arising from the clearance of those particular areas which the Board had already recommended for clearance." Rather, "[o]ur reaction to the intervention from London is the subject of a separate paper."[23] It should be noted that this phrasing clearly presents the genesis of the various documents as being intervention from London. The second paper, which would appear to be Housing Board Paper No. 49 for discussion by the Board on 1 March 1971, turned out to be more difficult to draft than expected. Tsui hoped that when Holmes saw the second report, it would be clear that "our views are not quite so inflexible as you fear." He agreed with Holmes' position that development plans should be changed to "clear nastier squatter areas earlier." However, the difficulty was that there was no convenient accommodation available for the Aldrich Bay (Hong Kong Island) clearance until 1973 unless they either "force the squatters to go to Kowloon, which seems hard to justify when the land is not needed and we know that convenient accommodation will be ready in about two years' time"; postpone the Tin Hau Temple Road clearance which the "Public Works Department need urgently"; or use space "required for the relief of overcrowding. This could mean a showdown with the Urban Council." Thus, while signaling support of the suggestion of non-development squatter resettlement, impracticalities were positioned to make actually doing so difficult, and likely to produce opposition from various parties and agencies.[24]

Housing Board Paper No. 49 was titled "Clearance of Squalid Squatter Areas." It followed up on decisions made on 24 August 1970, after Royle's letter but before the Governor's reply, to clear four squatter areas because they were "squalid," rather than because the land was needed for development. This indicates that some modest actions were being quietly explored after Prime Minister Heath's intervention, and possibly before it. The minutes of the Housing Board meeting held on 24 August 1970 has an agenda item on "analysis of squatter areas," which addressed Housing Board Papers No. 36 and 39 on the topic of environmental conditions. The squatter areas were ranked by environmental standards, an assessment that was "subjective and reflects mainly sanitary conditions in each area." They were also ranked on the number of water standpipes and latrines, whether they had electricity supply, and whether they were willing to accept resettlement.[25]

The minutes state that "[i]t was suggested that a start should be made with the worst squatter areas and that Government should build public housing specifically to clear squatters living on Crown land in these areas. Certain squatter areas are so repugnant to the public conscience that they ought to be cleared." It was agreed that the Board should recommend in its 1970 report that the government should compulsorily rehouse squatters on Crown land in bad housing and poor environmental conditions.[26] In this proposal, they made allowance in their rehousing planning for a total of 30,000 people to be resettled. The statement that these areas are "so repugnant to the public conscience" is intriguing: is this indicating the concerns from London, or local concerns that had emerged independently?

Three of the "squalid squatter areas" identified in this discussion were on Hong Kong Island, and one in Kowloon. Aldrich Bay was described as having acute congestion, with structures on stilts above stagnant water. Despite the poor conditions, only 50% of residents were willing to accept resettlement in Chai Wan, also on Hong Kong Island, and were strongly opposed to resettlement in Kowloon. The clearance did have development plans, as part of a larger harbor reclamation. Residents of Ngar Choi Hang on Hong Kong Island also objected strongly to Kowloon resettlement, despite the regularity of flooding they experienced. Many said that their livelihood depends on pig-breeding and "will strongly resist clearance . . . Unless some worthwhile use can be found for the site the Resettlement Department would be strongly opposed to clearing these people" because of hardships imposed on the squatters, the depletion of scarce housing supply for "persons who do both need and want it" and that "it would expose the Government to well-founded criticism if, as seems likely, their resistance to clearance attracts public attention." The one prospect in Kowloon had 3,000 out of 13,000 people living in poor

The Mangle of Policy Practice

environmental conditions. Most were engaged in pig-breeding, rattan ware production, cake baking, and market gardening. If resettled, they would have to give up their occupations, so for "this reason they are strongly opposed to being cleared. Compulsory resettlement of these people would cause great hardship." The general point made was that the Resettlement Department's view was that:

> when squatters are moved against their will for prestige reasons we should always be ready to say that the clearance is taking place to reduce fire and health risks and that the purpose may be to sell the land so that modern buildings can be built upon it . . . or details given of some other useful purpose . . . clearing sites and leaving them unused could be expected to have a serious effect on the morale of our clearance staff, who would find themselves in an impossible position trying to explain to the squatters why they were being cleared. The comparative smoothness and success of our present clearance operations is based mainly on the fact that the staff take great care to explain to the squatters why they have to move . . . The position would be very different if the only reason they were being moved was supposedly for 'their own good.'[27]

This report sheds useful light on the distinctive ways in which the advantages and (mostly) disadvantages of non-development clearances are presented. Concern for the desires and livelihoods of squatters are emphasized. This was not usually the case for conventional development clearances.

The comment about "prestige" points to the prestige of the British government more than that of the Hong Kong administration. It also seems to be a dismissive term, suggesting that a desire for prestige or image is frivolous compared to the real needs and demands of the population and the challenges faced by the government. Displacing people for image reasons only, with no intended use for the land, is presented as carrying risk of public criticism, which needs to be covered over with references to protecting public safety from fires and health risks. While there were probably genuine concerns that non-development clearances would increase difficulties for their staff, it seems likely that the problems are being heavily stressed from reluctance to embark on new approaches prompted by London's interventions. The concern for the psychological impact on squatter clearance officers' echoes worries that their morale was badly affected by the reaction of squatters to their destruction of their homes and often livelihoods.[28]

The District Commissioner NT, Denis Bray, responded to concerns about titling and improvement, stating that "[i]t is most unlikely that all squatters everywhere will be utterly opposed to being allowed to make some improvements to the quality of the buildings in which they live. In the redevelopment of huts under our jurisdiction, I conceive the granting of permanent tenure of land would act as an incentive to improvement, no matter from what sources the investments may come." For the New Territories, "many occupants of tolerated squatter huts would in fact be glad to be allowed to make improvements to their own buildings either by repair or by reconstruction and that in many cases we could authorise some increase in the space occupied or adjustment of boundaries." What was required, he thought, "is a procedure under which a tolerated squatter would be offered proper land tenure provided he reconstructed his building in accordance with some minimal standards." Bray noted that squatter dwellings on private land (usually agricultural leased land not authorized for building purposes) would need:

> special attention where existing procedures have not always led to regularisation of the buildings. If landowners withhold consent to regularize by issue of an M.O.T. [Modification of Tenancy] permit,[29] or other means, a threat of re-entry might stir things. Each building or application will have to be examined on its own merit and the initiative in this matter would be left to the squatters. There would thus be no question of enforcement of some unpopular measure – rather it would be a matter of granting approval for something that squatters want to do.

Bray argued that the type of tenure for the improved buildings should be "as generous as is required to stimulate rebuilding. Whether the annual permit is appropriate or offers sufficient incentive is a matter we should think about. I would not be averse to considering a 5-year lease renewable annually thereafter. If anything better than an annual permit is required then existing permittees should also be considered. It is the offer of more permanent title to the land that will attract private capital for investment" (offering well in advance an argument similar to de Soto's). To induce investment, it would only need "modifications of restrictions on the maximum quality of building" and "better land tenure."

Some squatters would be bought out by others, but they "should not however be allowed to squat elsewhere" and squatter control might have to be intensified. An early appreciation of the risk of what became known as gentrification is apparent here (Smart 2020). Bray noted that the effect on housing will be that the quality of "building on land now occupied by tolerated squatters will improve so that the poorest people who occupy some of these huts will move to property which will, in relative terms, become less attractive. We must however make sure that they are not allowed to sell out their rights and re-erect new squatter huts which will then be tolerated."[30] His memo is an incisive analysis of the risks of displacement and gentrification due to formalization, and the problem of resquatting if improvement creates housing ill suited to the balance of priorities for the poorest (Turner 1976). Bray also recommended classifying squatter areas into three types: (1) "areas due for clearance for permanent development – but only those required pretty soon for the rest are to get something new"; (2) "squatter areas not required for development but to be cleared to improve the quality of housing – i.e. squalid squatters"; (3) "the rest – i.e. areas where no immediate permanent development is contemplated and where the nature of the squatter huts is such that complete clearance would not be justified." He then turned to the inevitable administrative consideration: how much of an increase in staffing and funding would be needed, keeping in mind "the ramifications likely to be caused by speculation."

Bray also pointed out that "the directive of the Governor was not a directive confined to urban areas though the paper produced by the Commissioner for Resettlement appears to be." He encouraged NT District Officers to consider the problem and suggest responses.[31] There is a rich body of discussion focused on the NT situation, but this is mostly peripheral to the main narrative here, and will have to be relegated to a future publication.

The third alternative approach, technical improvement without tenure change, highlighted the importance of the Department of Public Works for such initiatives. The Director of Public Works responded to the Housing Board paper with suggestions and concerns. The first point was to stress the need for flexibility in the context of the diversity of individual areas. He began by saying that "I would have thought that it was unwise to adopt a hard and fast policy on the question raised in the paper since it seems to me that none of the three proposals provides a solution in itself." What he suggested as "necessary in practice is an approach addressed individually to the particular area in question. In some cases the condition is so bad as to call for clearance with no question of any attempt to improve" and should be seen as in need of a normal clearance for redevelopment. Other areas have conditions that "lend purpose to improvement although the extent of such improvement may well have to be more limited than that suggested in the C. for R.'s [Commissioner for Resettlement] third approach. There is little hope of making squatter structures technically acceptable and any attempt to do this would result in public money being mis-spent." Efforts should be concentrated on the "amenities of the squatter areas, coupled with re-housing."[32] The Director suggested that the key amenities to be provided should be: water for drinking and firefighting; precautions against fire and fire lanes (see Smart 2006 for a genealogy of interventions for fire safety back to the early 1950s); precautions against erosion; provision of latrines; and provision of area lighting. He argued for selecting a test case for improvement in order to test the effectiveness of this approach and suggested the area above Shaukiwan in eastern Hong Kong Island. The area's buildings were largely built of stone—that is, were of less temporary construction—and the steep terrain made it unlikely to be included in a redevelopment scheme for some years at least.[33]

One of the most interesting responses to the draft Housing Board paper came from the Secretary of Home Affairs, Donald Luddington. This post had only been renamed from the Secretary of Chinese Affairs in 1969 (created in 1913). His Memo to the Commissioner for Resettlement on 4 June 1971 began by agreeing that the paper's concerns about the difficulties of the first and second approaches were "for the most part valid" and agreed that their "third approach offers an effective practical solution which whilst not going as far as some would wish, nevertheless has the merit of being capable of execution." Again, the central value of practicality for the administration is clear here. The memo also acknowledges that the third approach is conservative and does not meet the aspirations of some within the bureaucracy, including the Governor. Luddington raised an alternative previously not discussed, asking whether consideration had been given to "the possible conversion of suitable squatter areas to cottage resettlement areas." He noted that a "detailed cost analysis" might find that "cottage resettlement is as expensive as multi-storey resettlement" particularly since the cost of site formation might make multi-storey projects "economically unattractive." Cottage areas were one of the initiatives used prior to the adoption of multistory resettlement in 1954. They suffered from being substantially less dense than either Resettlement Estates or squatter areas. No further mention of this possibility emerged from the files.

More importantly, he noted that "squatter areas use land which would otherwise be wasted and which house large numbers of people at minimal public expense. It has been claimed that squatter areas serve an extremely important function in that they provide an essential stabilising transitional period between rural life and urban life, which helps the rural dweller to adjust to the more regimented life of the city. To simply clear squatter areas which are themselves not to be used for development seems to me then to be inadvisable." Leaving aside the questionable assumption that most squatters came from rural contexts, his comments articulate one of the key rationales for the toleration of squatter areas: they serve essential services that neither government nor the (legal) private sector were capable of accomplishing for many during the first four postwar decades. He went on to say that while:

> squatting can be regarded as only one step above street sleeping, it is nevertheless an extremely flexible method of public housing in that space in squatter structures can be easily sold, rented, disposed of and converted to other use with the minimum of red tape and expense. Moreover, it would seem impossible for us to rehouse the estimated 345,000 squatters and licensed areas' occupants in the urban area . . . in the foreseeable future." Squatting, he concluded, "is going to be with us whether we like it or not, and it is surely right that we should do what we can to improve the basic amenities of the squatter areas to make the life of the squatter dweller more bearable. Economically he is an important member of Hong Kong society and he deserves a little more attention than he has received. The proposal which you have outlined in your 3rd approach are then a necessary first step.[34]

The Mangle of Policy Practice

Consideration of squatters' welfare is carefully couched within the practical advantages for Hong Kong more generally, rather than being based on social justice concerns, but it is important to acknowledge that the contributions of squatters are occasionally recognized in these administrative circles.

Luddington concluded by saying that "although it is necessary to examine the squatter issue in a realistic way, it is important also that political considerations" should not be overlooked. A "timely application of L.P.W. [the Local Public Works pilot scheme, mentioned in the Housing Board report] funds can gain considerable political mileage for Government and in this respect I feel it would be important for C.D.O.s [City District Officers] to be involved and kept informed." While "political considerations" here are somewhat vague in terms of whether it involves the politics of dealing with London and the FCO or with the local population, both the remit of the Secretary's post and the reference to City District Officers suggests that it was the latter which was being considered.[35]

The 1971 Housing Board Annual Report appears to mark the conclusion of the open-ended discussion of alternatives for dealing with non-development squatter areas. It modified the initial plan for rehousing 30,000 squatters through non-development clearances in the 1970 Report. It recommended a two-part "statement of aims." First, identification and clearance of squatter areas "where living conditions were bad" (repeatedly described in the files as "squalid"). Second, "consideration of the future of other squatter areas where conditions are not so bad." Later, Housing Board Paper No. 75 on "Improvement of squatter areas," drafted on 1 April 1973, stated that the adoption of the Ten-Year Housing Target overtook these recommendations, "with its provision for a complete solution to the squatter problem," leaving the Housing Board "only to consider if, in light of the newly recommended 'list of categories,' any further consideration need be given for recommendations made regarding the occupants of the so called 'squalid squatter areas.'"

The challenge faced was that under the Ten-Year Housing Programme, rehousing commitments for all categories in the six years from 1973 totaled 528,000, which "approximates to the building programme over the same period. Any major resettlement of squatters on Crown land not needed for development can therefore only be done at the expense of clearances of those included in the present categories. It is in this context that the Housing Board is now examining the question of housing priorities to see whether any higher priority can be given" to non-development squatters. This is a very weak and noncommittal form of Governor Trench's alternative of resettling all squatters. The focus was instead on "whether there can be any in situ improvement in the squatter areas themselves"—the third approach. In addition, it was necessary to "see whether it is possible to accelerate the housing programme by finding more suitable sites." This last option was not incompatible with any

126   *Hong Kong Public and Squatter Housing*

of the three alternatives. In practice, housing production acceleration faced a variety of challenges, including the exhaustion of sites in the urban areas, which would mean that:

> squatters will have to be prepared to move out of the metropolitan area if they are to be rehoused. Squatter areas are quite conveniently placed in relation to work in the urban area and there is no doubt that many squatters would prefer to stay where they are rather than move to outlying districts and in these circumstances they are likely to oppose enforced clearance. Siting of new estates will therefore add to the difficulty of clearances for development purposes and reduce the possibility of clearing for other reasons.[36]

Conclusions

In contrast to the squatter problem in the 1950s, the archives reveal that "intervention" from London and the FCO served to put the squatter problem onto the policy agenda in 1970. Policy discussions quickly coalesced around the issue of squatters on Crown land not needed for development, since London appeared to accept that Hong Kong had indeed been doing a great deal on the housing front, and that the squatter resettlement program was moving along approximately as quickly as possible. What remained was the problem of the "squalid" and "nastier" squatter areas, particularly those on steep hillsides for which conventional development would be difficult and which presented embarrassing images for visitors, journalists, MPs and members of the House of Lords. Since "something" had to be done, a short, open-ended period of considering relatively radical solutions was initiated by Governor Trench's two suggested approaches. Practicalities sidelined both, with a third approach emerging from the discussions: the technical approach of improvement without titling or entitling.

Returning to Andrew Pickering's metaphor of the mangle, we can see that Hong Kong's dirty laundry of the squatter problem had become increasingly difficult to keep out of sight. Intervention from London made it necessary to feed the particularly messy bundle of "squalid" and undevelopable squatter areas into the policy mangle. What came out of the deliberations cannot be seen as scripted or dictated by London, since multiple threads of constraints, contingencies and interests combined and tangled to determine what came out the other side. The first explanation—geopolitics—lacks hard evidence to support its plausibility. The second explanation—intervention from London—prompted action but had little influence on what kind of action was undertaken. The third alternative explanation for the end of new squatting focuses on policy mangles—first the Housing Board and then the discussions prompted by the Colonial Secretary's letter. Interventions from London certainly acted as a catalyst, but possible solutions proceeded through a series

The Mangle of Policy Practice

of policy discussions or mangles before sufficient consensus could emerge. A policy mangle explanation seems to accord with the empirical situation, and appears to have theoretical advantages, pointing to mechanisms by which the policies and practices we are concerned with could result. Where it is weak, though, is that it could apply to almost any specific causal explanation, as long as it is coherent and not contradicted by good evidence. The advantage of this approach is that if another alternative explanation is more specific, and accounts more directly for more features (or more crucial features) of the path taken, the mangle approach still offers a theoretical language of analysis within which this better account might be framed. As well it reminds us of the contingent nature of historical unfolding of policy.

In the next chapter we turn to another, more concrete and specific plausible explanation; that the changes result from imbalances in the supply and demand of two forms of public housing: permanent and temporary. These imbalances threatened the success of the housing reforms launched by Governor MacLehose. The supply and demand explanation focuses, first, on the challenges and failures faced by the Ten-Year Housing Programme. Second, how it affected the management of squatter areas, crucial as one of the main sources of land for development. Obstacles to squatter clearance and resettlement threatened this crucial reform project. Imbalances between public housing supply (both permanent and temporary) and demand provides the next part of the explanation for how the grinding of the colonial governmental works finally churned out a Squatter Occupancy Survey in 1984, as part of the solution for the long-standing squatter problem.

7

Supply, Demand, and Failures

I reconstructed the series of events, as a historian would do, from what happened in the process that led to the elaboration of the regulation whose effects I could see with the property sellers. I related the ensemble of pertinent events and only those, that is, the ones that need to be known in order to understand. In other words, it is not a formal account of proceedings, but an account of the events capable of explaining.

—Pierre Bourdieu, *On the State: Lectures at the Collège de France, 1989–1992* (2014, 18)

Introduction

This chapter will argue that public housing and squatter control policies adopted in the 1970s created serious imbalances in supply and demand for the two types of public housing: permanent and temporary. Attempts to fix the situation created new problems, resulting first in shortages of temporary housing and later in concerns about the fairness of allocation. Addressing these concerns, combined with the failure of squatter improvement (see Chapter 9), led to the end of new squatting. This was made possible by limiting the housing commitment entailed by the decision to resettle all squatters through a novel regulatory practice, the Squatter Occupancy Survey (SOS), finally adopted against previous precedent in 1984.

In the last chapter, we developed a mangle explanation of governmental decision-making, which is consistent with what we know about colonial Hong Kong governance, but is also compatible with a wide variety of potential explanations. To unravel the puzzle of ending new squatting in 1984, we need more specific diagnoses of how these outcomes came to be; how one path, resettlement for all (except for those specifically excluded for one administrative reason or another, particularly not being registered as a squatter structure occupant in 1984–1985), prevailed after it appeared to have been decisively rejected multiple times.

Supply, Demand, and Failures   129

In this chapter, we draw out a fourth rival explanation, based on supply and demand imbalances. It offers important insights into the empirical situation. Officials were keenly concerned about housing problems resulting from both market and regulatory failures. Imbalances emerged and required new governmental responses. The exclusion of many cleared squatters from permanent public housing created shortages of temporary housing. These shortages in turn constrained the rapid implementation of development clearances. Prompt squatter clearances were needed for the housing of an additional 1.8 million people. Fixing the imbalances ironically prompted more inclusiveness—one of the key topics addressed in this chapter—but this fix in turn created new political problems demanding exclusion, addressed in Chapter 8.

Ten-Year Housing Programme

The SOS was proposed in a memo for the Executive Council (ExCo) on the "Review of Public Housing Allocation Policies," which was discussed and approved on 4 September 1984.[1] This review arose from discussions around a report on "housing objectives" considered by ExCo on 22 October 1980. Its purpose was to review the Ten-Year Housing Targets adopted on 17 October 1972. These targets were one half of the Ten-Year Housing Programme, the other half being the merger of the Resettlement Department and the other public housing agencies, which significantly improved the quality of public housing management (Yip 2003).

The merger had been recommended by Governor Trench near the end of his term. Already in 1970, the Secretary for Home Affairs had pointed out the problems and inequity resulting from separating resettlement from low-cost housing, as well as other organizational problems.[2] At a meeting on these issues on 6 October 1971, near the end of his term, Governor Trench "took charge of this meeting from the start. He had obviously worked hard on the papers." He suggested the need for a better organized replacement for the Housing Board, which became the Housing Branch, and "that the Resettlement Department should gradually work itself out. No more Resettlement Estates as such should be built. Instead, new L.C.H. [Low-Cost Housing] and mixed estates" should be managed by a new authority with colony-wide responsibilities to take the place of the existing Housing Authority. This should be "much smaller and consist of officials, some unofficials elected by the U.C. [Urban Council], N.T. representatives and unofficial specialists. It should be chaired by the head of the department serving it." His rationales for these designs included that "the authority be more or less financially autonomous and able to use its basic funding and the estates rents for more building" and "that a general aim should be to reduce the absolute state of privilege enjoyed by those in Government and Government-aided housing."[3] The merger of Resettlement and Low-Cost Housing, the establishment of the new Housing Authority as policymaker, and the creation of an executive Housing Department thus were all presaged in this late-term meeting by Trench. It also set the scene for a conflict around eligibility distinctions between recent immigrants and established residents, considered in Chapter 8.

The merger ideas found fertile ground in a period when the FCO was promoting the reorganization of the Hong Kong government through modernized decision-making grouping functions to reduce the heavy load on the Financial and Colonial Secretaries and Secretariat. They were implemented by the new Governor (Ho 2011). When MacLehose began his governorship on 19 November 1971, he worked particularly to restore confidence in the colonial government by the people of Hong Kong (Yep and Lui 2010). In his first diplomatic report to London, he proposed that "the British should try to put Hong Kong's 'own house in order' by making it 'as prosperous and cohesive and contented and as free from legitimate points of criticism as possible' before 1980, the time MacLehose thought negotiations with China would occur" (quoted in Ho 2011, 194). Developing concerns about "the future of Hong Kong greatly accelerated the colony's social and housing development. As the time available was limited merely to a decade, what had to be done was enormous" (Ho 2011, 195). MacLehose's "specific idea" was to ensure the loyalty of the people of Hong Kong and strengthen people's identification with the government by "maintaining Hong Kong's living standards that lead China significantly" and by "cultivating responsible citizenship." As a result, social reforms to encourage loyalty were one of the primary focuses during MacLehose's governorship (Yu 2020, 487; see Chapter 8). A variety of social reforms were taken up, but the greatest spending was in the housing area,[4] the cornerstone of his reform agenda (Castells et al. 1990), and which he saw as the greatest source of unhappiness in Hong Kong (Akers-Jones 2004). It could be said that "prior to 1973 Hong Kong had a vigorous and purposeful public housing programme, but it did not have a housing policy" (Yeung 2003, 22). There was a new emphasis on higher quality housing, a subsidized home ownership system was established, and two New Towns were begun, allowing some decentralization of the overcrowded inner urban areas.

The key aims of the 1972 Housing Targets were "(a) to eliminate all squatter and licensed areas; (b) to allow for the redevelopment of cottage areas; (c) to provide a self-contained dwelling for all those households sharing accommodation in private tenements; (d) to relieve overcrowding in existing Government housing, including redevelopment and renovation of estates where some such form of renewal was essential; and (e) to provide housing for those people who had to be rehoused in consequence of other Government schemes and policies."[5] The prominence of squatters and former squatters in this agenda is obvious. If we accept government on its word in this case,

Supply, Demand, and Failures

the end of new squatting, and the beginning of its continual decline, after 1983, at the end of the Ten-Year Housing Programme, is simply a matter of policy implementation success. The first priority was not accomplished, but the conditions for getting the job done were formed by the end of the project's decade. Eradication, mostly through resettlement, was the path finally adopted, with no remaining trace of tenure change and only vestiges of improvement focused on infrastructure.

Despite its accomplishments, particularly on the organizational side (MacKay 2000), progress toward the Ten-Year Housing Targets was considerably slower than proposed, both in the provision of public housing and particularly in the elimination of squatter and licensed areas. The target was to house 1.8 million people over 10 years in permanent self-contained homes with good amenities and 3.3 m^2 of space per person. This would have required 400,000 public housing units to be built within the 10 years from 1973 to 1982. Only 220,577 units were completed (Yeh 1990). This shortfall resulted from "bureaucratic restructuring problems and the constraints of finance, manpower, and land resources in the early implementation stages of the programme." World recession and "the new wave of legal and illegal migrants from China made it difficult to achieve the programme target" (Yeh 1990, 442).

Already by February 1977, Governor MacLehose had become disturbed at slippages in completions. It was only in 1979–1980 that the level of housing production reached the average rate needed to meet the 1972 target.[6] Projections of housing need and supply showed a shortfall of 429,500 self-contained flats in 1979–1980 and 296,000 in 1984–1985. The Governor asked if the Housing Department (HD) could forecast what sites would be cleared, and when. In principle, he commented, "large groups of people should not be cleared until alternative public housing of some sort could be offered to them; i.e. clearance must be 'housing-led.'"[7] A severe shortage of building sites in the old urban areas of Hong Kong and Kowloon meant that the ambitious program had to rely on the development of New Towns in the NT, but their development "was much slower than envisaged."[8] Andrew Yu (2020, 498) argues that "it is understandable that MacLehose failed to build enough houses on schedule" due to the oil crisis, and the need to "balance the interests of private developers and public housing construction," plus the continued growth of illegal immigration which "lead to the growth of illegal squatters, which increased the pressure on the Government to solve the housing problems."

The 22 October 1980 Memo to ExCo on the review of housing objectives tried to be optimistic, noting that about 580,000 people had been given public housing by 1980, including 118,000 cleared squatters. An additional 57,000 squatters were moved into Temporary Housing Areas (THA; see Figure 7.1). Clearance had "released nearly 1,750 ha. of land for development, 370 ha. of which have been for public housing projects and 320 ha. for private development." Squatter clearance had been complicated because the "1964-surveyed huts are becoming increasingly difficult to identify on the ground and, indeed, after natural disasters, their identification is virtually impossible. Furthermore, the families occupying squatter huts were not registered at the time of the survey." A new survey was conducted in 1976, "when all huts, (but again not the occupants) were recorded. Because of the housing shortage only the occupants of the 1964 huts remained eligible for permanent housing, whilst families occupying those built after 1964 but surveyed in 1976 were eligible only for THA accommodation . . . The continued applications of the policy whereby only the occupants of 1964 huts qualify for direct public housing has thus meant a steady increase in the numbers eligible only for THA accommodation."[9] This is one of the earliest mentions of the difficulties created by surveying only squatter structures and not their occupants, but it does not get followed up at this time by a decision to do both, or even much discussion. What was more important at this time was the policy failure whereby limiting the permanent rehousing commitment for cleared squatters had generated unmet needs for temporary housing, which lead in turn to a bottleneck for development clearances. This new imbalance between permanent public housing and temporary housing shifted the course of discussions in novel directions that turn out to have been key to the success of formalization in the 1980s.

Figure 7.1: Temporary Housing Area, Kwun Tong, 1983. Copyright and provided by Alan Smart.

Supply, Demand, and Failures   133

Temporary Housing as an Obstacle to Permanent Public Housing Development

Regulations that made those in squatter dwellings built after 1964 eligible only for THAs resulted in a shortage of temporary housing, an unusual reversal of the general situation where it was permanent public housing that was in shortest supply (Smart and Chui 2006). The shortage of temporary housing was an obstacle to development clearances, including in the New Towns where the majority of new public housing estates were to be built. To alleviate the shortage of THAs, the Housing Authority:

> introduced a primary housing scheme, whereby families in the earlier Mark I/II estates are encouraged to transfer on a voluntary basis to modern, self-contained flats, so that the resultant vacancies can be utilised for displaced squatter families who are eligible only for THA space ... It is therefore necessary to review the criteria under which squatter and other displaced families are rehoused in order to restrain the demand for land for THAs and place more of these families directly into public housing but at the same time having regard to the pressures on public housing from all other categories.[10]

The tensions are clearly apparent here.

A key problem for the housing development plans was the "commitment to produce more and more land for low-rise THA accommodation" since so many squatters faced with clearance did not qualify for permanent public housing. As a result, the Housing Authority (HA) recommended in 1980 that the new criteria for resettlement to Permanent Public Housing (PPH) should be based on occupation of a 1976, rather than 1964, surveyed squatter hut and 15 years residence for the majority of adult family members, not including children born in Hong Kong.[11] The authors stated that the prior requirement of occupation of a 1964 surveyed hut "implies a minimum period of residence of sixteen years in 1980, and growing longer as each year passes. The introduction of the new fifteen-year rule, related to the occupation of a 1976 surveyed structure, will therefore have the effect of gradually increasing the numbers of squatter families eligible for direct public housing." The commitment to produce more land for "low-rise THA accommodation can be reduced but only at the expense of those families who might otherwise qualify for public rental housing through the Authority's quotas" via the income-based Waiting List. Besides highlighting the conflict between allocation through squatter clearance and the Waiting List, this statement represents a clear misunderstanding of squatter areas and the squatter property market operating in them, where many more recent migrants bought squatter dwellings. It is possible that a dwelling surveyed in 1964 might only shelter a household that had been resident continually since then, but it just as likely might have been sold to recent migrants in the interim, perhaps multiple times, or even subdivided into two or more units. Without a survey of the occupants, it would be impossible to make reasonable projections and estimates of how the new rules would change the relative demand on squatter clearance for permanent and temporary housing.

A Memo, dated 27 August 1981, for the Housing Authority's Operations Committee reveals important factors behind the adoption of these eligibility changes, as well as problems with their implementation. It states that the intention was to "accord priority for permanent housing to long-term Hong Kong residents, and it was estimated that the effect would be to increase the demand for permanent public housing from the emergency and compulsory categories by about 35%." If the assumptions had been accurate, demand for temporary housing would have dropped, and the "proportion of persons from the emergency and compulsory categories rehoused in permanent housing and temporary housing respectively should have changed from about 50:50 to about 70:30. However, this has not happened. Rather, because of the increase in the number of post-1976 squatter structures, there has been an increase in the proportion of families eligible only for temporary housing, both from the development clearance category alone, and from the emergency and compulsory categories as a whole."[12] There had been a large growth of immigration from China during this period, but squatter control changes adopted in 1976 seem to have been an even larger factor in the expansion of post-1976 squatting, thereby increasing demand for public housing. In addition, some squatters got into public housing through the Waiting List, and then sold their dwelling to others, often recent migrants.

It was concluded that despite the changes in the eligibility criteria, "there is a clear trend to a greater proportion of families in the emergency and compulsory categories becoming eligible for temporary housing, and a smaller proportion eligible for permanent housing. This is because the increase in the number of persons from surveyed structures eligible for permanent housing is more than offset by a substantial increase in the number of persons from unsurveyed structures eligible only for temporary housing." In 1979–1980, the proportion of those rehoused under emergency (fire, etc.) or compulsory (clearance, urban renewal) categories eligible only for temporary housing (TH) was 47%; for those in development clearances, it was 26%. By the first half of 1981, the proportions had increased to 53% and 40%, respectively. Given the continued use of existing criteria for permanent rehousing the proportion eligible only for TH would "continue to increase. If the supply of temporary and primary housing is insufficient, planned development clearances will have to be curtailed. Development clearances are the only component of the total demand for temporary housing which it is possible for the Government effectively to regulate and limit."[13] This point is crucial, since it highlights the importance of development clearances as a lever influencing

Supply, Demand, and Failures

imbalances; any additional delays would put the Ten-Year Plan even further behind.

More generally, there was a persistent priority placed on the development of land in government priorities, both before and after 1997 (Smart and Lee 2003). Previously, only a third of the land made available for development by squatter clearances was used for public housing (Drakakis-Smith 1979). This contributed to making resettlement at high density and minimal amenities affordable (Smart 2006). The predominance of making land available for development encouraged limiting the government's commitments for the provision of permanent public housing. It could do so primarily by making fewer of the squatter population eligible for PPH. This logic lay behind the initial decision to make those living in structures surveyed in 1976 ineligible for PPH. The supply and demand situation had changed by 1980, partly due to increased migration from China. The shortage of THAs consequently became a larger constraint on clearances, the crucial first step for building public housing. THAs had the problematic characteristic of being low-density, and thus occupied land that could otherwise be used more efficiently for multi-story housing. Ironically, regulatory changes had recreated the logjam presented in the early 1950s through the use of lower-density cottage areas and Licensed Areas to resettle those affected by the clearance of higher-density squatter areas (Smart 2006).

Attempts to Resolve the THA Shortage

One effort to resolve the THA shortage involved speeding up the production of THAs in the NT,[14] and another the 1980 change in eligibility to include those living in 1976-surveyed structures. These were still insufficient to solve the problem. Estimates of demand for TH and primary housing for 1981–1982 were 18,000 people, while supply "should be just adequate to meet demand. However, there is virtually no contingency reserve at all to cater for unforeseen commitments, for example a major squatter fire. Any such unexpected demand could be accommodated only at the expense of planned development clearances."[15] The following year was thought to be adequately accounted for, but "it will be touch and go again in 1983/1984. However, in practice, the situation is likely to be much more critical, as a result of possible slippage in development of future temporary housing area sites, reduced production of primary housing; and an increase in overall demand from the emergency and compulsory categories, mainly from clearance and squatter area fires. A considered judgement is that demand will exceed supply over the two-year period as a whole, and this will be a constraint on the development programme." This 1981 Operations Committee Memo concluded that there were only two possible solutions: "stepping up production of temporary housing, either by developing more land, or by increasing densities on the sites available for development" or "revising the criteria for admission into permanent housing so as to make a greater proportion of those rehoused through the emergency and compulsory categories eligible for permanent housing."

For the TH option, "there is clearly a limit to the amount of land which can be made available for this relatively low-density housing, and it is considered that the solution must lie in increased densities on future sites." New designs were being developed that would increase average density from 1,500 persons per hectare to 1,600 for a two-story model, with a projected three-story design that might manage average density of about 2,400 persons per hectare. Eventually, however, the need for high density temporary housing reached fruition in the high-rise interim housing completed in Tuen Mun and Tin Shui Wai in 2001 and 2003. These consist of about 17,800 flats accommodating about 52,000 people, with 17 blocks, each having 28 residential floors and 36 flats per floor. Each flat is self-contained with individual toilets and kitchens, with space per person of 5.5 m². The population in TH increased to 131,812[16] in 1982 before dropping slightly to 126,973 in 1984, then dropped sharply to 16,100 by 1998.

In response to the TH supply shortage, it was argued that:

> the eligibility criteria should be changed in order to reduce the demand for temporary housing. One possibility would be to change the eligibility baseline from the 1976 survey to the 1981 stocktaking survey. This, however, could greatly swell demand for permanent housing, would probably lead to an increase in new squatting, and would be seen as allowing recent squatters, who are overwhelmingly recent immigrants, to jump the queue for public housing. It is considered that the 1976 survey baseline should for the present be maintained.[17]

The imbalance could easily shift from excessive demand for TH to excessive demand for PPH, and managing the relative undersupplies had political dimensions and consequences.

A series of natural disasters magnified the supply and demand problems to crisis levels. In a minute to Governor MacLehose on 9 December 1981, the Colonial Secretary reported that "[t]he unprecedented number of fire victims [in squatter areas] this year . . . has given rise to a critical situation, viz: there is no [sic] sufficient temporary housing available to meet the existing commitment."[18] In the five years before 1981, fire victims in squatter areas averaged about 4,200 per year so that their rehousing "presented no major problem in the context of the overall housing programme. Approximately 30% would qualify for direct permanent public housing, which represented only a very small proportion of new flat lettings. The remainder, approximately 3,000 per year, were rehoused in temporary housing areas. This was manageable, given an overall demand for temporary housing of about 22,000 per year,

Supply, Demand, and Failures

and production of about 18,000 new person spaces per year in temporary housing—the balance being made up by turnover of temporary housing areas." In 1981, up to the end of November "almost 20,000 persons" were rendered homeless by squatter fires. Slightly over half "have to date been rehoused, because of a critical shortage of temporary housing accommodation. Because most recent squatter fires have occurred in Central and East Kowloon where most recent squatting, overwhelmingly by new immigrants, has occurred, at least 80% of fire victims on average qualify only for temporary housing." This produced serious problems: insufficient temporary housing, with 9,000 awaiting rehousing, with further fires expected in the dry season. Delays in their rehousing "has created a major demand for interim emergency accommodation in temporary shelters. Over 6,000 persons rendered homeless by the Tai Hom Wor fire in February this year will have waited for up to 10 months before being rehoused." Due to a high level of illegal immigration in recent years, and the unavailability of affordable housing for most recent migrants, they had become the predominant group of new squatters. Because of the eligibility rules, they could only qualify for TH in the NT, which was "precisely the problem – if it were not for the demand from fire victims for temporary housing in the New Territories, demand would not exceed supply."[19]

Delegitimizing Squatters and Migrants: Queue-Jumpers and Fairness

The discussion of the alternatives available for these problems is illuminating. Revision of eligibility to divert clearees from temporary housing to permanent housing had already resulted in residency requirements dropping from 15 to 10 years in 1981, but Governor Trench argued that "any further reduction at this stage would not be equitable in view of the average waiting time of over eight years for those on the Waiting List, and would encourage squatting even more as the easy way to jump the queue into public housing."[20] Equity for different categories of people living in Hong Kong and the fear of encouraging squatting were central to the calculus of decision-making here. Squatters were presented as unfairly advantaged over needy people waiting for public housing, and if squatters were recent migrants they were particularly unworthy of preferment or "the absolute state of privilege enjoyed by those in Government and Government-aided housing."[21] The "problem is essentially the new immigrant squatters who have arrived in Hong Kong, who should not be given priority for the best public housing."[22]

One way of delegitimizing squatter fire victims was to blame them for arson in the pursuit of public housing, although at this time squatters also accused the government of starting the fires in order to displace them without having to provide permanent public housing (Smart 2013). A paper for the Colonial Secretariat in 1981 stated that:

Although there is no hard evidence to substantiate this, it is the unanimous opinion of Housing Department squatter control and operations staff that recent squatter fires are not accidental. . . . The motivation is not clear; possibly racketeers are now building huts to be burned, and are selling new squatter huts not as homes, but purely as a right to resettlement when burned down. There would be plenty of buyers among recent immigrants. . . . In these circumstances, it is considered essential to make no concessions on eligibility; on the contrary, the new squatters and new immigrants must be rehoused, in accordance with normal eligibility rules, outside the urban area, Sha Tin and Tsuen Wan, this must be done as soon as possible, and announced immediately and unequivocally. This can be done only by establishing resite areas in the New Territories.

A police report, however, stated that Criminal Investigation Division Headquarters and Districts "have not found one shred of evidence to show that these squatter fires have been deliberately started."[23] Stigmatizing squatters as queue-jumpers was more successful.

Fires, Landslides, and a Crisis of THA Supply

Revision of eligibility to divert people from NT to urban temporary housing was seen as "not feasible, given the supply and demand position. Supply in the urban area is adequate for demand, but the small surplus comes nowhere near meeting the excess demand for N.T. temporary housing. In any case, this would also encourage new squatting, and (possibly) more squatter fires." Provision of more temporary housing was important but could not be done quickly. A "very much expanded temporary housing production programme is now under way, including three-storey T.H.A.s. Production in 1982/1983 is expected to be over 30,000 person spaces, the majority in the New Territories. In normal circumstances, this would be expected to meet all commitments, with plenty to spare." But there were doubts that even this would be sufficient. The extent of desperation is apparent in the alternative of allowing rebuilding on fire sites, something that had been resisted for decades. But it was only dismissed on practicality: "In practice, this option proves to be feasible in only a limited number of cases, usually small fires. Geotechnical objections . . . usually preclude rebuilding."[24]

The final option was resite areas: "Providing a suitable piece of land can be made available, resites can be effected much more quickly than building additional temporary housing." This was basically:

[a] reversion to old-style licensed areas which THAs replaced. Recently tried successfully at Chai Wan following a fire in early 1980 . . . Conditions are below the standard of temporary housing areas, but are far better than in most squatter areas, and can be considered acceptable. This option was

Supply, Demand, and Failures 139

previously considered by the Chief Secretary's Committee in July 1979 . . . but was not pursued at that time. . . . in present circumstances this option offers the best solution to the need to increase quickly the stock of temporary housing to cope with emergency rehousing commitments.[25]

Eliminating licensed areas, basically regulated squatting with self-building on allocated sites, was one of the 1970 Housing Targets, again displaying the sense of urgency of dealing with the fire crisis.

By March 1982, 12,000 fire victims still had not been rehoused. The Housing Department considered it essential that they be "rehoused by the autumn of 1982 at the latest, and that there should be a substantial stock of land in reserve by the same date for resiting future fire victims. This is because: (a) the situation in the transit centres, particularly Tuen Mun, is potentially explosive and can only get worse the more people who are housed there, the longer they remain there, and whilst they and we do not know when and where they are going to be rehoused." Transit centres were essentially homeless shelters, as were empty factories, warehouses, or army barracks where up to 10,000 people could be provided emergency accommodation (see Figure 7.2). If there was still "a large backlog of fire victims to rehouse at the start of the next dry season, and [we] continue to have fires on anything like the scale of this winter, we risk being completely unable to cope with the situation."[26]

Figure 7.2: Transit Centre, Kowloon, 1999. Copyright and provided by Alan Smart.

The solutions adopted to cope with the crisis were "(a) identifying and developing 10 hectares of land in the N.T. as resite areas; (b) obtaining additional accommodation for transit centre use; (c) proceeding with improvement works in squatter areas; (d) improving squatter control." Improvements were hoped to eventually reduce the likelihood of rehousing resulting from disasters, emphasizing firebreaks (Smart 2006) and slope stabilization (see Chapter 9). A. P. Asprey, Deputy Director of the Housing Department, wrote that:

> As regards (a), I assume there is no intention of going back on this decision, and revising eligibility either generally, or particularly for the fire victims, so as to allow more to go direct into permanent housing or into temporary/ primary housing in the urban area. It remains firmly my view and that of the Housing Authority that any such move, while it may make for an easier and quicker solution of the immediate problem, is bound to have very serious long-term consequences: queue jumping, increased squatting, more fires in squatter areas, serious interruption of planned development clearances, severe (and justified) public criticism.[27]

If the clearances in the New Towns were to proceed on schedule, necessary to maintain the momentum of the Ten-Year Plan (already far behind the housing production targets, but at last achieving the production levels needed), TH in the NT was indispensable. On 25 February 1982, the Housing Authority responded to the problem, which it described as a "very large rehousing commitment, predominantly for temporary housing in the New Territories" caused by the squatter fires, and which made it "apparent that the existing supply and planned future production of temporary housing in the New Territories would be insufficient to meet the demand, particularly in view of other demands on temporary housing from the emergency and compulsory categories." As a result, it was decided to "establish as a matter of urgency new emergency temporary housing areas in the New Territories to rehouse those made homeless in fires in squatter areas since 30 October 1981."[28]

Despite this urgency, and the strategic importance of the emergency THAs, their creation was relatively slow and impeded by interdepartmental politics. By 5 March 1982, HD Deputy Director A. P. Asprey complained that "[i]f 10 hectares of land had been quickly identified and allocated as resite areas following the decision in early December 1981, we would at least now see the way clear to achieving the objective. In fact, three months later, 3.5 hectares net have been allocated at Sheun Wan, Tai Po, which will enable us to accommodate at most 6,000 by the autumn of this year. No other sites have been allocated or even look like being offered, despite innumerable meetings." On 31 May 1982 the Director of Housing wrote to the Regional Secretary (NT) that "I cannot leave the fire victims in transit centres indefinitely, but must make arrangements for their rehousing. Some hard decisions

Supply, Demand, and Failures

now therefore have to be made. If I am not to be allocated land specifically for the rehousing of recent fire victims, I will have to make do with my existing resources . . . clearances in Tuen Mun and Yuen Long from about November onwards will have to be deferred"[29] until land for additional TH in those districts is developed.

The Housing Department decided, reluctantly, to use an additional site planned for a standard THA as another resite area, but this plan was disputed by NT departments. The original concept provided access, sanitary facilities, and services, with people building their own dwellings, but it was "considered more appropriate to construct standard part-built structures during the development of these areas." Once again, a top-level decision to adopt more radical approaches, accepting self-building if not tenure change, floundered against practical resistance. The more conventional THA approach was applied to all of the new emergency THAs, as well as all future sites. The added costs to replace self-building for the three sites was estimated at $12.5 million. The three sites would accommodate 12,077 people, at a cost of $40.9 million.[30] The Secretary for Housing was concerned that pressure from the HA and elsewhere had resulted in the HD being "driven to producing temporary housing schemes costing virtually as much as permanent housing. He stressed that temporary housing of permanent materials plus shops, roads and schools was moving into the realms of permanent housing and there would have to be a limit."

In response, the Secretary for Home Affairs suggested that the HD was "pushed by policies which generated demand for temporary housing beyond the point where land supply could satisfy it. Rather than build sub-standard housing, the policies creating the demand ought to be modified to bring the situation back in to balance." The Secretary for Housing replied that "this was not the case. He argued that most of the recent demand arose from fire victims who had less than three years' residence in Hong Kong and could not be given priority for permanent housing." The Director of Lands said "that whatever was done to the eligibility criteria for permanent housing, it would not result in more housing. Given an inadequate number of spaces in temporary housing, the only recourse was to enable more people who had to be provided with housing to go into permanent housing." The Secretary for Housing "replied that permanent housing was not available in the quantity which would be required." One plan to cope with these constraints was to design four-story THAs.[31]

Opposition to the emergency THAs came particularly from NT officials, with a strong voice from the District Officer of Tuen Mun, Billy C. L. Lam. Tuen Mun had developed rapidly as a New Town, with inadequate facilities and transport linkages. Lam felt his responsibility was to help the district to be planned and executed in a balanced and politically sensitive manner; he had "great reservations" because the plans would "seriously further strain the already extremely inadequate transport and ancillary facilities." The "intake of another 7 000 to 10 000 discontented victims most of whom have to travel to N.E. [Northeast] Kowloon for work amid the present volatile situation in Tuen Mun is likely to pose very serious security and management problems. The chances of yet another riot similar to the Yau Oi incident last July are very strong indeed."[32] This incident on 12 July 1981 involved a crowd of about 800 at the new housing estate in Tuen Mun protesting about their fear of crime. However, government officials interpreted the unrest as reflecting "the human and social problem about moving to Tuen Mun – the back of beyond – to a Kowloon dweller." While housing is "a priority and so terribly important, we cannot expect people to be satisfied with a home in the middle of nothing. A much greater effort is necessary to provide the other things in life that people who live in public housing need."[33] Tuen Mun had inadequate transport links to the old urban areas, and insufficient jobs. Without adequate services, social pressures could build up rapidly, with a risk of destabilizing the law and order that the government tried very hard to maintain. More broadly, the challenges of transferring tens of thousands of people a year to the New Towns were substantial, and posed additional obstacles to the housing production plans, particularly if resistance to New Town resettlement slowed the development clearance schedule.

Despite the chorus of opinions against changing eligibility rules to avoid encouraging squatting and unfairly advantaging recent migrants over established and poor residents facing years-long Waiting Lists for public housing, rules were again changed within months. In October 1982, a new policy was adopted so that all squatters affected by development clearances would be rehoused in the urban areas according to their eligibility for permanent or temporary housing. A staff worker of the Neighbourhood Advice Action Council who was involved in the incident and had good political connections, told Smart that he believed that a protest over a clearance in Tai Hom Wor (Diamond Hill) was a major factor in the policy change. The timing seemed to support this. Those who were not cleared until the second phase after protests were all relocated in the urban areas, with the recent migrants being housed at a THA in nearby Kowloon Bay (Smart and Chui 2006). However, behind a decision that seemed to be occasioned by the need to defuse political conflicts, there were structural problems whereby a shortage of TH in the NT—and the difficulties in establishing more quickly—had produced serious delays in a showcase social reform of key political importance. And these delays were happening just two years before the Ten-Year Programme was supposed to have achieved its targets, and near the end of the sponsoring governor's term. Political action by squatters and their supporters may have had an influence, but if so, probably more as an excuse to do what needed to be done for other

Supply, Demand, and Failures | 143

reasons. This illustrates the utility of finding out what was going on in confidential governmental circles to provide new, though belated, perspectives on the results of ethnographic research.

Creating Problems through Solutions, and Compromise from Problems

Policy choices that help solve problems in the short term may be likely to create larger or less palatable problems in the longer term, or even in the short term, as this chapter has illustrated. Overcoming their own reluctance to solve the TH shortage by making more squatters eligible for permanent public housing, Hong Kong colonial decision-makers increased other risks they feared: encouraging squatting and public criticism of the unfairness of PH allocation. In turn, this threatened that, rather than achieving the target of eliminating squatter areas, the numbers would rise further, reducing allocations from the Waiting List. This situation intensified the need to review housing policy objectives, with particular attention to public housing eligibility rules, which included discussion of the rationales that underlay them. These discussions began to emphasize and favor moving toward "fairer" treatment of long-term Hong Kong residents and giving more emphasis to those qualifying for public housing through the Waiting List. However, while public opinion supported reducing the priority of squatters, practical issues again cautioned against this, since it was strongly believed that such moves would increase the practical and political difficulties of development clearances. Such difficulties could further threaten the pace of the public housing construction program.

As we explore in the next chapter, a compromise was achieved in which the Waiting List income limits were not imposed on cleared squatters (at least, not until 1999), but all tenants would be evaluated at the end of each 10 years' period of occupancy and charged double rent if their incomes were double or more the Waiting List income limits. In this way, income limits would not be imposed on squatters at clearance, but they would still be treated equally on these criteria after 10 years, as would all those in public housing through the Waiting List.

This astute compromise resolved some of the political criticism about the inequity of squatter rehousing, but once again it threatened to continue or enhance the attractions of squatting. Even if full containment of new squatter structures could be attained and maintained, there was the risk of increasing populations within the persisting squatter areas. While squatter areas situated on easily developed land could be dealt with by conventional development clearances, the problem of squatters on land not needed for development would persist. Two innovations emerged. First, the announcement in 1984 that "a programme should be drawn up to clear and rehouse squatters currently living on the more vulnerable slopes over a period of about five years. This will be included in a 10-year clearance and rehousing programme for all squatters, including boat-squatters, in the urban area." This program would remove the need for the Squatter Improvement Programme, only established in 1982, the funds for which could be used to support the ambitious project of resettling all urban squatters, and it would be run down over five years, with continuing expenditure to be limited to fire and landslide precautions (see Chapter 9).[34] The three proposals raised in the 1971 debate over squatters on land not needed for development had been decided in favour of clearing and resettling all, rejecting the alternatives of tenure change/regularization of existing settlements, and improvement without tenure change.

The second innovation was the decision to do the Squatter Occupancy Survey in 1984 and impose registration of occupants at the time of survey as a new requirement for resettlement. This would put a cap on the number of squatters eligible for PPH. Indeed, it should ensure that the numbers would drop, as registered squatter occupants moved to public housing through the Waiting List or by purchase of a Home Ownership Scheme unit, or to private housing, or through development clearances, or death. As long as the policy was not changed, this would result in a ratchet of exclusion, inexorably squeezing down a key, and widely resented, component of housing commitments. There would only be a legacy problem, which would shrink, quickly or slowly depending on factors the government could influence. It seems likely that this decision to conduct the SOS was supplementary to the non-development clearance program, since the ambitious goal of resettling all urban squatters within 10 years could be undermined if the numbers continued to grow. Full containment would have to be extended to all remaining insufficiently controlled alternatives. Indeed, most of the problems of supply and demand imbalance could have been easily handled if all new squatting could have been ended. The remainder of this chapter addresses the challenges of squatter control, which attempted to limit new sources of public housing demand.

Ballooning Demand for Public Housing: Failures and Innovations in Squatter Control

Containing new squatting was a continuing problem until 1984. Full containment was often proclaimed only to be undermined by migration or leakages into the less patrolled niches of Hong Kong, such as squatting on rooftops. Squatting increased substantially in the early 1980s after the adoption of both the 1976 survey baseline and reduction of residence qualifications. Much of this increase was due to surging immigration, but other issues concerning squatter control exacerbated the problems.

Supply, Demand, and Failures 145

A 1976 Report on corruption in squatter control, produced by the Independent Commission Against Corruption, was prompted by complaints that "squatter control staff of the Housing Department may be bribed to tolerate illegal structures, whilst demolition Notices may be posted on the structures of those who are not prepared to pay." The policy of "selective containment" allowed "patrolling Housing Assistants, who are largely unsupervised, almost total discretion over the degree of control exercised in their areas." Various and "sometimes conflicting control measures employed in support of selective containment, e.g. 'token' demolitions, 'routine' demolitions, etc. afford opportunities to solicit and accept advantages not only to patrolling officers, but to any government officer or unscrupulous member of the public who may choose to exploit public uncertainty."[35] As elsewhere, reducing the discretion of junior frontline officers was seen as key to corruption prevention, and usually entailed more forms and mandated procedures (Smart 2018). Without reforms, squatting could be encouraged and control undermined.

Effective use of control personnel was crucial. In February 1976, the Housing Authority, with the approval of ExCo, "implemented new tactics on an experimental basis by which selected areas, known as Intensive Patrol Areas (I.P.A.s), were created. This enabled the H.A. staff to patrol the areas designated without effecting a total control over all squatters which would entail doubling the existing staff." The Commissioner of Police believed these new tactics to have "proved effective." These tactics and other reforms, it was argued, had largely resolved the corruption opportunity issues.[36] However, in 1982, ICAC still maintained that there was "a steady stream of complaints over the last eight years, many requiring investigation by Operations Department; and some resulting in prosecution."[37] The ideas behind the IPAs were "(a) to give the H.A.s [Housing Assistants] an achievable target, i.e. the prevention of new squatting (including extensions to existing huts) in manageable areas; (b) to freeze the situation in the development areas . . . ; (c) to allow each H.A. to have his own team of labourers so as to demolish new structures when they are found and before they are occupied; and (d) to be able to change over to the new system without having to employ large numbers of additional staff on a negative and unpopular function."[38] While the new targets might be achievable, they could not completely solve the problem of uncontrolled new squatting because of the geographical limitations of patrolling.

This 1976 Intensive Patrol Area policy modified the existing, but failing, policy set out in the 1964 White Paper on Review of Policies for Squatter Control, Resettlement and Government Low-Cost Housing to demolish all new illegal structures erected on Crown land or leased land and to provide licensed area accommodation for all persons rendered homeless in this way. Those built before 1964 were given formal tolerated status, but later ones ended up being informally tolerated (Smart and Aguilera 2020). In June 1976,

ExCo agreed with the proposal of Memo XCC(76)44 that this policy should be changed. The key changes were the toleration of structures included in the 1976 squatter survey; daily patrolling of land scheduled for clearance in the development programs; and "periodic patrolling of other land considered either saturated or inaccessible as total prevention of new squatting would not be practicable unless a disproportionate amount of staff and other resources were devoted to the job." The rationale for these changes were that:

> there seemed to be very little building of new squatter huts, and it was considered that, if there were no more large influxes of illegal immigrants, control could be maintained and the number of huts gradually reduced by clearance. However, what was *not* foreseen was the large-scale immigration of 1978 to 1980, which resulted in a substantial increase in squatting on land not scheduled for development and hence not patrolled on a daily basis. Some 115,000 new squatter structures have been built and left standing since 1976, notwithstanding that over 100,000 structures have been demolished over the same period.[39]

The 1976 policy concentrated on control of squatters on developable lands, with less intensive patrolling of squatters on lands not needed for development. Reduced patrolling increased the proportion and absolute number of new squatters on less developable land. This intensified the problems raised in the 1971 debate about non-development squatters. Squatting pressures were:

> most evident in the General Patrol Areas (GPAs). Five key areas of new mass squatting have been identified . . . The Squatter Control Division engages in a programme of 'shake-up' operations in which a very large workforce is organised to demolish the structures and destroy or remove all building materials. This system is usually an effective deterrent in GPAs, but in recent months 'shake-ups' have been found to be increasingly ineffective in these mass squatting areas. It is in these areas primarily that the racketeers operate. They are unperturbed by these shows of force, secure in the knowledge that it is not physically possible to patrol these areas daily, and it is not unusual for re-erections to take place on the same site the day after a 'shake-up'. Further, these re-erected structures are often found to be occupied by the following day.[40]

It is useful to think of the squatter problem, in the absence of affordable housing available to all (including recent migrants and singles), as being like squeezing a balloon, but one with a tough skin. It is easy to compress a portion of it, but the balloon will expand into other parts that are not being compressed. Intensified control over part of the territory combined with lessened control elsewhere could be predicted to move squatters into the less controlled regions, even if they were less attractive in terms of location, safety, or amenities. Controlling, and eventually deflating, the squatter balloon requires containing expansion into new areas or niches, while shrinking existing patches. Even with heavy repression, if the system fails to provide adequate amounts of affordable housing, the pressure behind the problem will tend to find new informal solutions, like the current issue of "cubicle homes"—tiny subdivisions of existing apartments (Wong and Chan 2019).

Initially, the 1976 patrolling plan appeared to have succeeded. Yet, assertions of full containment referred only to the control of land for which the Housing Department was responsible, with problematic consequences. The intensified patrolling of developable Crown land led to the resurgence of a long-standing problem. In the absence of viable housing alternatives for the low-income population—particularly recent migrants from China who were restricted from access to public housing through the Waiting List—heightened controls pushed demand into areas that were not being actively controlled, such as private agricultural land and Crown land outside the Intensive Patrol Areas (which increased the population of squatters on non-developable dangerous slopes). By 1979, particularly in Kwun Tong, "pressures are such that even Squatter Control saturation is unlikely to be able to contain, let alone totally prevent, new squatting. Squatters may be driven to more remote areas, thereby reducing the pressure on the urban area, but the problem will remain. If present trends continue, indications are that we will soon be approaching the position where we must perforce acknowledge that we are tolerating unlimited squatting, albeit by driving squatters out to remote areas."[41]

Squatting Outside Housing Department Areas of Control

In addition, there were problems with land that had been transferred to departments that did not adequately police them. Heads of departments were reminded in 1983 that "it is their responsibility to take all necessary precautions to prevent unauthorized occupation of land under their control," noting that "[i]t should not be the function of the Housing Department to clear squatters from allocated sites where squatting has occurred because of the failure of departments to assume their responsibilities for protecting land under their control."[42] There were also concerns about squatting at or under highway structures, which were "becoming a serious problem" because they could constitute fire hazards, obstruct inspection and maintenance, and become a nuisance. The HD insisted that they would not be the department for squatter control for highway structures since "all the present resources of HD were committed for clearing squatters over undeveloped lands and there was no spare capacity for highway structures." Owing to a "shortage of manpower, only those squatting problems with some sort of urgency should be touched as fighting against re-squatting is also a job requiring extensive resources."[43]

148   *Hong Kong Public and Squatter Housing*

In addition, there were growing concerns about rooftop squatting. Widespread complaints about unauthorized building on rooftops drew the attention of ExCo in 1983. The Secretary for Housing was asked if it would be useful to conduct a survey of illegal rooftop structures. He agreed it would be desirable and agreed to draft a report on it. The report, however, discouraged doing this kind of survey. Comments on the proposal were critical of the idea. One official wrote that:

> The secret to the success of squatter control surveys is that it is done very quickly so that new structures cannot be put up on any major scale when the survey is underway. Moreover, it is backed by effective control of the situation as recorded in the survey through the deployment of sufficient staff patrolling all surveyed areas. Without these two elements, a survey on rooftop structures will only help aggravate our present problem, as the word will get round that Government is doing a survey which will be construed to mean the basis of compensation and rehousing in future. I strongly object to the idea of doing a survey on a limited area since it does not meet the ExCo desire to have an idea of the extent of the problem while encouraging everybody to put up structures and worsening the situation.

He agreed, however, that there was a problem, noting that:

> The lack of Government action to contain the problem is a subject of serious public criticism and as the present exercise does nothing to improve the situation, we can expect more criticisms. I am certain that many people will respond to such views by erecting new structures, an experience encountered in squatter control surveys . . . It is a no-win situation and whether you do any publicity or not is not going to do any good. Any public explanation that such a survey does not in anyway confer any status to the structures covered will not be taken seriously by the public.[44]

Rooftop structures were the responsibility of the Building Ordinance Office, which took action on about 50 cases per month of unauthorized building works. But the report suggested that it seemed quite possible that 1,000 or more new cases could be found each month. It was stated that "[i]n the general economic conditions in Hong Kong, there are considerable advantages and potential profits to be gained from unauthorized building works, and as building owners must generally be aware of the restraints on action by the Building Authority and that therefore the risk of detection and removal is relatively slight, they are encouraged to take a gamble on discovery and add to the growing number of such abuses." The decisions were made to do a quiet sample survey to establish the extent of the problem, without publicity, and to establish a new Control and Enforcement Branch within the Building Ordinance authority.[45] New rooftop squatting did come under control by the mid-1980s, but Hong Kong's official census of rooftop dwellings showed that

Supply, Demand, and Failures   149

1,554 households (3,962 persons) still resided in this dwelling type in 2006 (Tanasescu et al. 2010).

Another exclusion from Housing Department squatter control concerned squatting in back alleys and other spaces in the interstices of the densely populated city. Clearances of these provoked several incidents of resistance in the 1980s since they were not eligible for rehousing prior to a policy change in November 1984. Previously, these environmental clearances had been implemented by the district management committees of the District Boards, and those affected were not entitled to any compensation, although those found to be homeless were accommodated in transit centres in the NT until room was available in THAs in the NT. The different treatment was because the clearances were done to improve the environment and did not make land available for development. After violent resistance by squatters in Kowloon City (1984) and Hang On Street (1983), David Ford, Director of Housing, was reported to be furious over the incidents and the effect that subsequent criticism had on the public image of his department. He refused to let his staff participate in these clearances, and a review[46] led to the transfer of these clearances to the Lands Department and the decision to offer rehousing comparable to that in development clearances (Smart and Chui 2006). However, because these structures had never been surveyed, eligibility for permanent public housing was based on length of residence only, as was being done at that time for rooftop structures affected by redevelopment clearances as well.[47]

The increased policing of the 1976 plan ultimately failed, or at most partially succeeded despite initial claims of achieving good control. The plans of 1976 joined a long history of failed plans to end the squatter problem since at least 1950 (Smart 2006). The hope to finally succeed in ending the squatter problem, encouraged by temporarily low levels of immigration from China, had faded, and new initiatives were needed to keep in sight the objectives of the Ten-Year Housing Target to eliminate all squatter and licensed areas.

By 1981, the failures had become clear, and a new set of policies was adopted to regain control of squatting outside the development areas. In order to "curb the construction of new squatter structures, and to introduce a unified system in the New Territories, the Squatter Control Division of the Housing Department was considerably strengthened to enable intensive patrolling of areas not included in the development programmes but vulnerable to squatting." This in effect reversed the 1976 decision to concentrate patrolling in areas scheduled for development. Despite this, the pressure of new squatting:

> is still intense. Racketeers are still very much in evidence, and are held in check only by a strong presence on the ground. In 1979, squatter control demolitions averaged 1,000 structures or extensions per month; by 1981 this had doubled to 2,000 per month. This year, demolitions have averaged over 4,000

150   *Hong Kong Public and Squatter Housing*

per month, and have reached nearly 5,000 in recent months. It is hoped that
the level of control now being exercised, together with the recently enacted
Crown Land (Amendment) Ordinance which provides heavier penalties for
racketeering, will deter hut building and reduce the number of demolitions
required each month.[48]

The SOS as Completing Containment

By September 1984, it could be proclaimed with better evidence that "[s]
quatter control is now fully effective. This means that new squatter structures
and illegal extensions are detected instantly and demolished immediately."
Even if it was possible to control any new encroachments on land, rooftops or
back alleys, however, there would still be possibilities for the squatter balloon
to expand within the envelope of existing squatter areas. That was because the
"current form of control" is "exercised over *structures* and not over occupancy.
Such control does not prevent squatter huts changing hands, nor does it prevent
additional people moving into existing huts. Under the present system, it is
possible for a number of squatters to 'jump the queue' into public housing by
moving into existing squatter huts before they are cleared for development."
As long as living in a squatter dwelling could provide a chance of access to
public housing, a shrinking supply could increase the demand for remaining
structures, potentially increasing density above the high levels already experienced. Beyond numbers, the new emphasis on "fairness" was being challenged
by such "queue-jumping." As a result, it was recommended that "[w]sith the
high degree of control now exercised by the Housing Department, it is now
considered opportune to carry out a survey of all *occupants* of squatter structures, so that their eligibility for rehousing may be established and so that the
rehousing commitment may be more clearly defined."[49] Making squatter areas
more visible through delineating their population as well as their structures,
and making PPH unavailable to those who moved in after the survey, would
create a permanent upper limit to the quotas used for clearing squatters. This
ratchet of exclusion would not only put a cap on this source of demand for
rehousing, but discourage prospective squatters, reducing pressure on squatter patrolling.

Demand, though, would persist until the SOS was complete, so it was "not
proposed that any publicity be given to the proposal to undertake a survey of
the occupants of squatter huts. Since public knowledge of such an intention
could have the effect of encouraging persons to move into existing squatter
huts in order to claim eligibility for rehousing upon clearance, it is considered that this exercise should remain confidential." Advance knowledge could
undermine their plans by creating new demand for both forms of public
housing. On 5 April 1984, the Operations Committee "recommended that

a survey of occupants of squatter areas should be undertaken." On 12 April 1984, the Housing Authority recommended that a survey of the occupants of squatter areas be carried out, "but that, in order to reduce the likelihood of false claims to squatter hut occupancy being staked, this proposal should not be included in the Consultative Document 'A Review of Public Housing Allocation Policy' for public discussion."[50] This absence of publicity is part of the reason we know so little about the SOS. What is known from the archives is discussed in Chapter 10.

Conclusions

This chapter has demonstrated the consequences of imbalances between supply and demand for permanent public housing and temporary housing. The high demand for temporary housing was largely a result of policy choices that excluded a growing proportion of squatters affected by clearance. At the same time, increased numbers of squatters resulted from policies that encouraged squatting, did not fully control new squatting, and failed to produce sufficient affordable housing. These policy failures stood behind the need to rebalance the problems that had been created, and which were inhibiting the production of the quantity of public housing promised in the Ten-Year Plan. The failure, or at best incomplete success, of one of the Governor's prominent social reforms threatened embarrassment. Behind these government failures were the market failures of the private housing sector, unable to produce enough cheap housing for the working class and even for much of the middle class, while displacing many through redevelopment. However, governmental interventions were major contributing factors to private market failure, particularly given the crucial role played by the government in making land available for development (Smart 1989).

The need to rebalance policy-induced demand for the two types of public housing resulted in a review of eligibility that attempted to make a larger proportion of squatters eligible for permanent public housing. Doing so, however, risked prompting more squatting, and making the failure of the first housing target—the elimination of squatter areas—even more apparent. Expanded eligibility of squatters for PPH was temporarily desirable, but was seen as objectionable in itself, and could cause excessive demand for PPH. The Ten-Year Plan could only succeed through expeditious clearances of squatter areas to make possible the building of new housing estates, creating tension with squatter resettlement as a means to the end of a massive housing program to instill loyalty among the long-term resident population. This conflict between ends and means also undermined the Housing Target to resettle all squatters, since clearances on non-development land would only increase the need for squatter rehousing without making useful land available. Chapter 9 will suggest that the failure, and expanding costs, of squatter improvement resulted in the 1984 decision to (eventually) resettle all squatters on land not needed for development. This commitment again risked an escalating housing commitment, which the SOS could help prevent.

Efforts to correct housing supply and demand imbalances, and the policies that created them, provide a specific and concrete mechanism for pushing the mangled policy processes toward the SOS and the turning of the tide for informal housing in Hong Kong. It thereby appears to have met the criteria for the best explanation available so far. However, this explanation leaves open the questions of why squatters were excluded and policies against rich tenants adopted. To explain this, issues of identity and governmental preferences about who should be helped offer viewpoints into discussions over fairness, but simultaneously about practicality.

In Chapter 8, we argue that identity issues and governmental preferences for who should receive public housing were a major source of the policy failures that created public housing supply and demand imbalances. These imbalances in turn were major influences on the changes of policy that led to the 1984 turning point for informal housing in Hong Kong. Behind these conflicts loomed the continuing failure to contain the squatter problem, with its balloon-like tendency to expand into any available niche that was not being adequately supervised. However, there is a strong possibility that both supply and demand and identity issues might both be part of a fuller and more complete explanation. Policy-induced demand imbalance could be the proximate cause of the policy shifts, while identity status discrimination/preference operated as a background cause of the policies that resulted in the imbalances and policy failures, and pointed the direction to a compromise that resolved the conflicts between fairness and practicality. The next chapter will address these issues, and examine how the two kinds of explanation interact with each other, whether one is clearly better than the other, or if their complementary strengths both need to be incorporated into a more complex but adequate explanation for the decisions that lead to the tide turning against squatting in Hong Kong.

8
Hong Kong Identity and Squatter Exclusion

> That communal world is complete in so far as all the rest is irrelevant; more exactly, hostile —a wilderness full of ambushes and conspiracies and bristling with enemies wielding chaos as their main weapons . . . It is there, to that wilderness, that people huddling in the warmth of shared identity dump (or hope to banish) the fears which prompted them to seek communal shelter . . . Communal fraternity would be incomplete . . . without that inborn fratricidal inclination.
>
> —Zygmunt Bauman, *Liquid Modernity* (2000, 172)

Introduction

As delineated in Chapter 7, a crucial consideration in the course of correcting housing supply and demand imbalances that pushed policy trajectory toward implementing the SOS was the growing concern for fairer treatment of long-term Hong Kong residents on the Waiting List compared to recent Chinese immigrants. The colonial government acknowledged, and may have helped foster, that concern and changed the eligibility for public housing. The upshot was squatter exclusion that exacerbated the PPH/TH imbalance in the early 1980s. In short, what we saw was an exclusionary turn in housing allocation and beneath it was a growing resentment of squatters and migrants, who were thought of as undeserving of scarce public housing. These changes (i.e., exclusion and resentment) are puzzling because, on the one hand, for most of its history Hong Kong has been an immigrant society and, on the other hand, acquiring public housing resources through squatter resettlement was an established practice that dated back to the 1950s. The exclusionary turn in housing allocation and the resentment of squatters and migrants thus beg several questions: How did such resentment of squatters and migrants come into being? Was the exclusionary turn inevitable? How did the preference for fairer treatment of long-term residents on the Waiting List come into being?

This chapter offers a broader assessment of the Ten-Year Housing Programme's motivations, outcomes, and failures; interrogates how identity issues entangled with the allocation of public housing quotas to generate resentment of squatters and migrants; and explicates the discursive role of the colonial government in managing the tensions that arise from allocation of limited public housing resources. We suggest that the identity issue is relevant as a complementary explanation to the implementation of SOS. Nonetheless, we argue that the tension between long-term residents on the Waiting List and recent Chinese immigrants had to be understood within the institutional context of housing allocation and the colonial government's discursive practices for maintaining legitimacy. The upshot of this tension and the state discursive practices that stigmatized the recent immigrants was that Hong Kong society became increasingly anti-immigrant: the Hong Kong Chinese began to see that they "deserved more attention [being given] from the government" (Mathews, Ma, and Lui 2008, 38). This served as an enabling condition for the colonial government's exclusionary tactics in protecting the local residents. In so doing, the colonial government could then divert public housing quotas to those on the Waiting List, a move deemed important in cultivating loyalty from the Hong Kong Chinese. It was in this way that the colonial government took a self-undermining move that further amplified the pre-existing PPH/THAs imbalance. The resulting problems pointed to a compromise that resolved the conflicts between fairness of housing allocation and practicality of increasing supply of affordable housing.

Ten-Year Housing Programme and Promoting Loyalty

To understand the formation of the preference for fairer treatment of long-term residents on the Waiting List that led to immigrant squatter exclusion, it is necessary to consider the imperative of promoting loyalty. Chapter 5 offered an overview of the changing colonial governing strategy and its relationship with the 1966 disturbance and 1967 riots, constrained and enabled by Cold War geopolitics. Bridging the gap between the government and the people was a crucial objective, but promoting loyalty began to demand distinctions between the "real" people and recent migrants, which we focus on in this chapter. In the course of promoting loyalty, the housing mission gained momentum under MacLehose's governorship. In a Government House meeting on 27 May 1972, Governor MacLehose "said that provision of housing was the biggest problem in Hong Kong" and the colonial government "should press as quickly as possible."[1] To his mind, "if adequate housing were available for all there would be greater stability and therefore as much as possible should be done in the next decade." In particular, he remarked that "the long term [housing] programme must take in the squatter population and the aim must be to mop up squatter areas." On 18 October 1972, the Ten-Year Housing Programme was announced in the Legislative Council to tackle the problem of "inadequacy

Figure 8.1: Government publicity materials, "Building Homes for a Hong Kong Million." Source: HKRS156/3/42. Graph compiled by the authors.

and scarcity of housing" that could remove "major and most constant sources of friction" that jeopardized "our civic pride and our political good sense."[2]

Governor MacLehose remarked in his 1972 annual report to London that the colonial government could not "aim at national loyalty" as the path to independence was out of the question, but "civic pride" could be a "useful substitute."[3] What he meant by civic pride was more than improving the standard of living, however. It meant convincing the populace that an alien authority could serve the interests of the local community within the status quo. In this way, promoting loyalty means more than cultivating a sense of belonging (i.e., identifying the colony as their home), but also a new form of colonial state-society relations where the colonial government attempted to be responsive to popular demands (at the same time that they tried to manipulate these demands through what Mok (2019a; 2019b) calls the "covert colonialism" of public opinion polls) so as to acquire a sense of legitimacy and consolidate colonial rule. In other words, promoting loyalty and being responsible are two sides of the same coin. What embodied such a new form of colonial state-society relations is a deformed citizenship that conferred the colonial subject a limited sense of entitlement without political power devolution (see Ku and Pun 2004). Indeed, Governor MacLehose noticed that people were increasingly aware of their "conditions of life" and "more expectant of Government."[4] In particular, he was aware that the demographic composition of Hong Kong had changed and a locally born generation was growing up. In contrast to their parents who came to Hong Kong by choice and "inclined to accept the status quo . . . for the sake of expediency," this baby boomer generation had a higher expectation of the performance of the colonial government and "the very thought of living in a political anachronism such as a colony makes them feel uneasy."[5] It was a situation of "growing impatience among young people with Government and the *status quo*."[6]

One manifestation of this higher expectation was that these baby boomers were more inclined to participate in social movements and challenge government policies that aroused considerable criticism and discontents. As an internal report published in 1971 revealed, "with dissatisfaction increasing, it is most likely that these young people would take a keener interest in the causes of dissatisfied groups and exploit such causes as issues for agitation."[7] Further complicating the issue is the rise of the New Left and "growing sentiments of pan-Chinese nationalism." Both had been sources of motivation that triggered agitation to redress the economic disparity and cultural discrimination in Hong Kong. In this way, the colonial government made sense of why students "made appearances at the strike of Cross Harbour Tunnel Workers . . . and again at the Tung Tau Tsuen [squatter] clearance" in 1971 and why the Chinese language movement could gather wide support. "Inadequacies in housing . . . are interpreted as sign of colonialism and proof that the wellbeing of the masses is subordinated to the interests of the minority which is in political and economic power."[8]

One conclusion of the report was that "there is an immediate need to bring [the moderates and the hitherto un-committed] much closer to the Government," otherwise they could side with the "very small minority [that] hold extreme views." In the long run, "there is a need for Government to have clear objectives" and "a programme of social reform and administrative actions should be established to meet the need." This would mean "much speedier progress in solving the housing problem [and the improvement of] the standard of the living environment." As the Secretary for Home Affairs succinctly summarized, the whole point was "humanizing the Government and making it and its officers feel more individually responsible . . . which gave Government [as in 1967] an aura of being run by people who cared."[9] Although people with a higher expectation for government performance could represent "a potential danger," Governor MacLehose saw this as an "opportunity to the Government if it sets out to meet them and is believed to be doing so."[10] It was within this framework that the Ten-Year Housing Programme announced in 1972 acquired a sense of political importance. To facilitate the implementation of the program, the colonial government subsequently reorganized the Housing Department's structure such that a single administrative authority (i.e., the Hong Kong Housing Authority, or HA) would be responsible for coordinating housing issues.[11]

The centralization was crucial for understanding the local community conflicts with immigrants in 1979 leading to the change of eligibility rule. This requires explication of the antecedent conditions for our discussion regarding the changes caused by it. Prior to April 1973, public housing provision and management were delegated to various individual agencies. These included mainly the Resettlement Department, the Housing Division of the Urban Council, the Housing Authority, and the (non-governmental organization) Housing Society. But it was the Public Works Department that built the bulk of the housing estates. These housing units built by the Public Works Department were then handed to the Housing Division of the Urban Council/Resettlement Department and the (old, pre-1973) Housing Authority for management (Pryor 1983, 33–34). There was a division of labor between the Resettlement Department and the Housing Authority/Housing Division of the Urban Council; the former was responsible for dealing with squatter clearance/resettlement and control, while the other managed Government Low-Cost Housing (GLCH) and Housing Authority programs aimed at the tenement poor (Drakakis-Smith 1979). According to a memo written by the Commissioner for Resettlement, the two had to be a "parallel operation" so that it would not have any "adverse effect" on the resettlement program.[12]

While the memo did not specify what "adverse effect" meant, the discussion seemed to refer to the political nature of squatter clearance and control, which often incited resistances that could destabilize the colony. In the 1950s, political calculations of guarding against the risk of destabilization in the context of the perceived unreliability of the Hong Kong Chinese was the crucial stimulus that led to the creation of the resettlement regime (Smart 1989, 2006) where squatters were no longer simply displaced but rehoused. To do so, however, there had to be a sufficient stock of public housing flats so that rehousing could be done "at the time" when "people [were] evicted from their homes."[13] Put alternatively, it would mean to shorten the time in which the clearees might gather and form a crowd (or sleep) in the street, which could create a confrontational situation. When public rental flats for rehousing were unavailable, Licensed Area sites—the forerunner of THAs—would be provided for self-construction to those whose homes were demolished by disaster or government action. This served as a political "safety valve" as well as to eliminate a "rally point for 'do-gooders' anxious to attack the Government."[14] "If there were no Licensed Areas . . . there would be many more confrontations (with the risk of disturbance) in clearance and squatter control operations." Thus, temporary housing was a "stop-gap measure" and "a holding area for people who are in the housing pipeline, but for whom accommodations are not immediately available."[15]

This timing consideration had crucial ramifications. First, rehousing at the time of eviction (i.e., being clearees) or after a disaster (i.e., being victims) implied that these categories of people were accorded a higher priority in the housing allocation process. Second, rent for resettlement housing was set at a level low enough for the poorest so that those evicted would not refuse resettlement on the ground of unaffordability (Hopkins 1972). While GLCH and the Resettlement program were both subsidized housing, GLCH was "entirely different in concept."[16] "What started resettlement was the need to clear squatter areas for development." This could yield economic benefits including but not limited to revenue from land sales. GLCH, though, "is a general social programme" intended to "provide decent housing for poor people now living in bad housing" and the allocation of this non-resettlement housing was "entirely on a basis of [housing] need" rather than matching "precise timing." Another difference between the Resettlement and GLCH program was the "outlook" of the tenants; the Resettlement program involved "tenants who have been obliged to move, often as a result of Government action" while GLCH program included those who "voluntarily moved to improve their conditions."[17]

The absence of such timing pressures for the GLCH program meant that "no obvious problems are produced by excluding the poorest who cannot afford the rent."[18] Admission to GLCH flats was based on a list of qualifications and disqualifications that acted as "upper cut-off points." These eligibility rules included assessed household income, and other conditions such as age and household size. In 1976, Waiting List applicants had to be "21 years of age or over," their family size no fewer than three persons, and all family members had to be Hong Kong residents.[19] Since Hong Kong's postwar industrialization relied on labor-intensive manufacturing and the colonial government had refused to introduce labor protection in order to maintain the colony's low wage economic advantage (Clayton 2006, 2007), the upshot was that there were "enormous numbers eligible for low cost housing . . . far more than can be housed."[20] Once the application was successfully filed, people applying for GLCH flats were then queued on a Waiting List and their entry to non-resettlement subsidized housing depended on the production rate of the GLCH flat.

Thus, the eligibility rule governing public housing allocation actually reflected the different natures of the GLCH and Resettlement programs. Comparatively, housing allocation to disaster victims and clearees was more lenient: one only had to prove that they were "genuine residents" and that there was "no income limit imposed." But eligibility rules for the GLCH were rather restrictive. It served to exclude households that "could easily be accommodated by the private sector" (Drakakis-Smith 1979, 96). The income limit therefore acted as a yardstick to determine which family deserved to receive housing subsidy and when the colonial government should stop intervening in the housing market.[21] Non-squatters and those living in overcrowded private sector flats could only receive housing subsidies by entry to the GLCH flat via the Waiting List channel. Given that the colonial government was reluctant to implement social and welfare programs, it was unsurprising to see that the colonial government financed the GLCH programs (i.e., those implemented by non-governmental organizations, such as the Hong Kong Housing Society and the pre-1973 Housing Authority) mainly through the Development Loan Fund while the Resettlement programs were funded mainly through tax revenue.

There was a subtle but crucial difference between financing through tax revenue or the Development Loan Fund. Agencies implementing the GLCH programs financed by the loans from the Development Loan Fund were required to repay the loans together with interest charges to replenish the Fund. As Skully (1982, 56) noted, social projects financed by the Development Loan Fund, unlike tax revenue, were "intended to be self-liquidating." This meant that projects financed through loans would not be a recurrent fiscal demand on government resources and the colonial government could force the agencies to adopt measures to become self-financing by refusing to offer additional financial support. For example, in 1971, the colonial government decided to "give no further financial support" to the Hong Kong Housing Society with the rationale that its "scale of operations" had reached a point "at which self-financing from rents should become possible" (Dwyer 1971, 38). Financing through the Development Loan Fund thus enabled the colonial government to limit its fiscal burden. Although the Development Loan Fund and tax revenue could both be categorized as government resources, it was crucial to recognize the fiscal implication that, in the long run, the Development Loan Fund could spare the colonial government's necessity to increase taxation as social projects became self-financing. It could also enable the colonial government to adjust the scope of the housing projects by manipulating the availability of fiscal resources in the Development Loan Fund.

In other words, the Development Loan Fund was a budgetary instrument to minimize the use of fiscal resources. When housing programs were financed by the Development Loan Fund, it would mean that the programs were always under budgetary constraints and therefore experienced a slower rate of expansion. Thus, although both GLCH and Resettlement programs were supported by government resources, the rate of production between the two was very different. From 1962–1963 to 1972–1973, the Resettlement program produced 162,857 units while the GLCH programs produced 61,446 units (Castells et al. 1990, 10–11). As Drakakis-Smith (1979, 97) observed, the GLCH program "had been underemphasized . . . [and thus] it was bringing fewer benefits for the tenement poor" (see also Yeh 1990; Goodstadt 2013).

By March 1971, there were 171,923 applications awaiting allocation of HA and GLCH flats.[22] Long Waiting Lists for HA accommodation began to attract "criticism from Western educated persons, expatriates and local alike" that "overshadowed" the colonial government's achievements introduced after the 1967 riots.[23] The Ten-Year Housing Programme was an endeavor of the government to cope with this situation. Being a colony-wide program, the colonial bureaucrats recognized that it was "necessary to ensure that we had the best organization to maximize our ability to build houses as required."[24] The centralization led to the formation of the HA in April 1973; it grouped together building, managing, and financing into one organization, which would be an independent statutory body.[25] Squatter clearance and control were also placed under the Hong Kong Housing Authority's jurisdiction.

Housing Shortfall, Different Commitments, and Competing Priorities

Two ramifications of this centralization are worth noting. On the one hand, the Financial Secretary was able to insert a fiscal cap that required the HA "to generate a net cash flow" by "moving toward financial self-sufficiency gradually."[26] Haddon-Cave was "worried . . . that such an independent Authority might embark upon ambitious new housing programmes which would not pay for themselves and the cost of these would have to [be] borne by Colony revenues but without the Government having any satisfactory means of controlling the expenditures." Stressing financial self-sufficiency "had the effect of placing upon the Housing Authority not only the full costs of future housing development . . . but also [the] unenviable task of eliminating the [housing] subsidies." From April 1973, financing methods of public housing programs thus became unified using a way similar to the one used in the GLCH program. In this way, the HA became indebted as the rents in public housing, especially resettlement estates, were so low that rent payment could not repay the funds borrowed from the colonial government's Development Load Fund without a substantial increase (Drakakis-Smith 1979, 115).

On the other hand, the distinction between the GLCH and the Resettlement program was removed and "squatters would be cleared into these estates which would be mixed estates" including both preexisting resettlement estates and GLCH estates.[27] Since then, all new flats would be simply called permanent public housing. It was in this circumstance that it became "necessary to decide a split of the allocation of accommodation between various categories of worthy people."[28] A review of categories was conducted in June 1972 for this purpose, and the allocation of housing quota was centrally administered.

The key difference before and after centralization was that the Waiting List category was integrated into a single list of eligible categories originally proposed in the 1964 White Paper. The timing consideration of providing housing at the time of eviction still prevailed. As Table 8.1 shows, there were four emergency categories for which "it is necessary to earmark [immediate] accommodation."[29] From category 4 to 6, people were "rehoused as part of a wider scheme [such as development clearance] . . . which will be delayed if accommodation is not available." The Waiting List category did not receive any favorable treatment. It was a residual category. Together with overcrowding and other unsatisfactorily housed categories, the Waiting List category had to compete for "the residue of public housing units left after the commitments of [former] categories 1–7 had been met." What further worsened the situation was the introduction of other categories such as civil servants and pensioners that further reduced the residue of public housing units remaining.

This administration of housing allocation through quota, therefore, put different categories of people in a competitive relationship that might engender conflicts, as increased housing allocation to a particular category would deprive the others (Drakakis-Smith 1979: 124). The discrepancy of eligibility rules, especially the income scrutiny, that governed the allocation of PPH between the Waiting List and non–Waiting List categories also created a built-in incentive that motivated those being excluded by the income limit to circumvent the government's exclusionary tactics and shorten the time to get PPH by becoming occupants of a surveyed squatter hut. Even middle-class households, which could afford the private sector rents and were thus ineligible, might also leverage this unique channel of squatter resettlement—originating from the discrepancy of eligibility rules—as a shortcut (Smart 2006, 179).

The competitive relationship could be seen in the case of the rainstorms caused by Typhoon Rose in June 1972. It led to twin landslides and 110 deaths, the third-highest number of dead since typhoon casualties were recorded (Royal Observatory Hong Kong 1973, 25). A reporter retrospectively described the event as "the day the earth moved"[30] and public sympathy sided with storm victims that urged the colonial government to give them top priority to rehousing.[31] The colonial government was dragged into offering emergency rehousing. In so doing, it created a "serious shortage of public housing" for which "a large part of the stock that was available in mid-1972 having been used to provide for families left homeless by the rainstorms of June 1972. This shortage means a longer wait for those families on the waiting list for public housing who could otherwise have been rehoused in 1972 or early 1973."[32] In other words, victims of fires and disasters involving a significant number of families could consume the quota remaining for residual categories that had gone through strict income scrutiny, and this could exacerbate the long wait for those on the Waiting List. Put differently, making victims ineligible for PH could minimize housing quotas being drawn away and, in this way, more PH flats could be allocated to the Waiting List.

Table 8.1: List of eligible categories for public housing before and after 1973. Compiled by the authors.

Category before 1973		Category after 1973	
Emergency Categories			
1(a)	Victims of fires and natural disasters	E.1	Victims of fires and natural disasters
1(b)	Compassionate cases	E.2	Compassionate cases
2	Occupants of squatter huts declared to be dangerous	E.3	Occupants of squatter huts and others declared to be dangerous
3	Former domestic tenants of building demolished as dangerous, and occupants of surveyed structures on the roofs of such buildings and in the side and rear lanes	E.4	Dangerous buildings
Development Categories			
4(a)	Present occupants of cottage, licensed, or resite areas, or occupants of tolerated structures on Crown land required for development	D.1	Development clearances
4(b)	Pavement dwellers in tolerated structures	D.2	Pavement dwellers in tolerated structures
5(a)	Tenants and subtenants of properties acquired in connection with Urban Renewal Schemes	D.3	Urban renewal
5(b)	Tenants of Resettlement Estates which are to be redeveloped	D.4	Redevelopment of Mark I/II blocks
Unsatisfactorily Housed Categories			
6	Occupants of certain squatter areas, selected because of particularly bad conditions	U.1	Occupants of certain squatter areas, selected because of particularly bad conditions
7	Reuse of licensed areas	U.2	Reuse of licensed areas (later, turning over of THA)
8(a)	Relief of overcrowding in Resettlement and GLCH Estates	U.3	Relief of overcrowding
8(b)	Persons unsatisfactorily housed who apply for public housing	U.4	Waiting list
		U.5 (M.1)	Civil servants and pensioners
		M.2	Miscellaneous

Hong Kong Identity and Squatter Exclusion

While victims of fires and disasters could "draw away" the housing quota, it was unlikely that, if there were no disaster at all, the problem of long waiting lists could be tackled before 1979, the year when the colonial government introduced residence requirements. It is intriguing to see that although the colonial government preferred catering to developmental needs and its rehousing implications over subsidizing those unsatisfactorily housed, it also acknowledged that "it would be wrong to use the total output of low-cost housing . . . for the current resettlement priority categories."[33] This ambivalence could be seen in the dispute between the Commissioner for Resettlement and the Commissioner for Housing in 1972, leading to the drafting of the "Reconciliation of Supply and Demand of Public Housing up to 31 March 1976."[34] The crux of the matter was about the former Housing Board Report's recommendation of building a total 700,000 public housing flats for distribution until 1976. However, by May 1972, it was anticipated that a substantial shortfall would occur in 1973–1974, which could be "a very bleak year as far as the production of public housing is concerned." The anticipated situation was that "only 10,000 individual units of resettlement accommodation and 13,800 individual units of low-cost housing accommodation will be forthcoming."[35] This created a problem of how to make use of housing quotas when shortage occurred.

To sustain the progress of clearance to free up urban land for redevelopment, the Commissioner for Resettlement requested on 6 January 1972 to use "all available Low-Cost Housing output in 1972/1975 . . . to meet resettlement commitments."[36] Such a request, the Commissioner for Housing recounted, could be controversial because "the Housing Board had recommended that not more than a third of the accommodation in any Low Cost Housing estate should be used for resettlement categories 1–4."[37] The point is that the GLCH program was intended for "voluntary applicants." As an established custom, "the public has been conditioned to this belief [that only Waiting List applicants could receive GLCH flats] and thousands have applied for this accommodation in the hope of improving their living conditions to a tolerable standard." To the Commissioner for Housing,

> it is of over-riding importance that the Government does not appear to break faith with these people, but this aspect of the matter does not seem to me to be receiving anywhere near the consideration which is its due, and I fear that the repercussions which could result from a public realization that they no longer have this opportunity [when the allocation of GLCH flats to waiting list applicants was halted]. There have already been complaints made in the press and by personal call at this office by applicants who resent the priority given to the resettlement categories. It is difficult to answer such complaints in a way satisfactory to the public . . .

What the Commissioner for Housing implied was that, instead of halting the allocation of housing quota, the colonial government had to increase the quota for the Waiting List category in order to maintain people's faith in the colonial government, not to mention to prevent the adverse effects such as damage to the public image of the colonial government.[38] However, in doing so, the colonial government would be unable to swallow the firm rehousing commitment generated from development clearance.

The colonial government was caught between these competing priorities and commitments. On March 1972, the Commissioner for Housing informed the Colonial Secretary that he was "being forced into an extremely difficult situation" and "[m]embers of the [Housing] Authority (including notably Mrs. [Elsie] Elliott) are following up enquiries by applicants whom they were told some time ago were on the point of being passed for allocation."[39] To rematch supply and demand, it was decided that allocation of public housing to Waiting List applicants should continue but that "the intake of Waiting List should not exceed 700 tenancies a month (about 4,500 units) during 1972/73."[40]

The dispute around the competing priorities and commitments in 1972 further clarified how conflicts between the Waiting List and non–Waiting List categories could arise. On the one hand, although fires and disaster victims could draw away housing quota, conflicts between priorities could still emerge because there were different governmental commitments. The need to meet rehousing commitments following the planned schedule of development clearance might press down the remaining housing quota for the Waiting List category. Victims of disasters only exacerbated the situation. On the other hand, the colonial government could not afford to entirely exclude the Waiting List category, which included those who were unsatisfactorily housed. The intake of this category into public housing not only meant that overcrowding could be relieved, but that former dwellers in private housing could also receive substantial housing subsidies and greatly mitigate the burden of high rents. This could enhance the colonial government's image and thereby support the imperative of promoting loyalty. Alternatively, failure to allocate public housing to the Waiting List category would attract attacks from critics like Elsie Elliott and trigger public outcry. These could undermine the goal of promoting loyalty.

These circumstances would mean that the colonial government had to maintain a dedicated balance of quota distribution between the Waiting List and non–Waiting List category. It was politically impossible to use all housing quota for development clearance; but allocating all quota for the Waiting List was also impractical because it would obstruct the progress of development clearances.[41] The centralization enabled the colonial government to alter the preexisting housing quota arrangement that GLCH flats would only go to the Waiting List applicants. While this enabled the colonial government to flexibly arrange and administer housing resources to suit its needs,[42] it also made the overall rate of production of public housing—in other words, the availability of housing units—more crucial, and politically salient, than before.

However, as discussed in Chapter 7, the Housing Programme failed to produce sufficient public housing. As expected in 1972, the production of PH flats dropped to the lowest level in 1973–1974 and 1974–1975 when only 8,495 and 9,786 housing units, respectively, were completed (Castells et al. 1990, 10–11). In other words, the PH building program "had been retarded."[43] On 8 July 1975, the Secretary of Housing reported that "a further 109,000 flats in the public sector" would be needed to meet the target of the Ten-Year Housing Plan.[44] This housing shortfall prompted the colonial government to review the Housing Programme, conducted by the Housing Programme Plan steering group, and start regulating the demand side to minimize rehousing commitment.

Being Responsive to Changing Popular Opinion

Yet, what concerns us here are the questions of how this shortfall shaped the dynamics of housing quota distribution and, more importantly, whether the THA shortages that occurred in 1979 were inevitable. Figure 8.2 records the public housing flats allocated to the Waiting List applicants, development clearees, and fire/disaster victims. The numbers must be treated with caution because they do not tell us the original quota planned to allocate to that category.[45] Even so, the figure is still useful in showing the trend of PH flat allocation. From 1974–1975 to 1984–1985, PH allocation to fire/disaster victims did not change much; it consistently received no more than 1,000 PH flats. Between 1975–1976 and 1978–1979, PH flats allocated to Waiting List applicants dropped from 6,733 to 2,237, but the number of PH flats allocated to development clearees gradually increased from 1,678 to 7,258. Hence, from 1975–1976 to 1978–1979, PH allocation demonstrated a contrasting trend where availability of PH flats to the Waiting List applicants declined while the housing shortfall did not undermine PH allocation to development clearees.

One immediate consequence of the decline of PH provision to Waiting List applicants was the considerable increase in waiting time. By April 1979, with around 2,000 new applications received monthly, the waiting time increased from around 63 to 84 months in 1976–1977 to around 75 to 96 months.[46] It is crucial to recall that members of the HA, especially Elsie Elliott, had already expressed grave concern about insufficient housing provision to the Waiting List applicants before the shortfall. But the Secretary of Housing was able to pacify the critics by promising that "when the 10-year housing programme gained momentum [in 1976] . . . there would be a substantial amount of

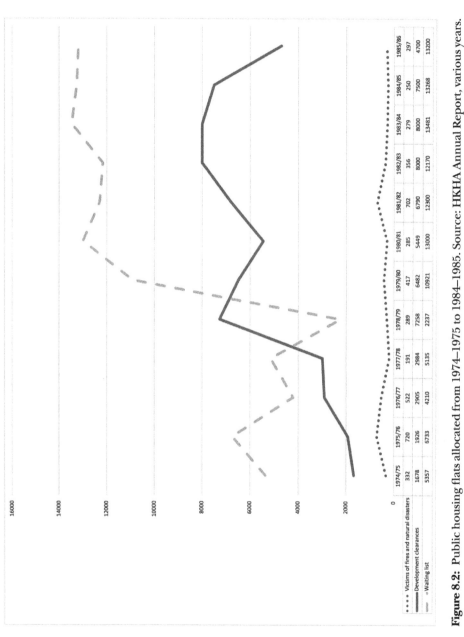

Figure 8.2: Public housing flats allocated from 1974–1975 to 1984–1985. Source: HKHA Annual Report, various years. Graph compiled by the authors.

allocation to the discretionary categories, including the Waiting List applications, after meeting emergency and development needs."[47]

By March 1976, Elliott "was disappointed at the small number of flats available for Waiting List applicants."[48] To her, the HA "should aim at allocating 50% of the available stock of housing to the Waiting List applicants" so that the waiting time could be reduced to around 44 months.[49] She was also discontent that "all cheaper accommodation was given to clearees, thus giving Waiting List applicants no choice but to accept new accommodation at higher rent." Other HA members also recognized that the Waiting List method "provides the principal solution to the general housing problem of people in Hong Kong" and "much of the public sees the Waiting List as a fair and proper method of allocating housing."[50]

It is difficult to give a comprehensive assessment of the scale of the problem. However, circumstantial evidence indicates the situation was acute. The *South China Morning Post* reported in September 1976 that there was an average of 10,000 inquiries "each month about its waiting list, which now contains approximately 100,000 families."[51] In April 1979, the Waiting List increased to 114,103 applicants, as an internal government document from the Management Committee of the HA revealed.[52] Another source provided by the Hongkong Observers—a group of critics—suggested that the Waiting List figure could be as high as "some 150,000," and described the housing situation as a "mess" in November 1979.[53] Interestingly, the Hongkong Observers also suggested that it was due to the government's failure to deal with the housing shortage that "the poor turn[ed] to illegal squatting." Regardless of which figure was closer to the reality, it could reasonably infer that the situation until late 1979 was deteriorating as both figures showed an increase from "approximately 100,000 families" in 1976.

Moreover, it is crucial to notice that the Waiting List figure actually included at least two types of families. On the one side, there were families who applied for rehousing from old resettlement blocks to the newly built and larger flats of public housing; on the other side, there were families who wished to move from the private to public sector housing. Thus, the situation was not only deteriorating but the scale of the problem could be widespread, affecting families who lived in private and public housing sectors. Thus, it was not surprising to find that, in a note submitted by the Secretary for Housing, it acknowledged that, by September 1979, "too little housing, too late" and "low priority [being] given to waiting list applicants" were the frequent points made by critics of the colonial government.[54]

Indeed, the declining proportion of PPH provision to the Waiting List applicants, as Figure 8.2 shows, also changed the perception of the public: the colonial government's reputation as being a benevolent authority was undermined. According to a covert opinion polling report published in August

1976, even though the Ten-Year Housing Program was previously seen as a "benevolent act of Government" when it was announced, the people gradually became "disillusioned" due not only to the long waiting time but also to public housing rent increases since 1974.[55] While the rent policy provided grounds for pressure groups such as the Society for Community Organization to criticize the authority and therefore amplified the growing dissatisfaction, "[f]amilies living in unsatisfactory conditions are also unhappy because they feel that victims of fires, natural disasters, etc. are allowed to jump the queue, when they have been on the waiting list for many years." The middle-income groups were dissatisfied because "they pay substantially more tax . . . and yet they are deliberately excluded from any form of subsidized or aided housing."[56] Low-income groups also held critical attitudes as they considered that the colonial government failed to meet the expected "social and moral obligation to provide cheap housing for families struggling along on meagre incomes." From August 1976 to June 1979, public housing continued to be a major reported concern for the low-income groups, as they saw it as "their best chance of getting good accommodation at a reasonable price."[57]

The contrasting trend of PH provision between the Waiting List applicants and development clearees from 1975 to 1979 also combined to generate a situation: the Waiting List method was seen as a fair and proper method, and receiving housing subsidies could relieve distress created by high private housing rent, but preferential allocation favoring development clearees and fire victims made this method of acquiring housing subsidies "unrealistic."[58] The long waiting time "removes much of the incentive for applying in this way, and encourages many people to squat or to make demands for priority housing by other means." Thus, long waiting time—originating from the discrepancy of eligibility rules for quota allocation—also contributed to the building of new squatter huts. The most troubling issue was that, as the Secretary for Housing had reported, the space for THAs, especially in the urban areas, was already in shortage since 1973, but the colonial government could not undertake a new squatter survey to review "the 1964 deadline" due to the PH shortage.[59] Without a new baseline during a period of proliferation of post-1964 squatter structures, it was inevitable that more occupants would fall into the channel toward the THA in the course of development clearance and squatter control. As the wheel of development clearance trundled, (unfulfilled) demand for THAs would only increase (see Figure 8.3).

By February 1976, it was clear that squatter control was ineffective. To improve, the colonial government instituted new tactics of intensive patrolling in selected areas (i.e., the Intensive Patrol Areas) to contain the situation and regain squatter control (see Chapter 7). Yet, it was also ruled that, in connection to squatter control improvement, "the question of eligibility of domestic squatters for public housing on clearance must also be considered at the

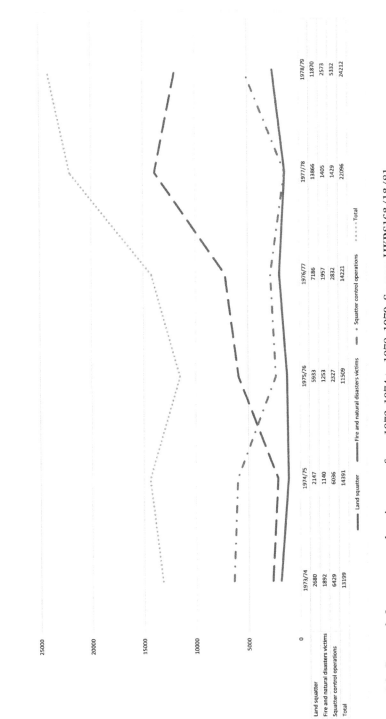

Figure 8.3: Demands for temporary housing areas from 1973–1974 to 1978–1979. Source: HKRS163/13/81.

same time."[60] This prompted the colonial government to review eligibility for housing allocation and, retrospectively, this was arguably the moment when the colonial government could avoid the THA shortage that occurred in 1979. What was needed was to undertake a new survey to include post-1964 illegal structures and confer eligibility for PH to the respective occupant. In this way, rehousing demand generated from post-1964 structures could be channeled to PPH instead of urban THAs. This was reasonable because, without an extension of eligibility, the number of ineligible squatters found in squatter clearances had increased to "almost as great as" the eligible ones. It made clearance more difficult as "it is difficult to get either the squatters or the public [to] accept the justification for this differential treatment for people whose circumstances on the face of it appear much the same."[61] "Even worse, when the structures cleared are operated as shops or workshops" as non-eligible commerce squatters would "get nothing at all" and, to avoid organized resistances in the course of development clearances, "the Housing Department has had to postpone indefinitely some clearances where there are large numbers of unsurveyed structures used as shops or workshops."

If the decision to extend the baseline from 1964 to 1976 were taken at this juncture, then more housing quota would be allocated to cleared squatters and, in so doing, the colonial government could temporarily ease the demand for THAs generated from squatter control and clearance. The extension would "add a future 10,000–12,000 persons, or 2,000 odd extra flats out of the year's total supply of 15,000" and these additional flats could be provided by drawing quotas from other categories.[62] The danger of extending the baseline was threefold, however. First, it would "inflate the rehousing commitment in clearance" as "the public might conclude that the only avenue into public housing is to become a cleared squatter." Second, "any reduction or inadequacy in its quota, at a time when public housing is said to be becoming more plentiful, would be likely to attract unfavourable comment." Third, it meant that people on the Waiting List for public housing had to wait longer. Hence, it would be "difficult to see how the [Housing] Authority's acknowledged policies [of providing affordable housing to all] can be pursued if further obligations are accepted at this stage." In the words of the Director of Home Affairs, "it is because of the plight of people living in tenements paying high rents who have been waiting for public housing for many years that we have to be careful that new squatters and people in licensed areas are not allowed to force their way into public housing years ahead of other people simply by kicking up a big row."[63] Under these rationales, the imperative of promoting loyalty by providing PH to Waiting List applicants intertwined with the necessity to regain squatter control, blocking the extension of survey baseline that might otherwise ease the demand for THAs.

Identity Politics and Reconfiguring the Ratchet of Exclusion

As development clearances proceeded in 1976–1977 without changing the survey baseline, the demand for THAs from land squatters found in clearance surged from 7,186 to 13,866. As the Research and Planning Division of the HA reported in 1977, "a limit [of the provision of the THAs] has nearly been reached" and it had to "increase the quota for turnover of population in existing T.H.A." to ease the demand.[64] The position was further exacerbated by the influx of Chinese illegal immigrants to Hong Kong from 1977, leading to another proliferation of post-1964 squatter structures and therefore another tide of demand.[65] The scale of the illegal immigration could be seen in the increase of arrests of illegal immigrants, growing from 1,200 in 1974 to 8,200 and 89,920 in 1978 and 1979, respectively (Mok 2021, 357). The housing situation in January 1979 was particularly severe due to another slippage, so that "only 10,467 flats [about half of the expected figure] had been completed" and it was apparent that "there will not be sufficient flats available to fill all quotas [set in 1978–1979]."[66] Yet, it was agreed in February 1979 that "a far larger share for the Waiting List" had to be allocated when clearance commitments were reduced.[67]

Scholars have recognized that the government successfully acquired legitimacy and maintained stability during the MacLehose era. King (1973; 1975) argued that the City District Officer Scheme enabled the colonial government to co-opt local elites into the consultative networks and incorporate public opinion into the decision-making process to achieve societal integration by means of what he coined "administrative absorption of politics." Lau (1984) described Hong Kong society as a "minimally integrated socio-political system" that enabled an autonomous colonial regime to govern without significant interference from societal pressure.[68] Scott (1989) argued that increased administrative penetration enabled the colonial government to implement social reforms to shore up popular support. Although they capture some crucial features of colonial governance, they failed to specify the mechanisms that actually translated provision into loyalty. Mok's (2019a; 2019b) thesis of "covert colonialism" demonstrated how the incorporation of public opinion took place through the intelligence apparatus inside the Home Affairs Department, and argued that such penetrative intelligence work enabled the colonial government to be more attentive to changing popular sentiment amongst different social classes and age groups.

However, these works still paid insufficient attention to how the intelligence apparatus could inform and shape the colonial government's discursive practice for maintaining legitimacy.[69] As Wyrtzen (2017; see also Thomas 2005; Bayly 1999) argued, legibility tool kits such as the census enhanced the colonial state's infrastructural power to render subjugated society legible. Classifying

172   *Hong Kong Public and Squatter Housing*

the population into different social units and activating those constructed boundaries such as ethnicities, the colonial state could recast the claims that could possibly be made by dissenters. Indeed, the colonial government was well aware that its policy "could not please everyone" as "there are [problems of] conflicting rights and interests, and the ideal solution from one point of view may be unsatisfactory from another."[70] In such a scenario, the aim "is to be as fair as possible to the greatest number." The underlying rationale was that only in doing so could the colonial government implement policies in "the context of the favourable climate of opinion towards Government so created that unfavourable reactions . . . can be restrained and contained."[71] This could be done by a "variety of methods . . . to ensure that its policies are understood and to show that they are aimed at the best interest of the public," but as the Defence Secretary noted, these methods were crucial "not only in correcting misapprehensions but also in preventing them before [they] arise."[72] In other words, along with the will to know and ascertain the changing public opinion, the colonial government also realised the need to mold the perception of policy.

This molding of the policy perception could be seen in the case of the 1974 Kowloon Bay fire, where "the majority of those who came forward for registration admitted that they had only been in the Colony for not more than 6 months and some had only been here for 2 weeks."[73] A government radio program was prepared to air the "question of immigrants from China and the housing problems created by them." Beginning with the question of "where do all these new immigrants live?" and the answer of squatter areas, the script of the radio program then went on to say

> Housing Department has reported a considerable increase in the building of squatter huts . . . when the squatter control teams come and knock down the illegal hut, the family in it has to be offered a space to build a new legal hut in a licensed area. After that, the new immigrants are in effect on the Hong Kong housing list . . . but how does that affect the rest of Hong Kong's population? Although the Government has a 10-year housing plan, it seems to be taking a bit of time to get into top gear, and 60,000 [i.e. the number of new immigrants in 1973] is about the same number of people who were housed in public housing last year. So, if things go on as they are . . . in a few years' time, practically all the public housing will have to be used to house these new immigrants, leaving precious little for the long-suffering Hong Kong resident. This certainly isn't what most people would describe as social justice . . . these immigrants are now Hong Kong's problem, and it is time the Government did something about them.[74]

Mok (2021, 535) found that the colonial government used particular rhetoric to portray "Chinese illegal immigrants as undesirable elements and external threats to society" and such ways of blaming the illegal immigrants were not only used in the housing domain but also in areas including but not limited to law and order, cultural integration, and other social services. The underlying rationale for using such rhetoric was, as she argued, to manufacture anti-immigrant popular sentiment so that the colonial government could justify the repatriation of Chinese illegal immigrants. She also suggested that the colonial government successfully manufactured anti-immigrant popular sentiment as indicated, on the one hand, in covert opinion polling reports and, on the other hand, seen in the increasing use of anti-immigrant rhetoric in mass media.

Echoing Mok's analysis, the radio script quoted above exemplifies how the colonial government's discursive practice framed the immigrants as a cause of the housing problem. It also provides a valuable vantage point for us to examine closely the underlying logic of the anti-immigrant rhetoric. On the one hand, it concealed the institutional rule of housing allocation that put the Waiting List applicants in an unfavorable position. Instead, the new immigrants were portrayed as the cause undermining the colonial government's efforts in tackling the housing problem. On the other hand, the anti-immigrant narrative amplified the tension between the local residents and the new immigrants by representing the latter as the sole but undeserving beneficiary of the housing resource. Implicitly, it used one's resident status to define which category of people deserved the housing resources. By guiding the local community to perceive the new immigrants as a problem, the script called for remedial actions to protect the local residents. These included forcing the new immigrants to be rehoused to the new towns, which were seen as undesirable areas for public housing allocation, and requesting them to register so that the new immigrants would be on the queue to receive public housing in due course.

One could, therefore, see how the colonial government leveraged the categorical difference between the local residents and the new immigrants to mold the public perception of housing policy. The construction of such categorical difference could be traced back to the colonial authorities' early efforts at border and political control (Mark 2007; Madokoro 2012). But it was not until the 1970s that the colonial government was able to finally reclassify the population by creating the "Hong Kong belonger" notion in 1971 and implementing the "reach-base" policy in 1974, such that place of birth could be seen as distinctive in a city of immigrants (Ku 2004; Mok 2021). The upshot of these changes was that Chinese whose place of birth was not in Hong Kong would be regarded as new immigrants (*xinyimin*), even after registering their identity. They could legally become Hong Kong belongers after satisfying the requirement of having seven years of length of residence, but those who failed to register yet stayed in Hong Kong were categorized as illegal immigrants. In this way, the Hong Kong Chinese were seen as one group (i.e., us) "with the same history and aspirations" while new immigrants (i.e., them) were seen as outsiders and a threat to the local community (Ku 2004, 351).

It should be noted that such bifurcation, until the recent decade, was far from clear-cut. As Lui (2019) observed, the Hong Kong Chinese held a peculiar brand of national consciousness that distinguished allegiance toward a regime in China and the Chinese community sharing a similar cultural lineage. The outcome of this decoupling was an ambivalent subjectification wherein many Chinese in Hong Kong identified with China as an abstract cultural construct but politically distanced themselves from it (Mathews 1997; Chan 2014; Fung 2004; Ma and Fung 2007). At the heart of this ambivalence is a hybrid identity, as the term *Hong Kong* Chinese epitomized. It also connotes a growing host mentality that people came to conceive, identify, and eventually take for grant that Hong Kong was their "home" (Leung 2004, 92; Mathews, Ma, and Lui 2008, 36). A survey done by Lau and Kuan (1988, 178) indicated that a significant proportion of Hong Kong people came to identify themselves as a community different from the mainland Chinese by the mid-1980s. To be sure, Hong Kong Chinese in the 1970s included people born in the mainland but having stayed in Hong Kong for a long time. Whether the recent immigrants could be seen as Hong Kong Chinese, however, depends on a complex web of factors such as class, level of education, and lifestyle (Siu 1996; 1986).[75] Nonetheless, the cultural landscape that the bifurcation created has an enduring impact on the dynamics of postcolonial politics. Without the categorical difference as a schematic building block, it would be difficult for the locals to imagine themselves as a semi-ethnocratic group (Sautman 2004; Ip 2015) and resist the new sovereign ruler's nation-building and regional integration project (e.g., Yew and Kwong 2014; Fong 2017; Fung and Chan 2017; Dupré 2020; Ortmann 2017; Chan 2000).[76]

The question of when and how Hong Kong identification emerged has been addressed by numerous scholars. Some traced it back to the prewar era and argued that the established Chinese elites demonstrated a Hong Kong identification (Carroll 2005; Law 2009). Though insightful, it should be cautioned that the broader rise of Hong Kong identity, as a popular phenomenon, seems to have emerged gradually after the 1962 border crisis and the 1967 riots (Turner 1995; Lee 1998; Tsang 2004). It is at this point the scholarly answers diverged. One approach focuses on societal changes and argues that the emergence of Hong Kong identity was accelerated by the growing economic superiority of Hong Kong over China, made apparent by visits to family in the mainland (Ma 1999). Popular culture and expansion of education also played a significant role in fostering a common linguistic pattern and an image of recent migrants as uncultured, thus facilitating formation of Hong Kong identity among the baby boomers who had no experience of living in China (Ng 2001; Mathews, Ma, and Lui 2008: 36–37). Later, the 1984 Joint

Declaration further intensified the tendency to self-identification as *heunggong-yan*. Another approach underscores the role of the colonial state in citizenship and identity management and, in doing so, provides a more nuanced understanding of the formation of Hong Kong identity as a product of state-society interplay (e.g., Smart and Lui 2009; Leung 2004; Ku 2004; Vickers 2002; Fung 2022; Tong 2016; Ho 2004; Ip 2004; Tse 2004). This approach highlights the state's interest, rationale, and (in)action in propagating a distinctive kind of citizenship in the course of colonial governance. A common theme in these works is that governmental efforts to foster loyalty from Hong Kong people reinforced the trend of the emergence of Hong Kong identity.

Our analysis here echoes the second approach but also goes further by underscoring what Foucault (1991) called the "technologies of power" that the colonial government used to transform the conduct of the subjugated population. Previous works on identity formation/citizenship management argued that these are correlated to housing policies of the colonial government (Erni 2016; Leung 2004; Mathews, Ma, and Lui 2008). For instance, Erni (2016, 334) argues the mechanism of "included-out" in the postcolonial era should be traced back to the earlier history of Hong Kong, where immigration and housing policies combined to generate exclusionism against citizen-subjects who were inside Hong Kong but extremely marginalized.[77] Similar to others (e.g., Law and Lee 2006; Chiu 2002), Erni rightly underscored the role of the host mentality for the government exclusionary tactics, but what remains unclear is the question of why this host mentality would turn defensive or even hostile against the recent immigrants in the late 1970s. It is in this sense that the role of the colonial state's discursive practice and debate about public housing eligibility played a significant but largely neglected role in strengthening the local/migrant distinctions.[78]

Although it is difficult to quantitatively ascertain the discursive influence of these state-disseminated anti-immigrant narratives, archival evidence indicated that the role of the colonial state was indispensable in revaluing these categories. In July 1974, the Director of Immigration wrote to the Director of Information Service to argue for preventing illegal immigrants from entering, so as to "provide a better way of life for our own people."[79] The influx of Chinese migration was conceived as a threat because the incoming immigrants who received low wages could not contribute "by way of taxation," while this additional population would mean additional housing demands and thus stretch the housing program.[80] With limited resources, this meant that "additional demands for housing will remain unsatisfied for many years and immigrants which obtain public housing accommodation can do so only at the expense of the local population." In November, the government Information Service produced an internal note about the effects of Chinese immigration on various social reforms and recorded that popular sentiment was changing as the "community-minded citizen" urged "something should be done to tackle the problem of illegal immigration."[81] In a Directorate meeting later, it was ruled that the note prepared by the Government Information Services should "be used as a guideline for use in response to queries and unavoidable comment."[82]

By October 1975, the local community began to articulate a similar discursive logic echoing the colonial government's discursive practice, and the anti-immigrant sentiment took root in Hong Kong society. "The total size of illegal immigration occasions concern. Many people, including low-income groups, see this as an impediment to the fulfilment of long-term social service projects such as the 10-year housing programme. Rapid growth of population will keep changing the target dates, and deprive them of services they need badly."[83] As people were increasingly critical of the colonial government's efforts in dealing with the housing shortage, they were also becoming anti-immigrant. Those who were paying high rent were particularly "disgruntled that no scheme has been devised to take care of them" as they paid "more tax than the underprivileged groups and are many of them residents since birth who should have a strong claim compared with illegal immigrants."[84]

Tension between local residents and new immigrants emerged, or intensified, in 1976, but it was another tide of Chinese immigrant influx between 1978 and 1980 due to the liberalization policies in China (Siu 1986) that realized the "apparent threats from without" (Mathews, Ma, and Lui 2008, 37). A City District Officer admitted on 4 October 1980 that "[g]overnment has been only too successful in convincing people that the flood of illegal immigrants has caused us grave housing problem" that affordable housing was not coming according to the schedule (Hong Kong Housing Authority 1979, 7).[85] As Governor MacLehose's 1980 annual address revealed, numerous people still had to live in "sub-standard accommodation" by the mid-1980s, implying that the housing program had failed.[86] However, he claimed that this failure was due to the influx of immigrants that created additional demand, and that the colonial government would continue to improve the housing situation. Blaming the illegal immigrants would be misleading because it obscured the colonial government's decision to "intentionally cut back" the housing production in 1973–1974, leading to significant drops in housing production.[87] This "inaccurate publicity" had been adopted because the colonial government was "reluctant to draw public attention to the cut back." Meanwhile, playing up the colonial government's "determination to make every effort to provide better housing for the public at large" could also guard against pressure groups' attacks and public criticism.[88]

Nonetheless, the influx between 1978 and 1980 intensified the local community's "psychological anxiety" where "illegal squatting activities . . . is thought to be directly associated with Chinese immigrants," and "the public believed that the Government will have to provide immigrants with temporary housing at the expense of keeping up the public housing programme," implying that the waiting time for public housing would be increased.[89] As the Secretary for New Territories reported, there was a "hardening" of public opinion that accused "the government . . . of being over-humanitarian" toward the illegal immigrants.[90] The *South China Morning Post* simply asserted, on 2 August 1979, that "illegals [were] jumping homes queue."[91] Against this backdrop of "hardening" of public opinion against illegal immigrants and the decision to deliver a larger share of public housing to the Waiting List applicants made in February 1979, housing allocation intersected with identity politics so that the colonial government decided to exclude the illegal immigrants so as to prevent queue-jumping. Although the need to curb the institutional channel that enabled queue-jumping through emergency rehousing was well acknowledged in early 1974, it was rejected because "discontinu[ing] the provision of housing for disaster victims would be extremely adverse" when "public sympathy is with the victims."[92]

Yet, the cumulative shortage of urban THAs from 1976 to 1979 prompted the colonial government to reevaluate the situation, leading to the reconfiguration of the ratchet of exclusion to exclude the new arrivals from receiving PH flats in the course of emergency rehousing. On 13 July 1979, the Housing Branch submitted a proposal to the Chief Secretary's Committee known as "Revision of Squatter Clearance and Housing Allocation Policy" to recommend imposing a seven year residence requirement in the course of emergency rehousing.[93] The situation was that, "through being caught up in development clearances, squatter control action and natural disasters [new arrivals] are able to gain early entry into new public housing . . . at the expense of longer term residents living in unsatisfactory conditions in private premises or old resettlement estates." In short, the problem was that the new arrivals fall "into the 'bona fide' category" such that they, in sharp contrast with the Waiting List applicants, could take up PH/THA units without income scrutiny.[94] Hence, it was necessary "to devise a means of allocating this [current] stock [of PH flats] in such a way that preference is given to persons of longer residence in Hong Kong."[95] The situation was further complicated by the insufficient stock of urban THAs so that "when the THA is turned-over or cleared [to provide land for new development]" it would not only enable queue-jumping of the new arrivals but also encourage further squatting and building of illegal structures by racketeers.

The situation was so acute that a change of eligibility rules was needed. This was because there were three consecutive squatter fires that happened in Lei Yue Mun, Ma Chai Hang, and On Lok Tsuen in October 1979, and the one at Ma Chai Hang was claimed to be "the worst ever since the disastrous Shek Kip Mei fire" as it destroyed about 630 squatter huts and left 5,263 people homeless.[96] This characterization is inaccurate since the Tai Hang Tung fire of 22 July 1954 left 25,000 homeless and the 1 October 1954 Lei Cheng Uk fire destroyed the homes of 7,000 (Smart 2006, 129, 143). Nonetheless, according to a follow-up paper submitted by the Housing Branch in January 1980, "about 900 of the 3400 victims registered were issued with ID cards after 1976" in the case of the Ma Chai Hang fire and "the majority of the huts destroyed were recently occupied by new immigrants [having no ID cards]."[97] Meanwhile, there were pressure groups organizing boat squatters whose dwellings had been destroyed by a typhoon to press for rehousing, which could reduce the housing quotas available to the Waiting List applicants.[98] Consequently, it was ruled in July 1979 that an eligibility rule of seven years' residence requirement for more than half of the household would be established in the course of emergency resettlement.[99] This new policy was announced publicly in December 1979.[100] For those who failed to meet this additional requirement, they would be resettled to resite areas and THAs in the New Territories. In this way, "allocation policy of new housing [could] be changed in favour of the longer-term residents" and "the same qualification would in the interests of equity be applied to occupants of 1964 surveyed structures."[101]

The imposition of the residence requirement was a practical solution that enabled the government to retain those available housing quotas in 1979 for the Waiting List category, which was deemed important in terms of promoting loyalty. In this way, housing quotas would not be drawn away by other prioritized categories (i.e., the E1 category). Such improvisation could also spare the colonial government's need to alter the allocation institution itself, such that development clearees could still remain as a category having higher priority. Finally, in view of "a more abundant supply" of THAs in the New Territories such as Tuen Mun, the new residence requirement—as a "distant land policy"—could also ease the demand on urban THAs, as clearees would be resettled to the New Territories. Interestingly, this is exactly the policy proposal suggested in the radio program prepared after the 1974 Kowloon Bay fire. In this way, on the one hand, the residence requirement could force the relatively new arrivals (i.e., those who stayed in Hong Kong without the possession of an identity card) to "wait their turn." On the other hand, it would also "reduce the incentive to squat in the main urban areas" and "assist in the build-up of population in the New Towns."[102]

The anti-immigrant sentiment of the late 1970s against new arrivals from China had been crucial because it not only called on the colonial government to intervene to protect local residents, but also opened a window of opportunity for the colonial government to implement exclusionary tactics without being seen as acting against public sympathy. This seems to explain why "public support" was written, with a tick nearby it, on the "Revision of Squatter Clearance and Housing Allocation Policy" paper. The Housing

Branch was very confident that, even though the imposition of the residence requirement could trigger protests, "it is felt that these are far outweighed by the likely support for the [fairness] principle behind." The anti-immigrant sentiment was therefore a societal condition that enabled the reconfiguration of the ratchet of exclusion in the name of the protection of the local community. The contextual change reconciled the practical need for exclusion and the imperative of promoting loyalty. Being responsive to this particular demand for protection, the colonial government could institute the exclusionary tactics without jeopardizing the imperative of promoting loyalty. Indeed, a public opinion polling report indicated that "public response [to the imposition of the residence requirement] was favourable."[103]

The residence requirement enabled the colonial government to reserve a large proportion of housing quotas to the Waiting List category. The intake in 1979–1980 increased by about five times the record in 1978–1979. However, the change of eligibility also created new problems. On the one hand, the application of the distant land policy triggered protests, and pressure groups found fertile ground to organize the masses for more favorable rehousing (e.g., Lui 1984, Chapter 5). However, as Smart and Chui (2006) argued, whether squatter protests could gain concessions was contingent on whether there was popular support through media campaigns. In an increasingly anti-immigrant society, the government could argue that offering concessions to illegal squatters who were recent immigrants could be unfair to the local residents and, in doing so, fend off the challengers by using stigmatization. Still, the protests themselves and their media campaigns could shine light on the government's actions and potentially undermine its credibility.

The change of eligibility rules was an exclusionary tactic that only altered the rehousing proportion but failed to resolve the housing problem stemming from the shortage of affordable housing. The application of a residence requirement pushed the displaced squatters to the New Territories, but the sustainability of this exclusionary tactic depended on the stock of THAs in the New Territories. Without adequate supply of affordable housing, people would squat and thus lead to an increase in demand for squatter huts. Consequently, racketeers would be in a position "to take advantage" and further push the limit of the THA space in New Territories.[104] When there was an indication that the limit was approaching, the colonial government again altered the eligibility rule from "1964 surveyed structure cum the seven year length of residence" to "1976 surveyed structure cum 15 years length of residence" for the majority of the adult family members in January 1981, so as to swing demand from THA in New Territories to PH/THA in urban areas.[105]

Unexpected numbers of fire incidents in 1981 further exacerbated the situation and forced the colonial government to quietly lower the length of residence requirement to 10 years.[106] This was followed by another attempt to lower the residence requirement from 10 to seven years, as mentioned by the Director of Housing, David Ford, during an internal meeting on 12 April 1984.[107] On the same occasion, Ford also raised the possibility to apply "income eligibility criteria to the emergency and compulsory categories" and for those unable to meet the additional income eligibility rule, they "would be offered a removal allowance" that could be "used as a deposit to purchase H[ome] O[wnership] S[cheme] flat." In doing so, the measure could have "the advantage of limiting rental housing only to those satisfying the income criteria" but it could be "controversial" and generate "strong reaction from affected residents." Even so, the colonial government was able to gradually introduce these new measures. The seven years' residence requirement was made effective on 6 April 1989.[108] Applying income eligibility to clearees was made effective, but not until September 1998.[109] In a nutshell, exclusivity became prominent in the government's policy toward squatter settlement, and the imposition of residence rule could be considered as a formative point of the process where a new regulatory regime would later emerge (see Chapter 10; Smart 2001).

These consecutive attempts of changing the eligibility rules were ways to adjust the degree of exclusion. The colonial government could thus retain a sufficient stock of public housing units for rehousing squatters and intaking Waiting List applicants. The rich tenant policy could be seen as an extension of the exclusionary trend that began since the late 1970s. The "rich tenants" issue was more about whether "well-off public housing tenants" could continue to receive government subsidy.[110] It was decided that "the objective of public housing programme was to assist those in need so that they would benefit as a result" and thereby "enhance social stability." Ford's rationale was that, given the scale of the public housing shortage, it would be "unfair" to those on the Waiting List to suffer while tenants, capable to satisfy housing need in the private sector, could continue to benefit from "subsidized accommodation." In short, the policy was to set up a measure so that undeserving tenants could be identified and unfairness corrected. However, it was also considered that "eviction of over-income tenants would be politically unacceptable and impractical to apply." After the public consultation in 1985, the rich tenant policy was fully adopted by the colonial government in 1992 to subject tenants having 10 years or more tenancy to regular household income scrutiny. The result of this decision was that although clearees were free of the income limit on initial clearance, they would be equally subject to it after 10 years' tenancy. This generated a delayed equal treatment with those accessing public housing through the Waiting List while avoiding adding difficulties to the clearance process. A Subsidy Income Limit was set such that tenants whose household income exceeded the limit had to pay a higher level of rent and, after 1993, those who were found owning assets could be evicted from subsidized accommodation (see Lau 2003, 183–184, 186).

Hong Kong Identity and Squatter Exclusion   181

To be sure, the expression of the "rich tenants" issue was different from the queue-jumping of clearees. However, both are functionally equivalent: the colonial government targeted and excluded undeserving categories of people so that they could be screened out to ensure sufficient public housing stock be retained for those on the Waiting List. Nonetheless, these exclusionary efforts failed to improve the overall situation. The Secretary for Housing revealed on 4 March 1982 that there was an "extreme urgency of the present situation" and that THA space in both New Territories and urban areas was insufficient.[111] An extension of the baseline from 1976 to 1982 was then proposed so that the colonial government could again alter the rehousing proportion.[112] In the meantime, it was apparent that the solution to the squatter problem would mean more than changing rehousing proportions through exclusion. It entailed a more radical approach that could contain pressure generated from rehousing.

Conclusion

This chapter demonstrated how the issue of identity and housing supply/demand imbalances interacted and traced how the government preference for long-term residents came into being. The identity issue is clearly relevant and must be considered as a part of a fuller and more complete explanation of the gradual demise of squatter housing in Hong Kong. It not only complements the supply and demand imbalance explanation but accounts in large part for why the imbalances developed in the first place. It demonstrates that avoiding further deterioration of the Waiting List performance, which was instrumental for the imperative of promoting loyalty, blocked the colonial government's attempt to correct the supply/demand imbalances in 1976. After that, the colonial government endeavored to provide greater housing quotas to the Waiting List category, which echoed the imperative of promoting loyalty.

Subsequent parts of this chapter illustrated how the colonial government took advantage of the emergence of the Hong Kong identity. As Mathews, Ma, and Lui (2008, 37) observed, the Hong Kong Chinese "had become defensive and self-protective" and demanded government protection against the backdrop of the influx of Chinese immigrants in the late 1970s. Scott (1989, 157–158) also observes a similar change of social ethos and the importance of forcing "new immigrants from China to take their place in the [housing] queue" for maintaining government legitimacy. Yet, Scott failed to specify why and how this change happened. As we argued, tension between local residents and new immigrants and the anti-immigrant sentiment must be considered as, at least in significant degree, outcomes of the quota allocation and the colonial government's effort in molding policy perception. The former generated conflicts, the latter amplified the tension by framing the recent immigrants as the cause that undermined the governmental effort in tackling the housing problem. This constituted a protection demand for the long-term residents in receiving housing subsidies. It also created an opportunity that enabled the colonial government to selectively exclude the recent immigrant squatters to ease the housing supply/demand imbalances. In other words, the formation of Hong Kong identity, as an outcome of promoting loyalty, in turn served as a societal condition that enabled state exclusionary tactics.

While the use of exclusionary tactics could temporarily mitigate the pressure in the urban areas by forcing squatters who failed to meet the residence requirement to move to the New Territories, it failed to improve the overall situation. The crux of the matter was still the supply of affordable housing, and this had much to do with the overall supply of PPH. This was clearly shown in 1982 when the stock of THA space in both New Territories and urban areas became insufficient. It was apparent to the colonial government that a more radical approach had to be adopted to contain the squatter problem. New policy thinking thus emerged in the early 1980s. To "get on the top of squatting and the racketeering associated with it . . . and to reduce the risk of large scale squatter fires," the colonial government would have to institute more effective squatter control, a stronger deterrence against racketeering, and an improvement of squatter area administration that could guard against fire risks.[113] The first two approaches seem reasonable because, as discussed before, what Governor MacLehose had in mind in 1972 was to "mop up squatter areas." Thus, effective squatter control and deterrence against racketeering would remove the incentive to build and occupy a squatter hut. But when it comes to the improvement of squatter area administration, the idea was no longer that straightforward. Given that squatter areas would eventually be gone, what was the point of improving them? How did the improvement of squatter area administration contribute to the formalization process? If the aim of improving the squatter areas was to reduce the risk of squatter fires, which one could see throughout the 1970s, then what explained the scheme's belatedness? These are the questions for the next chapter.

9

Squatter Area Improvement

> Despotism is a legitimate mode of government in dealing with barbarians, provided the end be their improvement, and the means justified by actually effecting that end.
>
> —John Stuart Mill, *On Liberty, Utilitarianism and Other Essays* (2015[1859], 13)

Introduction

This chapter has three objectives. First, it offers a description of one of the main paths to formalization in Hong Kong: Squatter Area Improvement (SAI). This emphasizes formalizing the infrastructure, while leaving the legal status of the dwellings unchanged. Second, it considers another possible explanation for formalization: the colonial desire to improve problematic spaces and places. More generally, this is related to what James Scott (1998) describes as "seeing like a state," making its territory visible and accountable through "rational engineering of all aspects of social life," with an assumption that this would "improve the human condition" (Scott 1998, 88). For rulers and officials that he considers to be "high modernists," an "efficient, rationally organized city, village, or farm was a city that looked regimented and orderly in a geometrical sense" (16). As we will see, the problem with this explanation lies in the belatedness with which such desires took hold in Hong Kong, and in squatter areas (for Singapore, see Loh 2009b and Chapter 11), and the need to offer further reasons for why it took place at the time that it did. The third objective is to use the case of Squatter Area Improvement to consider the strengths of some of the other plausible explanations posited in previous chapters.

Long before there was a squatter area improvement program in Hong Kong, squatter areas (and squatters) were seen as in dire need of improvement, both by London and in Hong Kong's Government House. The most desired way to improve these areas was to demolish them completely and permanently and replace them with something legally ordered. There were various constraints to this, particularly on land that was difficult to develop, as discussed in the last three chapters. Improvement in the absence, or delay, of demolition became a more attractive alternative after other solutions to the squatter problem failed, sometimes repeatedly. At the least, squatter improvement could help avert London's gaze and criticism from the squatter problem. It would be seen as doing something positive, with the advantage of being photogenic, even amenable to ribbon-cuttings. Government would be addressing the problem, and the evidence could be presented in Annual Reports, with pictures of stabilized slopes, improved roads and water supply for fire department access, and new blocks of latrines. In Hong Kong, improvement like this was projected to be only temporary, for the time being and without continuing commitments. Without a definite timeframe for persistence, though, the value of infrastructure spending in tolerated squatter areas could not be adequately calculated, making them riskier and less attractive investments. Therein may lie part of the answer to why the program had such a short life (1982–1984), although with a longer gestation and afterlife, since long delays in clearance after 1984 prolonged the need for infrastructural improvements.

The British colonial enterprise itself (as with others) was generally presented as helping to improve places where the natives had failed to do so. As Tania Li (2007, 5) explains, the "will to improve" involves trusteeship, the effort, real or putative, to develop the capacities of another. The "claim to expertise in optimizing the lives of others is a claim to power." Yet, in colonial Hong Kong's squatter areas, improvement risked undermining progress elsewhere in the urban landscape, as scarce resources,[1] including the land on which squatter areas were built, were diverted from permanent housing and other elements of the built environment. Future squatting might also be encouraged. In the limited form adopted in Hong Kong—squatter upgrading without the provision of tenure security to the occupants—improvement could only be temporary, a liminal state between "wild" squatter areas and modern legal buildings and districts. To translate the will to improve into explicit programs requires identifying deficiencies that need to be rectified, which was readily done for the squatter problem. More difficult is the practice of "rendering a problem technical," turning it through definitions and collecting information into a situation that is not only problematic, but which can be addressed with the resources available to intervention agents (Li 2007, 7). A program of intervention is not the straightforward product of a will to improve but is rather "situated within a heterogeneous assemblage," a contingent set of practices and institutions that emerge from contentious pasts and presents. Rather than following a grand plan, they are usually "pulled together from an existing repertoire, a matter of habit, accretion, and bricolage" (Li 2007, 6). This clearly can apply to the emergence of the SOS. Can we explain the adoption of the Squatter Area Improvement (SAI) Programme as resulting from efforts to render technical vulnerable slopes and settlements, to fix the squatter areas through infrastructural improvements? If this explains the adoption of the SAI, how should we account for its subsequent rapid rejection?

Improvement is hard to criticize as a goal, even if the consequences are often disastrous. At the same time, many people, including squatters, have a will to be improved and thus support interventions in hope of a more "normal" life (Jansen 2014). For example, a 1983 survey of residents in the first two SAI pilot projects found that about two-thirds wanted legal electricity, 52% improved sanitation, and 48% legal water supply (Leung 1983). Tania Li (2007, 2) suggests that a central feature of *programming* (the design and implementation of programs to try and improve something) is "the requirement to frame problems in terms amenable to technical solutions. Programmers must screen out refractory processes to circumscribe an arena of intervention in which calculations can be applied." This is reminiscent of Stanley Milgram's (1970) argument about "urban overload," where overstimulation requires people to selectively attend to only parts of the situation and screen out the rest. Both programmer and urbanite tend to focus on what is useful for them. Programmers, in particular, need to focus on those aspects of a "problem" that appear amenable to being changed: no room is provided for utopian proposals, so practicality focuses attention on certain kinds of actions and problems rather than others.

In the context of the trajectories traced in this book, improvement without tenure change offered another option to the dominant response to the squatter problem, which was demolition, generally combined with some varieties of resettlement after 1952. In terms of Governor Trench's two alternatives, infrastructural improvement first avoided the massive expenditures required for resettling all squatters. Second, it tamed the more radical suggestion of giving title, or even time-limited licenses, to squatters, which could cause problems for the property revenue-dependent government and economy (Smart and Lee 2003). Instead of regularizing squatter structures, SAI would concentrate on bringing the infrastructure into greater conformity with the formal system, reducing the squalor that drew the attention of London to the squatter situation, while offering the hope of reduction in the frequency and severity of fires and landslides, thereby reducing demand for temporary housing. As Chapter 6 described, the question of "squalid" squatter areas had been broached in the period between Edward Heath's expression of concern about the squatter situation and Governor Trench's suggestion of two alternative solutions. The SAI can trace its genesis back to this 1970 policy mangle.

The minutes of the Housing Board meeting held on 24 August 1970 had an agenda item on "analysis of squatter areas," which addressed Housing Board Papers No. 36 and 39, including the topic of environmental conditions. Squatter areas were ranked by environmental standards, an assessment that was "subjective and reflects mainly sanitary conditions in each area." They were also ranked on the number of water standpipes and latrines, whether they had electricity supply, and whether they were willing to accept resettlement.[2] A discussion on the same topic on 1 June 1970 reported Father Fergus Cronin saying that his "main concern was with people living in sub-human conditions and also to make it possible for squatters who wanted to move to improve on their housing conditions. He was not convinced that it would be right to move squatters simply because they were squatters if their housing was reasonable even if temporary." The Chairman, K. A. Watson, said that there were clearly a "wide range of squatters areas and of types of squatter accommodation varying from very bad to quite good." Mr. Whitelegge, Deputy District Commissioner NT, raised the issue of "just how far one was justified in forcing better housing conditions on people who would be quite happy if left alone."[3]

After discussion of Housing Board Paper No. 45, which reported on the same topic, the Housing Board concluded "that three squatter areas on Hong Kong Island and one squatter area in Kowloon are considered to be of such a poor environmental standard as to be incapable of amelioration . . . In some areas there is a health as well as a fire hazard. The Board considers that these squatter areas are so repugnant to the public conscience that they ought to be cleared and therefore suggests that a start should be made with the worst squatter areas."[4] However, this pilot program involved identifying settlements on land not planned for development, and clearing them, so that their improvement involved their disappearance. The problem, though, was that in the absence of development, the space that was opened up would be a continual attraction for resquatting. Improvement by demolition and resettlement created new costs of surveillance and control if no immediate use for the land existed.

The 1970 Housing Board Report proposed rehousing 30,000 squatters through non-development clearances. The 1971 Housing Board Annual Report modified this plan with a two-part "statement of aims." First, the "identification and clearance of squatter areas where living conditions were bad" (repeatedly described in the files as "squalid"). Second, "consideration of the future of other squatter areas where conditions are not so bad." These analyses distinguished different settlements on the basis of how badly they needed improvement. While this influenced the pilot clearance of four settlements diagnosed as particularly squalid, the larger influence came from the Commissioner for Resettlement's proposal of the third approach to London's challenge.

To briefly summarize our account in Chapter 6, the Resettlement Department proffered this third approach, framed as less ambitious but more realistic than either resettling all squatters or changing the tenure of squatter structures. This would involve expanding an existing scheme, introduced in NT squatter areas in 1968, of minor improvements through Local Public

Works "votes"; that is, budget lines. This scheme was an "experiment" severely limited by the rules and by the size of the budget, at that time only $100,000 a year. In the Local Public Works model, improvements were only carried out where the squatters could perform the job themselves or contribute toward payment for labor and supervision charges. Government contribution was limited to providing construction materials.

Considerable discussion on squatter improvement in the early months after the Colonial Secretary's 11 November 1970 letter proposed improvement along with some kind of tenure change, perhaps on the model of permits and licenses given in the NT. But pursuit of this approach in the urban areas was soon abandoned (see Chapter 6). Afterward, the discussion continued primarily on the topic of improvement without titling or other change in tenure. The Director of Public Works advised against a "hard and fast policy" since he thought "none of the three proposals provides a solution in itself."[5] He suggested an approach addressed individually to specific areas: conditions might be "so bad as to call for clearance with no question of any attempt to improve." Other areas had conditions amenable to improvement but advised that it be limited, since there is "little hope of making squatter structures technically acceptable"; any such attempt would misspend public money. The Director suggested the key amenities to be provided: water for drinking and firefighting; precautions against fire; preventing erosion; latrines; and area lighting. This foreshadowed the actual course of improvement in the 1970s, but mostly through piecemeal programs dealing with specific kinds of infrastructure separately until 1982.

The Secretary for Home Affairs argued in June 1971 for improvement as preferable to non-development clearances, from the perspective of appreciating the positive contributions of squatting (see Chapter 6).[6] Eight years later, similar arguments continued to be advanced in important policy venues. A 1979 Memorandum for the Executive Council argued that:

> previous assessments of the housing situation have neglected the role played by the temporary sector in providing housing for the people of Hong Kong. The assumption has been that housing built of temporary materials is a short-term unsatisfactory housing solution which has to be replaced as early as possible. To many households, however, housing of this type can be quite acceptable, since it is usually unshared, at nil or low rent, and often combine advantages of location and sometimes amenity over permanent housing.[7]

Other documents promoted the revival of resite areas as a temporary solution during the housing challenges intensified by the record influx of 276,363 people from China in 1978 and 1979, and the squatter area disasters of 1981 and 1982 (see Chapter 8).

Earlier, though, Housing Board Paper No. 75 on "improvement of squatter areas," drafted on 1 April 1973, stated that the adoption of the Ten-Year

Housing Target Programme overtook these recommendations for improvement, since it proposed "a complete solution to the squatter problem," leaving the Housing Board "only to consider if, in light of the newly recommended 'list of categories', any further consideration need be given for recommendations made regarding the occupants of the so called 'squalid squatter areas.'"[8] If all squatter and licensed areas were to be eliminated within 10 years, expenditure on improvements would seem wasteful unless urgently necessary. Yet if areas were dangerous and excessively insalubrious, would not clearance, even in the absence of development plans, seem to be more sensible? Despite this position, various improvements did take place throughout the 1970s. One set of reasons derives from the failures of the Ten-Year Housing Programme; if it had ever been believed that the complete end to the squatter problem could be achieved by 1983, this belief was dashed by the resilience of new squatting, particularly when illegal migration surged.

Specific programs of improvement were advanced during the 1970s, particularly electrification and safety improvements, including fire watch teams. Each strand of legal infrastructure provision is complicated, and not apparently central to the course of improvement as an alternative pathway to formalization, so we restrict our account of them to indicative examples and interesting aspects that emerge from the records.

One intriguing issue concerned unauthorized wiring at Chai Wan Resettlement Estate, on Hong Kong Island. Fortunately, there are photographs in the file on the problem that help visualize the remarkable situation (Figure 9.1).

These wires stretched from individual dwellings in the Estate to the licensed area and squatter area across the road. The number of illegal wires were calculated as 310 crossing Chai Wan Road, plus 140 between telephone poles, and 90 to hawker stalls. The situation emerged as a problem that had to be dealt with when a letter was sent to the City District Commissioner by the Hongkong Electric Company on 30 September 1972, following up on a prior complaint. They stated that the "connections present an unacceptable hazard to the public and to our street lighting maintenance engineers." The Hong Kong Telephone Company had also complained of the danger to their maintenance staff and equipment. The situation was complicated because only the second phase of the Estate was serviced by the Hongkong Electric Company, while the first 15 blocks were under direct government control.

> [Prior] experience at Chai Wan has shown that unless the squatter huts and the unauthorised wires are completely removed at the time of disconnection, they will be reconnected soon after any inspection by us has been completed. Our consumers simply have to disconnect the unauthorised wire from the power sockets to restore their installation to a condition which would have to be accepted by us. We do not wish to make supplies available to the squatter

Squatter Area Improvement

Figure 9.1: Illegal electrical wiring, Chai Wan. Source: HKRS934/9/38.

area as it now stands, as many of the structures themselves and their haphazard locations make them unsafe for an electrical installation to be put in.[9]

But if government paid for all costs, they would be prepared to provide supply, under "certain conditions." They also wanted government to apply strict control "to prevent reconnections of unauthorised wires being made."[10] The Hong Kong Telephone Company threated to cut their services unless the problem was resolved. At a meeting on the issue on 9 October 1972, Fire Services representatives "expressed extreme dissatisfaction with the situation." They stressed that not only did a "bad fire hazard exist but that the wiring would make it very difficult to use life saving equipment in the event of a fire. Thirty-one electrical fires had been recorded in the area in the last eighteen months; the existence of the illegal wiring being a major factor." The bus company had also lodged serious complaints. Superintendent Li of the Police commented that "it could be argued that it was morally wrong to cut a supply which Government had, by its inaction, permitted to exist for a considerable time. He considered that the possibility of a public disorder existed if precipitate action was taken." It was agreed that since the area would not be cleared until April 1973, earlier action had to be taken. Coordinated action to remove the wiring was agreed, as well as following up with Hongkong Electric Company to provide legal electricity.[11] After some delays, the Electric Company agreed to supply the licensed and squatter areas, although they reminded government that this would be uneconomical for them. The City District Commissioner commented that "the distinct possibility of the Chai Wan Resident's Association installing generators to provide a private supply of electricity to the area has at last galvanized Hong Kong Electric Co. into action. The Company has secured clearance from Crown land to undertake" the work. The wiring removal was finally concluded on 18 December 1972 "without any opposition or trouble."[12]

Tensions between private utility suppliers seeking profits and the government seeking improvements at minimal cost to themselves continued throughout the 1970s. A Working Party on Electrification in Squatter Areas was established in November 1975. Its importance is made clear by a published Report on Squatter Area Improvements in 1982, which stated that "[m]any of the principles adopted by the [SAI] Division owe their origin to [their] excellent report."[13] The Working Party developed a pilot scheme; one of the first issues they had to deal with was that the law obliged electrical companies to "exercise all due precautions to ensure safety . . . these regulations have deterred the supply companies to provide a legal source of electricity to structurally unsound huts in squatter areas." In order to "overcome this problem of criminal liability, the Attorney General advised that a new set of regulations . . . should be made for supplying power."[14] To protect the companies, the law was amended, and a procedure developed that a squatter area which "has been designated by the Secretary for Housing as a 'special area' for legal power supply will be subject to . . . special regulations . . . whereby power companies will be relieved of the criminal liability incurred in supplying structurally unsound huts in squatter areas." The memo to the Executive Council emphasized that "[t]here has recently been a growing unease about the lack of a properly organised electricity supply in squatter areas, and the dangers to life arising from the present widespread illegal connections. This paper sets out proposals for providing a legal, metered supply into such areas in a practical way which requires the active participation of the squatter-hut consumers."[15]

Connecting individual squatter structures to the newly installed system was a difficult task, and the City District Office and the Housing Department each tried to leave the responsibility to the other.

> [While the] ideal solution would be for the company to provide and control all wiring within the squatter area up to the consumer's structure (with the meter in the structure), but in practice this would require an excessive amount of subsequent supervision by the company, to disconnect illegal connections and to require defective wires etc. to be replaced . . . Because of the difficulty of effective control inside the squatter areas, the consumers will be expected to maintain their wiring systems on their own initiative.[16]

Rather than having the utilities install connections to dwellings, procedures for authorizing other companies to do the work were established, with concerns for both the costs to the squatters, and the danger of corruption. All of this shows the complexity of formalizing infrastructure while maintaining the informal status of the structures. It also reveals the complications created by having a private company involved that needs to protect itself from risks, both legal and of unpredictable, ongoing maintenance costs.

Since the adopted model required the participation of squatters, Home Affairs was concerned about the amount of work that would be carried out by City District Officers and District Officers (in the NT); it preferred that the Housing Department be responsible for the required liaison and supervision. The process still ended up with heavy involvement by City District Officers. Effective participation "by local villagers was of vital importance in the pilot scheme. Villagers as a whole had to make applications, appoint contractors to install their wiring, arrange for postal deliveries of electricity bills and oversee the subsequent maintenance of the consumers' installations."[17] A local Mutual Aid Committee had to be organized by the CDO if it did not already exist. A compromise on subsequent work resulted in the creation of an Implementation Subcommittee, involving the CDO, HD and the power company. Given the hilly site, an airlift of bulky equipment by the Royal Air Force was required. However, City District Officers and District Officers would still be the "prime movers" and "responsible for the coordination of such schemes and for liaison with all concerned."[18] As late as 1978, however, the CDO reported that "they have encountered difficulty in liaising with both the Squatter Control Section and Hongkong Electric; the latter two did not appear to be fully briefed on what role they were expected to play."[19]

Electrification was pursued steadily, but not as quickly as the power companies desired. Sir Lawrence Kadoorie, Chairman, China Light & Power Co. wrote to the Chief Secretary, Jack Cater, on 30 June 1981, on concerns about electricity in squatter areas. Since 1976, "electricity has been afforded to 4,900 families in nineteen areas. However, there are at present at least twenty-four areas (representing some 11,500 families), which have not been provided with legal electricity supplies and where the squatter population resorts to theft in order to obtain supplies."[20] The areas with electricity through "theft" were of concern because of "the high risk of fire and danger to the general public arising from the substandard and illegal connections used to abstract power from the Company's network"; these "unauthorised connections frequently result in loss of supply to the Company's legal consumers in the general areas," and China Light "loses significant revenue each year due to theft of electricity," an estimated $300,000 a month. Frequent exercises in conjunction with the Hong Kong Police to remove illegal connections "had little effect because within a few days the connections are replaced." Kadoorie and his colleagues held the view that the only real solution to the problem is to expedite the provision of legal electricity supplies to squatter areas . . . the designation of such areas by Government has not proceeded as quickly as we would have wished." He felt that "a more drastic solution is required – particularly as it would appear that squatter areas will be with us for a long time. My proposal is, in essence, that the requirement for designation is discontinued and that China Light is permitted to supply squatter areas . . . as and when the requirement for supply arises.[21]

The Secretary for Home Affairs sent a memo to the Secretary for Housing on this issue. He found that 58 of 138 squatter areas (around 60% of the squatter population) were covered by the electrification scheme and had been or would be provided with legal electricity supply. Another 44 areas (10% of the squatter population) not covered by the scheme were considered "adequate" in electricity supply in the 1980 Survey, leaving 36 areas with 30% of the population in which it was considered inadequate or non-existent. He found the last group "particularly worrying. To prevent these deprived areas from turning into 'trouble spots', of illegal tapping, among other things, you may wish to consider including them in the electrification scheme" and setting target completion dates for each.[22]

The City District Officer for Sham Shui Po commented on China Light's proposal, agreeing that to dispense with formal designation (gazetting) would speed things up; but it was not practical to simply let things proceed independently. There were necessary steps that could not be skipped: confirming the expected life of the squatter area to ensure financial viability; the geotechnical office had to confirm the stability of slopes and whether it would be affected by proposed works; and making available a site for a meter room, perhaps through a clearance. Additionally, "initiative for legal electricity supply comes from the residents (usually the Mutual Aid Committee, sometimes on our instigation), and it is the City District Office that leads the effort and coordinates Government department action. This action is not going to change, even if the China Light is allowed to supply squatter areas without going through gazetting."[23]

Firebreaks, and other fire prevention measures, were one of the longest standing improvements implemented in squatter areas. After a large fire on 11 January 1950 in Kowloon City left over 17,000 people homeless, the Fire Brigade Chief Officer warned of a possible holocaust resulting from squatter fires and called for an expenditure of HK$245,990 to extend water mains, provide fire hydrants and water storage, extend firebreaks through squatter areas, and control dangerous industrial premises and goods. The Colonial Secretary's response was that "fire precautions are getting a little out of hand" and "[i]f a large number of them were burnt down we should probably have to take steps to assist the occupants in re-provisioning themselves, but we can hardly overlook the fact that the effect would be no bad thing politically." The

Financial Secretary concurred, seeing it as "crazy" to spend so much money on protecting "structures that are a perfect curse from every point of view and which we are anxious to eliminate. We should concentrate on fire breaks and lanes" (Smart 2006, 66). This concentration on creating open spaces, in hope that fires would not jump over them and so limit the damage, persisted for decades and was still a key part of the SAI Programme.

A report on the issue by the Director of Housing on 20 November 1979 noted that experience had found that "to be effective fire breaks of about 50 ft. are needed for approximately every 100 ft. of squatter hut concentration. The figures might vary of course with the terrain it might be possible to reduce the break to about 30 ft . . . the 20 ft. break provided by the road at Ma Chai Hang proved to be no barrier to the fire spread."[24] In plans for five squatter areas, the estimate of the number of residents to be cleared was over 15,000, which would require 3,400 PH flats, "about half of the houses for a whole year's development clearance program." For example, for the firebreak program in Tai Hom Village in Diamond Hill, with 8,570 structures, 1,998 would be cleared (23%), and out of a population of 35,236, 24% would be cleared (8,633).

The cost of creating these firebreaks can "be measured in terms of the cost of development clearances that would have to be postponed, as it would be necessary to utilize a large portion of the . . . Development Clearance housing quota each year to create them." The cost also included maintaining control after the firebreaks are created. It would be "essential to incorporate the breaks into new Intensive Patrol Areas or they would very quickly be reoccupied by other squatters. Present squatter control policy would not permit this" because of the expenditure necessary to keep the breaks clear, leading to "the conclusion that desirable though the breaks are it is a risk we simply have to take unless we are prepared to invest a very considerable amount of housing and financial resources at the expense of other development."[25] Firebreak creation proceeded on an ad hoc basis when appropriate circumstances presented themselves, such as after fires, but often on a scale too small to prevent the fires that bedeviled the temporary housing demand in 1981 (Chapter 7).

Attitudes toward other prevention measures, including the provision of water supplies, changed over the decades. In 1950, the Social Welfare Officer supported only firebreaks, noting that "no official encouragement should be given to the formation of local voluntary fire-fighting units in any non-tolerated squatter area. To do otherwise would be to encourage the squatters to count on and to trade on official recognition of their 'rights'" (Smart 2006, 67).[26] By 1979, policy had moved to the encouragement of fire watch teams in squatter areas. As part of a Fire Prevention campaign, a meeting on 18 July 1978 agreed that the most suitable targets for them would be squatter areas.[27] By 1979 there were 15 teams, with plans for another 11. Team members were expected to patrol areas in their spare time to ensure fire equipment in proper condition and keep fire escape routes clear from obstruction. In case of a small fire, they would hopefully "keep it from spreading before the arrival of Fire Services personnel."[28]

In a meeting on fire prevention held on 24 October 1979, the Director of Fire Services noted that "[t]he provision of rudimentary fire lanes and the use of tin sheets on the outside of the structures had helped but access to the fire scene continued to be a problem . . . if fire hydrants, access roads and fire breaks were provided in these areas, his department's problems would be reduced . . . it was important to create fire breaks and sub-divide large squatter areas to reduce the risk of fires spreading." The Assistant Director of Housing responded that the "creation of such fire breaks would necessitate rehousing the people affected and this would strain public housing resources." The Director of Fire Services countered that "if fires broke out and large numbers of people were rendered homeless, as in the case of recent fires, this would also have a serious effect on the housing programme."[29]

Fire watch teams received more emphasis in the absence of serious expansion of firebreak efforts, but these were plagued by disagreements and minimal provision of resources. Multiple memos circulated around who was responsible for recharging fire extinguishers provided to the teams, for example. Because the Fire Services Department refused to accept the responsibility, the Home Affairs Department and the New Territories Administration had "no other alternative but to agree at the Fire Prevention Campaign Publicity Working Group meeting on 31 August 1979 to take on the work."[30]

In Diamond Hill in the early 1980s, several fire watch teams were fairly active, partly due to the NGO Neighbourhood Advice/Action Committee promoting them. Another factor was the policy change in 1979 that squatter fire victims were only eligible for rehousing in the New Territories. This resulted in fear that a fire would displace them before a clearance could occur, since in the latter case they would be rehoused in the urban areas. Smart was told by several residents that they thought that the frequent fires at the time were being caused by government arson, since this would reduce their rehousing commitments, given the severe shortage of urban PPH and TH. Simultaneously, of course, the government speculated that squatters were themselves the authors of the fires to obtain rehousing.

After a decade of experimentation, the Squatter Area Improvement Division was established within the Housing Department in late 1981 (Leung 1983). In September 1982, ExCo decided that "since it was unlikely that major squatter concentrations would be cleared in the next few years, measures were being taken to introduce fire and landslip safety measures and certain basic improvements in squatter areas."[31] Yet, only two years later, the decision was made to "run down" the program over five years and divert the funds to

Squatter Area Improvement 195

support a plan to clear all urban squatters and resettle them in accordance with their eligibility, which had become more generous after 1982.

Discussions within the Working Group on SAI, and submissions to and comments on the Working Group, reveal some of the tensions involved around the improvement alternative for the squatter problem. Improvement is hard to criticize as a goal in general, even if the consequences can be disastrous. Yet, even if not criticized explicitly, expenditures on it can be sidelined because of problems of practicality. In 1982, a minute on the SAI Programme, then still under discussion, states that "[t]he ExCo Paper says little that we do not know already. It does however surprise me slightly in that it gives a general impression that the improvement programme is a foregone conclusion – very little argument is put forward why Government should undertake to spend such a large amount of money on people who are, after all, illegally occupying Crown land."[32]

However, not improving had costs as well. The District Officer of Wong Tai Sin—where Smart's field site, Diamond Hill, was located—argued that "many pockets of squatters will remain, where it would be expensive to provide basic services. Notwithstanding the Housing Department's current position . . . that clearance rates a higher priority than improvement, nonetheless, the work of the Squatter Area Improvements Division has created expectations of improved services that are difficult to refuse. It would seem desirable in some cases at least to clear a whole village where a major part is required for development."[33] This note reveals a conflict between economizing on resources and investment in improvements. Complete clearance of a village could be seen as a better option because of the expectations of squatters themselves.

One discussion paper prepared for the Interdepartmental Working Group provides insights into thinking about costs and benefits. It began with estimates of the "current costs of providing services to squatter areas, the cost of inefficient use of resources in these areas, and the cost of squatter fires." This recognized that the status quo also involved substantial costs, which could "be partially offset against the costs of a Squatter Area Improvements programme if the latter is approved." The calculations are more complex than this, though, since "in practise, there will be scant savings as resources channelled by departments into squatter works would be legitimately deployed elsewhere, reabsorbed into existing work, or continue coextensively with the new SAI projects." The new program would need to take on the responsibility for funding some activities already being carried out, but without those resources necessarily being transferred to the SAI. The main categories were direct costs of expenditure on squatter areas for capital and maintenance ($19.96 million); indirect costs of wastage of resources and income in squatter areas ($45.57 million); the costs of fires in squatter areas ($67.42 million); and racketeers' estimated income ($97.06 million). These costs were thought to be conservative and indicative, rather than actual expenditure, and did not include the cost of recent landslips nor any assessment of "how the services which are put into squatter areas return money into the economy," for example, through squatter industries.[34]

It was observed that what was "spent on providing services to squatter areas is far smaller than the cost of dealing with disasters," while "More money is left uncollected, and resources allowed to run to waste, than is spent on installing and improving the efficiency of services." Moreover, the "considerable cost of rehousing fire victims could be spent on a planned programme of rehousing, using land and other resources more efficiently, if squatter fires were reduced in number and size." Finally, and probably most dubiously given the persistent failure to provide evidence for widespread racketeering in the production of squatter dwellings, the "lack of government services leaves open the opportunity for considerable racketeering, which makes life in squatter areas inherently unstable." A 1982 Home Affairs survey of squatters asked how they acquired their huts: "no mention is made in the report of racketeers" and most huts were reported as being purchased or self-built.[35] In Smart's ethnographic research, "racketeers" were involved in the production of new huts, but not in their resale (Smart 1986).

Some of the details of the calculation of costs and benefits for 1981–1982 are intriguing. Regarding direct costs, local public works were counted at $7 million (likely projects that benefit the wider region in which the squatter area is located), while improvements to squatter areas were only $300,000. Cleansing drainage ditches of silt and slope repair was calculated as $1,060,000, but a note acknowledges that this "cost is not strictly to do with squatter areas per se – the works happen to occur in squatter areas." Indirect costs include "wastage through tapping where legal supplies exist" ($2,250,000) and potential revenue where no legal electricity is available ($6,380,000). The costs of fire were predominantly based on the provision of temporary housing and ex gratia allowances at $52,173,000, but also included Fire Services expenses of $7,692,000 and the opportunity costs of underuse of land for THAs over six years ($6,066,000). Racketeers' incomes were estimated at $61,090,000 for hut construction, $12,577,000 for water supplies, and $23,380,000 for electricity provision.[36]

Another discussion paper for a meeting held on 19 August 1982 assessed the appropriate size of the SAI Programme. The squatter problem was put in context, estimating that squatters represented 42.6% of the 1,392,000 people who were inadequately housed, with the second-largest group being the 439,000 in private tenements. With prevailing policies, the proportion was estimated to increase to 53% squatters by 1986. The report outlined six main options for dealing with the problem: "continuing as at present; improvements to basic services which do not affect the structure; wholesale resiting of squatters; HD rebuilding of areas to Temporary Housing Area standards; HD rebuilding of areas to sub-Temporary Housing Area standards; and allowing squatters themselves to rebuild in more permanent materials." "No change" was rejected, since the SAI was "set up partly in response to a general feeling that present arrangements were unsatisfactory. Nothing has been found to contradict this." Land was unavailable to resite all squatters into purpose-built temporary housing. Rebuilding to THA standards was "feasible but expensive." The cost would be approximately $7,000 to $8,000 per capita "which is 50% more than costs for normal Temporary Housing Areas" due mostly to site formation costs, while the HD considered that it would be "unacceptable to build anything more basic than the current Temporary Housing design." With regard to allowing squatters to rebuild, the "recent rainstorms have demonstrated the fragility of unformed hillsides with even light structures on them. Allowing reconstruction in more permanent and therefore heavier materials would be unwise. The density of squatting makes proper ground treatment and foundation work impractical,"[37] although possible in the rural areas.

Whether the benefits outweighed the costs depends in part on how long an improved squatter area can be expected to persist. The criteria used in the squatter electrification schemes focused on length of tenure before development, size, and need. It was proposed to follow this model, so that a "life span of at least two years is the required minimum" with higher service standards for areas likely to remain more than five years. At least initially, only areas with more than 500 people would be included, and they would be graded for need. Using this criterion, the program would have to cover about 150,000 squatters over five years, at a cost of $300 million.[38] The types of improvements to be provided were "designed to provide temporary relief to squatter settlements which will eventually be cleared for development."[39]

A major factor in the creation of the SAI Programme clearly appears to have been the spate of fires and landslides that had taken place in squatter areas in 1981 and 1982, magnified by increased awareness of the financial and political costs of allowing the status quo to remain for squatters on vulnerable slopes. We saw in Chapter 7 how squatter fires that destroyed the homes of 20,000 people (with three deaths) between October 1981 and March 1982, were a major contributor to the shortage of temporary housing. This shortage in turn imperiled the progress of development clearances for the New Towns that were crucial to building the housing promised in the Ten-Year Plan. Six thousand squatters were evacuated following serious rainstorms in 1982. The landslides resulted in 16 deaths. Landslides have generally been more deadly than fires for squatter areas, since occupants are much less likely to have advance warning of the disaster when large portions of a hillside slip away instantaneously (Lumb 1975). Landslides did not only affect squatter areas, but also legally built structures on steep hillsides, which accounted for the majority of Hong Kong's land, particularly if land reclaimed from the sea or estuaries is excluded.[40] Most landslides resulted from severe rainstorms and affected slopes that were not well built or well maintained. Most "reported landslips in Hong Kong occur suddenly during rainstorms and move rapidly . . . experience has shown that even small failures create severe hazard in certain circumstances, e.g., in close proximity to squatter dwellings" (Malone 1997, 2). They were responsible for more than 470 deaths between 1948 and 1997. The worst disaster occurred in June 1972. An intense rainstorm killed 67 people when a 12-story private apartment building collapsed, while 71 people were killed in a licensed area in Sau Mau Ping, East Kowloon. Although this licensed area should have been better planned than an unregulated squatter area, an engineer with the Geotechnical Control Office later wrote that "[t]he temporary, flimsy dwellings occupied by squatters on many of Hong Kong's steep hillsides are particularly vulnerable to landslides" (Brand et al. 1984, 276).

A commission of enquiry was established in response to a "public outcry" and by the end of 1972 a group of civil engineers had been assigned "to vet the geotechnical aspects of private development submissions" to the Building Ordinance Office (Malone 1997, 3–4; Yang et al. 2008[1972]). In 1976, another serious landslide had occurred in a Sau Mau Ping (Kwun Tong) licensed area, killing 18. Investigation found that the collapse was because "the earth fill forming the face of the slope was in loose condition, having been placed by end-tipping without compaction." In response, "the Governor established an Independent Review Panel on Fill Slopes . . . which recommended the creation of a central policing body to regulate the whole process of investigation, design, construction, monitoring and maintenance of slopes in Hong Kong" (Malone 1997, 4). The Geotechnical Control Office (GCO) was created in July 1977. Subsequently, the previous rule of a permissible angle for cut slopes was replaced with requirements for justification by "use of soil mechanics analysis, based on a ground investigation report" (Malone and Ho 1995, 132). Studies of selected squatter areas by the Public Works Department led to the evacuation and rehousing of 16,000 squatters. The Mid-Levels of Hong Kong Island was considered to be so problematic (because of its geology and the large number of past excavations of poor quality) that a comprehensive geotechnical study was carried out over the entire area, and a moratorium was imposed during the study, from 1979 to 1982 (Malone and Ho 1995).

With 3.25 metres of rain, 1982 was the wettest year since Hong Kong's records began in 1884 (Brand et al. 1984). In May and August, almost 700 landslides were reported; 27 people died, of whom 23 were squatter occupants. These events "brought recognition of the need for concerted effort to tackle the landslip risk to squatters and the realization that the only effective disaster preventive action is to clear squatter dwellings and re-house the occupants"

(Malone and Ho 1995, 138). In 1983, ExCo approved a plan for the GCO to devise a "scientific method of zoning squatter areas in terms of their potential danger from geotechnical hazards."[41] An initial survey of landslide risks in squatter areas distinguished between Category A (dangerous slope failure areas where "the slope has a gradient of not less than 30 degrees and a height of more than 5 metres or where, because of other terrain conditions, a danger is obvious from a visual inspection"), and Category B (slopes that indicated an element of risk). There were 67 slopes, 3,692 huts, and 11,976 persons in Category A, and 13 slopes, 652 huts, 1,681 persons in Category B.[42]

A later more comprehensive study of squatter areas on slopes classified them into three categories of relative potential hazard, providing "for the first time, a rational basis for prioritized inspections of the squatter areas on hillsides." This led to about 65,000 squatters being cleared from steep slopes "at a rate controlled by the capacity of the public housing programme," a number that increased to 72,000 by 1997 (Malone 1997, 138). The result was that the proportion of landslides affecting squatters dropped from about 50% in 1985 to about 10% in 1993. The landslide fatality rate was reduced by about 90% between the mid-1980s and 2001, largely due to squatter clearance (Cheung and Shiu 2003). A Landslip warning system had been introduced in 1977 to encourage precautionary evacuation of vulnerable squatter settlements at critical times, with broadcasts on radio and television and the deployment of staff to danger spots when necessary (Malone 1997).

Acknowledging the "need to improve conditions in the major squatter concentrations which are likely to remain in existence for some years," a small planning unit was established in the Housing Department in 1982 to "undertake as a matter of urgency fire and landslip safety measures in the larger squatter areas" and investigate the "feasibility of effecting other improvements to basic services in squatter areas, and to recommend how this might best be done." In February 1982, the Finance Committee approved a new special expenditure for improvements to squatter areas with a commitment of $21.9 million to "meet the cost of the planning team and safety related works in selected squatter black spots in the urban area."[43] This planning team was either the Squatter Area Improvements Interdepartmental Working Group or a smaller group that quickly grew into it. It should be noted that these decisions were made in advance of the May 1982 rainstorms, although the influence of public concern over the 1976 disaster in Sau Mau Ping was probably lingering. However, the squatter fires of 1981 were probably a more direct influence on these decisions.

The Working Group Report noted that community involvement is an "essential pre-requisite to the successful implementation of this type of project"; squatter cooperation and participation "will be required if the scheme is to be implemented with the time scale envisaged, and is to operate successfully thereafter." However, consultation with the City District Office suggested that this would require well-organized Mutual Aid Committees and to assume this would be "optimistic." There were also outstanding legal questions, such as the "extent to which improvements may be construed as government acceptance of occupation of land by squatters which gives the squatters a right to occupy land,"[44] and the procedures to be used in removing illegal water pipes and electrical connections.

Pilot studies were a key part of the planning for a more ambitious SAI program. In early 1982, projects began in two areas in Kwun Tong (Sau Mau Ping and Lam Tin) and Nga Choi Hang in Causeway Bay, Hong Kong Island (Leung 1983). After the initial pilot studies, but before the decision to launch the full SAI program, several more improvement projects were initiated, focusing on fire and safety works. The minutes of the 19 August 1982 meeting of the Interdepartmental Working Group on Squatter Area Improvements noted that a project in Shau Kei Wan, Hong Kong Island, would begin in spring 1983 when housing became available, and that work in Sau Mau Ping and Lam Tin would be finished in September 1982 (see Figure 9.2). Of personal interest was the short mention of Diamond Hill, where Smart conducted his doctoral ethnographic research on squatter clearance. The "proposed main firebreak follows the line of Social Avenue; this will incur the problem of clearing shops."[45] This was the geographic focus of his study, and the shopkeepers were indeed unhappy with the project (Smart 1992). He wanted to understand the impact of clearance by living and researching in an area due to be affected, and how it influenced those cleared. The registration of those to be cleared took place in August 1983, so the proposal took a year to be put into action.

A clearance requires physical surveying to ensure where lot boundaries are and how they relate to the jumble of temporary structures covering the land. Even the Lands Department was reluctant to guarantee the maps that they produced for the Housing Department, since they had doubts about previous cadastral surveys and many markers had been dug up or built over. The clearance was carefully planned to avoid involving any private land, which would have required resumption procedures. Preparations "had to be done carefully enough so that on the day of the registration, dozens of officials involved in the 'blitz' would unerringly go to the right dwellings. This is never an easy task in a squatter area. Secrecy is a major consideration in the clearance planning. Since all those registered in the clearance registration are eligible for some form of relocation compensation or rehousing, the Housing Department tries to ensure that no one knows in advance that a clearance will occur" (Smart 1992, 137).

There were protests against the firebreak clearance, which succeeded in postponing and modifying it, and all of the protesters were shopkeepers and small manufacturers. They approached local leaders and the District

Office with their complaints and managed to set up meetings with Housing Department officials. The shopkeepers stressed, at these meetings and many times to Smart, "the economic dislocation that the clearance would cause. They also did not think that it was fair that they were to be resettled now for a firebreak, when the whole area was going to be cleared within a few years, according to government plans" (Smart 1992, 145). In fact, the last parts of Diamond Hill were not cleared until 1999 (Smart 2001). When cancellation was clearly impossible, they tried to renegotiate the location, but were told that advisors had recommended this location, without explaining why. Social Avenue was lined on both sides with shops and was the main commercial area for Diamond Hill, which then had about 50,000 people. The main "justification given for the building of the firebreak along the main road of Diamond Hill was that it would allow Fire Department vehicles to enter the area more easily in case of a fire, as well as the larger open space reducing the risk of a fire spreading uncontrollably" (Smart 1992, 145). In fact, "the worst bottleneck of all, at the junction of Grandview Road and Social Avenue, would remain unaltered. This part of the road (barely ten feet wide at the junction) was always terribly congested at peak times, both before and after the project's completion. Just to walk the fifty feet from Leung Cheung Road [a highway bisecting Diamond Hill] to the junction could take ten minutes of squeezing past the almost immobile goods trucks and stepping through the front part of the shops on this stretch of the road" (Smart 1992, 145).

The completed project also suggested that the rationale was not achieved. Instead of the cleared space being used as a wider road, it was cemented and enclosed behind non-movable traffic control fences, which allowed pedestrians but not vehicles to enter the newly cleared area so that, though it was a firebreak, it did not seem to be effective in improving firefighting access. Another criticism from the shopkeepers was the clearance of the north side of Social Avenue, where most structures had been for at least 15 years, while on the south side they had been rebuilt 10 years previously after a fire and were more of a fire hazard. In an interview with a SAI Division officer, though, it was explained that the south side structures were on Crown land, but this stretch was only 10 feet wide and behind that was 20 feet of private land. On the north side, the Crown land formed a 20-foot strip. The official said that "since this ten-foot strip was not wide enough for the plans, if it was taken it would still be necessary to clear the north side as well" (Smart 1992, 148). Private land, which included about 75% of Diamond Hill, particularly in the lower sections, was avoided because of the added complications. This also explained why most of Diamond Hill was not cleared until 1999, except when affected by fires. While the shopkeepers were mostly unsuccessful in their protests, they did manage to delay the clearance for five months. The consequences were reduced by an agreement that allowed those whose property extended farther north past the 20-foot strip to keep the additional space, rather than the whole structure being removed as in the original plans. These experiences echoed the concerns of the Sau Mau Ping planning report about consultation and legal issues.

We did not come across this report in the files we have consulted, but Smart received a copy from the Housing Department during his fieldwork between 1983 and 1985. It was commissioned on 4 March 1982 and completed in May 1982. The project would affect about 1,800 people living at a density of 1,500 persons per hectare. About 10% of the huts were present before 1976. The main objectives were to improve fire and slope safety and provide basic services such as drinkable water, toilets, refuse collection, legal electricity, improved footpaths, and lighting. In addition, a rather modest objective was that "stability of existing slopes is not to be made worse by proposed works, and wherever possible stability is to be improved." A key underlying objective was that while every attempt should be made to keep costs to a minimum, the solutions proposed should be the "most cost effective after due consideration of technical options and of geotechnical, programming and implementation (such as minimising clearance of existing structures)." It is worth noting that based on a visual inspection of pipes discharging from huts, it was estimated that up to half the dwellings had some form of private toilet. In addition, although half of the pilot area was covered by a legal electrification scheme, few dwellings had been hooked up and most huts had an illegal electrical connection. To encourage the replacement of these with legal connections, it was proposed that "illegal connections will be removed within a fixed period – say 28 days of legal communal services being available." Some adaptation to local conditions was envisaged: a "main aspect of the design approach is to improve and make better use of facilities that have already been provided by squatters, where these facilities do not represent an undue fire hazard or endanger slope stability." In addition, it was acknowledged that the standards applied "should be appropriate for the improvement scheme . . . rather than simply being adaptations of existing approved standards . . . The test of any standard adopted will be whether in the judgement of the engineer, it is technically acceptable, given fire prevention and slope stability requirements, rather than whether it fulfils current Government requirements."[46]

Establishing the SAI

In response to the various inputs resulting from the studies of squatter areas on dangerous slopes, in 1982, ExCo considered a report which proposed changes to squatter control policies. This memo reported that the squatter population was an estimated 580,000 and that "since it was unlikely that major squatter concentrations would be cleared in the next few years, measures were

Figure 9.2: Electrification, Sau Mau Ping squatter area, 1983. Copyright and provided by Alan Smart.

being taken to introduce fire and landslip safety measures and certain basic improvements in squatter areas." However, "low priority has been accorded to squatter areas, and conditions in many of these areas have deteriorated greatly as a result of extensive new squatting following the large-scale immigration of 1978 to 1980. It was mainly the new squatter areas . . . which suffered devastation from fire in the winter of 1981/82 and from landslips during the May rainstorms of 1982." The measures to that point had been inadequate because "[r]esponsibility for the provision of basic services in squatter areas has hitherto been divided between a number of Government departments and the public utility companies."[47] The Working Party on Slope Preventive Works in Squatter Areas was established in 1983. As some of the issues considered in relation to it seem to have influenced the policy shift toward early clearance of all squatters on dangerous slopes in 1984, we leave discussion of it until Chapter 10.

Edward Youde began his term as Governor on 20 May 1982. Briefing notes had been sent to him in advance, with the longer-term housing issues described as allocation of public housing to new arrivals versus Hong Kong belongers; supply of temporary housing to be increased; and eligibility for the Home Ownership Scheme. However, those in the category of issues likely to come to a head in the next six months were quite different. These more urgent questions were development clearances, "a number of major and difficult clearances are in the offing, including Tai Hom Wor . . . and squatter areas in North Point, Shaukeiwan, Sheung Shui, Fanling and Tsuen Wan"; rehousing of boat squatters; squatter control "moves to tighten control on hut-building racketeers"; squatter area improvements, "pilot measures in four squatter areas and preparation of comprehensive report on improvements in all squatter areas in September 1982"; Tuen Mun transit centre, where "conditions will have to be monitored during summer"; and further review of rent control.[48] The centrality of the squatter problem in this briefing is quite striking.

While fires and landslides were the most pressing concern, and had impacts on the entire housing program (see Chapter 8), another report to ExCo in February 1983 argued that beyond the danger of disasters, "the most serious problem in squatter areas is lack of sanitation. This arises from the absence of mains water, drainage, and sewage. Most squatter areas are highly insanitary. Human and animal sewage together with rotting garbage clog stream courses or seep onto the open hillside until flushed away in the rainy season." Reliance on natural drainage for waste disposal and the absence of organized refuse collection presented a "serious and worsening health hazard." The absence of drainage "exacerbates slope stability problems. Very few squatter areas have a metered mains supply of water. Apart from those so high on the hillside that pump systems are needed, most areas do have access to a communal standpipe. However, in almost all cases water is illegally tapped and redistributed from the standpipes" which increased the risk of contamination. Water supply was "invariably organised and charged for by racketeers. A similar problem exists with regard to electricity. Although there are arrangements for providing legal supplies, these could not keep pace with the expansion of squatter areas between 1978 and 1981 so that, in many places, illegal tapping and overloading increase the risk of fire. Work is now in hand, however, to catch up on the backlog."[49] These dangers and inconveniences to squatters were supplemented by risks to society more broadly, such as disease, fire, destabilized slopes, and the promotion of illegal service provision through racketeers.

The conclusion from these points was that it was "considered that these conditions cannot be allowed to continue in the interest of public health and safety and that systematic improvements must be attempted."[50] The question, though, was how such improvements should be provided. Clearance of "the worst squatter areas in advance of the land being required for permanent development is considered to be impractical in the foreseeable future, given the very large numbers who would have to be rehoused, and the many other demands on permanent and temporary public housing, particularly from essential development clearances." This rejection would itself be overturned within a year. Reconstruction of squatter areas to the "standard of existing temporary

Squatter Area Improvement

housing areas would require very extensive and costly site formation, and, in most cases, it would be possible to reaccommodate on the same site only a proportion of the existing residents. This solution would also involve long term management by government staff." While management by government staff was seen as an excessive expense, self-management was also problematic: "Permitting rebuilding in more permanent materials is not practicable . . . the density, layout and topography of most squatter areas preclude the site formation and foundation work necessary for this type of development," while rebuilding without "extensive site formation and foundation work could not be permitted in view of the vulnerability of many areas to landslip."

After rejecting the other apparent alternative paths to squatter area improvement, it was "considered that the long-term aim should remain the clearance and rehousing of these squatters. It is, therefore, recommended that no change should be made in the legal status of squatters." Once again, the second alternative proposed by Governor Trench in 1970 was raised only to be dismissed. The reasons for this rejection were that any attempt to legalize the occupation by squatters of Crown land "would be very expensive in terms of staff," would not further the "prevention and control of new squatting, and might indeed exacerbate the situation," and would "require that the Government was reasonably satisfied as to the safety of the structures, which in most cases is not possible. For similar reasons, it is considered that formal management of squatter areas by the Housing Department would be impractical and inadvisable." Improvements were "essential in order to alleviate the serious environmental hazards presented by inadequate water supplies and an absence of proper drainage and sanitation. And, as neither reconstruction nor immediate rehousing is feasible, it is considered that these improvements should be carried out *in situ*."[51] Again, any kind of tenure change was being rejected.

The priority clearly was on safety improvements: "The density of construction, the type of materials used and the difficulty of access make the risk of fire high and fire fighting difficult. Similarly, the method of construction on the steeper slopes, without adequate retaining walls or drainage, increases the risk of localised landslips. These parallel dangers were starkly illustrated by the devastating fires at the end of 1981 and the tragic events of the 1982 rainstorms. Quite apart from the personal losses involved, disasters on this scale are enormously disruptive to the normal work of clearance and rehousing for development projects." Even sanitation was considered in part in these terms: in addition to inadequate drainage and sewage systems presenting "a serious and worsening health hazard," it also "exacerbates slope stability problems." It was estimated that the average cost of these improvements would be $2,500 per "head." The proposal, which was approved, was that this "programme should be phased over five years and that it should aim to complete improvements for

8,000 squatters in the first year, and about 20,000 squatters in each subsequent year" at a total cost estimated at $300 million.[52]

The SAI proposal was not accepted without criticism. At a Housing Authority discussion on 24 March 1983, "Mrs. Elliott questioned whether, since squatters did not pay rent, they should be required to pay something towards the cost of improvements. The Chairman said that such payment would be seen to confer on them a right of tenure which might cause trouble to future clearances." Another non-official member said that the Wong Tai Sin District Board had visited the SAI pilot projects and felt that "the work done was over-expensive. As most of the improvements would only benefit new immigrants, rather than long-time residents, it was considered unfair, particularly as the District Board itself wanted to make certain improvements, such as installing better public lighting, but Government would not agree to pay." In response, "Mr. Denny Huang and Miss Maria Tam both thought that the Housing Department should not discriminate against new immigrant squatters."[53] An assessment of the possible public reaction suggested that there may be some adverse reaction from "sections of the press who are more critical of Government's policies." They might question why government did not do this earlier: "Why should Government pay $2,500 a head ($63 million a year) to improve the living conditions of people who occupy Crown land illegally and who pay no rent?" In addition, they might query if this is a "replacement rather than an addition to part of Government's public housing programme, and if so, will not more deserving sectors of society lose their chance of being given public housing within the near future? Would it not be better to put the money towards more permanent public housing?" As well, the question might be posed if it will "increase the number of squatters and act as an enticement for people not to apply for public housing?"[54]

Despite such concerns, the SAI Programme was put into place and funded, although it did not last long. To establish "objective priorities for the improvement work, an assessment has been made of the conditions in all squatter settlements in the urban area and Tsuen Wan. Based on three criteria – degree of need, size of population and length of tenure before clearance – a priority list has been drawn up for the residual 100,000 squatters around the main urban areas who will not be cleared for development over the next five years."[55]

Conclusion

This chapter considered the course of the improvement path to regularizing squatter areas. In this approach, rather than achieving greater conformity with legal rules through resettlement or tenure change, the squatter structures and their residents would remain in the gray area of toleration for the time being, but their infrastructure would be upgraded to be more consistent and

Squatter Area Improvement

compatible with formally developed areas. This can be seen as a limited form of one of the two main paths to formalization of the informal: regularization. Rather than regularizing informal housing by squatter titling or other forms of tenure change, or by modifying building and other regulations, it is only the infrastructure that is regularized, bringing it into closer conformity with the infrastructure of the formally developed parts of the city. Ultimately, though, squatter area improvement was only a temporary holding measure, intended to improve conditions or to reduce the likelihood of disasters, but with the dominant path to formalization in Hong Kong: a combination of demolition and resettlement, constantly casting a shadow of demolition and/or resettlement, achieving formalization through removing informally used space.

How strong is the will to improve as an explanation of the formalization of informal housing in Hong Kong, or more narrowly, as an explanation for the use of squatter area improvement to regulate non-developable squatter areas? If we leave aside improvement through demolition and resettlement, then improvement in the form of better infrastructure for safety and sanitation was always a minor part of the overall strategy to deal with the squatter problem. It was applied only to those squatter areas that were hard to develop conventionally, initially those that were evaluated as being excessively "squalid" and later primarily those on slopes vulnerable to landslides; as well as to insert fire precautions such as firebreaks and improved access. Despite being proposed by Governor Trench in 1970 (in the broader form that included tenure change) and by the Commissioner for Resettlement in 1971 (in the narrower form that precluded tenure change), it took a decade before it developed into a division and a program. Prior to that, limited forms of improvement took place through legal electrification and legal water supplies and modest safety interventions. Then, after being adopted as a substantial program in 1982, the decision was made only two years later to opt for resettlement of all squatters on vulnerable slopes instead, and to run down the program as a much more modest and residual project.

More generally, high modernist improvement by government was belatedly and often reluctantly adopted by the Hong Kong colonial government. Leo Goodstadt (2006) points out that until the 1970s, Hong Kong's government collected as few statistics as possible. Officials "regularly claimed that a non-interventionist colonial administration in an open economy did not need the sort of statistics routinely compiled by governments elsewhere." Goodstadt (2006, 3) argues that, to the contrary, "laisser-faire principles were not the dominant factor in the colonial administration's reluctance to compile statistics." Instead, officials "resisted the collection of data whenever they believed that the figures would empower their local critics or create additional excuses for British ministers and officials in London to interfere with Hong Kong affairs" (3). The tendency might better be described as "not seeing like a state"

(Steenberg 2016). For example, no census was conducted between 1931 and 1961. Standard understandings of the governmental will to improve assumes that the collection of detailed information is crucial, but Hong Kong's practices seem to assume that it was often better not to know things in detail, so long as the administrative elite felt that they adequately understood the situation. It was preferable not to visibly know things that one did not desire to do anything about.

More likely than an inherent desire of government to improve squatter areas that remained as squatter areas, the will to improve them arose from the concerns of others about these problematic and highly visible parts of Hong Kong's urban fabric, whether that concern came from London or the "public" in Hong Kong itself. However, we think that even this indirect will to improve (or perhaps more accurately, the will to avoid influential criticism from those who want to see improvements) is relatively weak compared to other explanations. One extremely important cause would seem to be the way in which fires and landslides in squatter areas could exacerbate the public housing supply and demand problems examined in Chapter 7. Disasters in squatter areas were unpredictable in timing, even if they were to be expected eventually in general, and thus could create sharp spikes in demand for temporary housing that could derail the development clearance program. The next chapter considers the management of disasters as one of the influences on the sharp turns in policy about the squatter problem between 1982 and 1984.

10
The Squatter Occupancy Survey

[I]nstead of deducing concrete phenomena from universals, or instead of starting with universals as an obligatory grid of intelligibility for certain concrete practices, I would like to start with these concrete practices and . . . pass these universals through the grid of these practices.

—Michel Foucault, *The Birth of Biopolitics: Lectures at the Collège de France, 1978–1979* (2008, 3)

Introduction

This chapter has two objectives. The first is to examine the crucial policy changes between 1982, when the Squatter Area Improvement (SAI) Programme was put into place, and 1984, when it was decided to instead phase out the SAI over five years, resettle all squatters on vulnerable slopes, and carry out the Squatter Occupancy Survey (SOS). These decisions were influenced by growing awareness of the political and economic costs of managing landslide risks affecting squatters, as well as considerations of legal liability. The second objective is to consider how the SOS was implemented.

The SAI was intended to improve squatter areas, in part to manage criticism over the conditions of life in them, and in part to avoid the difficulties and costs of non-development clearances at a time when the failure of the Ten-Year Programme to meet its goals had become very clear. By 1983, however, the HA was setting new records for the number of flats constructed and the number of squatters cleared (Housing Authority 1984). New plans for dealing with the housing situation were being explored and adopted in the early 1980s, so devoting resources to clearing squatters from land that was not easily usable for development was not an obvious priority. However, the serious problems caused by fires and landslides in 1982, with attendant public concern, pushed the problem higher on the policy agenda. At the same time, studies into squatter areas on dangerous slopes were making it clear that the very modest slope stabilization efforts included in the SAI Programme would be insufficient to significantly better matters. This situation undermined the

210   *Hong Kong Public and Squatter Housing*

attractions of squatter improvement as a way of managing these residual squatter areas, since it would be unlikely to avoid future loss of life in disasters, while even modest increases in slope safety would be expensive. At the same time, legal issues emerged about the duty of care of government for squatters. These studies of slope safety, and the Working Party that they prompted, acted as additional "policy mangles" that brought together disparate issues and resulted in new policy directions.

Dangerous Slopes

Minutes of a meeting of the Chief Secretary's Committee had already noted in 1981 that "[t]he problem was the allocation of public housing, which did not provide for the early removal of squatters living under dangerous slopes." The Secretary for Housing said that although the housing supply was continuing to increase, "each recipient sector demanded a still greater allocation." The Chief Secretary "said that an enormous amount of effort has been devoted to the squatter problem but that the problem was far from solved" and asked the Secretary for Home Affairs, the Secretary for New Territories, and the Secretary for Housing to "consider what might be done."[1] The slow pace of clearing squatters in high or moderate danger areas received internal criticism from the Principal Government Geotechnical Engineer, E. W. Brand. In a letter commenting on an early draft of the first report on landslide dangers to squatters, he argued against a narrow plan for "first-aid" slope stabilization. If this was restricted to work within the squatter areas, it would be inadequate since work "must also be carried out on those peripheral areas immediately outside squatter areas where there are obvious hazards to the squatters." Previously, the Landslip Preventive Measures Programme managed by the Geotechnical Control Office (GCO) had "not undertaken major works where potential hazards threaten squatter areas only, and recommendations for clearance have been made where such major hazards have been identified."[2] As a "result of the casualties that occurred in squatter areas in May and August 1982" the Housing Department asked the GCO to consider "the possibilities of zoning squatter areas to enable localised landslip warning to be given in future." That study began in July 1982 and led to a Memo to Executive Council on 31 August 1982. ExCo directed the GCO to "find a methodical and scientific technique for zoning Hong Kong in order to identify the most potentially serious areas." This led to the report on "Landslide dangers to squatters in Hong Kong and Kowloon," completed in November 1982.[3]

    This report concluded that 25% of urban squatters (54,000) were on dangerous slopes, where the chance of landslides causing casualties was high.[4] Brand stated that the dangerous areas "should ideally be cleared as a matter of urgency. Failing this, they should feature high on the Housing Department's priority list of areas for improvement." As a consequence, he stated that if the SAI Programme tackled the dangerous areas, "the average cost of the improvement works will certainly exceed" the estimate and "extra provision will be necessary for the external slope stabilisation works required." Most crucially, the draft ExCo paper "dismisses clearances of the worst squatter areas as impractical . . . A viable alternative would seem to be to relocate squatters on land prepared with the basic site formation work, drainage and services . . . The Geotechnical Control Office could readily identify safer patches of land for the relocation exercise. On these prepared sites, squatters could build their huts in much safer conditions than those in which they presently live."[5] At most, modest concessions to this critique were undertaken for the final version of the Report to ExCo, and the concern for practicality over safety persisted. The SAI Programme was expected to be delivered to 8,000 squatters in the first year, and about 20,000 squatters in each subsequent year. In addition, under then current development proposals, approximately one-third of squatters on dangerous terrain in the urban areas were likely to be cleared over the next five years, leaving between 35,000 and 40,000 squatters on dangerous slopes in the urban area.

Some key points arise from the October 1982 geotechnical study. It found 25% of urban squatters (54,000) were on dangerous slopes, 15% on marginal slopes where the chance of casualties was moderate, and 55% were on safe ground where the risk was low.[6] Hong Kong's slopes are mostly "residual soil overlying weak rocks," characteristic of tropical areas. Little research had been done on it by that time. The high permeability of these soils "means that their shear strength changes rapidly during times of rainfall." It was noted that it "is probably true . . . that there is nowhere else in the world where such dense urban development occurs on steep residual soil slopes which are subjected to such intense rainfall. In this respect, Rio de Janeiro . . . probably most closely resembles Hong Kong, although building development on slopes is generally less dense than here. That city also suffers considerably from rain-induced landslides, with frequent casualties."[7] A Landslip Preventive Measures Programme was established in 1977 under the control of the Geotechnical Control Office, with over $600 million spent by 1986 on slope stabilization works. Expenditure was "continuing at a rate of about $65 million per year. In addition, more than $40 million per year is being spent on slope maintenance."[8]

Estimating the likelihood of landslides is complex because the geology itself is complicated, and, before comprehensive and expensive geotechnical surveys are conducted, mostly uncertain. Before 1977, most of the architectural modifications to the slopes had been based on rules of thumb rather than clear scientific knowledge. In their study of roadbuilding in Peru, Harvey and Knox (2015, 94) discovered that "[o]ne of the most powerful effects of the material engagements that engineers encounter in the field, as opposed to in the classroom, is an ongoing relationship with material qualities and their pressing social effects." They often "heard engineers talking about the battles they had with the earth" and their job required them to "transform this site-specific and embodied experiential knowledge of substance in action into a mathematical description that would make the terms of its unstable qualities knowable, and the possibilities for its stabilization calculable." The "powers of the numbers they were working with came from their capacity to mediate between the specific social and material circumstances found on the ground and the legal, financial, and engineering standards to which infrastructural projects had to adhere" (Harvey and Knox 2015, 86). In deliberations over safety improvement versus rapid clearance, these multiple factors operated in a complex interplay between estimates of material degrees of safety, costs, the likely longevity of an improved squatter area and concerns about the public opinion consequences of further disasters. This kind of policy mangle is clearly affected by diverse material qualities that may offer possibilities for diverting policy decisions from existing pathways.

Despite the research and public concern over landslide dangers, "only a small amount of stabilisation work has so far been carried out specifically to safeguard squatters, but there are good reasons for this in addition to those of resources and priorities. On many of the steep slopes occupied by large numbers of squatters, it is not feasible for large-scale stabilisation measures to be carried out, simply because the squatters need to be cleared before the works can progress. Once clearance has been effected, there is generally no need for the preventive works to be undertaken." This resembles Joseph Heller's classic idea of a catch-22, where bureaucratic tangles make resolving a problem impossible.[9] The impasse lead the GCO to recommend to the Housing Department "that squatters be cleared from such slopes, but these clearances can obviously only be undertaken within the capacity of the housing programme, and priority is given to the clearance of squatters occupying slopes where there is an immediate danger to life and limb. Government continues to give high priority to the rehousing of squatters. However, there are several hundred thousand of squatters in the Territory, and it will be some years before all of them can be properly housed."[10]

An exchange of memos about the legal liability of government for landslides on Crown land also played into the situation. The discussion was initiated by a Memo from the Registrar General on 24 September 1982, about liability for slope maintenance in regard to a slope cutting for a highway. He described Leakey and others vs. National Trust [UK] (1980) as the "leading case on this subject" and summarized it as the principle that "wherever a state of affairs has arisen on land which constitutes a hazard to neighbouring property, the occupier of the land once aware of, or if he ought to become aware of, the hazard is under a duty to take reasonable steps to remove the hazard."[11] In that case, "Mrs. Leaky noticed a big crack appear in the bank above her house. She informed the National Trust and offered to pay half the cost of making it safe. Her offer was rejected. A few weeks later there was a large fall." The National Trust were found liable by the Court of Appeal, the decision stating that

> The defendant's duty is to do that which it is reasonable for him to do. The criteria of reasonableness include, in respect of a duty of this nature, the factor of what the particular man – not the average man – can be expected to do, having regard, amongst other things, where a serious expenditure of money is required to eliminate or reduce the danger, to his means. . . . But this can only be in the way of a broad, and not a detailed, assessment; and, in arriving at a judgment on reasonableness, a similar broad assessment may be relevant in some cases as to the neighbour's capacity to protect himself from damage.[12]

On 22 July 1983, the Secretary for Lands and Works wrote a Memo to the Attorney General concerning the government's legal responsibility for consequences of slope failure on Crown land hillsides occupied by squatters. This memo raised the issue of duty of care again. Given the timing, it is possible that the timing was due to the initiation of the Working Party on Slope Preventive Works in Squatter Areas (addressed below). The question to the Attorney General was whether, in the context of its allowing squatters to remain on slopes until the areas are required for development, the government as landowner could "be held liable for damage or injury caused by the consequences of the failure of slopes on which structures have been erected without its consent and which are occupied unlawfully, which unlawful occupation is tolerated by the Government as a matter of policy as being a lesser evil than rendering the occupants homeless."[13]

Prior to expressing an opinion, the Attorney General asked for information about the nature of the conditions under which squatters were tolerated, and was given some intriguing documents about the legal nature of squatter toleration. These were the result of an initiative by the Secretary for Home Affairs in 1976 to consider "bringing a number of commonplace but illegal activities as far as possible within the law, the social consequences of which appeared generally acceptable to the majority of the public," including squatting.[14] The Housing Branch, in a report titled "Regularisation of tolerated squatters," questioned the assumption that "long 'tolerated' squatters on Crown Land were in breach of the law i.e., they were committing an offence." This had indeed been the case before the Amendment of the Crown Lands Ordinance in 1972, when a squatter on Crown land committed a trespass. Policy after the 1964 squatter survey was that surveyed structures would be tolerated, "i.e., the occupants would be left in peaceful occupancy until such time as Government required them to cease occupation. It is suggested that this action gave them an implied licence to remain," which could give a defense against trespass. Structures built after 1964 did not receive this formal toleration. It was "not possible to take effective action against every illegal occupation . . . but at no time did the authority (at least in the urban area) acquiesce to this presence." The Secretary for Home Affairs mooted making all squatters licensees by issuing a license, but this "would entail many administrative difficulties and the costs and resources involved and possibility of abuses would outweigh any advantages." An alternative to bringing squatters within the law would be by "merely deeming them to be licencees for them to be licencees . . . This would give them an express licence (as opposed to an implied one)." Since the "policy of 'toleration' and its practical effect is well known to the squatter" (that the policy will, on clearance, bring an offer of compensation), this practice is "perhaps more germane to him than his strict legal rights." Their conclusion was that there was no real benefit "to amend the law merely to deem a squatter a licencee just to bring the law into line with the policy." It could have negative consequences, such as encouraging squatting and racketeering. When "things are understood and working then one should leave well alone may be . . . as good a course as any to take in this matter."[15] And there the matter stood until landslides shifted the legal questions.

The Attorney General's legal advice was that "in principle, Government could be held liable for injury or damage to persons or property caused as the result of a slope failure on Crown land." The Privy Council had held since 1967 that "there is a general duty of care upon occupiers of land in relation to hazards, whether natural or man-made, occurring on their land." The legal status of tolerated squatters extended this duty of care to them, and possibly to unsurveyed squatters. This duty goes beyond what is done by the owner to include "a defect in the land" of which the owner is aware or should have become aware if "he had acted with ordinary and reasonable care." The principle of reasonableness prevents general conclusions beyond there being a duty of care, "but one cannot say without specific facts whether there has been a breach of duty." From this, "the size of the problem with potential landslips will be relevant as will the size of Government's resources and its ability to provide manpower and alternative accommodation." If government has "acted in accordance with available resources," it could "make out a good case . . . that it has discharged its duty."[16] The implication of this advice is that in leaving squatters on vulnerable and unimproved slopes, it might be in breach of duty, but also that the token nature of slope stabilization measures in the SAI Programme might have to be made more substantial. Given this, squatter improvement might be more expensive than a residual management of squatters on undesirable land could justify. More aggressive clearance efforts could have legal as well as public opinion and financial advantages.

It is likely that these considerations influenced the course of deliberations by the Working Party on Slope Preventive Works in Squatter Areas. In February

1983, the Housing Department maintained that clearance of all squatters in dangerous areas was "impractical in the foreseeable future," in part because the "features which make terrain dangerous render it generally unsuitable for permanent development," and due to "the very large numbers who would have to be rehoused, and the many other demands on permanent and temporary public housing, particularly from essential development clearances."[17] By 7 December 1983, though, the HD and the GCO "seemed to be becoming more sympathetic towards clearing squatter areas on dangerous slopes and he suggested that DOs [District Officers] consider whether any areas in their districts should be cleared on these grounds."[18] The May 1982 landslides led to a "vast commitment" of staff resources for clearing evacuated huts that had been affected, and arranging emergency housing for those evacuated. This had a "combined effect on the drain of a [sic] substantial housing resources at the expense of normal clearance commitment and other categories."[19] The change in attitude may have been at least partly due to the establishment of a Working Party on Slope Preventive Works in Squatter Areas, chaired by the Director of Engineering Development after submission of the November 1982 Geotechnical Control Office Report on Landslide Dangers.

A Memo from Lands and Works Branch on 29 March 1983 agreed with proposed objectives for the Working Party: "to decide on any immediate actions which need to be taken; and . . . to consider ways in which priorities for squatter clearance and squatter area improvements can be adjusted to take account of the findings of the study."[20] However a Memo in November 1983 stated that the Secretary of Lands and Works had "suggested that one of the Working Party's objectives should be to consider ways in which priorities for squatter clearance and squatter area improvements can be adjusted to take account of the findings of the study . . . Despite this recommendation the clearance aspect has been left out of its terms of reference . . . which are very much 'works' orientated."[21] This kind of calculation could have contributed to the downsizing of the improvement commitments announced in September 1984 that "a programme should be drawn up to clear and rehouse squatters currently living on the more vulnerable slopes over a period of about five years. This will be included in a 10-year clearance and rehousing programme for all squatters, including boat-squatters, in the urban area." As part of the announcement, it was stated that this new program would remove the need for the SAI Programme, the funds for which could be used to support the ambitious project of resettling all urban squatters. It would be run down over five years, with continuing expenditure to be limited to fire and landslide precautions.[22]

The reasons underlying this change of direction are not well explained in the documents, so we again have to resort to the most plausible explanations. The shift seems to be due to the collapse of earlier hopes that the SAI could be a cheap holding action to put off dealing with squatters on land not needed for development, while reducing the embarrassments of squalor and lessening the unexpected and sudden demand on both permanent and temporary housing caused by fires and landslides.

These hopes were submerged by new information. The geological studies made clear that achieving safe slopes would be much more expensive than had been hoped, while the legal advice pointed out the risks of leaving the situation unchanged. A proposal presented to the HA's Operations Committee on 24 February 1984 stated that "[a]lthough the long-term aim is to rehouse all squatters, there is no existing programme to clear squatter enclaves outside development areas. Of these, squatters on dangerous slopes pose a special problem since many dangerous slopes lie outside areas scheduled for development." It was noted that under the SAI, "some $25 million per annum is spent in carrying out minor preventive works (of a safety-cum-first-aid nature) and providing some basic facilities. The clearance of squatters from dangerous slopes would reduce this commitment." To clear all squatters on dangerous slopes within five years would require approximately 1,000 public housing units each year, plus 3.6 hectares for temporary housing. After completion, "a residue of squatter huts that are situated neither within development zones nor on dangerous slopes will remain. At that stage consideration could be given to extending the dangerous slopes clearance programme to include these areas. But it is envisaged that some squatter areas in the remote parts of the New Territories would remain in the foreseeable future."[23]

Awareness of the costs of an SAI adequate to resolve the environmental problems dawned during the first years of Governor Edward Youde's term, which began on 20 May 1982 . Compared to MacLehose, Youde continued the concern to maintain confidence in the context of the negotiations for Hong Kong's future but was more fiscally conservative. In this, he was likely reinforced by the Colonial Secretary, Philip Haddon-Cave, who in his previous post as Financial Secretary had been the architect of the concept of *positive non-interventionism,* a reworking of a more traditional principle of laissez-faire. In Youde's October 1982 address to LegCo, he said that the government would probably only break even, rather than have the expected (and usual) surplus, due to a sluggish world economy. The economy was forecast to grow by 4% in real terms, revised from a prior budget forecast of 8%. Youde announced an intention to "place a renewed emphasis on the value-for-money criterion to move away from the habit of automatically refilling posts whenever they become vacant . . . and to keep under critical review the size and composition of the public service as a whole" (quoted in Cheek-Milby 1982, 219). As part of this, a planned expansion of the civil service was cut due to the pressure from some unofficials in the Legislative Council "over their perception of a burgeoning public sector in Hong Kong" (Cheek-Milby 1982, 219). Under these relative budgetary constraints, and due to new awareness of costs for an SAI Programme effective enough to resolve the problems it was intended to address, it may simply have no longer seemed a cheap option. If squatter improvement and doing nothing were both rejected as options, clearing squatters on dangerous slopes may then have seemed like the obvious, or only, option. However, deciding to resettle all squatters on dangerous slopes—and within 10 years to clear all additional remaining squatters in the urban areas—created an increased risk of expanded rehousing commitments. This situation would have made it more desirable or necessary to develop procedures that could help end continual growth of rehousing commitments and make the financial implications of the decision calculable.

It must be acknowledged that in many years before 1984, the government claimed that it had succeeded in containing new squatting. It had done so temporarily (although usually with exceptions outside the Housing Department's areas of responsibility); but new squatting had always reemerged before 1984. The 1982/83 Annual Report of the Housing Authority stated that the number of "new huts found and demolished each month dropped sharply, from about 5,000 in the early part of the year to less than 2,000 at the end. . . . By the end of the year, new illegal squatting had been effectively contained" (8). The Crown Land Ordinance amendment of 1982 sharply increased penalties for "racketeers" building squatter structures, while reducing the evidentiary requirements for proving profit from such activities. Part of the rationale was that despite "full control . . . pressure of new squatting is still intense. Racketeers are still very much in evidence, and are held in check only by a strong presence on the ground."[24] The wording of the Bill was broad enough to make the Crown Counsel worry that it could include help in construction by family and friends.[25] In 1984, the HA requested 16 additional clearance staff in part to undertake non-development clearances. The number of squatters cleared had increased to 87,536 in 1982–1983, a 61.6% rise from the previous year. It rose another 64,730 in 1983–1984.[26] This expansion does occur before the Joint Declaration but after negotiations had begun with Beijing, so it might offer some circumstantial evidence for geopolitics enabling more repressive action against squatters. Since July 1982, all "new squatter structures are being quickly discovered and immediately demolished. This has had a marked deterrent effect on new squatting as can be seen from the following record of squatter control demolitions" dropping from 4,455 in July 1982 to 1,851 in March 1983.[27]

The 1983/84 HA Annual Report noted that various measures to speed up rehousing squatters were under consideration and that "the Authority hopes to reduce the total number of squatters by half within the next five years" (11). The 1984–1985 edition asserted that "[t]otal control over squatting has been maintained—there were no incidents of mass squatting or racketeering in the building of squatter huts. The key to this success lies in the well-established system of policing, with vulnerable areas covered by daily patrols." However, it acknowledged that "[p]erhaps the only drawback is the fact that control is still based on the structure rather than on its occupancy. To overcome this a registration exercise on all squatter inhabitants was set in hand during the year with a view to tightening up the eligibility criteria for rehousing. This should prevent queue jumping and, indeed, a start has been made whereby the occupancy of squatter huts is frozen once a family obtains permanent housing through the Waiting List" (13).

This statement clearly identifies the SOS as significant for plugging a loophole that remained after squatter control had become otherwise fully successful, thereby putting one of the last nails in the coffin of new squatting. It would also reduce the costs of resettling all squatters on dangerous slopes, and eventually all squatters in the urban areas. However, history supports some skepticism about the claims for the containment of new squatting. This had been repeatedly asserted over the years (as discussed in Chapter 7), yet when substantial new demand for this housing option boomed, either due to private housing redevelopment, migration, or housing costs, intensified squatter control mostly served to slow and divert the "squatter balloon" to areas under lighter control. This might have happened once again. The SOS not only closed this final loophole, but also reduced the attractiveness of squatting; after 1985, it would no longer offer a route to permanent public housing.

The discussions of the SOS in the files offers some insights into the rationale for adopting the Survey. There is less information than might have been hoped for, perhaps because of the distraction of the Sino-British negotiations going on during this period. On 5 April 1984, the HA's Operations Committee approved a recommendation that "a survey of occupants of squatter areas should be undertaken." This recommendation was approved by the full HA, but it decided that the plan "should not be included in the Consultative Document 'A Review of Public Housing Allocation Policy' for public discussion" in order to "reduce the likelihood of false claims to squatter hut occupancy being staked."[28] This concern to avoid publicity certainly contributed to the lack of public and academic discussion of the SOS.

The main rationale for carrying out a survey of squatter occupants, despite the claim that new squatting was already contained, was that "the survey of squatter *huts* does not prevent them changing hands either by being sold by racketeers or by the squatters themselves. This loophole in the present system enables a number of people to 'jump the queue' into public housing. Nor is there any way of controlling the increase in the numbers of people occupying existing surveyed structures." It was claimed that registration of squatters would produce several advantages: "(a) the size of the squatter population would be controlled other than by natural increases in family size; (b) as there would be no advantage in buying squatter structures the sale of these would be much reduced; (c) the eventual rehousing commitment of squatters could be accurately quantified; and (d) during the survey the opportunity could also be taken to encourage all squatters to submit waiting list applications." Statistics of the squatter population were "based upon the number of surveyed structures multiplied by an estimate occupancy rate of 4 persons per structure. The present estimate stands at 586,000 persons, but this is obviously a very approximate figure. (Note: this figure excludes the housing demand from other sectors e.g., tenement buildings, boat squatters and rooftop structures)."[29] Within this total estimate, 72,000 were in Hong Kong Island, 86,000 in Kowloon, 38,000 in Tsuen Wan, and 389,000 in the rest of the NT. Squatters were 11% of the total population of Hong Kong, compared to 14% in 1976 and 12% in 1982.

The disadvantages of the survey were that "there could be inevitable 'stake-claiming' and, hence, an increase in the squatter population might be expected"; it would not be practical to control "actual occupancy"; and preclearance screening would still have to be done. Clearances "could become more difficult as some squatters initially registered might subsequently be found to be ineligible for rehousing," due to insufficiently long residency in Hong Kong. Elsie Elliott said the "survey must not be misinterpreted by squatters as an exercise in rehousing; otherwise, this would only benefit racketeers who built structures for sale." Lee Lo Yuk-sim was "worried about partitioning of existing structures," while other members were concerned that "any survey would swell the number of squatters because of anticipation that an amnesty could be forthcoming. They expressed reservations as regards the publicising of this proposal." Elliot argued that "control should be further tightened by requiring squatters to register on the Waiting List." While there was some support for this point, the Secretary for Housing elaborated on some of the difficulties it would present, particularly that "in a clearance operation, Government was responsible for rehousing persons who were genuinely homeless." The proposal for the survey was supported, with a recommendation that adequate publicity should be given to advise squatters to register on the Waiting List.[30]

A full survey was estimated to require four to six weeks and a task force of 1,200 part-time staff, with an additional 250 housing assistants and 50 assistant housing managers. This estimate was based on a pilot survey in eight squatter areas in May 1984. Surveyors on that pilot claimed to have identified about 6–9% of interviews as involving *overclaims* (more occupants than actually resident) and imposters. It also found that an average of two structures could be enumerated in one hour, so that the total survey would require 72,500 man-hours. An alternative was to "survey squatter areas which will be affected by development clearances, with a lead time of, say, two years. Experience has shown that, in any such exercise, there will be those who 'stake claims' and hence result in a consequential increase in the squatter population, but this effect could be somewhat minimised by maintaining the element of surprise in the timing of the registration exercise."[31]

The advantage of the alternative survey methodology, conducted by existing Squatter Control staff, would be that it would be a "valuable aid in enabling squatter control field staff to gain a better knowledge of the people residing in the surveyed structures. . . . there is much to be gained in conducting periodic 'follow-up' visits within squatter control districts." These visits will "provide a means of either verifying or discounting claims to residence on behalf of persons not present at the time of the initial survey, and will also help in familiarising field staff with the regular occupants of squatter structures in addition to (as at present) their becoming familiar with only the structures. The occupancy records . . . will become an important source of information to be incorporated into subsequent pre-clearance surveys of individual squatter areas at the time squatters are rehoused." Information obtained in "the survey and subsequent visits should be entered into the 'HATMIS' computer, thus facilitating information retrieval and permitting cross-checks to be made in areas such as public housing applications and allocations." The second survey approach was adopted, with the emphasis on the urban areas first, but it is not clear if follow-up visits occurred. From Smart's interviews with Squatter Control officers in 1999, it does not appear that they did, although he did not specifically ask. The survey commenced on 12 September 1984 "on a low-key basis i.e., by Housing Assistants during their daily patrols, and would be completed within 12 months."[32]

The SOS was completed for the urban areas in September 1985. In a report on its administration, the procedure was that "[p]articulars of all members of each household who are living in the domestic structures were recorded on a printed registration form . . . The completed form was then shown or explained to an adult member of the family who was requested to sign the form to confirm that the information recorded was authentic and correct" (see Figure 10.1). The total survey found 123,626 families with 477,184 persons. Of these, 14.1% were in Hong Kong Island, 24.3% in Kowloon, 3.5% in Shatin, and 8.0% in Tsuen Wan, while 50.1% were in the rest of the NT. The large number in the NT was the result of growth in areas where control had been lightest. It was recognized that some occupants might be missed, so that "[s]hould the bona-fide occupants re-appear and apply for registration, their claims will be examined. If sufficient and convincing proof is provided with valid reasons for being absent at the time of the survey, they will be accorded."[33]

After the SOS, government direct control over actual occupancy of the surveyed structures was not considered to be "practical because: (a) this would necessitate the introduction of some 'licensing' system with the implication

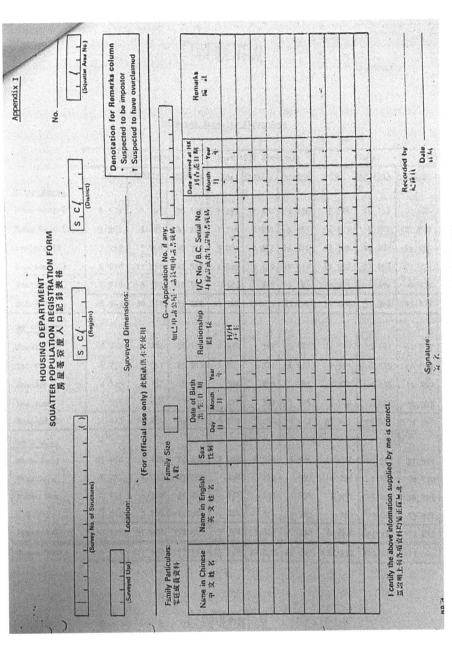

Figure 10.1: Squatter population registration form. Source: HKRS696/3/127.

that the Government formally accepted liability for the safety and well-being of all squatters; and (b) day-to-day control to check and contain 'licensed' occupancy would be a near-impossible task and could well be criticized as an invasion of privacy and result in strong objections."[34] Instead, it would be possible for people to move in to squatter structures after the SOS, but this would be discouraged and penalized by the change of policy. The squatter survey "together with the application of residential and income criteria . . . would be the basis for establishing those eligible for permanent public housing. These measures should greatly minimise but might not completely prevent the claims for belated registration on the basis of alleged absence during the time the survey is carried out. It is considered that preclearance surveys and detailed screening would still be necessary before clearance is carried out. But the workload should be reduced."[35]

Beyond registering squatter occupants, the SOS was tied to a major policy change. Once the "squatter population was so registered, any person not recorded as an occupant of a surveyed structure would not be eligible for permanent housing in a subsequent clearance exercise or if the hut in question is destroyed by fire or landslip. In other words, despite meeting the prevailing residential qualification, such a person, if found to be genuinely homeless, would only be offered temporary housing and would only become eligible for permanent housing (through trawling or clearance)."[36] Although it had been the intention from the decision to conduct the SOS to use it to limit eligibility for PPH, it was only in September 1986 that the formal decision was taken to "use the 84/85 occupancy survey as an additional rehousing criterion."[37] The new eligibility rules are summarized in Table 10.1.

Table 10.1: New rehousing arrangement after the SOS in 1984. Compiled by the authors.

	Region	Eligibility Criteria	Rehousing Categories
(i)	Urban Area	1982 Survey Structure + 10 years' residence + Occupancy Survey	Urban Permanent Public Housing
(ii)	New Territories	1982 Survey Structure + 10 years' residence + Occupancy Survey	New Territories Permanent Public Housing
(iii)	Urban Area	1982 Survey Structure + less than 10 years' residence + Occupancy Survey	Urban Temporary Housing
(iv)	New Territories	1982 Survey Structure + less than 10 years' residence + Occupancy Survey	New Territories Temporary Housing
(v)	Urban Area and New Territories	All others	New Territories Temporary Housing

The Squatter Occupancy Survey   223

It was also necessary to deal with the issue of registered squatter occupants who had moved from one surveyed structure to another between the SOS and the announcement of the policy. It was decided that such squatters could apply to change their registered dwelling, but the dwelling must be surrendered to HD for demolition "or for occupancy freezing if the structure cannot structurally be demolished." It also could not take place after posting of clearance notices, and no transfer from the NT to the urban areas would be allowed. These conditions were to discourage people from moving for other than very genuine needs. The decision attempted to minimize a number of potential problems: queue-jumping ("[s]quatter may take the opportunity to move to areas with imminent clearances so as to obtain housing offers ahead of others"); hut sales ("this will give rise to speculation and more sales of huts"); and if "many people tried to move into imminent clearance areas, they could generate unpredicted rehousing commitment in that area, thus upsetting clearance plans." Furthermore, "If the structure to be vacated by the applicant is not surrendered for demolition or cannot be demolished because of structural linkage to another, there is the chance for reoccupation by new squatter families thus leading to additional rehousing commitment upon clearance in future." The guidelines for changing place of registration were thought to "answer individual needs of squatters in a humane manner but provide adequate checks to prevent abuse of the system." Such transfers would be possible subsequently, but it was hoped to discourage it as much as possible. A check on the amount of movement between the SOS and the implementation of the new eligibility criteria across numerous pre-clearance surveys, however, found that 16.4% of residents had moved in since the SOS. It was hoped that the new criteria would sharply reduce such movements.[38]

Policy changes after the implementation of the SOS and the new eligibility criteria, however, created the potential for new loopholes through which the squatter balloon could expand further. In particular, new rehousing commitments for "back-lane" squatters subject to environmental clearances and for rooftop squatters (see Chapter 7) were created by two decisions to equalize their rehousing eligibility with that of ground squatters in 1986.[39] It was noted that "[b]ack lane squatters were excluded from the 1984/85 Occupancy Survey, but were surveyed in April 1986. Rooftop dwellers have never been surveyed. Under the criteria proposed . . . these squatters would only qualify for TH in NT upon clearance. This would be unacceptable,"[40] although precisely why was not unspecified.

The change for rooftop squatters faced opposition; it had a "sticky passage partly because of the Chairman's hobby-horse of absolute support for waiting list applicants, at the expense of squatters (all of whom he sees as 'illegal') and partly because of the unfortunate and very insensitive attitude" of the Building Ordinance Office representative. There were also worries about "taking on a commitment for rooftop squatters other than those in 'dangerous' buildings," but generally the "disparity of treatment was recognised, as well as the fact that the proposed quota is a very modest one. After much discussion it was agreed that the freezing survey" of rooftop squatters should be carried out. The Chairman of the HA Operations Committee had "commented that the proposal was unfair for Waiting List applicants who had to wait for years and pass through the income test in order to obtain public housing."

J. W. Hayes pointed out that some rooftop structures had been erected for 20 to 30 years and were "tolerated by relevant government departments of necessity. The occupants were required to pay rates and stamp duties as the residents of private properties. He felt it would be reasonable to accord the rooftop squatters the same housing arrangements as those involved in development clearances and dangerous buildings. He said that the Building Ordinance Office had encountered considerable resistance in squatter clearances, and it would be necessary for other departments concerned to provide appropriate support." E. B. Wiggham remarked that the proposal would treat all squatters alike: "The purpose of the paper was to balance the competing demands from various categories of people rather to suggest any preferential treatment for the rooftop squatters." HD "had agreed to take over the responsibility of environmental clearances with effect from 1 April 1986. In order to be consistent, it would be advisable to bring the arrangement for the rooftop squatters in line with those for other squatters."[41]

In both cases, however, it was decided that to avoid encouraging increased squatting in these sectors, a "freezing survey" similar to the SOS would be needed. Structures on rooftops, lanes, pavements, roads, boat squatters and structures on private building land had been excluded from the SOS: "The reason for their exclusion is that control of these structures do not fall within the responsibility of the Housing Department."[42] Seven thousand six hundred and thirteen back-lane structures were found, but only 1,854 of these were domestic; 96% were in urban areas.[43] For both back-lane and rooftop squatters, if their resettlement eligibility was equalized with ground squatters, and no "freezing survey" like the SOS was carried out, there would be new niches in which squatting could once again expand. So the logic of the SOS had to be extended to these other sectors if new squatting was truly to be ended.

There was, however, one final loophole that would eventually be closed only in 1995. Before then, squatter clearees not eligible for PRH were rehoused to THAs upon clearance. Upon clearance of the THAs, eligible residents were rehoused to PRH. Thus, squatter occupants not included in the SOS could still have the chance of getting into permanent public housing if the THA they were resettled in was demolished for redevelopment. On 23 September 1995, the Housing Authority approved the policy that all residents rehoused to THA or Interim Housing sites that were announced after 23 September 1995

The Squatter Occupancy Survey

(that is, those THA clearances already in progress at that time were exempted from the new exclusion) had to register on the Waiting List. Any subsequent rehousing to PRH for them would depend on their position on the Waiting List and their "fulfillment of the WL [Waiting List] eligibility criteria. Since then, THA/IH [Interim Housing] licensees have not been automatically rehoused to PRH [Public Rental Housing) upon clearance." Those whose Waiting List applications are "not yet mature are only rehoused to another THA or IH [Interim Housing]." This "9.23 Policy" was intended to "eliminate the possibility of queue-jumping by squatting and to ensure rational allocation of public housing resources."[44] Why the closing of this two-step loophole was delayed for a decade would be an interesting research question we cannot answer at this point, but it may simply have been another example of "out of sight, out of mind" or the "turning a blind eye" form of toleration (Smart and Aguilera 2020).

These innovations and policy reactions enabled a bureaucratic ratchet of exclusion that could reduce the total stock of squatting in additional to ending new squatting. Ratchets are tools that can only turn in one direction, so they can tighten[45] without slipping in the other direction. The SOS provided a similar mechanism. After it was completed, and even if full control on new squatting was maintained through expansion of surveillance and demolition, people could still move in and out of existing squatter structures. It remained possible to subdivide squatter dwellings to accommodate additional individuals or families. The squatter property market did not disappear, although the prices dropped in response to the disappearance of clearance as a path to permanent public housing; the attractions to middle-class people greatly diminished (Smart 1988). This was particularly true after the 9.23 Policy was imposed in 1995, since even the indirect path to PPH through THAs would be closed to those with incomes above the Waiting List limits. But as registered occupants moved out or died, others could still move in. There was an effort to demolish the dwellings of those who obtained public housing through the Waiting List, but this was only possible if the structure was not subdivided or shared. Even when there was only the one family resident, destroying the dwelling could endanger adjacent structures that relied on each other for physical integrity or stability. Otherwise, people moved in, but the crucial change was that they would only be eligible for temporary, not permanent, public housing, and only in the NT. As clearances escalated, for development as well as for the new program of non-development clearances, the number of squatter structures dropped. While the total population of surviving structures could increase through greater crowding, in general the squatter population declined gradually but inexorably. These circumstances also reduced the incentives for new squatting elsewhere. In combination with intensified squatter control, these factors resulted in the end of new squatting. A goal that had been sought for four decades, and which had periodically been prematurely declared, had finally been accomplished and made to stick, right to the present.

Conclusion

Improvement of squatter structures and settlements, other than by demolition and replacement, was only at the forefront of Hong Kong policy for a brief time in 1971. Although it temporarily eclipsed Governor Trench's two suggestions for dealing with non-developable squatter areas, the launching of the Ten-Year Housing Programme sidelined it. It reemerged in 1982, because the policy-induced imbalances of public housing between supply and demand made resettling all squatters on land not needed for development infeasible. Squatter improvement of infrastructure could reduce the "squalor," while delaying adding them to the increasingly unmanageable and politicized queue for scarce housing. Yet, the material features that made it difficult to deal with these areas through conventional development clearances also raised increasingly unacceptable risks because of their concentration on dangerous slopes. The price tag for squatter improvement soared, making expedited clearance seem relatively more attractive.

Resettling all squatters, though, could only be practicable if new squatting was brought to an end. Otherwise, the policy would encourage new squatting, thereby increasing the costs of the policy innovation. It is possible that a substantial expansion of resources devoted to controlling new squatting could have been successful, particularly since geopolitics was stripping away external sources of support for squatter resistance, while the rise of local Hong Kong identity was reducing their internal support. However, as the persistently failing War on Drugs demonstrates, when demand persists for something—whether heroin or prohibited forms of housing—intensified repression, even when largely successful, usually just increases prices and encourages greater effort to supply the demand (Heyman and Smart 1999). It would be more effective to combine heightened squatter control with actions that could close loopholes that encouraged squatting. In this respect, the SOS was, at a minimum, of great importance to the ending of new squatting.

Without the registration of occupants of squatter areas, and the exclusion of unregistered occupants from permanent public housing, the last important loophole would have persisted (since the back-lane, rooftop and two-step THA loopholes were only the consequence of the partial coverage of SOS-enabled exclusion). New occupants moving into existing squatter areas would have gained access to permanent public housing on clearance, adding to the housing commitment, which would have complicated the extension of the non-development clearance program. It would also have increased the cost of the plan to clear all urban squatter areas prior to 1997, although that did

The Squatter Occupancy Survey

not actually occur. Remnant populations remained in urban areas in 2022, with hundreds of thousands in the NT (see Conclusions). The SOS, then, may not have been indispensable to achieving the goal of ending new squatting, but it played an important role in facilitating it. It did so in part by reducing the attractions of new squatting, as well as by reducing the costs of the non-development clearance program. It also by extension spurred more effective controls on other types of illegal occupation, leading to "freezing surveys" on back-lane (environmental) and rooftop squatters.

For a policy change that has had so much impact on the making of late colonial and contemporary Hong Kong, it is remarkably poorly known outside the Hong Kong government (and probably within it, as well). Besides considering its adoption and impact on the ending of new squatting in 1984, this chapter has also documented how it was implemented. It still exists and operates in contemporary Hong Kong, but this is not the place to address that non-historical question. We will touch on it in the Conclusions. However, an adequate account of it would require another—ethnographic as well as documentary—research project.

Prior to the Conclusions—which will bring together the various plausible explanations of the turning of the tide against informal housing and draw out some of the implications of this book—in the next chapter, we broaden our perspective by considering the management of squatters in other Asian cities. This effort will help to make clear what aspects of the Hong Kong story are unique, what similarities can be identified, and how much variation exists in the region. It also will make clear how squatter management approaches in Hong Kong could have taken very different paths, with diametrically different possible outcomes.

11

Managing Squatting in Other Asian Cities

> Urban land is distinctive in that social and economic pressures almost compel it to become real estate . . . proximity increases the impact of externalities, which requires the regulation of land use, construction and occupancy. Regulation requires a greater role for the state and, by extension, more potential informality. In a village, amateur builders are unexceptional; in a city, they may become unacceptable.
>
> —Richard Harris, "Modes of Informal Urban Development:
> A Global Phenomenon" (2018, 268)

Introduction

The explanations for how and why Hong Kong managed to end new squatting in 1984 were developed specifically for that historically distinctive situation. Some aspects of our account could be applied in other contexts, which might highlight additional types of explanation and spur new lines of inquiry for understanding squatter management in Hong Kong and elsewhere. In this chapter, we make an initial effort—which would require more time and space (and locally knowledgeable research collaborators) to fully develop—to work toward a model to better understand the diverse methods used to control squatting. We consider only the squatting of land, by far the most common form in the Global South, omitting the squatting of existing buildings, more common in the Global North, particularly Europe (Aguilera and Smart 2016). We concentrate on governmental management and control of squatting, which have more in common, rather than the architecture, history, social organization, and individual experience of informal housing in different Asian cities—aspects with much greater diversity (Smart and Aguilera 2020).

Prior to describing squatter control and the situation for formalization in each case, we begin by applying two prior efforts to develop typologies for this field. The first considers three different modes of forced eviction. The second focuses on varying forms of toleration of informal housing. Toleration allows residents of illegal settlements to remain in their unconventional shelter "for the time being," without providing security of property rights or entitlements. Toleration, in a way, allows the administration to have its cake and eat it too, allowing some people to provide housing for themselves without allowing a permanent loss of the space from governmental control.

These varieties of tolerated squatting are situated on a spectrum between complete repression/eradication (in other words, all squatting is demolished without undue delay) and legalization of all existing squatter structures. Underlying these strategies are also issues of state capacity (Smart and Aguilera 2020). Even if the policy toward squatting is one of zero tolerance, as in Kuala Lumpur, governments usually fail to implement such a policy due to repressive incapacity: there may be too many people squatting for authorities to demolish all structures; resistance or political divisions may inhibit aggressive actions; or foreign funders such as the World Bank may sanction those who engage too harshly in forced eviction. On the other end of the spectrum, generous programs of squatter upgrading and titling may have limited success because of the reluctance of squatters to take up the legalization options available to them (Varley 2002). In addition to the position on the spectrum, there is variation of whether toleration is explicitly acknowledged or implicit in practices and in its trajectory. In many contexts, if a squatter area can survive the difficult first years, it begins to acquire services, residents improve their dwellings, and it gradually becomes difficult to visually distinguish from legal, low-income neighborhoods—a process that can be called "inexorable whitening" (see Yiftachel 2009). In Hong Kong, survival never led to legalization, but gradually increased the chances of explicit toleration.

There are three main modes of eviction of those illegally occupying urban space (Smart 2002). The political mode emphasizes confrontations mediated through power and coalitions of support—a situation frequently found in Latin America. It was common for politicians and even ruling parties to organize "invasions" of land, in support of social justice or to gain blocks of reliable supporters, since continued toleration or the provision of services could be contingent on active support for sponsoring brokers and patrons. Squatters may retain their hold on space, or even obtain legal tenure, through their ability to cause trouble or because of their utility to certain political groups—as blocks of votes or political labor, embarrassments to one's rivals, or showcases of progressive policy. The bureaucratic mode is less common and emphasizes specialized agencies that administer and control. These agencies may tolerate illegal occupation or provide compensation or resettlement when residents are evicted, but such compensations are maintained as ex gratia concessions, rather than entitlements or rights. The result is that few issues or cases surrounding illegal settlements in Hong Kong or Singapore have involved court cases or lawsuits—the main arena of the judicial mode—which is dominant in liberal democracies such as the United States. Instead, the focus of conflict

230   Hong Kong Public and Squatter Housing

has been on administrative practices and guidelines, on mobilizing political support to modify the policies and practices used to administer squatter clearance and resettlement.

Our selection of cases is partially driven by the availability of adequate research; but it also aims to cover a large range of variation. We combine comparison of most similar systems and most different systems (Smart 1989a). Singapore has the greatest similarities to Hong Kong's squatting experience. China, despite its geographical and cultural proximity to Hong Kong, is a considerably different example because of its political economy. India is the most different case culturally but shares the British colonial influence. There is a large variation in wealth, which could affect state capacities to respond to squatting. In 1984, Singapore had the highest per capita GDP at US$7,228, followed by Hong Kong at US$6,208. As city-states, they are difficult to compare with the other cases, as nations with large rural sectors. China in 1984 was the poorest, with GDP per capita of US$251, followed by India (US$277), the Philippines (US$595), and Malaysia (US$2,234).

Chinese Cities

Squatting is largely absent from post-1949 China, but illegal building is not, particularly after 1979. The forms taken by illegal building in China are very different from those found in Hong Kong after 1954. The People's Republic of China was unusual among low-income countries in that it did not develop large, uncontrolled squatter settlements. In part, this was because of restrictions on urbanization, so that the urban population stayed relatively low as a proportion of the total before the twenty-first century, and partly due to the greater capacity of the communist state to control activities compared to the capitalist Least Developed Countries (LDCs, now usually called the Global South). Since economic reforms were adopted in 1978, migration to the cities grew massively. And because most lacked household registration in the cities, illegal building has also increased substantially, with illegal land use accounting for about 10% of the total changes in land use between 1993 and 1999 (Tang and Chung 2002, 47). Comparison with capitalist LDC cities offers insights into various dimensions of the Chinese reform urban landscape. The relevance of LDC experience particularly applies to situations where central control has eroded, and irregular and illegal spaces have come into being and persisted despite various efforts to eradicate them or reassert control (Zhang 2001).

The process of creating markets for real estate in early reform China, particularly during the 1980s, shows similar dynamics in a very different context. Illegal building must be seen in the context of contestation over the classification of "grey" practices (Zhu 2002). There were widespread expectations that local practices for developing land would eventually become "white," as had other economic projects that "pushed the envelope" of acceptable practice under the reforms (Smart 2000). Unlike Hong Kong, most illegal land use resulted from the activities of rural collectives and state organizations on land they had use rights for. Some practices, such as secondary market exchange of allocated land, eventually became legal, while others eventually became a black market. The system of property rights in land have become more routinized, particularly since the Land Administration Law of 1998 (Xie, Parsa, and Redding 2002). But illegal building is still pervasive in the form of what have become known as urban villages or villages in the city (as well as building on arable land in the countryside). While the state usually sees urban villages as a problem, their distinctive property rights have "enabled indigenous villagers to build inexpensive housing units in order to start small rental businesses and . . . provide low-rent housing for migrants" (Sheng, Gu, and Wu 2019, 339). Demolishing these neighborhoods can have very damaging consequences for migrant livelihoods. Some cities, such as Shenzhen, appear to have a greater understanding of the contributions of urban villages, probably because its explosive growth rates could hardly have been sustained without such informal expansion of the housing supply. Without local registration, migrants are easily removed when considered problems, although migrants could go underground. However, avoiding detection is becoming harder in a world of ubiquitous cameras linked to biometric ID cards and the world's most effective facial recognition system (Curran and Smart 2021).

Demolition is massively used for redevelopment: out of 10.2 million *forced evictions* worldwide from 1995 to 2005, 4.1 million occurred in China (Advisory Group on Forced Evictions 2007). The continued ubiquity of demolition has prompted descriptions of "bulldozer urbanism" characterized by "escalated demolition and displacement under the joint forces of a socialist state and neoliberal market" (Ling 2020, 1142). The predominant planning tendencies include biases against migrants, informally developed urban villages, and "low-end" populations and built environments in general. These preferences are associated with the promotion of land uses that meet central government targets, look modern, and generate as much revenue as possible for real estate-dependent local governments.

It appears that little new illegal building takes place at present. Toleration of urban villages and illegal building has also gradually been reduced as China is trying to project a modern and prosperous image. The influence of local village leaders and the utility of these spaces for accommodating migrants results in temporary toleration, but demolition, resettlement (usually to the urban fringes), and redevelopment appears to be the ultimate fate of most if not all urban villages. Guo et al. (2018) reveal Liede urban villagers in central Guangzhou as "major players in redevelopment." The villager as developer and/or rentier has largely been neglected in the dominant narrative of rural/urban citizenship divisions as oppressive to those unable to escape rural status (Smart and Smart 2017b). In recent years, the housing boom has come under both political and economic pressure. Macroeconomic conditions combined with the large increase of developed land result in decreased demand for land and dropping land lease fees. The Guangzhou government, according to Guo et al. (2018), blamed the 21 approved urban village redevelopment schemes, which were planned to supply an additional 11.9 million m² of building land. The fear is of more "ghost cities" of the type that are haunting accounts of China's newly shaky expansion, raising fears on stock markets and commodity exchanges around the world (Lin et al. 2019).

The mode of eviction in Chinese cities has primarily been political, with better connected urban villages persisting longer while those that are visible "eyesores" are targeted earlier, such as before the Beijing Summer Olympics. However, there are signs of a trend toward the dominance of a judicial mode, through the development and enforcement of clearer controls on building, but with China's distinctive form of jurisprudence. Toleration of urban villages was seen as transitional, facilitating migration and fast urban growth (Zhang 2001), but is now disappearing and being replaced by efforts to "formalize and regularize such informality in pursuit of modernist city images and higher property returns" (Liu and Wong 2018, 161). There are local examples of upgrading and regularization of them, such as Liede urban village in central Guangzhou. Rather than resettlement to more peripheral districts, one-third of the site was reserved for high-rise in-situ resettlement of all villagers, while another third was used for a hotel which would generate income for village shareholders, and the final third was commercially developed to pay for the redevelopment costs of the first two thirds. In addition, Guangzhou informally tolerated illegal building above a maximum eligible for resettlement compensation. But the migrant tenants were ignored in the process (Hu et al. 2020). However, demolition, resettlement in the fringes, and redevelopment is by far the dominant path to formalization (Liu and Wong 2018).

Singapore

Of the cities we consider, Singapore was the first to end new squatting, by the mid-1970s (Loh Kah Seng, personal communication)—a decade before Hong Kong. A 1947 colonial government report stated that "Singapore had one of the world's worst slums, 'a disgrace to a civilised community,'" with about 300,000 people in "temporary squalid dwellings in squatter areas with no sanitation, water or any of the basic health facilities and another 250,000 in ramshackle shophouses within the city area, in neighborhoods such as Chinatown" where gross overcrowding was common (quoted in Yuen 2007, 273). Brenda Yeoh

Managing Squatting in Other Asian Cities

(2003) has extensively documented the colonial efforts to control the sanitary problems created by overcrowded shophouses. As late as 1968, about 20% of the population lived in temporary structures (Yeung and Drakakis-Smith 1974). The situation changed rapidly after Singapore separated from Malaysia in 1965, following serious ethnic riots between Chinese and Malays (Nagata 1979). Public housing was adopted as a key mechanism for nation-building. By 1965, 23% of the population lived in Housing and Development Board (HDB) units (Loh 2009b), while, in 1985, 85% of Singaporeans lived in publicly provided housing, and 85% of these were in government-assisted home-ownership on a 99-year lease (Chua 2000). As Singapore sought to become a multiracial, multilingual society, public housing allocation since 1960 has been premised upon balancing a mixture of different major ethnic groups (Yeung and Drakakis-Smith 1974).

Singapore adopted a bureaucratic mode of forced eviction, even more so than Hong Kong. The authority of the HDB was inclusive and considerable. Under the 1966 Land Acquisition Act, the government can compulsorily acquire any land for public interest. The act provides for compensation determined by the state, with no account taken of "any potential value for more intensive uses, only the existing use or zoned use is considered, whichever is lower. The prices paid by the HDB for the acquired lands are therefore usually much lower than the market price" (Yuen 2007, 277). These powers, and the decline of a left-wing party that had supported the resistance of rural landowners, resulted in the disappearance of political support for resistance to land acquisition and resettlement. The Singaporean government increased its ownership of land from 40% when the British left to 85% by the end of the twentieth century (Chua 2000). The dominance of housing provision by the HDB has given the government a "very strong hold on the material interest of the vast majority of the population, making it very difficult for opposition forces to find a crack in its political power over the people" (Chua 2000, 58). Public housing became the "chief instrument of social change after the war," intended "to mould the semi-autonomous residents into model citizens of the high modernist nation-state." (Loh 2009a, 140).

The population of the urban *kampongs* (as they were known locally) grew from 127,000 in 1947 to 246,000 in the mid-1950s, in large part due to migration from China and Malaya. By 1955, growing resistance to eviction lead the City Council to designate areas "with wooden houses and the adjacent vacant lands as 'attap areas,' in effect authorising these lands for settlement" (Loh 2009a, 146), tolerating them. We might consider this to be what Smart has called "reluctant toleration." There were plans to regulate utilities and house forms, similar to Hong Kong's licensed areas, but little implementation occurred. The Singapore Improvement Trust was aggressive in clearance and established 18 squatter resettlement areas (Loh 2009a). It also established "tolerated attap areas" in 1955. Dwellings in these kampongs were supposed to meet strict housing standards. In the late colonial period, two rural associations were crucial in helping to forge a potent alliance of workers, students, and wooden house dwellers against colonial rule in the mid-1950s. The People's Action Party, which has been the ruling party ever since Singapore became self-ruling in 1959 (with full independence in 1965), mobilized low-income Chinese kampong dwellers, which "was instrumental in its resounding victory in the 1959 general elections" for home rule without formal independence (Loh 2009a, 151). However, as a ruling party, it continued the British clearance practices even after the HDB replaced the Singapore Improvement Trust. The policies continued to experience serious resistance, and the building program faced an impasse that limited land acquisition. This "impasse was broken by the outbreak of Singapore's biggest fire at Kampong Bukit Ho Swee on 25 May 1961, destroying 2,200 dwellings and rendering 15,694 people homeless" (Loh 2009a, 151), paralleling developments around the 1953 Shek Kip Mei fire in Hong Kong. Anti-communist actions against supporters of the squatters crushed effective resistance. Loh Kah Seng (2009a, 155) argues that in Hong Kong, the "presence of a tentative colonial administration undermined the squatter clearance campaign. In Singapore, by contrast, the program was much more robustly pursued by a postcolonial government that had acquired the mantle and methods of colonial kampong clearance but also possessed a singular will to reconfigure state-society relations." He describes the "basic political motivation behind the development of public housing in Singapore" as being to "transform the semi-autonomous urban kampong population into a model and integrated citizenry" (Loh 2009b, 619).

During the colonial period and in the first years of independence, there was a significant degree of toleration of squatter structures, sometimes explicitly. This was occasioned by repressive incapacity, particularly during the British period, because of the support of strong anti-colonial forces for the resistance of squatters against eviction. In a manner similar to the Shek Kip Mei fire in Hong Kong, the 1961 Bukit Ho Swee fire broke the logjam of the need to displace squatters to facilitate large-scale public housing construction (supply and demand imbalances). The main difference was that the Singaporean public housing plans were much more ambitious, and the rehousing of squatters was part of a nation-building project. With the great majority of residents of Singapore accommodated in public housing of higher quality than that in Hong Kong, the need for new squatting was greatly lessened and the demolition of squatter areas was facilitated (Aldrich 2016).

Early resistance to rehousing by squatters could be violent and dangerous (Loh 2009b). In the early years of squatter rehousing, more affordable household expenses and lifestyle familiarity outweighed the advantages and facilities available in the new housing estates for many. It was a "wrenching experience

Managing Squatting in Other Asian Cities 235

for them in personal, social, and economic terms. At times, the squatters would refuse to move and frustrate plans of redevelopment." To ease resettlement, squatters were "offered resettlement terms and encouraged to move, failing which action would be taken in the courts to obtain warrants for eviction" (Yuen 2007, 288). Eviction was the last measure and resettlement policy was "continually reviewed to provide a better deal in resettlement compensation so that 'there will be no room left for pro-Communist elements to instigate the farmers and squatters against the Government.'"[1] Here we can see evidence of judicial and political modes of eviction, but by the end of new squatting in the 1970s, the situation had stabilized into a classic example of a dominantly bureaucratic mode of eviction. As opposed to Hong Kong, which had used the Squatter Occupancy Survey to end new squatting through exclusion, Singapore had completely ended the squatter problem by making increasingly high-quality dwellings available to almost all squatters. By the end of the twentieth century, 90% of Singaporean citizens or permanent residents qualified for public housing (Chua 2002), although foreign workers—1.3 million out of 5.07 million total population—are not included and are often housed in crowded dormitories. While we have been unable to find details about how new squatting was ended, a combination of generous rehousing and strict policing seems likely to be the means by which this early ending of new squatting was achieved, perhaps a decade before Hong Kong accomplished it.

Kuala Lumpur

In his comparison of Southeast Asian squatters, Brian Aldrich (2016, 496) concluded that, unlike the other cities he considered, "Singapore, Hong Kong and Kuala Lumpur, with an integrated elite and no mobilized squatter organizations with resources, rehoused all or almost all of the members of the informal settlements." Kuala Lumpur has fewer similarities with Hong Kong than Singapore but shares British colonial history. The issue of squatters was a major problem in the urban areas in Malaysia, particularly Kuala Lumpur. A 'Zero Squatter by 2005' Program had managed to relocate almost all squatters in the extended Kuala Lumpur area by about 2006 (Abdullah et al. 2017, 26). Although sporadic incidents of new squatting occur, enforcement appears to be reasonably effective in Kuala Lumpur and environs. In 2015, there were still 68,861 squatter families (284,892 individuals) in Malaysia (increased from 64,129 in 2013), and the zero date has been extended to 2020 for the country (Abdullah et al. 2017).

While small numbers of squatters have long existed in the Malayan Peninsula (Bunnell and Nah 2004), the growth of squatter areas (known locally as *perkampungan setinggan*) exploded during the Great Depression of the 1930s. During the "Malayan Emergency" from 1948 to 1960, about one million rural dwellers, mostly squatters and 86% of them Chinese, were forcibly moved into 600 New Villages, to combat the threat of Communist anti-colonial action (Sandhu 1964; Scott 1998).[2] The pre-independence "squatter problem" was almost completely about the Chinese, since Malays and Muslims could often obtain use rights to unoccupied land. After the Federated Malay States' Enactment of 1897, however, such rights were limited to land in rural areas of less than 100 acres. The subsequent Federated Malay States Land Code 1926 reduced this limit to plots not exceeding 10 acres (Bunnell 2006). For non-Muslim immigrants, however, obtaining land legally was difficult. Squatting was a common solution but left them in precarious situations. There were an estimated 400,000 Chinese squatters, dropping to about 150,000 by 1950 (Sandhu 1964).

Malaysia's 1971 New Economic Policy fostered high levels of rural-urban migration, but failed to provide sufficient affordable accommodation, so that squatter settlements spread and became denser, as in Hong Kong. The highest number of squatters was in Kuala Lumpur. Kuala Lumpur's population in 1968 included 32% squatters, which later increased to 37% in 1971 (Abdullah et al. 2017). Malay rural migrants arriving in Kuala Lumpur/Klang Valley after 1970 moved to existing squatter areas and opened up new ones on government or privately owned land (Bunnell 2002, 1689). The numbers continued to rise during the 1970s and 1980s, with much of the increase "accounted for by the expansion of the Federal District and the resulting incorporation of peripheral settlements" that had developed under a "traditional Malay land rights system which gave 'ownership' to anyone occupying and/or improving 'dead land'" (Aldrich 2016, 499). These rights were restricted after independence from the British (Bunnell and Nah 2004). The relationship between customary law, colonial law, and colonial interpretation of customary tenure is contested and too complicated to address here (Zaki et al. 2010). This is particularly true for the Kuala Lumpur region, which is a Federal Territory carved out of the Selangor state. Many "squatters" still believe that they have rights to the land despite the changed legal system, which had dispossessed them in the early Independence Era (Abdul Aziz 2012). When such beliefs have influence on the breaking of rules, and by consequence also on those administering the land, we may think of this as *ambiguous toleration* (Smart and Aguilera 2020). That form of toleration applies when an activity is considered by the public to be legitimate despite governmental definition of it as illegal. In this kind of situation, toleration results in part from authorities' reluctance to anger citizens or voters who do not want resources used to clamp down on practices they do not think should be illegal. Such circumstances increase the likelihood of toleration through repressive incapacity.

Although administrative techniques and technologies can push problematic conduct in desired directions, government often fails in such efforts, particularly when popular ideas of legitimacy differ from governmental ideas of legality (Smart 2001). When intervention fails, though, there are usually consequences that may have to be responded to once again. For Kuala Lumpur, Tim Bunnell (2002, 1687) shows how "[t]he persistence of city kampungs and putatively 'kampung conduct' reveals both the limits and the limitations of the authoritative urban(e) code in contemporary Kuala Lumpur." Such codes can be used to delegitimize residents of squatter areas, even those established prior to the new land regime instituted in 1965 (Bunnell 2002). Such discursive efforts reduced popular support for squatters. Combined with a policy of subsidizing rehousing for squatters, more repressive policies became feasible.

A surge of evictions developed in the late 1980s, when land for development became a more important resource for the state governments while Kuala Lumpur and surrounding areas of the state of Selangor were fast expanding (Abdul Aziz 2012). Although often not meeting their targets or providing the quality of housing promised, the Malaysian government has been "relocating evictees into low-cost houses and flats since the 1980s. Evictees were initially placed in temporary settlements known as *rumah panjang* (long houses). These supposedly temporary transit shelters were to be occupied by these former *kampung setinggan* dwellers for a period between six months and two years while the government developed their new low-cost settlements" (Abdul Aziz 2012, 38).

Tim Bunnell (2002, 1690) argues that the official goal of making Kuala Lumpur into a squatter-free city is "bound up with broader governmental attempts to realise *Melayu Baru* (the 'new Malay') through appropriate urbanisation." The city's policy since the 1990s has been to resettle squatters into planned residential environments with modern amenities and facilities. The promotion of low-cost high-rise blocks in Kuala Lumpur "represents a programme of modernist regeneration which may be considered moral as much as infrastructural." Squatter relocation was associated with attempts from the 1990s on to (re)image Kuala Lumpur as a suitable destination for hypermobile global investment capital (Bunnell 2006).

In 2001, the Selangor state government, which surrounds but does not include the Kuala Lumpur Federal Territory, launched the Zero Squatters 2005 program, through which all squatter settlements in Selangor would be eradicated. The aim of the program was to improve the quality of life of former squatters and to "ensure that every single person living in Selangor is entitled to a house or a place of shelter. Squatter dwellers were to vacate the land they were illegally occupying and be relocated to various housing schemes." A key motivator was that "failure to solve the issue of squatter settlements would have an effect on the state government's credibility in achieving Selangor as a developed state by 2006" (Abdul Aziz 2012, 1). Two main strategies were used to achieve the zero squatters goal: resolving issues in existing squatter settlements; and preventing the construction of new squatter settlements.

Selangor had previously attempted to solve the issue of squatters but had never succeeded, as more squatter settlements were built over the years. Squatters "were regarded as an indicator of an imbalanced development of the state, but at the same time, squatter dwellers make a big contribution to the state's economic growth, especially through the industrial and production sectors" (Abdul Aziz 2012, 149). In addition, politicians had frequently supported and protected the squatter areas.

A squatter census, similar to Hong Kong's Squatter Occupancy Survey, was carried out in 2001 and found 43,547 families in Selangor. Subsequently, the state government announced it would eradicate without notice any new squatter settlements erected after 1997 (Abdul Aziz 2012, 37). After the census, it was discovered that new squatter dwellings were found each time they visited, or "when it was time for demolition. These new squatter dwellers would then claim that they too were eligible for compensation and low-cost housing units. However, as they had records of original squatter dwellers collected during the planning stage, the problems were easily resolved" (Abdul Aziz 2012, 151). By 2007, Selangor demolished 93.6% of squatter settlements throughout the state; 44,701 of the 47,756 squatter families were evicted (Abdul Aziz 2012, 37).

The considerable success of the program was due to the relatively generous (at least in comparison to Hong Kong, although the quality has been widely criticized) relocation arrangements. All squatters, except illegal immigrants, were eligible for relocation to low-cost housing developments, although some could not afford the subsidized mortgage payments and stayed in transit centres even after the new developments were completed. Although most relocations went fairly smoothly, there were still many people who compared their new accommodations negatively in comparison to their established squatter communities. Even though their "occupation of the land is illegal, the settlers still voice their rights over the settlements. The situation is worsened when politicians from opposing parties and 155 non-government organisations also support the dwellers in the form of promises and even providing legal support." To ensure a smooth relocation process and to prevent any conflicts, in the Zero Squatter 2005 program, "negotiations between the dwellers with the state assembly member and developers were often conducted. The negotiation revolved around matters regarding the price and the design of each housing unit, temporary shelters and other compensations and claims" (Abdul Aziz 2012, 155). A state government officer "stated that if any former squatter dwellers decided to take the matter to court and lost, they were not eligible for any compensation or low-cost housing unit." (Abdul Aziz 2012, 155). We can see in these descriptions a shift away from a political mode of eviction toward a bureaucratic mode, as well as an effort to avoid the involvement of the judicial system.

Toleration had been extensive prior to the 1980s, out of recognition of the need for the labor of migrants to the cities (reluctant toleration), combined with an inability to end squatting without a very large expansion of state-subsidized affordable housing (repressive incapacity). There may also have been some recognition of the dispossession that the transfer of customary land to the control of the Sultans in 1965 and the persistence of claims to the land (ambiguous toleration). The ability to pursue a zero-tolerance campaign against squatters, with considerable success, was facilitated by a generous rehousing policy, by conducting a squatter survey that fixed eligibility for the future, and by the increasing wealth of the Malaysian state.

Manila

Manila has relatively little in common with Hong Kong. It has a distinct colonial experience and one of the most vibrant democracies in Southeast Asia, which has translated into powerful and influential squatters' movements. It shares, though, extremely high densities and a persistent shortage of affordable housing.

Informal settlements, the locally preferred expression for squatter areas, sprang up after 1945, with official estimates of 46,000 in 1946, 98,000 in 1956, and 283,000 in 1963. The historic center of Intramuros was badly damaged by bombardments during the Second World War and occupied by squatters (Pante 2020). By 1990, there were 654 squatter areas, but many lived in clusters with small numbers outside these squatter areas. Van Naerssen (1993) estimated a total of 2.5 million in Metro Manila, about one-third of the population. At this time, he found that squatting "on land and building a shelter on it is not easy. By consequence, many poor families try to find a place in already established spontaneous settlements" so that population densities steadily increase (4). In 2010, there were more than half a million squatter households, about 20% of the total households in Metro Manila (Jensen et al. 2020, 394). In 2017, the estimate is 2.8 million informal settlers in Metro Manila (Du and Grieving 2020).

Government responses trace back to 1947, when the People's Homesite and Housing Corporation was set up by the government of the Philippines to provide cheap houses. By 1969, it had administered 19 projects. Only 12,000 sites for housing had been prepared or sold to relocated squatter families. The "prices were based on the actual costs and therefore out of reach for poor families. In fact, middle income families took advantage of the schemes" (Van Naerssen 1993, 5). A Slum Clearance Committee was established in 1950, which evicted squatters and transported them to sites outside the Metro Manila area. There were large evictions, particularly between 1960 and 1964. This neither helped the affected people nor resolved the problems, since the majority had little choice but to return to Manila and squat again (Berner 1996). These evictions occurred "despite promises by the then President Ramon Magsaysay that the squatters would be able to buy the land they occupied. This promise never materialized and instead, widespread struggles for land and against evictions ensued, followed by the equally violent suppression of squatter movements" (Jensen et al. 2020, 393).

In 1975, President Ferdinand Marcos passed a law (repealed in 1997) that declared squatting a criminal offense. This "stick" was "combined with the promise of carrots: For the first time, the state went to appreciable expenses in the housing sector" (Berner 1996, 5). The National Housing Authority (NHA) was founded in 1975 to serve the housing needs of the poorest 30% of the population. Its performance in the Marcos years "was outright pathetic"; between 1975 and 1985, a total of 4,054 new housing units were "constructed in NHA administered projects in all of the Philippines . . . To make things even worse, construction costs were far too high to meet the needs of the target groups" (Berner 1996, 5).

Under President Marcos (1973–1986) in situ squatter upgrading and sites-and-services proffered alternative approaches to formalization, with encouragement and financial support from the World Bank and the Asian Development Bank (Van Naerssen 1993). The World Bank used the Philippines to pilot its new strategies—self-help housing, sites-and-services, and squatter upgrading—that were influenced by the work of John Turner but were also criticized by him (Smart 2020). This involved the identification of 415 "blighted areas" in Metro Manila, with 1.6 million people, of which 253 were designated Areas for Priority Development (Berner 1996, 5). The Zonal Improvement Program (ZIP), initiated in 1977 and funded in part by the World Bank, was designed to upgrade the legal, environmental, social, and economic conditions of slum residents, with minimum relocation. It planned for 15,000 upgraded plots per year (150,000 persons/year) between 1983 and 1998 to eventually serve 2.2 million people (World Bank 1980). How much of this came into existence is unclear, but it was certainly much less than planned. The NHA upgraded only 1,020 informal settlement units in 2019. The Philippine Development Plan 2017–2022 budgets upgrading for 2.53% of NHA's housing production, while resettlement is allotted 35.86%. There has been a strong decrease in investment in informal settlement upgrading from the 1980s to the present (Du and Greiving 2020).

Other programs that provided alternatives to demolition and resettlement to peripheral areas have also had mixed results, such as the Community Mortgage Program (CMP) launched in 1989, which allowed squatters "to buy the land they occupy without compulsory, costly upgrading measures and decongestion that would displace 'excess' population" (Berner 1996, 7). It has benefitted 189,000 families since 1989 (Du and Greiving 2020). Without a government subsidy, and without compulsory expropriations of private land, it cannot "solve the sharpening contradiction of skyrocketing land prices and the low incomes of a large majority of the population. Under market rules, it would at best produce middle class settlements at the urban fringe" (Berner 1996, 8). This conclusion presages the widespread displacement of informal settlements in Manila described by Alvarez and Cardenas (2019).

These varying initiatives, and the constant increase in the number of squatters, makes it clear that repressive incapacity has been a major factor in the implicit toleration of squatting through benign neglect, particularly before squatting was made illegal in 1963. This is a good example of market toleration, where governments acknowledge the inability of enforcement to end lucrative markets where demand is strong, and thereby do not devote the resources that would be necessary to control it; as well as a situation of ambiguous toleration where there is widespread recognition of the justice of squatting when there are no viable alternatives. In comparing Manila's and Hong Kong's responses to the squatter problem up to the early 1960s, Denis Dwyer (1965, 166) argued that colonial rule in Hong Kong "enabled government officials to work within an atmosphere of benevolent despotism rather than one in which it is necessary to trim public policies carefully in response to pressure groups." Manila was also subject to considerable fragmentation of authority between local governments and central agencies, whereas Hong Kong could concentrate power within the Resettlement Department.

Finally, democratic politics in the Philippines empowered squatters as mobilizable blocks of votes. Government officials might sell land informally to new settlers, or settlements might be sponsored on government land by politicians (Ortega 2016). Hong Kong squatters had fewer political avenues to encourage toleration and better treatment, although geopolitics played a role in deterring repression before 1984 (Chapter 3, Smart 2006). Denis Dwyer suggests the greater ability of Hong Kong to resettle massive numbers of squatters compared to Manila was the result, in part, of the political apathy of Hong Kong's squatters. This attribution of "apathy" neglects the considerable degree of resistance to squatter clearance in the 1950s and later, and inappropriately reads back into the past the higher degree of compliance once resistance had forced the government to begin resettling rather than simply clearing, thus reducing the intensity of resentment (Smart and Lui 2009).

Manila has perhaps the most effectively organized squatters' movements in Southeast Asia, creating both a considerable obstacle and an incentive to offer better resettlement arrangements to make valuable land available for development (Aldrich 2016; Berner 1996). However, the considerable stigma attached to informal settlers (Garrido 2019; Ortega 2016) has tended to produce programs that disproportionately benefit the less poor within the communities. One result is a tendency to create divisions within the squatter movement, while its impact "either dwindled or morphed into patron-client relations" (Jensen et al. 2020, 404). The Philippine state either attempts to eliminate social movements by repression or uses patron-client relationships to co-opt them within the existing system (Van Naerssen 1993). The claims that informal settlers could make on the state and the elite decreased considerably "at the moment of resettlement. The informal settlers were no longer in the way of metropolitan dreams, elite accumulation, or a healthy city. They no longer posed a 'problem' needing to be managed. Rather, they were confined to areas outside the immediate interest and purview of the state and the elite" (Jensen et al. 2020, 405).

Toleration, irresistible demand, and politics resulted in the number of informal households in Metro Manila increasing for decades, with spikes of growth between 1980 and 1990. Since 2000, this "growth rate has declined along with a significant drop in the percentage of informal households" (Ortega 2016, 40). Their political claims to stay in their communities have "largely been trumped and/or co-opted by business interests," resulting in numerous demolitions of "thousands of homes to accommodate large-scale public-private partnership infrastructure projects and profitable developments" (Ortega 2016, 41). Informality is being annihilated, "undergirded by neoliberal-global developmentalism and facilitated by post-colonial relations on land and the state" (Ortega 2016, 48).

In 2009, tropical storm Ondoy revealed another way in which informal settlers are becoming delegitimized. The Chief Engineer of Quezon City (a major suburb of Manila) argued that local governments and the national government should cooperate to drive "informal squatters away from rivers, ponds, canals, esteros, and easements of other major waterways" (quoted in Alvarez and Cardenas 2019, 237). The disaster and following debates lead to a Metro Manila plan to relocate 104,219 informal settler families living in danger zones. Informal settlements, "which carried with them legacies of stigmatized landscapes and populations, were thought to endanger not only their own residents but the city's residents too" (Alvarez and Cardenas 2019, 238). Yet, this obsession with the dangers caused to the rest of the city by the transgressions of the informal settlers "ignored blockages generated and aggravated by the informalities and illegalities of private developments and elite landscapes. Malls, luxury condominiums, gated residential developments, and mixed-use enclaves for Manila's upper and middle classes have also been built along the Marikina River and the shores of Manila Bay, in some instances right on the edge of waterways or directly on top of tributaries" (Alvarez and Cardenas 2019, 241). Such elite spaces were not classified as dangers because they did not look like sources of danger. Selective interpretation and omission of facts supported a disaster risk-management strategy premised on the eviction of informal settlers. Alvarez and Cardenas (2019, 245) see this as the use of aesthetic governmentality (discussed in the next section) by building on elite and expert biases that saw "the slum as the source of urban flood risk via the territorial stigmatization of the slum-as-blockages." Social justice becomes submerged by management of risks, and the risk of flood becomes a compelling reason for resettlement in the periphery rather than on shorelines, which are highly prized spaces in any world-class city. Although only 6,171 informal settler families in these zones were evicted between July 2011 and February 2016, rather than the 104,219 informal settler families in danger zones targeted by Metro Manila, it seems likely that this emerging rationale will have continuing influence. Ironically, the United Nations Office for Disaster Risk Reduction (UNDRR) describes the Philippines as a leading country in integrating disaster risk-reduction into national laws and harmonizing processes, as well as methods to enable coherent implementation of the New Urban Agenda (Du and Greiving 2020, 19).

Despite these myriad setbacks, from a comparative perspective, it is striking that battles to retain informally settled land that is highly valued due to its location continue, and that not all informal settlers have yet been displaced into less desirable peripheral locations. Manila is a case that most clearly illustrates the political mode of eviction, which emphasises confrontations mediated through power and the ability to construct coalitions of support. Squatters may retain their hold on space, or even obtain legal tenure through their capacity to cause trouble or their utility to certain political groups (e.g., as blocks of votes or as political labor, embarrassments to rivals, or showcases of progressive policy).

Indian Cities

This section, like the one on Chinese cities, does not focus on a single city, because the informally housed population is much more widely distributed among many large cities, and the wealth of excellent research on squatter management has been conducted in different places. The main commonality between Hong Kong and Indian cities is the British colonial legacy. Several important urban planning innovations were first tried in India, such as the Bombay and Calcutta Improvement Trusts (Home 2013), which, via Singapore, influenced Hong Kong ideas about public housing. This legacy has also meant that there were large amounts of state land, which could both be more easily squatted and more easily redeveloped.

The number of squatters in India is difficult to estimate because of alternative and competing labels and definitions, which vary by state and city as well as across time. Squatter settlements are frequently called *jhuggi jhopri* (JJ) "which are largely built on land occupied outside formal processes" (Datta 2016, 6). However, most governmental efforts are targeted at slums, which are either notified (officially identified) by states or fit the census definition: "poorly built congested tenements, in unhygienic environment usually with inadequate infrastructure and lacking in proper sanitary and drinking water facilities" (quoted in Patel et al. 2020, 3). While many of these may have been illegally occupied or have informal tenure, the proportion is unclear. *Jhuggi jhopri* "clusters, urban villages, unauthorized colonies and even resettlement colonies are often classified under a more generic language of 'slum,' yet the everyday experiences of law, regulation and urban development for those living in JJ clusters differ sharply from those in other types of slums on account of their relationship with law" (Datta 2016, 6).

The 2011 Census of India reported that the slum population of the country amounted to 5.4% of the total population. India's official estimated urban slum population decreased from 54.9% of the total in 1990 to 24% in 2014 (Li et al. 2021). Rather than relying on the official census's estimate of slums, Patel et al. (2020, 6) used the more detailed 1% household survey by the census to generate their national estimate based instead on the United Nations definition of *slum* and the specific housing data. They found that 171.2 million people lived under at least one deprivation with their modified definition—"more than 2.6 times larger than the slum count given by the Census."

This underestimation applies to individual cities as well. Delhi is a good example. Of Delhi's population in 1959, 200,000 are estimated to have been squatters—13% of the total population (Dwyer 1965). In 2000, 47% of the total population of Delhi live in JJ and slum-identified areas. However, such counting may miss some inhabitants who sleep on the streets and those who reside in unidentified informal settlements (Padhi and Mishra 2021). It also misses many who encroach on or develop land without required authorization. According to Ghertner (2015, 6), "a comprehensive statistical summary of the size and distribution of Delhi's slum population has not been reported since 1998. The Delhi government itself is unaware of the total number of jhuggi colonies in Delhi and therefore continues to report 1998 numbers as if they were valid to this day." Just over 2 million people lived in JJ clusters in Delhi in 2000 (Datta 2016). Delhi's Municipal Corporation claims that "70 percent of all land development in Delhi—by jhuggi dwellers and wealthy property owners alike—violates the Master Plan. Indeed, most of the privileged few in Delhi who own private land received it at highly concessional rates from the government. Furthermore, the vast majority of the land used outside of the formal oversight of the state is occupied by the wealthy" (Ghertner 2015, 53). A 2006 report concluded that 80% of houses in Delhi "are illegal; they were built without permission, or violate existing building bylaws. Furthermore, 75 to 80% of space usage infringes on zoning laws, with prohibited activities of trade, industry, or service" (Rao 2013, 762). Benjamin and Raman (2011)

Managing Squatting in Other Asian Cities

describe a similar situation in Bangalore, and reveal how the push for clear digital land titles is best seen not as a technical fix but an interested intervention, permitting large corporations to assemble big tracts of land for information technology related development. Majumdar (2017, 84) says that "[i]n India in particular, a squatter or a jhuggi is quite simply another word for a seemingly incomprehensible heap of legal ambiguities, messy politics and abject poverty," which seems to be true, but only if you neglect the ambiguities and mess of the land encroachments of the rich and powerful.

After independence in 1947, if government intervention into housing and settlement

> was thought imperative at all, there were no adequate legal and policy instruments that could be used for this purpose ... Poor migrants occupied (public) land as they had done before. Land owners subdivided and sold their land without 'authorisation'. . . . It was a continuation of the old ways of doing things. In the meantime, new laws have been passed, new organisations established, public policy documents and discussion papers have been prepared, and a host of land and housing schemes have been implemented. Still, in the larger share of the Indian cities, the delivery of residential land takes the form of squatting and illegal or semi-legal land subdivision. (Baken 2003, 2)

In the first decades of independent India, then, repressive incapacity was linked with pervasive ambiguous toleration.

Understanding the patterns of squatter management in India is complicated by the federal system, which results in very different treatment between states. In addition, the categories have been blurred to the point that *squatter* has become more a term of abuse than a technical legal term. Data on illegal settlers is poorly compiled and often ambiguous. Roy (2002, 27) captures this omission with a quote from a supervisor of slum surveys in Calcutta who told her that: "Our study deliberately excluded all squatter settlements, studying only pavement-dwellers and slum-dwellers. We are concerned that studying squatters will give them a false sense of legitimacy. We cannot acknowledge their presence." Informal housing policy has become focused around "slum designated areas," which are settlements given a statutory status under India's 1956 Slum Act and include settlements ranging from "JJ clusters to historic neighbourhoods with 'slum-like' conditions. These places are eligible for formal intervention by the state in terms of infrastructure and housing and not all of these are informal or illegal. 'Unauthorized colonies' can also include elite gated communities built on illegally occupied land or in violation of the masterplan ... On the other hand, regularized-unauthorized colonies are those informal/illegal colonies which have been given legal tenure retrospectively" (Datta 2016, 6). Housing legality is an unstable category that is "unsettled not only by the survival strategies of people in crisis, but also by the countless slippages in bureaucratic processes" Even new suburbs created by official resettlements often result in "vigorous and ongoing renegotiations of what can count as permitted ways of living in the city" (Rao 2013, 760). In a reversal of the process of "inexorable whitening" (Smart and Aguilera 2020) in Latin America—where favelas that survive long enough can come to be indistinguishable from legally developed areas and have sufficient de facto tenure security to reject formal titling—formal resettlement communities can become progressively less distinguishable from informal settlements and can come to have substantial numbers of squatter structures within them (Datta 2016). However, for unauthorized developments by corporations and elites that look modern and "world-class," "whitening from above" (Yiftachel 2009) often takes place. As Ghertner (2015, 7) says, "[m]alls appear planned even if they violate planning law; slums look unplanned even if they conform with land-use plans."

Robert-Jan Baken (2003, 46) describes how in twentieth century Indian cities, politicians "specialised" in influencing the implementation of policies. Because the residents of illegal settlements have the greatest need for protection from the implementation of rules, the "most important role of local politicians . . . in the field of housing is to protect and guide squatters." Most of the low-income housing provision in Indian cities in the second half of the twentieth century was created through squatting, along lines continuous with colonial forms of governance. Politics around land claims is "likely to be a major factor in the very high voter turnouts by 'slum' inhabitants in municipal elections: 95–98% in Bangalore" (Benjamin 2008, 724). Those living on disputed land, or aspiring to, form "vote banks" for ambitious local politicians, a pattern widely criticized by governments, developers, and NGOs wishing to transform Indian cities into modern and globally competitive places, rather than scaring investors off with what Benjamin (2008) calls "occupancy urbanism."

Resettlement has been the dominant way of dealing with squatters and slums, but the nature of the resettlement process and housing varies greatly and may even offer conditions inferior to the community from which they were evicted. Often, only slum dwellings that have been "notified" by respective municipalities, corporations, local bodies, or development authorities are eligible. This notification is described by De (2017, 994) as formalization of the land tenure "which differs from common titling programs that provide full property title. It only guarantees occupancy and entitlement to basic services but not rights to develop, inherit, sell, lease or mortgage houses." It appears to be similar to explicit toleration. Eligibility for resettlement also seems to be less clear-cut than in Hong Kong. For example, in a massive slum clearance undertaken to prepare Delhi for the Commonwealth Games in 2010, "[s]ixty percent of the displaced families were eligible for a resettlement plot and yet less than half of these had the resources to take advantage of the offer to relocate" (Rao 2013, 760). Often a ration card is required as proof of eligibility, which might exclude both those who had not been "notified" but also many more affluent squatters (although the affluent may illegitimately obtain ration cards; Gupta 2012).

These variations—and the fragmentation of authority over slum clearance—clearly indicates a political, rather than a bureaucratic, mode of eviction, and the high rate of voting among poor slum dwellers also suggests a very heavy level of politicization related to competitive politics. Both in-situ and off-site forms of resettlement take place, but the latter is predominant, particularly when the slum is centrally located and makes valuable land available for redevelopment. Because slum dwellers often invest in improving their dwellings, they may "reject any slum upgrading option because either in situ upgrading or slum relocation would lead to either temporary displacement or permanent relocation and the loss of the investment they made in their dwelling" (Li et al. 2021, 16). The World Bank supported the Bustee Improvement Program from 1970, focusing on the conversion of service latrines, connection of water taps, development of surface drainage facilities, construction and widening of roads and pathways, and provisioning of street lighting and waste disposal facilities on the basis of the cost recovery principle. The results were promising until the early 1970s but "gradually became worse" (De 2017, 991). In 1972, a federal scheme for the Environmental Improvement of Urban Slums through Community Empowerment was undertaken to provide services including water supply, sewage, drainage, and street pavements in 11 cities in India. Basic Services for Urban Poor (BSUP) was launched in 2005 to provide "security of tenure at affordable prices, improved housing, water supply, sanitation, education, health and social security" (De 2017, 991). There is evidence that improvement of de facto tenure security is "crucial for slum improvement." Notification fosters improvement of housing. However, "full property rights are not transferred through notification of slums. Hence, the threat of displacement due to market forces and eviction persists, especially when slums are well connected to the rest of the urban area." Desirable location reduces de facto security, which "in turn reduces the investments for housing. Housing development also triggers improvement of other services in the slum. Hence, notification, meant for improvement of basic services in slums, is not sufficient. Transfer of full property rights is essential to safeguard slum dwellers from eviction and incentivize them to make private investment" (De 2017, 1009).

Such displacement of slums on coveted land has intensified in the last two decades. "Slum-free cities have become a policy narrative for governments at all levels. Governments are driving slum dwellers away from the cities" (Li et al. 2021, 3). This dynamic is particularly strong in the largest and most globally connected cities, such as Bangalore (Benjamin 2008), Calcutta (Majumdar

2017) and Delhi (Datta 2016), creating some fascinating shifts in both the mode of eviction and the character of toleration.

In the late 1990s, courts in Delhi and elsewhere reacted to "the dismal and gloomy picture of such jhuggi/jhopries coming up regularly," and in 2002 observed that "it would require 272 years to resettle the slum dwellers" according to existing procedures (quoted in Ghertner 2015, 13). These conditions were "incompatible with Delhi's imagined world-class future," so the courts responded by intervening in slum matters and rebuking state agencies for failing to address the "menace of illegal encroachment" and slums. But when the "courts pushed state agencies to more aggressively clear slums, judges were befuddled by messy ground realities, missing government records, and incomplete surveys" (Ghertner 2015, 13).

Bypassing these complex and politicized "calculative procedures, the courts started using a surrogate indicator to identify illegality: the 'look' of space." Judges began to rule that "settlements of jhuggis were illegal not just because they occupied public land, a position that had proven ineffective in remedying the growing menace of slums, but because they violated the world-class aesthetic" (Ghertner 2015, 14). Jhuggi dwellers became "objects—nuisances, encroachers—to be managed, not citizens warranting equal protection" (Ghertner 2015, 17). After 2000, slum demolition in Delhi accelerated, displacing "as many as a million jhuggi dwellers by 2012. Until this time, the decision to raze a slum had been the almost exclusive domain of Delhi's various land-owning agencies." In millennial Delhi, these branches of government had "little say in determining the legal and political status of such settlements. Instead, court-issued demolition orders became the primary mechanism of slum removal, in most cases issued in response to resident welfare associations' . . . petitions requesting the removal of neighboring slums" (Ghertner 2015, 99).

Eviction had shifted from a political mode to a judicial one, but an unusual judicial process that adjudicated on a subjective sense of aesthetics and desired futures rather than the precisions of property law (which had become confused and politically entangled in the previous decades). Toleration for anything that did not fit with a claimed and aspirational image of world-class cities had declined, and resettlement became a way of facilitating the movement of nuisances to margins, where they could be ignored and neglected. The irony is "that squatters realize that their struggles for legitimacy cannot now be realized through informality or political patronage," but only through engagement with formal processes (Datta 2016, 8), at a time when the courts are adopting a kind of processual informality that also reduces squatters' chances for social justice.

Despite their common British colonial legacies, independent India and Hong Kong differ greatly in their squatter management approaches. New

Managing Squatting in Other Asian Cities   249

squatting in India appears to be continuing, although perhaps not in the central areas of the wealthiest cities. Although resettlement is a core part of responses to the squatter problem in both territories, the management of India's resettlement colonies is much less centralized and effective, sometimes allowing them to become similar to jhuggi clusters and requiring another round of resettlement. As well, eligibility for resettlement is much less clear and more politicized in Indian cities, and the categories of illegal encroachment have become intensely ambiguous. These differences create a lack of clarity of reasons for toleration of squatting, since squatting becomes perceptually lost in a confusion of other kinds of nonconforming land uses and physically dilapidated but legal slums.

Conclusions

There are advantages to comparing a set of things, such as squatting in Asian cities, with significant degrees of similarity (Gilbert 2002; Grashoff and Yang 2020), but there are also disadvantages, since it is less likely to reveal the full range of variation or important issues that do not arise among the subset. The cities considered in this chapter are all close to the repressive pole of the repression/legalization spectrum, with Manila the closest to the legalization pole. If we had included Latin American or African cities, we would have had clearer cases of squatter titling and "inexorable whitening," where the longer squatter settlements persist, the stronger their practical tenure security and the greater the likelihood that improvements of buildings and infrastructure will gradually make the areas look more like legal neighborhoods.

Another similarity is the common importance of ambiguous toleration. Although this may be universal when squatter areas persist, it can be modulated when other forms of toleration are of greater importance. This is apparent in these case studies because the social legitimacy of squatting as a survival tactic among non-squatters diminished significantly in several cases. In Kuala Lumpur and Indian cities, in the last two decades, the rejection of slums as an impediment to claiming world-class status and to the construction of new modern developments facilitated the delegitimization of informal housing areas. In the Philippines, informal settlements in flood zones that exacerbated flood risk to legal property also made it easier to displace squatters as sources of risk.

A thorough comparison of these cases with the Hong Kong situation would take considerable effort, and space. However, our initial consideration shows the potential for a comparative perspective on these disparate cases. The cases also make clear that the pathway taken in colonial Hong Kong, far from being inevitable, involved choices from a broader spectrum of squatter management strategies, which would have resulted in very different urban configurations.

12
Conclusions

> [H]istorical research takes us into a world of detail, inevitable incomplete-
> ness and nonlinearity. . . . If storytelling reflects our need to organize our
> knowledge into modes of explanation (or refutation) that make sense of this
> world, then it will always need to elide or flatten some of the detail. Research,
> however, remains closely bound up with what we do not know, as well as what
> we do.
>
> —Peter N. Miller, *Peiresc's Mediterranean World* (2015, 25)

Introduction

The natural tendency is to assume that the path Hong Kong took was the
path it had to take. Yet, it is possible to imagine it as a place where public
housing is as small a component of the housing stock (less than 5%) as in the
United States or Canada. This outcome is perhaps even more probable than
the reality, given the emphasis in Hong Kong on positive non-interventionism
(Smart 2006). With only a tiny residual public housing sector, almost everything else about the landscape, economy and society would be different in
many ways. Without an alternative to private sector accommodation, high
housing prices could have undermined the territory's labor-intensive manufacturing boom. Alternatively, without the safety net, housing prices might
have been lower, undermining the profits (and perhaps the concentration) of
the private property development sector. As a third possibility, the facilitation
rather than repression of villager-controlled building on agricultural land in
New Kowloon and elsewhere could have produced an outcome closer to the
urban villages in reform China. Conditions might also have led to a much
greater reliance on public housing to promote loyalty, as in Singapore. There
is no inherent reason why squatter management could not have taken any of
the paths discussed in Chapter 11, all of which would have made Hong Kong
a very different place.

Even the path that Hong Kong was on in the late 1970s, if continued,
would have contributed to a very different contemporary Hong Kong.

Conclusions

Squatter control could have continued its leakiness with new squatting alternately contained and pushing through the loopholes. This would have been particularly likely if Beijing and Hong Kong had not cooperated in curbing large uncontrolled movements from China into Hong Kong. This straight-line projection of the 1970s would fit less well with media images of the global city and would score lower in terms of aesthetic governmentality. But it might have offered more opportunities for small and medium enterprises to start up and grow, while also providing housing opportunities, especially for migrants and the growing number of asylum seekers (Mathews 2014) who do not qualify for public housing.

Not as much has changed about the squatter problem as might have been expected. It was the stated intention to clear all remaining squatter areas by 1996, but squatter structures and squatter residents are still around in large numbers. This fact is probably surprising to many, because of their virtual invisibility in public discussion and government documents, except in more rural parts of the NT affected by developments such as the high-speed rail link. Nonetheless, the squatter problem does not just go away. It stays. In urban areas, three squatter areas still exist in Kowloon East, located at Cha Kwo Ling, Ngau Chi Wan, and Chuk Yuen United Village, where the numbers of surveyed squatter structures are 475, 266, and 49 respectively.[1] They are likely to be gone soon as the government announced in 2019 plans to redevelop them into high-density public housing. On Hong Kong Island, Pok Fu Lam Village (population about 3,000), is a possible exception to this disappearance, due to the history of the pre-colonial village with agricultural land leases. Its profile was increased by being listed by the World Monuments Fund in 2014 "to raise awareness of its significance and scarcity in the modern metropolitan Hong Kong."[2] We explore the contemporary situation in the second half of this chapter. Prior to that, however, it will be useful to summarize our conclusions about the explanation of the end of new squatting, as concisely as possible.

The squatter problem was like a tough balloon: squeezing in one area prompted expansion elsewhere. The pressure in the balloon resulted from various conditioning circumstances, particularly the shortage of affordable housing, migration from China, and the reliance of the government on land-based revenues. Unless the pressure could be reduced, control of its spread required thorough control of all the niches and places in which illegal encroachments or illegal building could take place. We could consider this to involve building an adjustable cage around the squatter balloon, with squatter control and clearances attempting to squeeze down the size of the balloon. However, before 1984, leaks in the cage were rampant. In the 1950s and 1960s, at least, geopolitics restricted how aggressive the force applied on the balloon could be. From 1954 on, squatter resettlement made clearances less politically and diplomatically risky.

Clearance, however, was constrained by its focus only on developable land. Using part of the land made available while auctioning the rest to the private sector affordably financed the Resettlement Programme, which in turn made clearance politically feasible. The stage was set for the public relations problem of squalid squatter areas on land not needed for development. Intervention from London created a need to do something about them, but what was done derived from local preferences and deliberations. London's pressure, though, created a policy mangle in 1970, out of which initially emerged neither of Governor Trench's two suggestions, but rather a new approach of infrastructural improvement. Only modest improvements took place, however, as the first-listed Ten-Year Housing Target of 1972 set the objective to eliminate all squatter and licensed areas. In the circumstances, this implied resettling all squatters, since clearance without any rehousing would be politically contentious, perhaps impossible; but in any case, delays would result. This target was not achieved (and still has not been achieved) with 477,880 squatters in 1984.[3] The failure was due to public housing supply and demand imbalances, particularly the impeding of essential development clearances by shortage of temporary housing. Shortage was in turn induced by growing exclusion of squatters from eligibility for permanent public housing.

Dealing with the increasing proportion of cleared squatters eligible only for the less dense temporary housing was complicated by a growing sense of the unfairness of public housing allocation to squatters and new migrants, rather than long-term Hong Kong residents. Resettling all squatters in a short time frame would sharply reduce PPH access through the Waiting List, while squatter area improvement could delay the need for resettlement. However, this holding action failed due to reports that made clear the escalating costs of any improvement that would reduce the risk of landslides and fires, which had been adding pressure to the TH shortage in the early 1980s.

The other alternatives had failed or been seen as impractical, so the decision to resettle squatters in non-development zones came to be seen as the only option. Resettling all squatters would also be impractically expensive, however, if new squatting continued. The SOS could plug one of the largest remaining holes in the cage containing squatter rehousing commitments, and thus followed quite obviously from the prior decisions. Along with other squatter control measures, making registration on the SOS a new criterion for PPH was a key action for ending new squatting. In doing so, the tide turned against housing informality.

This summary of our argument makes clear that none of the plausible explanations that we have developed and evaluated in this book were adequate in themselves to account for the adoption of the SOS and the ending of new squatting. Instead, they explain at most one part of the troubled path of efforts to deal with the squatter problem. The loosening of the geopolitical

Conclusions 253

constraints on more repressive solutions was perhaps necessary but not sufficient, since it does not appear to have been explicit in squatter policy discussions in the early 1980s. It seems to have been a conditioning factor, like the continuing shortage of affordable housing. Intervention from London about the image problem of squatting in 1970 influenced when the debate had to be undertaken, and therefore the attendant issues that were being addressed during that period. This intervention thus influenced the course of this policy mangle, but the solutions adopted were locally formed. The greatest weight of empirical evidence is lined up in support of the supply and demand imbalance explanation, which clearly had a major influence on the decisions made in the 1970s and set the path toward formalization. However, the shortage of temporary housing due to exclusionary policies cannot be explained without turning to another major influence: rising concern about fairness and greater allocation of PH to long-term residents, rather than recent migrants and squatters. Improvement in general is a relatively weak explanation of the empirical situation, other than improvement through demolition of illegal uses of Crown land. It was, however, critical in creating a situation where it finally became clear that resettling all squatters on land not needed for development was the only viable way forward. It was the final failed experiment that resulted in policy learning. The policy mangle approach—although weak as a predictor of empirical outcomes, since it can usually be shown to be consistent after the fact—does have an important contribution to our explanatory goal. It helps us to understand why no single explanation manages to account for the road to formalization. It sensitizes us to the contingency of crucial policy decisions, because they generally were made through policy mangles (inquiries, working parties, or reports) that feed together heterogenous issues and concerns as necessary contextual considerations for conclusions about what interventions might be practical and desirable. One mangle leads to new problems, which may result in additional mangles so that contingencies and accidents multiply. Outcomes may result that are unexpected from the programmatic starting points of the process. Tracing such tangled mangles has been one of the challenges of this book, but also one of its rewards. Unexpected linkages have shed new light for us at various junctures, and beyond helping us to make sense of our initial questions, have unearthed new questions for us to pursue in the future.

The Situation in the 2020s

We include a brief discussion of the contemporary situation in Hong Kong because it helps to disclose what was changed and what continued about the conditions that formalization was expected to accomplish. Two features of the contemporary situation are particularly pertinent to our concerns in this book. First, that there are still many squatters in Hong Kong. Second, that surprisingly little is known about them, even allegedly by the government itself, and certainly by the general public. The Secretary for Development, Carrie Lam (the Hong Kong's Chief Executive, July 2017–June 2022), responded to a question about the number of squatters in LegCo in 2010 by stating that "[t]he Government has not conducted other statistical survey on squatter occupancy since the Squatter Occupancy Survey conducted in 1984. As such, the government is unable to provide the current number of residents in squatter huts."[4] All she could offer as an answer was that the current number of squatter huts for residential use was 2,713 on Hong Kong Island, 1,542 in Kowloon (see Figures 12.1 and 12.2 for persisting examples), 32,475 in New Territories East, and 48,844 in New Territories West, for a total of 85,574. Using the 2016 census finding for average number of occupants of a temporary quarter (2.577) gives us an estimate of 220,525 people. For Hong Kong Island and Kowloon, it would be 10,965. These numbers are much higher than for people living in the census definition of temporary quarters (54,596).[5]

The Lands Department's Squatter Control Quarterly Statistics for March 2016 include 772 squatter areas, with 388,497 surveyed squatter structures erected on unleased government land (126,369) and private agricultural land (262,128). Of these, 84,369 were for domestic use, 32,575 on government land and 51,794 on private agricultural land.[6]

The Lands Department took over squatter control responsibilities for Kowloon, Hong Kong and Islands from the Housing Department Squatter Control Offices in April 2002, with the remainder transferred in April 2006. The justification given for this was to simplify the workflow of government's land control function and enhance overall efficiency. A report from the Audit Commission in 2017 was quietly critical of squatter control effectiveness. They did site visits to check whether squatter control patrols had ensured that squatter structures were compliant with policy. In one visit, they found 50 apparently noncompliant structures. Five structures on private land were not 1982 surveyed structures, and another 19 cases were non-compliant. Of these, 12 had been noted before and enforcement actions were ongoing. Another 21 cases were still under investigation to confirm whether they were non-compliant or not. The noncompliance involved extensions rather than new structures, but some had been converted from storage to domestic use. Either extension or conversion could expand the number of people living in them. It was also noted that only one of the seven Squatter Control Offices kept records for the source of identifying non-compliance; in that Office, 88% of the 206 cases originated from public complaints or referrals from other government bureaus or departments.[7]

This report implies rather low efficacy in controlling squatter structures. It also indicates that, when the squatter problem becomes virtually invisible in the

Figure 12.1: Squatter structures, Chuk Yuen Heung, Kowloon, 2019. Copyright and provided by Alan Smart.

Figure 12.2: Structure with squatter survey markings, Ngau Chi Wan, Kowloon, 2019. Copyright and provided by Alan Smart.

media domain, the government could revert, though perhaps only temporarily, to toleration in dealing with the squatter problem until it becomes a public scandal prompting government actions and/or the government resumes the land for redevelopment. The former scenario is evident in the case of Mak Sai-yiu, who lived in a squatter house in Tung Ah Pui village, a place near Tai Tam on Hong Kong Island. As the Hong Kong Free Press reported on 9 June 2016, Mak lived in the village since 1981 and made his way to the hut, which had been subsequently turned into a luxurious building, through purchasing.[8] A staff member of the Lands Department contacted by the Press disclosed that the Department was aware "of the occupation of government land" but "had not taken action because of the identities of residents" because it was "afraid of doing squatter control work." Mak is not the only squatter resident in the village, as the Press also reported that some wealthy businessmen also lived there by purchasing squatter huts. The case of Mak triggered a public outcry, not only because he was formerly a civil servant but also because the case seems to involve complicity. On 10 June, the Secretary for Development, Paul Chan (now the Financial Secretary), instructed the Lands Department to follow up on the "allegations" and handle the case seriously.[9] Some land justice-concerned activists took this occasion to demand another round of surveys of occupants, but the political momentum was insufficient to materialize the demand.[10]

Rather than responding to the activists' demand, the Lands Department announced on 22 June 2016 that it would "raise the effectiveness of enforcement work over squatter structures."[11] In 2021, the Lands Department restated that it had "strengthened squatter control measures. Specifically, if there is evidence showing that a new extension has been completed after [22 June 2016], actions will be taken such as cancelling the squatter survey number instantly and demolishing the whole unauthorized structure on government land immediately upon detection without giving any opportunity to rectify, or taking lease enforcement actions against cases involving newly extended structures on private land as appropriate."[12] Other than cancelling the squatter survey number, this mostly reaffirms the prior policy, if not the actual practice. Cancelling the survey number means that no future occupant could claim to be living in a surveyed structure. The case thus illustrates—similar to Smart's (1992) earlier study and what we discussed in previous chapters—that public attention to the squatter problem could open up a politicized occasion, but it does not determine the outcome. Going back to our squatter balloon metaphor, in the postcolonial era, it seems that the scandal derived from public attention to the squatter problem is more likely to lead to the strengthening of the adjustable cage around the balloon, potentially further squeezing down the size of the balloon.

Conclusions

A subsequent Audit report also found in 2017 that of the 1,582 government man-made slopes posing landslide risks to squatter and licensed structures, the Civil Engineering and Development Department "had not commenced upgrading works for 940 (59%) slopes." As well, the Buildings Department may issue a Dangerous Hillside Order to a "private-slope owner requiring him to carry out slope upgrading works within a specified period." However, as of January 2017, 210 Dangerous Hillside Orders on private slopes posing landslide risks to squatter and licensed structures "had not been satisfactorily complied with. Of these, 34 (16%) had been outstanding for 10 to 21 years" (ix).[13] The risk of dangerous slopes that had prompted both the Squatter Area Improvement Programme and the non-development clearance program has rather remarkably persisted 30 years later. All of this suggests that the actions of the 1980s, once they had succeeded in ending new squatting, had left most squatters on land not needed for development neglected. Restrictions on occupants improving their dwellings, however, were still in place, so that rebuilding in permanent materials could result in demolition.

Smart (2002, 338) wrote that while globally, many housing programs have attempted to encourage and facilitate the residents of squatter areas to improve their dwellings, Hong Kong by contrast "has consistently and stringently attempted to prevent squatters from improving their dwellings with better materials, and continues to devote significant resources in order to control the improvement of housing quality of squatter dwellings, many of which are expected to persist indefinitely into the future. . . . improving one's dwelling is one of the occasions on which summary demolition can result. Much of the work of squatter control officers is devoted to preventing such improvements." Remarkably, the system of squatter control still operates in a way that creates both living conditions that are poorer than necessary and which leaves many still exposed to landslide risks and greater risk of fire. LegCo member Lau Kong-wah's question to Carrie Lam in 2010 included this point: "given that most of the squatter huts have been built for a long time and many of them are dilapidated, whether the Government will consider compassionately the housing needs of the residents, relax the existing policy on maintenance of squatter huts and allow the residents to carry out repairs with more solid materials; if it will, of the details; if not, the reasons for that." Her reply seemed perhaps less than compassionate in relation to problems created by control policy:

> Investigating the conditions of squatter huts is not within the working ambit of the SCU [Squatter Control Unit]. If a squatter hut is at risk of collapsing, the occupant has to arrange for repair on his/her own. But if the occupant has difficulty in housing because his/her squatter hut is at risk of collapsing, the SCU will refer the relevant case to the Housing Department or the Social Welfare Department so that the relevant department can arrange rehousing

for the occupant in temporary shelter, interim housing unit or public housing unit.[14]

What is not explicitly stated in the reply, however, is the fact that rehousing of squatter occupants has to undergo income scrutiny, and there is no guarantee that rehousing would be in situ. We traced how income scrutiny and the so-called "far shore policy" were introduced by the colonial government to redress the imbalance of PPH/THA shortage and discourage urban squatting. The reason we call for attention to these institutional legacies here is that, without acknowledging these historical legacies, it would be difficult to comprehend the current situation of squatter resettlement. Under these institutional legacies, those whose squatter huts are at risk of collapsing would not have much motivation to apply for rehousing because they have been excluded by these rehousing barriers. This accounts for why squatter residents of Cha Kwo Ling, after fire incidents in January 2006 and December 2016, would insist to stay rather than being rehoused elsewhere even though this means that squatter residents would continue to be exposed to a greater risk of fire.[15] Some squatter residents also worried that they could not pass the income scrutiny and therefore, in the course of rehousing, they would have to move to sub-divided units in the same district or at worst become homeless. The same could be seen in the cases of squatter residents of Ngau Chi Wan who worried that they would not receive "appropriate compensation" and thus they would prefer to stay.[16]

We come back to the issue of subdivided units later, but the upshot here is that, under these inherited institutional arrangements, voluntary rehousing would not appear to be an appealing choice for these residents of remaining urban squatter areas. While the change in the status quo could be initiated by the exposure of a public scandal that prompted government actions, the government could also initiate changes in the status quo by resuming lands occupied by squatter residents.

Carrie Lam announced in her Policy Address of 2019 plans to "increase land supply" for public housing by resuming the urban private lands occupied by squatter residents; these residents would be compensated and rehoused "in accordance with the prevailing policy" (13).[17] Without altering the inherited institutional arrangements discussed above, such a unilateral move could create a potentially confrontational situation. This is best seen in the cases of Cha Kwo Ling and Ngau Chi Wan. In both areas, residents formed a concern group, demanded rehousing in situ, and opposed means-testing in the course of resettlement to public housing.[18] Interestingly, some squatter residents in Ngau Chi Wan would also like to see the reimplementation of Squatter Area Improvement, so that the environment of the squatter area could be improved.[19] These demands could not be easily met by the government, as they might increase the cost of resettlement and obstruct the land resumption

Conclusions 259

process. Therefore, it could lead to a head-on situation. It is too early to draw any conclusions because the process of resettlement is still ongoing. Yet, one insight that we can draw here is that the colonial institutional setups are durable and could complicate the processes of urban restructuring in contemporary Hong Kong, even after the formal end of colonial rule. In other words, these colonial institutional setups are what Stoler (2016) called "imperial duress," shaping the life worlds that we are now inhabiting.

Nonetheless, we are not implying straight continuity where everything is the same. For example, the issue of maintenance of squatter huts has been addressed recently. From 28 June 2021, the Lands Department has streamlined the procedures for repairing and rebuilding. Before commencing, occupiers of Surveyed Squatter Structures are required to complete and submit a Notification for Repair/Rebuilding of Surveyed Squatter Structure(s) to the relevant district Squatter Control Office. Repairs still cannot involve a change from temporary to permanent materials.[20] Rebuilding is only allowed in the NT. If the NT surveyed structure was recorded in 1982 as being built with permanent material, "the rebuilt structure will lose the status of the Surveyed Squatter Structure," but successful applications will receive "a Short-Term Tenancy (STT) for government land or a Short-Term Waiver (STW) for leased agricultural land to replace the original SC Survey Record." It will then become a regularized licensed structure. Repairs or rebuilding without following the procedures "will render the structure non-conforming with the SC [Squatter Control] Survey Record . . . which may result in the loss of its status as a Surveyed Squatter Structure. The consequence is that the SC Survey Record will be cancelled and the structure will no longer be tolerated. As the structure constitutes unauthorised occupation of government land or is an unauthorised structure on leased agricultural land, it will be subject to appropriate enforcement actions by the Government without any compensation including ex-gratia allowance."[21]

The fate of the SOS has also been less auspicious than its origins promised. The Audit report discussed above revealed that the registration had not been used to keep track of changing occupants of Surveyed Squatter Structures. It certainly has not served as a panoptic system of surveillance over squatter residents, nor has it been used in conjunction with occasional revisits by Squatter Control Officers in 1983 (see Chapter 10). Even more remarkably, its role as a criterion for access to housing—a key element of its ability to contribute substantially to the ending of new squatting—disappeared in December 2002. The Housing Authority adopted a new policy for rehousing occupants of 1982 surveyed structures who had not been covered in the 1984–1985 Occupancy Survey, under which occupants who have lived in affected structures for two years prior to the date of announcement of a clearance operation are eligible for the HA's rehousing scheme, provided that other public rental housing eligibility criteria are met.[22]

Another change relevant to the SOS is the Squatter Occupants Voluntary Registration Scheme in effect from 1 November 2018 to 31 October 2022. This applied to households residing in non-domestic structures surveyed in 1982, allowing them to voluntarily register. This voluntary measure allows "eligible households to benefit from compensation/rehousing, while freezing the occupation of non-domestic structures for domestic purposes." Households registered in this way will be eligible for compensation/rehousing if their structures are affected by development clearance. So long as there is "neither any change in their household status, enforcement action will not be taken against these non-domestic structures in respect of change of use into domestic purposes."[23] It would be tempting to consider the Squatter Occupants Voluntary Registration Scheme as an indication of a relaxation of the cage around the squatter balloon. Yet this understanding is unlikely the case because the targets of the Scheme are those domestic occupants residing in "licenced non-domestic structures or in squatter structures recorded for non-domestic uses" included in the 1982 structure surveys.[24] The majority of this form of squatting (domestic occupants and non-domestic structures) could be found in the NT.[25] Essentially, despite the SOS, an undisclosed amount of new squatting had occurred through the conversion of non-domestic structures into domestic accommodation after 1985. This new Registration Scheme combines a new round of specific toleration with a "freezing survey" (see Chapter 10) and belatedly closes an additional loophole that had been allowed to emerge.

While some of those struggling with access to housing may still move into the remaining squatter housing stock (so long as the sellers have not been allocated public housing units), its relatively small size compared to the total population means that it can at most play a modest role in meeting the vast need. Our focus here is not on the housing situation in general, but on the ways in which the pressure of demand is creating new forms of informal housing in the absence of a new squatting option.

Hong Kong has always had very high housing costs. The private housing rent index increased from 73.6 in 2003 to 182.6 in 2017 (Wong and Chan 2019). It now has the world's highest rental housing costs per square metre— with rents of US$7,267 compared to US$6,867 in London (second)—as well as for housing price and rent-to-price ratio.[26] Even migrants who earn good wages often find their housing conditions worse than in their prior place of residence, since they struggle to afford private housing and are not eligible for public housing until at least half of the family members have lived in Hong Kong for seven years. Yung and Lee (2012, 407) quote a woman in a shared apartment: "Of course, [I am] not satisfied with [my present housing]. When I

Conclusions

lived in mainland China, a room was bigger than my present housing in which 3 persons [now live]."

One of the most notorious options at the bottom of the "housing ladder" in the private sector is the "caged men apartments" or "bedspace lodgers" (Kornatowski 2008). As Cheung (2000, 236) indicates:

> Within the fantasy and the realities of skyscraper penthouses and land deals, perhaps the most ironic phenomenon in Hong Kong is the destitute and solitary human being who lives in a cube measuring six by three by four feet surrounded by a metal grill . . . Under the regime of hegemonic fetishism, "spatial entitlement" has become the signifier of social status, defining class and implying the worth of persons who possess and control space.

The costs for such limited spaces in 2000 were surprisingly similar to the comparable rent for luxury housing relative to the unit size.

The type of informal housing that appears to have been growing most rapidly in the last decade is the sub-divided unit, which is produced by dividing units originally designed for a single household into two or more smaller rental units (Leung, Chung, and Lai 2020). There are "around 209,700 people (around 2.86% of the total population) living in them according to the 2016 by-census. They are often "unauthorized building works" which breach the building code in various ways (Wong and Chan 2019). A 2013 survey on 1860 buildings found that their living areas ranged approximately from 4.6 to 10.8 m^2/capita, with an average of 6.2 m^2/capita (Wong 2018, 1159). The rent-to-income ratio of subdivided units was 39.81% in 2018 (Leung, Chung, and Lai 2020).

In July 2021, the government announced a bill that would put rent-control limits on certain subdivided flats, specifically excluding those with illegal structures or unauthorized building works. This change, and perhaps some of the initiatives discussed above around improving squatter control policy, may have been influenced by Beijing. It is becoming increasingly outspoken about the need for Hong Kong's government to do more for "the improvement of people's livelihood, and effectively solve prominent problems such as housing, employment, medical care, and the gap between the rich and the poor," as Xia Baolong, the director of the cabinet-level Hong Kong and Macau Affairs Office in Beijing, said in a high-profile event in Hong Kong on 16 July 2021. He singled out his hope that "[i]n particular, the housing problem that we are worried about now will be greatly improved, and we will bid farewell to 'cage homes,'" he said, referring to "the city's infamous, coffin-like subdivided apartments for the poor" (Lindberg 2021).

These comments follow on multiple reports that Beijing is concerned about the problems caused by unaffordable housing in Hong Kong, and in particular the worry that the housing and precarious income problems of youth may have been a major contributing factor to the unrests in recent years, particularly in 2019. Such Beijing influence on housing and land policy is purely speculative, even if plausible, given the political situation. Nonetheless, local factors are also important in the shaping of the trajectory of policy development, as we demonstrated for colonial Hong Kong in previous chapters. But if that is the case, an interesting question would be: what are the local factors that are powerful enough to defy, or divert, the initiatives from Beijing?

Considering the squatter and housing situation in the 2020s, unlike the situation in the 1960s (see Chapter 4), forces us to rely on evaluating publicly available documents and commentary by informed individuals. We can generate interesting possibilities and plausible explanations of the twists and turns of policy changes, but we cannot see the mangle in operation, nor get a clear sense of disagreements and discussions. Questions emerge but answering them is another matter. Whether in 30 years we will have the quality of information to answer these questions that we found in our research for this book (which was already much diminished from the richness of the archives for the 1950s that Smart discovered) is uncertain, but the signs are worrying. Transfers of Hong Kong government documents to the Public Records Office have been much less common and subject to major gaps, such as for the office of the Chief Executive, which failed to hand over any official records at all for eight of the 20 years since 1997 (Wu 2017).

Consequences

We argued in the Introduction that informality was central to Hong Kong experience and development prior to 1984. It made major contributions to Hong Kong's economic and social miracles. In the rest of the book, we concentrated on informal housing and how new squatting was ended in 1984. Here, we briefly return to the broader question of the turning of the tide against informality in the 1980s. It is difficult to adequately document the extent of decline of informality in general, but the proliferation of rules and regulations in almost every domain of everyday life would suggest a substantial degree of increased formality. At the same time, rules tend to generate new informal workarounds. In the narrower context of the informal economy, though, it seems clear that its share of the overall economy has diminished. The traditional informal sectors of squatting and illegal street vending have certainly shrunk. The residual urban squatter areas house only small numbers, and even the subdivided flats house only a small percentage of the population (less than 3%). As well, not all of those flats are operating informally. The sharp decline in manufacturing activities in Hong Kong has also reduced the opportunities—and consequences—of outwork, domestically based production, and informal networks of collaboration. Finance has been increasingly important

Conclusions 263

to the Hong Kong economy, with the proportion of GDP from financial services (only part of the broader sector including business services) rising from 10.4% in 1996 to 19.7% in 2018 (Liu 2020), while manufacturing only contributed 1%. The major component of this finance involves the rest of China. Hong Kong continues, on paper, to provide over half of China's foreign direct investment. However, much of this involves corporations (including Chinese state-owned enterprises) exploiting legal loopholes by using offshore bases to channel their capital back into China, so that their investments can benefit from the tax holidays and other preferential policies for foreign investment—a pattern called "round-tripping" (Smart et al. 2015). This and more illicit forms of money laundering represent a new kind of financial informality, but one that is rarely available to the ordinary resident of Hong Kong.

Finance creates fewer jobs than manufacturing: only 7% of total employment in 2020. The jobs are also hugely polarized between highly skilled and unskilled. The economic shift has led to a greater reliance on low-paid and often precarious positions, especially for the young, who increasingly rely on the "gig economy," which offers little chance of upward mobility compared to the flexible production system of the 1960s and 1970s. Hong Kong's Gini index of income inequality was 0.539 in 2021, as high as Brazil's, whereas in the 1970s it was relatively low. In this context, the shrinking availability of informal opportunities may be restricting livelihoods in significant ways. Becoming a street vendor or buying a tiny squatter cubicle are options that are not readily available to those struggling with the world's highest housing prices and a shortage of middle-income jobs.

For example, the number of licensed street hawkers has declined from 70,000 in 1946 to about 20,000 in the late 1980s, and further to about 6,000 in 2022 (Fall and Sam 2014; Kwok 2019). Unlicensed street vending, ubiquitous in the 1970s and before, has mostly disappeared, other than at the margins: furtive sales of copy watches, the sale of used goods on Apliu Street (Coppoolse, 2021; Ta 2017), and small clusters of vendors appearing at transit hubs after the routine anti-vendor Food and Environmental Hygiene Department patrols end in the evening. With strict enforcement actions against unlicensed hawking activities, the estimated number of unlicensed hawkers decreased from more than 5,500 in 1995 to around 1,500 at the end of 2013 (Lam et al. 2015, 38). Even licensed hawkers almost invariably engage in informal, rule-breaking tactics to expand their small three-by-four feet stall spaces, using different techniques to temporarily obtain more space while avoiding detection by the Hawker Control Task Forces (Kwok 2019).

During Chinese New Year in 2016, the so-called Fishball Revolution brought local activists to the densely populated district of Mong Kok in Hong Kong to protect local "traditions" (Lim 2017). These traditions involved both the food served and the precedents of toleration for cooked food hawkers at this time of year. The spark—or excuse, depending on interpretations of the events—was a police crackdown on illegal street vendors. Unlike year-round food stalls, the ones that emerge at New Year "are not licensed and do not pay rent, but generally the authorities turn a blind eye to this." In 2015, a similar crackdown on unlicensed stalls failed. "This year, they tried again. News of the plan reached local activists who were keen to oppose any moves they deem to be threatening local traditions. On Monday, one group posted a video of the night market on its Facebook page, urging its supporters to come down and protect it. Dozens of people had gathered to defend the vendors by the time the inspectors turned up" (BBC News 2016).

This celebratory attitude toward disappearing hawkers—objects of intervention to "free" the streets for traffic by colonial and Hong Kong Special Administrative Region governments alike—is echoed in a broader nostalgic interest in the informalities of the past. Seng (2020, 15–16) notes a growth of work on "issues concerning heritage and the informal as well as a renewed interest in the rediscovery of the Walled City and Chungking Mansions" and associates it with a "renewed search for identity in post-British Hong Kong, particularly in light of the physical and spatial 'disappearance' that is threatening the city." Since 1997, there has emerged a widespread call for making Hong Kong not just a business center with efficient transportation, but a livable and vibrant space that respects local history and memory and tries to preserve some of the more distinctive spaces, like Wedding Card Street (Smart and Lam 2009).

Implications for the Study of Informality and Formalization

Beyond Hong Kong, we believe that our book offers some significant insights for the broader field of study. Clearly, colonial Hong Kong is a distinctive case, with many differences from the diverse global settings of widespread squatting and other forms of informal housing. However, beyond increasing our (currently quite thin) knowledge of squatter management in colonial regimes, there are parallels with postcolonial cities that are becoming wealthier without democratic political systems. In particular, it is very unclear from the literature on most cities if, when, and how they managed to end new squatting, as opposed to the broader issue of formalizing existing squatter populations.

One area where more work would be valuable is the provision of better knowledge of how governments formulate and implement their attempts to formalize informality. A careful reconstruction of Hong Kong's experience based on confidential government documents may offer lessons for the continuing global situation of over 1 billion squatters. The idea of the policy mangle may be helpful here: rather than considering policy decision-making only in terms of the specific issues of the domain of informality being

Conclusions 265

addressed, it highlights the reality that the broader contexts of policy debates and discussions become entangled with the specific questions addressed. But even a fine-grained dissection of a specific policy mangle is only part of the story, since policy mangles are entwined with other mangles. The past constrains and enables viable resolutions to problems, and in turn influences the future paths that are likely to be taken.

Although our focus in this book has been on government policymakers and implementers, since this is where the largest gaps in our knowledge lie for colonial Hong Kong, it does not mean that the informal populations being targeted do not influence the policy outcomes. Governmental control efforts meet responses from people trying to reduce the resulting negative consequences for them. They may take advantage of opportunities created unintentionally. Those working informally pursue advantages and may push the limits of where, when, and how they do business. Informal practices transgress official boundaries. Informal practices are everywhere but are more common when people are confined to undesirable positions, with opportunities for mobility (social or spatial) blocked. Informal practices may allow those who are confined, such as residents of Gaza subject to import blockades (Pasquetti and Picker 2017), to reach out for resources denied them. In turn, controlling informality usually attempts to *confine* informal practices in ways that *conform* to boundaries, such as zones of toleration.

Our emphasis on the utility of being aware of constraints does not mean that we are encouraging narrow pragmatism—such as the fetishization of "practicality" by colonial Hong Kong officials we regularly encountered—at the expense of more social justice-oriented policy objectives. Rather, we believe that even the most idealistic, even utopian, policy goals would benefit from understanding the practical concerns and limitations of those forming policy, so that their tactics can increase the viability of their strategic objectives. Social movements can alter the terrain of practicalities, as the Hong Kong riots and disturbances in 1966 and 1967 suggest.

Marco Solimene (2019, 1) observes that scholarly attention has "shifted from a focus on (in)formality and (il)legality as facts to the processes through which these phenomena are produced." Such a focus usefully goes beyond the (limited but crucial) recognition that (in)formality is a duality rather than a dualism, with a spectrum of greater or lesser degrees of informalness in between. His emphasis on process rather than stable state (or *fact*) echoes Herzfeld's (2021) critique of the problematic methodological legalism in the use of the label of informality. But we believe that the term *informality* can be used without rejecting the analytical and empirical utility of attending to the consequences of labelling something as informal rather than illegal. A processual approach also helps us to think about both formalization and informalization as simultaneously governmental and popular tactics and strategies

(Roy 2005). Methodological legalism may obscure the reality of governmental actions against marginalized communities, but it can also impede arbitrary evictions, as can be seen with the various interventions by Hong Kong's Attorney General on whether tolerated squatters could be considered to be in "breach of law," or if the government had a "duty of care" toward squatters on dangerous slopes (see Chapter 10). The legal perspective may obscure the realities on the ground, but it can also provide resources for resistance or inducing governments to do things that they would prefer not to do, or to refrain from actions they would prefer. So long as we do not unquestionably accept the accounts of methodological legalism from above, we can recognize that its use from below can accomplish useful things, as with Manila's squatter movements (see Chapter 11).

Notes

Preface

1. One of the anonymous reviewers of this volume suggested that sterilization may have continued after 1997 as well, although we have no independent knowledge of this happening. For post-1997 files, a growing problem has been the reduction and delay of accession of documents to the Public Records Office, raising concerns about future archival research.
2. Carlo Ginzburg et al. (1993, 28) see microhistory, which has influenced our perspectives in this book (see Preface), as an approach that accepts the severe limitations of evidence while using this very limitation as part of its contribution to methodology, which becomes incorporated in its narrative, such as the distortions and screen of the inquisition documents for understanding the accused heretics.

Chapter 1

1. We should clarify here the rationale for our use throughout this book of the term *squatter*, which is now widely avoided as a derogatory term that ascribes wrongdoing to those coping with the inaccessibility of legal housing. However, the widely used alternative, *slum*, is misleading because it lumps together inadequate forms of housing with very different legal statuses, and incorrectly implies that all squatter dwellings are physically inadequate. *Informal housing*, while less stigmatizing, likewise fails to specify the tenure and legal particularities that are crucial to understanding the dynamics of its creation and maintenance. Spontaneous, irregular, and other alternatives have different limitations, and generally fail to clarify the legal situation. However, "squatting" is often misapplied by governments. In colonial Hong Kong, it was possible to be a squatter on your own land, if it was on an agricultural land lease rather than a building land lease. For these reasons, we treat the term as an "emic" or "member's" concept rather than an analytic (etic) concept, while also recognizing that the legal definitions, precedents, and conditions do have consequences for residents in squatter areas.
2. See Chapter 12.
3. For example, neither squatting nor informal are listed in the index of G. A. Bremner, ed., *Architecture and Urbanism in the British Empire* (Oxford: Oxford University Press, 2016), and even vernacular housing is given cursory discussion in only a few of the chapters.

268   Notes

4. Licensed Areas, discussed in Chapter 9, resemble this pattern but differ since the government directed cleared squatters into areas that were controlled through certain government-imposed rules and conditions, rather than trying for legal changes after uncontrolled prior settlement.

5. The precise label for the Survey is variable from document to document, sometimes the Squatter Occupant Survey, sometimes the Squatter Occupancy Survey. In a memo proposing it to the Housing Authority, it was referred to as "The Survey of Occupants of Squatter Areas": Memorandum for the Operations Committee, 5 July 1984, HKRS 696/3/125, HKPRO [HKPRO]. On the forms actually filled out for Occupants it is labeled the "Squatter Population Registration Form." We adopt Squatter Occupancy Survey except where other terms are used in quotations.

6. Extract from Draft Record for S. for S. [Secretary of State] of Mr. Royle's Private Conversation with H.E. [His Excellency], 11 October 1970, HKRS 163/9/653, HKPRO.

7. Extract from Draft Record for S. for S. [Secretary of State] of Mr. Royle's Private Conversation with H.E. [His Excellency], 11 October 1970, HKRS 163/9/653, HKPRO.

8. We follow the common practice in international studies of metonymy, where the part (London or Beijing) stands in for the whole (the government of the United Kingdom or China). This usage will be restricted to situations where a part of the government acts with the authority of the executive power of that government. For example, when we refer to "Hong Kong" doing something, it is a shorthand for either the governor acting or some entity acting with his implicit or explicit approval.

9. A related problem is the risk of following the documentary stones and neglecting the river in which they are located, a danger we were warned against by one of the anonymous reviewers of this book's submission draft.

10. We contemplated attempting to locate and interview people who had been registered in the SOS, but COVID-19 complicated this. We concluded that it would be better to undertake that task as part of subsequent research on the current situation of squatters in contemporary Hong Kong that we are contemplating.

Chapter 2

1. We omit stateless societies here because there must be authoritative rules for how something should be done for there to be informal alternatives. See Alan Smart, "Anthropology of Law," *The Sage Handbook of Cultural Anthropology*, ed. Lene Pedersen and Lisa Cliggett (London: SAGE, 2021b), 348–363. It is possible to argue that societal norms could have a comparable impact, but we leave that aside here.

2. We do occasionally dabble with the latter, but more in passing than with any thoroughgoing rigor.

3. If space permitted, we would have enjoyed expanding further on what is known about the varieties of economic informality in Hong Kong during this period. Rather than doing so, we point the interested reader to work by Chu (1992),

Notes   269

Cooper (1988), Howell (2004), Leeming (1977), Salaff (1995), Scott (2007), Topley (1964), Ta (2017), and Watson (1975).

4. See Smart and Tang (2014) for details.

5. Quoted in Smart (2018, S38).

6. Quoted in Smart (2018, S43).

Chapter 4

1. Memo from Commissioner for Resettlement C. G. M. Morrison to Secretary, Standing Committee on Departmental Gradings and Superscale Salaries, 23 October 1963, HKRS163/3/87, HKPRO, emphasis in original.

2. The high land-price policy is an example of an implicit principle that is widely assumed by many, but which is never publicly acknowledged by government spokespeople.

3. Councilor Sir Y. K. Kan complained in a Legislative Council meeting, "I believe it is Government's policy to resettle squatters only if the land they occupy is needed for development. There are of course minor exceptions such as victims of natural disasters or dangerous buildings. This conservative policy was necessary at the time when Hong Kong was beset by a serious refugee problem and acute housing shortage. Government's efforts in rehousing over a million squatters in the ensuing years have been gigantic and creditable. I personally have no actual figures of the number of squatters who are desiring and are still awaiting resettlement, but their number cannot be so great as to make it impossible for us to cope with it if we are determined to make an all-out effort to do so" (Official Report of Proceedings, 11 March 1970, *Hong Kong Hansard*, 401.)

4. Special Committee on Housing Final Report 1956–1958, pp. 12–13. HKRS934/9/40, HKPRO.

5. *Review of Policies for Squatter Control, Resettlement and Government Low-Cost Housing*, 1964. HKRS874/5/39, HKPRO.

6. "Working Party on Housing Report" CO [Colonial Office] 1030/1178, TNA.

7. *Review of Policies for Squatter Control, Resettlement and Government Low-Cost Housing*, 1964. HKRS874/5/39, HKPRO.

8. Memo by Paul K.C. Tsui, Assistant Commissioner for Resettlement to Working Party on Housing, 3 May 1963. HKRS260/2/39, HKPRO.

9. Memo by Paul K.C. Tsui, Assistant Commissioner for Resettlement to Working Party on Housing, 3 May 1963. HKRS260/2/39, HKPRO.

10. *Review of Policies for Squatter Control, Resettlement and Government Low-Cost Housing*, 1964. HKRS874/5/39, HKPRO. 1963 refers to widespread outbreaks of "mass squatting." Subsequent quotes from this section are also from this file.

11. Notes on Border Control, attached in Memo from Immigration Planning Officer, Colonial Secretary to Political Adviser, 21 March 1960, HKRS298/1/2, HKPRO.

12. Dame May Curwen, Chairman of the British Council for Aid to Refugees, 1 June 1957, HKRS40/3/459, HKPRO.

13. See also Peterson (2008) who stated that the Hong Kong government refused to use the word *refugee* to describe asylum-seekers from China, preferring instead the

term 'squatter'. While this may have sometimes been the case, more commonly we have encountered the usage of "illegal migrant" as the preferred alternative.

14. Memorandum for the Working Party on Housing – The Resettlement Programme: 1963 Review, HKRS934/9/40, HKPRO.
15. Notes of meeting on 11.1.67, HKRS935/1/1, HKPRO.
16. Secret Memo from Colonial Secretary, 16 November 1967, HKRS934/5/33, HKPRO.
17. Secret Memo from Colonial Secretary, 16 November 1967, HKRS934/5/33, HKPRO.
18. Memo from Colonial Secretary to Director of Commerce and Industry, 11 September 1963, HKRS298/1/2, HKPRO.
19. Minute from Secretary for Housing to PAS(H), 15 December 1975, HKRS163/8/19, HKPRO.
20. Memo from Secretary for Chinese Affairs, 10 August 1964, HKRS874/5/38, HKPRO.
21. Memo from SCA to DCS, 26 June 1962, HKRS156/1/10388, HKPRO.
22. Memo for ExCo XCC No. 142, 6 December 1960, HKRS163/1/1090, HKPRO.
23. Commissioner for Resettlement C. G. M. Morrison to Supt Crown Lands & Survey, 19 June 1962, HKRS156/1/10388, HKPRO.
24. Supt Crown Lands & Survey to SCA, 10 May 1962, HKRS156/1/10388, HKPRO.
25. Memo from DPW to DCS, 12 September 1962, HKRS156/1/10388, HKPRO.
26. SCA to Supt Crown Lands & Survey, 29 May 1962, HKRS156/1/10388, HKPRO.
27. Supt Crown Lands & Survey to SCA, 2 June 1962, HKRS156/1/10388, HKPRO.
28. J. P. Aserappa, DCNT to SCL&S, 18 June 1962, HKRS156/1/10388, HKPRO.
29. Report by P. B. Williams, 11 October 1963, HKRS874/5/38, HKPRO.
30. Telegraph from H.E. to Secretary of State for the Colonies, 16 September 1963, HKRS874/5/38, HKPRO.
31. Telegram from H.E. to Secretary of State for the Colonies, 12 December 1963, HKRS874/5/38, HKPRO.
32. Memo from CS to HE 24 August 1963, HKRS874/5/38, HKPRO.
33. Memo from Commissioner for Resettlement C. G. M. Morrison to CS, 29 August 1963, HKRS874/5/38, HKPRO.
34. Memo from Commissioner for Resettlement C. G. M. Morrison to CS, 29 August 1963, HKRS874/5/38, HKPRO.
35. Memo from SCA to CS, 20 September 1963, HKRS874/5/38, HKPRO.
36. Memo from SCA to CS, 20 September 1963, HKRS874/5/38, HKPRO.
37. C. P. Sutcliffe ACP/K to Commissioner of Police, 23 September 1963, HKRS874/5/38, HKPRO.
38. Memo from Director of Special Branch to Commissioner of Police, 26 September 1963, HKRS874/5/38, HKPRO.
39. Memo from Commissioner for Resettlement to Attorney General, 22 July 1963, HKRS874/5/38, HKPRO.
40. Memo from Legal Department to Commissioner for Resettlement, 25 July 1963, HKRS874/5/38, HKPRO.
41. Memo from Sgd. A. B. McNutt, 15 July 1963, HKRS874/5/38, HKPRO.
42. Report by P. B. Williams, 11 October 1963, HKRS874/5/38, HKPRO.

Notes

43. Memo from CS to Commissioner for Resettlement, 7 November 1963, HKRS874/5/38, HKPRO.
44. Memo from CS to Commissioner for Resettlement, 7 November 1963, HKRS874/5/38, HKPRO.
45. Memo from Secretary for Chinese Affairs, 10 August 1964, HKRS874/5/38, HKPRO.

Chapter 5

1. To use Žižek's (2014, 9) usage as the "surprising emergence of something new which undermines every stable scheme," which seems to apply well to all three of these situations.
2. It is certainly common to refer to temporally extended periods of unrest or reform as "an event" such as the 1789 French Revolution.
3. Official Report of Proceedings, 27 February 1957, *Hong Kong Hansard*, p. 22.
4. The Government in Hong Kong: Basic Policies and Methods, attached in memorandum from the Defence Secretary to D. C. C. Luddington, 12 May 1970, HKRS742/15/22, HKPRO, quoted in Fung (2022, 6).
5. Governor to Secretary of State for Foreign and Commonwealth Affairs Michael Stewart, 23 April 1970, FCO40/292, TNA.
6. Memorandum by James Murray, 16 October 1968, FCO21/538, TNA. Also see Mark (2017).
7. The nature of the post-1997 state is one of the issues we do not address in this book, although some of our findings seems relevant to comparing it with the late colonial state.
8. The Government in Hong Kong: Basic Policies and Methods, attached in memorandum from the Defence Secretary to D. C. C. Luddington, 12 May 1970, HKRS742/15/22, HKPRO.
9. Murray MacLehose to the Secretary of State for Foreign and Commonwealth Affairs, 4 January 1974, FCO40/547, TNA.
10. Murray MacLehose to the Secretary of State for Foreign and Commonwealth Affairs, 27 May 1974, FCO40/547, TNA.
11. "Address in the Legislative Council, 16 October 1974, *Hong Kong Hansard*," quoted in Faure (1997, 308).
12. "Address in the Legislative Council, 16 October 1974, *Hong Kong Hansard*," quoted in Faure (1997, 308).
13. The Abercrombie Report was the first urban plan for Hong Kong. It was funded by the Colonial Office under the Colonial Development and Welfare Scheme and intended to help the Hong Kong government in the development aspect of its post-war administration. For reception, see HKRS156/1/3425 'Town planning – report of Sir Patrick Abercrombie on' 19 November 1949.
14. "Planning Paper on Future of Hong Kong (Part D)" 1976, FCO40/704, TNA.

Chapter 6

1. The earliest approximate citation is to John Godfrey Saxe in 1869, with a slightly different phrasing as "Laws, like sausages, cease to inspire respect in proportion as

we know how they are made." Bismarck, Chancellor of the German Empire (1871–1890), was not associated with that witticism until the 1930s. Quote Investigator, https://quoteinvestigator.com/2010/07/08/lawssausages/.

2. Draft record of Royle's private conversation with the Governor on 11 October 1970, HKRS163/9/653, HKPRO.

3. Telegram from Secretary of State for the Colonies to Governor Trench, 20 November 1970, HKRS163/9/653, HKPRO.

4. Governor Trench to Deputy Undersecretary Leslie Monson, 7 January 1971, HKRS2021/1/52, HKPRO.

5. Personal from Acting Governor, 9 December 1970, HKRS2021/1/52, HKPRO.

6. Personal from Acting Governor, 9 December 1970, HKRS2021/1/52, HKPRO.

7. Worker-Student Action Committees were apparently of some significance during the Paris uprising of 1968, and this Committee may have been inspired by that, but some search does not indicate that they were of any great importance in the UK, at least under that label. However, the letter does reveal considerable interest and knowledge of the Hong Kong situation.

8. Chairman of the Housing Board to Colonial Secretary, 11 November 1970, HKRS2021/1/52, HKPRO.

9. Draft Housing Board paper, 1971, HKRS2021/1/52, HKPRO.

10. Draft Housing Board paper, 1971, HKRS2021/1/52, HKPRO.

11. Draft Housing Board paper, 1971, HKRS2021/1/52, HKPRO.

12. Draft Housing Board paper, 1971, HKRS2021/1/52, HKPRO.

13. Draft Housing Board paper, 1971, HKRS2021/1/52, HKPRO.

14. Housing Broad Programme of Work 1970–1971, Housing Board Paper no. 47, 19 December 1970, HKRS163/9/653, HKPRO.

15. Housing Board Minutes, 1 February 1971, HKRS174/1/10, HKPRO.

16. Housing Board Minutes, 20 January 1971, HKRS174/1/10, HKPRO.

17. Housing Board Minutes, 20 January 1971, HKRS174/1/10, HKPRO.

18. Draft Housing Board paper, 1971, HKRS2021/1/52, HKPRO.

19. Draft Housing Board paper, 1971, HKRS2021/1/52, HKPRO.

20. Draft Housing Board paper, 1971, HKRS2021/1/52, HKPRO.

21. Draft Housing Board paper, 1971, HKRS2021/1/52, HKPRO.

22. Commissioner for Resettlement Paul Tsui to Secretary for Home Affairs Ronald Holmes, 15 February 1971, HKRS156/3/83, HKPRO.

23. Draft Housing Board paper, 1971, HKRS2021/1/52, HKPRO.

24. Localization of the civil service began in Hong Kong in 1950 with the enactment of the Public Service Commission Ordinance. Since the 1950s, expatriates were recruited on permanent and pensionable terms only when there was no likelihood that local officers could be found to fill these posts in the foreseeable future (Lo 1995). The exception to this rule was that half of vacancies for administrative officers should always be filled by British officers.

25. An Analysis of the Squatter Areas in Hong Kong and Kowloon, Housing Board Paper No. 39, undated, HKRS174/1/9, HKPRO.

26. Draft Report of the Housing Board 1970, Housing Board Paper No. 45, undated, HKRS174/1/10, HKPRO. The report was submitted and discussed at 31st meeting of the Housing Board on 21 September 1970.

Notes 273

27. Housing Board Paper No. 49, for discussion on 1 March 1971, HKRS156/3/83, HKPRO.
28. "Working Party on Housing Report," 7 April 1971, CO 1030/1178, TNA (The National Archives).
29. This system was put in place after villager protests from 1923 to 1926 against the proposal to impose premiums on building land. The compromise was that villagers requiring additional land for building had to apply for this permit upon payment of increased Crown Rent. Crown land licenses could also be used for similar building purposes. See A. Chun (2002).
30. District Commissioner, N.T. to Colonial Secretary, 7 April 1972, HKRS2021/1/52, HKPRO.
31. District Commissioner, N.T. to Colonial Secretary, 7 April 1972, HKRS2021/1/52, HKPRO.
32. Director of Public Works to Colonial Secretary, 27 May 1971, HKRS2021/1/52, HKPRO.
33. Director of Public Works to Colonial Secretary, 27 May 1971, HKRS2021/1/52, HKPRO.
34. Secretary of Home Affairs to Colonial Secretary, 4 June 1971, HKRS156/3/83, HKPRO.
35. Secretary of Home Affairs to Colonial Secretary, 4 June 1971, HKRS156/3/83, HKPRO.
36. Improvement of Squatter Areas (Draft), Housing Board Paper No. 75, 1 April 1973, HKRS163/9/653, HKPRO.

Chapter 7

1. Review of Public Housing Allocation Policies, Executive Council Draft Memo for discussion on 4 September 1984, attached in Memo from Secretary for Housing, 9 August 1984, HKRS696/3/4, HKPRO.
2. Minute from D. C. Bray, District Commissioner, NT for Secretary for Home Affairs Luddington, 7 November 1970, HKRS934/5/33, HKPRO. He strongly criticized the housing situation in this minute, describing "the lack of direction of this mammoth programme. We seem to be building houses as fast as we can, putting in no doubt worthy people but without any great system about it, and proceeding with some fairly unrealistic ideals in the backs of our minds."
3. By this privilege he meant that once obtaining a flat, they could continue occupation despite income increases, an issue that became crucial in the 1980s "well off tenant" debate. "Notes of a meeting held at Government House on 6.10.71." HKRS934/5/33, HKPRO.
4. Government spending on housing during the program increased to $2.43 billion in 1980–1981, 29.2% of social expenditure, and 10.4% of total government spending. However, in 1963–1964, spending on housing accounted for 38% of social expenditure, and 15.5% of total government spending (Lui 2017).
5. Review of Housing Objectives, Memorandum for Executive Council, 9 October 1980, HKRS696/3/3, HKPRO.

6. Review of Housing Objectives, Memorandum for Executive Council, 9 October 1980, HKRS696/3/3, HKPRO.
7. Notes on Briefing at Housing Department HQ on Friday 11 February 1977, attached in Memo from Secretary for Housing to Private Secretary G. H., 17 February 1977, HKRS696/3/3, HKPRO.
8. Review of Housing Objectives, Memorandum for Executive Council, 9 October 1980, HKRS696/3/3, HKPRO.
9. Review of Housing Objectives, Memorandum for Executive Council, 9 October 1980, HKRS696/3/3, HKPRO.
10. Review of Housing Objectives, Memorandum for Executive Council, 9 October 1980, HKRS696/3/3, HKPRO.
11. This change was approved by the Housing Authority's Operations Committee on 31 July 1980, following a recommendation in Paper OC 26/80, and later by ExCo. See, Eligibility for Permanent Public Housing of Emergency and Compulsory Categories, Memorandum for the Operation Committee, 27 August 1981, HKRS696/3/3, HKPRO.
12. Eligibility for Permanent Public Housing of Emergency and Compulsory Categories, Memorandum for the Operation Committee, 27 August 1981, HKRS696/3/3, HKPRO.
13. Eligibility for Permanent Public Housing of Emergency and Compulsory Categories, Memorandum for the Operation Committee, 27 August 1981, HKRS696/3/3, HKPRO.
14. Paper on Possible THA Site at Tuen Mun Area 44 for Consideration by Members of Temporary Housing Sub-Committee of Land Development Policy Committee, attached in Memo from Director of Housing, 5 May 1982, HKRS934/8/85, HKPRO.
15. Eligibility for Permanent Public Housing of Emergency and Compulsory Categories, Memorandum for the Operation Committee, 27 August 1981, HKRS696/3/3, HKPRO.
16. Housing Authority Operations Branch Quarterly Report OC 2/83, 31 January 1983, HKRS394/29/227, HKPRO.
17. Eligibility for Permanent Public Housing of Emergency and Compulsory Categories, Memorandum for the Operation Committee, 27 August 1981, HKRS696/3/3, HKPRO.
18. Minute from CS to HE on "Squatters and Squatter Areas," 9 December 1981, HKRS696/3/1, HKPRO.
19. Paper on "Squatter control, improvements and re-housing in disasters, etc." for discussion in CS Office, 28 November 1981, HKRS696/3/1, HKPRO.
20. Paper on "Squatter control, improvements and re-housing in disasters, etc." for discussion in CS Office, 28 November 1981, HKRS696/3/1, HKPRO.
21. Governor Trench in "Note of a meeting held at Government House on 6.10.71.," HKRS934/5/33, HKPRO.
22. Paper on "Squatter Control, Improvements and Re-Housing in Disasters, etc." for discussion in CS Office, 28 November 1981, HKRS696/3/1, HKPRO.
23. "A CID Criminal Intelligence Report on Squatter Fires" submitted to ExCo for discussion on 8 January 1982, 30 December 1981, HKRS696/3/1, HKPRO.

Notes 275

24. Paper on "Squatter control, improvements and re-housing in disasters, etc." for discussion in CS Office, 28 November 1981, HKRS696/3/1, HKPRO.
25. Paper on "Squatter control, improvements and re-housing in disasters, etc." for discussion in CS Office, 28 November 1981, HKRS696/3/1, HKPRO.
26. Memo from A. P. Asprey Deputy Director/Operations, 5 March 1982, HKRS696/3/1, HKPRO.
27. Memo from A. P. Asprey Deputy Director/Operations, 5 March 1982, HKRS696/3/1, HKPRO.
28. Rehousing of Those Made Homeless in Recent Fires in Squatter Areas, Memorandum for the Operations Committee, HA Paper OC 13/82, 25 February 1982, HKRS696/3/1, HKPRO.
29. Memo from Director of Housing to Regional Sec (NT), 31 May 1982, HKRS696/3/1, HKPRO.
30. Construction of Emergency Temporary Housing Areas, HA paper BC 70/82, 21 July 1982. HKRS696/3/2, HKPRO.
31. Minutes of the 85th Meeting of the Land Development Policy Committee on 23 March 1982, HKRS696/3/1, HKPRO.
32. Memo from D. O. Tuen Mun Billy C. L. Lam to Regional Secretary N. T., 24 March 1982, HKRS696/3/2, HKPRO.
33. Report on an Incident at Yau Oi and On Ting Estates, Tuen Mun: 12 and 13 July 1981, 15 July 1981, HKRS886/1/4, HKPRO.
34. Review of Public Housing Allocation Policies, Executive Council Draft Memo for discussion on 4 September 1984, attached in Memo from Secretary for Housing, 9 August 1984, HKRS696/3/4, HKPRO.
35. Squatter Control—Crown Land in the Urban Area, Corruption Prevention Department Assignment No. 44/75, 22 June 1976, HKRS163/15/65, HKPRO.
36. Memo from PAS(H) E. Chia to Secretary for Housing D. P. H. Liao, 16 October 1976, HKRS163/15/65, HKPRO.
37. Letter from P. B. Williams, Commissioner ICAC to Secretary for Housing D. P. H. Liao, 1 October 1982, HKRS163/15/65, HKPRO.
38. Memo from Commissioner of Police A. J. Schouten on "New Policy for the Control of Squatters," 4 September 1976, HKRS695/2/8, HKPRO.
39. Review of Policy for Controlling Squatting and Rehousing of Squatters, Memorandum for ExCo for discussion on 21 September 1982, 10 September 1982, HKRS394/29/227, HKPRO.
40. Housing Branch Paper for Chief Secretary's Committee—Squatter Control, 3 December 1979, HKRS394/29/225, HKPRO.
41. Housing Branch Paper for Chief Secretary's Committee—Squatter Control, 3 December 1979, HKRS394/29/225, HKPRO.
42. General Circular No. 9/83 Protection of Land under Departmental Control, issued by J. C. A. Hammond, Director of Councils and Administration Branch, 8 February 1983, HKRS695/2/8, HKPRO.
43. Meeting Minutes of Squatting at or under Highways Structures on 28 April 1983, attached in Memo from Commissioner of Police R. A. Williamson, 16 May 1983, HKRS695/2/8, HKPRO.

44. Comment by AS (HK & K) on Memo by SHA, 23 September 1983. HKRS394/29/227, HKPRO.

45. The Problem of Rooftop Structures, Review of Policy for Controlling Squatting and Rehousing of Squatters, Note for ExCo, 4 November 1983, HKRS394/29/227, HKPRO.

46. Another mangle, but one that space does not allow the consideration of here. See Smart and Chui (2006).

47. Rehousing of Squatters Affected by Environmental Clearance, Memo for the Operations Committee of the Housing Authority, 13 September 1984, HKRS696/3/125, HKPRO.

48. Meeting Minutes of Squatting at or under Highways Structures on 28 April 1983, attached in Memo from Commissioner of Police R. A. Williamson, 16 May 1983, HKRS695/2/8, HKPRO.

49. Review of Public Housing Allocation Policies, Executive Council Draft Memo for discussion on 4 September 1984, attached in Memo from Secretary for Housing, 9 August 1984, HKRS696/3/4, HKPRO, emphasis in original.

50. Survey of Occupants of Squatter Areas, Memo for the Operations Committee of the Housing Authority, 5 July 1984, HKRS696/3/125, HKPRO.

Chapter 8

1. Brief Note of a Meeting at Government House on 27 May 1972 to discuss the Housing Programme, HKRS477/6/28, HKPRO.

2. Official Report of Proceedings, 18 October 1972, *Hong Kong Hansard*, p. 4.

3. Letter from Murray MacLehose to Sir Alec Douglas-Home, 1 January 1973, FCO40/439, TNA.

4. Murray MacLehose to the Secretary of State for Foreign and Commonwealth Affairs, 4 January 1974, FCO40/547, TNA.

5. Chinese Youth behind the Current Agitation: Their Grievances, Motivations and Aspirations, 18 September 1971, HKRS1071/1/11, HKPRO.

6. Public Relations Standing Committee Working Paper, Current Public Attitude to Government, Secretary for Home Affairs, 3 May 1971, HKRS163/9/531, HKPRO.

7. Chinese Youth behind the Current Agitation: Their Grievances, Motivations and Aspirations, 18 September 1971, HKRS1071/1/11, HKPRO.

8. Chinese Youth behind the Current Agitation: Their Grievances, Motivations and Aspirations, 18 September 1971, HKRS1071/1/11, HKPRO.

9. Secretary for Home Affairs to CDC (K), 23 August 1971, HKRS934/2/75, HKPRO.

10. Murray MacLehose to the Secretary of State for Foreign and Commonwealth Affairs, 4 January 1974, FCO40/547, TNA.

11. Official Report of Proceedings, 18 October 1972, *Hong Kong Hansard*, p. 6.

12. From Commissioner for Resettlement to Hon. Colonial Secretary, 28 March 1961, HKRS890/1/11, HKPRO.

13. Housing Aims and Policies by Secretary for Home Affairs, October 1970, HKRS934/5/33, HKPRO.

14. Class II License Areas, 26 May 1972, HKRS1588/9/50, HKPRO.

Notes

15. Housing Situation as Reflected by Recent Squatting by the Resettlement Department, December 1972, HKRS934/12/47, HKPRO.
16. Housing Aims and Policies by Secretary for Home Affairs, October 1970, HKRS934/5/33, HKPRO.
17. Commissioner for Housing to Hon. Colonial Secretary, 14 January 1972, HKRS1588/9/51, HKPRO.
18. Housing Aims and Policies by Secretary for Home Affairs, October 1970, HKRS934/5/33, HKPRO.
19. Application for and Allocation of Flats in Public Housing Estate, Corruption Prevention Department Assignment No. 7/76, 1 October 1976, HKRS163/15/74, HKPRO.
20. Housing Aims and Policies by Secretary for Home Affairs, October 1970, HKRS934/5/33, HKPRO.
21. From D. C. Bray to Hon. Secretary for Home Affairs, 20 January 1971, HKRS934/5/33, HKPRO.
22. The Housing Authority Public Meeting, 30 September 1971, HKRS934/12/112, HKPRO.
23. Current Public Attitude to Government, Public Relations Standing Committee Working Paper prepared by Secretary for Home Affairs, 3 May 1971, HKRS163/9/531, HKPRO.
24. Notes of a meeting at Government House on 28 June 1972 to discuss reorganization of housing administration, undated, HKRS934/8/123, HKPRO.
25. Memorandum for Executive Council: Reorganisation of Housing Administration, 19 September 1972, HKRS934/8/123, HKPRO.
26. Background Paper on Public Housing Rentals by Director of Home Affairs, 25 October 1976, HKRS488/3/23, HKPRO.
27. Record of a meeting at Government House to consider the reorganization of public housing, 6 October 1971, HKRS934/8/123, HKPRO.
28. District Commissioner in the New Territories to Hon. Secretary for Home Affairs, 20 January 1971, HKRS934/5/33, HKPRO.
29. Eligibility for Government Housing: Review of Categories, undated, HKRS934/12/44, HKPRO.
30. "Catalogue of a Disaster: The Day the Earth Moved," *South China Morning Post*, 15 June 1975, p. 6.
31. "The Rainstorm," *South China Morning Post*, 1 July 1972, p. 2.
32. Current Pressures towards Squatting and the Class II Licensed Areas, Memorandum for the Operations Committee, 22 June 1973, HKRS934/12/47, HKPRO.
33. District Commissioner in the New Territories to Hon. Secretary for Home Affairs, 20 January 1971, HKRS934/5/33, HKPRO.
34. Reconciliation of Supply and Demand of Public Housing up to 31st March 1976, 5 May 1972, HKRS1588/9/51, HKPRO.
35. Reconciliation of Supply and Demand of Public Housing up to 31st March 1976, 5 May 1972, HKRS1588/9/51, HKPRO.
36. Commissioner for Resettlement to Deputy Colonial Secretary, 6 January 1972, HKRS1588/9/51, HKPRO.

37. Commissioner for Housing to Hon. Colonial Secretary, 14 January 1972, HKRS1588/9/51, HKPRO.

38. See Minutes of 62nd Meeting of the Housing Board held on Wednesday 14 June 1972, HKRS1588/9/50, HKPRO.

39. Commissioner for Housing to Hon. Colonial Secretary, 21 March 1972, HKRS1588/9/51, HKPRO.

40. Colonial Secretariat to Commissioner for Housing, 23 May 1972, HKRS1588/9/51, HKPRO.

41. Squatter Clearances—Current Policies and Practices, Memorandum for the Housing Authority, 4 June 1973, HKRS394/29/224, HKPRO.

42. Allocation of Public Housing: 1st April 1973 to 31st March 1975, Note for Executive/Legislative Councils, 29 March 1973, HKRS1588/9/50, HKPRO.

43. Letter from Murray MacLehose to the Chairman of Hong Kong Housing Authority, 4 February 1976, HKRS163/8/96, HKPRO.

44. Memorandum from the Secretary for Housing to Colonial Secretary, 8 July 1975, HKRS163/8/21, HKPRO.

45. For example, the colonial government planned to allocate 500 new flats to fire/disaster victims in 1975–1976 that could "accommodate anything from 2500 to 5000 persons" depending on the size of the flat, but the number of allocated flats turned out to be 720. See, Assistant Director, Squatter Control to Secretary, Housing Authority, 2 January 1975, HKRS934/12/44, HKPRO.

46. Waiting Time for Waiting List Applicants, Memorandum for Management Committee, 4 April 1979, HKRS1693/4/6, HKPRO.

47. Minutes of the meeting of the Hong Kong Housing Authority held on Thursday 7 June 1973, HKRS934/12/112, HKPRO.

48. Extract from minutes of the Meeting of the HA Operations and Management Committees held on 4 March 1976, HKRS1693/4/6, HKPRO.

49. Extract of Minute of meeting of HKHA Management Committee on 10 February 1977, HKRS1693/4/6, HKPRO.

50. Quotas for Waiting List Applicants, Memorandum for the Management Committee, 4 February 1977, HKRS1693/4/6, HKPRO.

51. "100,000 Families on Waiting List," *South China Morning Post*, 26 September 1976, p. 7.

52. Waiting Time for Waiting List Applicants, Memorandum for Management Committee, 4 April 1979, HKRS1693/4/6, HKPRO.

53. "Time to Tidy Up Housing Mess: Hongkong Observers' Forum," *South China Morning Post*, 19 November 1979, p. 2.

54. Housing in Hong Kong, Secretary for Housing's Notes, 20 September 1979, FCO40/1123, TNA.

55. Policies of the Housing Authority under Fire, Part I, by Home Affairs Department, 19 August 1976, HKRS925/1/1, HKPRO.

56. Policies of the Housing Authority under Fire, Part II, by Home Affairs Department, 20 August 1976, HKRS925/1/1, HKPRO.

57. Current Trends in Living and Thinking in Hong Kong, 20 June 1979, HKRS925/1/1, HKPRO.

Notes

58. Quotas for Waiting List Applicants, Memorandum for the Management Committee, 4 February 1977, HKRS1693/4/6, HKPRO. The colonial government was conscious to the existence of such a loophole and how people could make use of it. As a City District Commissioner reported in 1974, "as time goes on people will lose patience on the housing list and they will, to an ever-increasing degree, 'reserve' space in squatter areas probably preparing evidence to support any claim and sit tight to await a fire or the screening for clearance of the squatter area, at which time they will come forward for housing." See, From City District Commissioner (Kowloon) to Director of Home Affairs, 1 February 1974, HKRS934/12/47, HKPRO.

59. From Secretary for Housing to Director of Housing, 19 June 1974, HKRS934/12/44, HKPRO. See also, Director of Public Works to Secretary for Environment, 9 October 1976, HKRS934/12/46, HKPRO.

60. From Director of Housing to Secretary for Housing, Secretary for the New Territories, and Director of Home Affairs, 24 February 1976, HKRS934/12/46, HKPRO.

61. Memorandum (53) from the Director of Home Affairs to DD/AD(2)/AO(L), 1 March 1976, HKRS934/12/44, HKPRO.

62. Eligibility for Public Housing on Clearance, Memorandum for the Operations and Management Committees, 27 February 1976, HKRS934/12/46, HKPRO.

63. Memorandum (53) from the Director of Home Affairs to DD/AD(2)/AO(L), 1 March 1976, HKRS934/12/44, HKPRO.

64. Assessment of Possible Rehousing Commitments and Supply of Public Housing, Research and Planning Division, 5 October 1977, HKRS1588/9/38, HKPRO.

65. A Review of the Problem of Temporary Housing, LDPC Paper, 29 February 1980, HKRS163/13/81, HKPRO.

66. Housing Allocations 1978/79—Third Review, Memorandum for the Operations Committee, 19 January 1979, HKRS1588/9/38, HKPRO.

67. Extract from Notes of Heads of Branches' Meeting held on 22 February 1979, HKRS1588/9/39, HKPRO.

68. For a critique of the "minimally integrated socio-political system" thesis, see Lam (2004).

69. An exception is Lee and Chan (1990). However, their attention is the political communication between state and society after the Sino-British Joint Declaration. Thus, the linkage between housing provision and legitimacy is not included in their discussion.

70. Aims and Policies of the Hong Kong Government, September 1970, HKRS742/15/22, HKPRO.

71. Director of Home Affairs to Director of Housing, 13 October 1976, HKRS488/3/23, HKPRO.

72. Aims and Policies of the Hong Kong Government, September 1970, HKRS742/15/22, HKPRO.

73. From City District Commissioner (Kowloon) to Deputy Director of Home Affairs, 11 September 1974, HKRS934/2/77, HKPRO.

74. Talk for "Viewpoint," attached in City District Commissioner (Kowloon) to Deputy Director of Home Affairs, 11 September 1974, HKRS934/2/77, HKPRO.

75. Acceptance of immigrants also varied with factors such as class. For example, immigrants from Shanghai in the late 1940s were welcomed by the colonial government as they brought capital to Hong Kong. This facilitated the economic transformation of the colony from an entrepot to an industrial colony (Wong 1988).

76. It should be noted that not all the locals and localists embraced the idea of ethnocracy. Rather, some drew distinction by embracing civic values (Veg 2017). For the changing faces of localism, see Chen and Szeto (2015). Despite this, the basic schema still remained as the locals versus the national/China.

77. Erni's analysis focuses on the right of abode controversy leading to a constitutional crisis in 1999. On the right of abode controversy, see Chan, Fu, and Ghai (2000). The crux of this controversy has to do with the question of how to handle cross-border interactions and marriage, see Smart (2003a), So (2003), and Law and Lee (2006).

78. One could see an interesting historical parallel of the immigrant influx in 1979 and the right of abode controversy. In both cases, the government leveraged the categorical difference to justify exclusionary tactics. For the case of the right of abode controversy, see Chan (2000).

79. Director of Immigration wrote to the Director of Information Service, 26 July 1974, HKRS163/8/13, HKPRO.

80. The Economic and Financial Implications of Immigration, 3 October 1974, HKRS163/8/13, HKPRO.

81. Notes on the Problem of Illegal Immigration, Government Information Services/Public Relations Division, November 1974, HKRS163/8/13, HKPRO.

82. Extract of Minutes from Directorate Meeting held on 2 December 1974, HKRS163/8/13, HKPRO.

83. Illegal Immigration: Public attitudes gradually turning anti-immigrant, 9 October 1975, HKRS934/4/1, HKPRO.

84. Policies of the Housing Authority under Fire, Part I, by Home Affairs Department, 19 August 1976, HKRS925/1/1, HKPRO.

85. From City District Officer (Yau Ma Tei) to Director of Home Affairs, 4 October 1980, HKRS934/5/19, HKPRO.

86. Official Report of Proceedings, 1 October 1980, *Hong Kong Hansard*, p. 15.

87. From Member of the Housing Authority John Walden (Director of Home Affairs) to Chairman of the Housing Authority Alan Scott (Secretary for Housing), 10 July 1979, HKRS696/3/3, HKPRO.

88. City District Commissioner (KW) to AD (CR), 2 October 1980, HKRS934/5/19, HKPRO.

89. Effects of Immigration from China in Hong Kong, attached in Commissioner for Census and Statistics to Assistant Political Adviser, 22 January 1980, HKRS163/8/176, HKPRO.

90. Minutes of the Governor's Committee Meeting held on 4 July 1980, HKRS508/3/6, HKPRO.

91. Extract from *South China Morning Post* dated 2 August 1979, HKRS1693/4/6, HKPRO.

92. From Secretary for Home Affairs to Director of Home Affairs, 28 January 1974, HKRS934/12/47, HKPRO.

Notes

93. Revision of Squatter Clearance and Housing Allocation Policy, Paper for Chief Secretary's Committee, 13 July 1979, HKRS163/13/81, HKPRO.
94. Squatter Control, Paper for Chief Secretary's Committee, Housing Branch, 30 January 1980, HKRS163/13/81, HKPRO.
95. Revision of Squatter Clearance and Housing Allocation Policy, Paper for Chief Secretary's Committee, 13 July 1979, HKRS163/13/81, HKPRO.
96. "Second Major Fire in Four Days Leaves 5,263 Homeless," *South China Morning Post*, 14 October 1979, p. 13.
97. Squatter Control, Paper for Chief Secretary's Committee, Housing Branch, 30 January 1980, HKRS163/13/81, HKPRO.
98. From City District Commissioner (Kowloon) to Director of Home Affairs, 21 September 1979, HKRS163/13/81, HKPRO.
99. Squatter Control, Paper for Chief Secretary's Committee, Housing Branch, 30 January 1980, HKRS163/13/81, HKPRO.
100. "Outsiders Face Long Homes Ban," *South China Morning Post*, 7 December 1979, p. 18.
101. Revision of Squatter Clearance and Housing Allocation Policy, Paper for Chief Secretary's Committee, 13 July 1979, HKRS163/13/81, HKPRO.
102. Revision of Squatter Clearance and Housing Allocation Policy, Paper for Chief Secretary's Committee, 13 July 1979, HKRS163/13/81, HKPRO.
103. Flashpoints, 10 December 1979, HKRS934/10/42, HKPRO.
104. Squatter Control, Paper for Chief Secretary's Committee, Housing Branch, 30 January 1980, HKRS163/13/81, HKPRO.
105. Review of Housing Objectives, Memorandum for Executive Council, 9 October 1980, HKRS696/3/3, HKPRO. Statistics on Eligibility, From ADC to DDO, 2 April 1981, HKRS1693/4/6, HKPRO.
106. Eligibility for Permanent Public Housing of Emergency and Compulsory Categories, Memorandum for the Operation Committee, 27 August 1981, HKRS696/3/3, HKPRO; "Residency Policy for Fire Victims Quietly Relaxed," *South China Morning Post*, 29 December 1981, p. 1.
107. Notes of 11th District Officers Meeting held on Thursday, 12 April 1984, HKRS696/3/4, HKPRO. On 27 April, the colonial government announced a review of housing policy through public consultation. Lower residence requirements as well as applying means-testing to clearees were included. See also "Policy Is Reviewed in Five Areas," *South China Morning Post*, 27 April 1984, p. 14.
108. "Squatters Demand Equal Treatment," *South China Morning Post*, 26 May 1989, p. 10.
109. Housing Department, Rehousing Policy for Squatter Clearees, Information Paper for LegCo Panel on Housing Sub-committee on Rehousing Arrangements for Residents Affected by Clearance of Squatter Areas, January 2000, Appendix I, available at https://www.legco.gov.hk/yr99-00/english/panels/hg/cl_squat/papers/a728e02.pdf.
110. Notes of 11th District Officers Meeting held on Thursday, 12 April 1984, HKRS696/3/4, HKPRO.
111. Minutes of the Meeting of the HKHA Operations Committee held on Thursday, 4 March 1982, HKRS696/3/123, HKPRO.

112. Eligibility for Public Housing: Emergency and Compulsory Categories, Memorandum for the Operations Committee, 23 July 1982, HKRS696/3/123, HKPRO.

113. Rehousing of Recent Fire Victims, 27 November 1981, HKRS696/3/1, HKPRO.

Chapter 9

1. Temporary housing "should be viewed as a scarce resource and be subject to firm rules." See Minutes of the Fifth Meeting of the Working Group on Housing Demand and Production held on 18 March 1980, attached in Memo from Secretary for Housing, 28 March 1980, HKRS163/8/176, HKPRO.

2. An Analysis of the Squatter Areas in Hong Kong and Kowloon, Housing Board Paper No. 39, undated, HKRS174/1/9, HKPRO.

3. Minutes of the Housing Board meeting. HKRS174/1/9, "Housing Board – confirmed minutes & numbered papers."

4. Draft Report of the Housing Board 1970, Housing Board Paper No. 45, undated, HKRS174/1/10, HKPRO.

5. Memo to Commissioner for Resettlement, 17 June 1971, HKRS156/3/83, HKPRO.

6. Memo to Commissioner for Resettlement, 17 June 1971, HKRS156/3/83, HKPRO.

7. Demand and Supply of Public Housing, Memorandum for the Executive Council, attached in Memo from Director of Housing to Secretary for Housing, 14 April 1980, HKRS163/8/176, HKPRO.

8. Improvement of Squatter Areas (Draft), Housing Board Paper No. 75, 1 April 1973, HKRS163/9/653, HKPRO.

9. Letter from Assistant Chief Engineer D. M. Allingham, 30 September 1972, HKRS934/9/38, HKPRO.

10. Letter from Assistant Chief Engineer D. M. Allingham, 30 September 1972, HKRS934/9/38, HKPRO.

11. Notes on Departmental Meeting to Discuss Action on Illegal Electric Wiring in Chai Wan Resettlement Estate, attached in Memo from Colonial Secretariat, 9 October 1972, HKRS934/9/38, HKPRO.

12. Memo from City District Commissioner (HK) to CS, 21 November 1972, HKRS934/9/38, HKPRO.

13. Squatter Area Improvements Division (1982).

14. Memo from Secretary for Housing, 26 April 1976, HKRS684/1/9, HKPRO.

15. Provision of a Legitimate Electricity Supply in Squatter Areas, Memo for ExCo for discussion on 15 June 1976, 1 June 1976, HKRS684/1/9, HKPRO.

16. Memo for ExCo XCC (76)32, "Provision of a legitimate electricity supply in squatter areas." Discussion on 15 June 1976, HKRS684/1/9 Electrification of squatter areas. HKPRO.

17. Report of the Working Party on Electrification in Squatter Areas 1976, enclosed in HKRS684/1/9, HKPRO.

18. Report of the Working Party on Electrification in Squatter Areas 1976, enclosed in HKRS684/1/9, HKPRO.

Notes 283

19. Notes of Meeting to discuss Electrification of Squatter Areas on Hong Kong Island held at the office of City District Commissioner (Hong Kong) on 9 September 1977, 16 September 1977, HKRS684/1/9, HKPRO.

20. Letter from Chairman of the China Light and Power Company Limited Sir Lawrence Kadoorie to Chief Secretary Jack Cater, 30 June 1981, HKRS413/4/15, HKPRO.

21. Letter from Chairman of the China Light and Power Company Limited Sir Lawrence Kadoorie to Chief Secretary Jack Cater, 30 June 1981, HKRS413/4/15, HKPRO.

22. Memo from Frankie Lui for Secretary for Home Affairs to Secretary for Housing, 23 October 1981, HKRS413/4/15, HKPRO.

23. Memo from City District Commissioner (Shamshuipo) Stephen Ip to Director of Home Affairs, 15 July 1981, HKRS413/4/15, HKPRO.

24. Report by Director of Housing on the Possibility of Creating Fire Breaks in Squatter Areas, 29 November 1979, HKRS934/7/62, HKPRO.

25. Report by Director of Housing on the Possibility of Creating Fire Breaks in Squatter Areas, 29 November 1979, HKRS934/7/62, HKPRO.

26. From DCS to CS, 14 December 1949, HKRS163/1/1231, HKPRO.

27. Fire Prevention Campaign – Fire Watch Scheme, undated, HKRS934/7/62, HKPRO.

28. Fire Prevention Campaign – Fire Watch Scheme, undated, HKRS934/7/62, HKPRO.

29. Minutes of a Meeting held in the Acting Chief Secretary's Office on 24 October 1979, attached in Memo from Secretary for Security, 26 October 1979, HKRS934/7/62, HKPRO.

30. Letter from Secretary for Home Affairs John Walden to Director of Fire Services F. M. Watson, 15 December 1979, HKRS934/7/62, HKPRO.

31. Review of Policy for Controlling Squatting and Rehousing of Squatters, Memo for ExCo for discussion on 21 September 1982, 10 September 1982, HKRS934/10/9, HKPRO.

32. Minute from AS(D)1 M. L. Wong of the City and New Territories Administration (CNTA), 10 November 1982, HKRS934/10/9, HKPRO.

33. District Officer (Wong Tai Sin) to Director of Housing, 22 January 1985, HKRS934/10/9, HKPRO.

34. Discussion Paper for Squatter Area Improvements Interdepartmental Working Group, undated, HKRS696/3/13, HKPRO.

35. Summary of HD comments on the Home Affairs Branch Survey on Squatting, 17 June 1982, HKRS696/3/13, HKPRO.

36. Summary of HD comments on the Home Affairs Branch Survey on Squatting, 17 June 1982, HKRS696/3/13, HKPRO.

37. Assessment of the Size of the SAI Programme, Discussion Paper for Squatter Area Improvements Interdepartmental Working Group, 10 August 1982, HKRS696/3/13, HKPRO.

38. Assessment of the Size of the SAI Programme, Discussion Paper for Squatter Area Improvements Interdepartmental Working Group, 10 August 1982, HKRS696/3/13, HKPRO.

284   Notes

39. Squatter Area Improvements Division (1982).
40. A full half of the flat land in Hong Kong—that is, with elevations of less than five degrees—is reclaimed from the sea (Brand et al. 1984).
41. Improvements to Squatter Areas, Memo for ExCo for discussion on 1 February 1983, HKRS696/3/13, HKPRO.
42. Report No. 1, Landslides in Squatter Areas: Precautionary measures, undated, HKRS934/8/67, HKPRO.
43. Improvements to Squatter Areas, Memo for ExCo for discussion on 1 February 1983, HKRS696/3/13, HKPRO.
44. Minutes of the Interdepartmental Working Group on Squatter Area Improvements, 19 August 1982, HKRS696/3/13, HKPRO.
45. Minutes of the Interdepartmental Working Group on Squatter Area Improvements, 19 August 1982, HKRS696/3/13, HKPRO.
46. Squatter Area Improvements, Sau Mau Ping Pilot Area: Report and preliminary designs, Housing Authority. May 1982. Document received by Smart during fieldwork, 1983–1985.
47. Review of Policy for Controlling Squatting and Rehousing of Squatters, Memo for ExCo for discussion on 21 September 1982, 10 September 1982, HKRS934/10/9, HKPRO.
48. Major Issues, attached as enclosure (1) in Letter from Philip Haddon-Cave to Edward Youde, 7 April 1982, HKRS163/14/156, HKPRO.
49. Improvements to Squatter Areas, Memo for ExCo for discussion on 1 February 1983, HKRS696/3/13, HKPRO.
50. Improvements to Squatter Areas, Memo for ExCo for discussion on 1 February 1983, HKRS696/3/13, HKPRO.
51. Improvements to Squatter Areas, Memo for ExCo for discussion on 1 February 1983, HKRS696/3/13, HKPRO.
52. Minutes of the Meeting of the Hong Kong Housing Authority held on Thursday 24 March 1983, HKRS696/3/120, HKPRO.
53. Minutes of the Meeting of the Hong Kong Housing Authority held on Thursday 24 March 1983, HKRS696/3/120, HKPRO.
54. Minute from AS(D)1 M. L. Wong of the City and New Territories Administration (CNTA), 10 November 1982, HKRS934/10/9, HKPRO.
55. Improvements to Squatter Areas, Memo for ExCo for discussion on 1 February 1983, HKRS696/3/13, HKPRO.

Chapter 10

1. Minutes of the 276th Meeting of the Chief Secretary's Committee held on Monday, 29 June 1981, HKRS934/2/91, HKPRO.
2. Letter from E. W. Brand, Principal Government Geotechnical Engineer to Secretary for Housing, 20 November 1982, HKRS696/3/13, HKPRO.
3. Landslide Dangers to Squatters in Hong Kong and Kowloon, Geotechnical Control Office of the Engineering Development Department, November 1982, attached in Memo from Director of Engineering Development to Secretary for Housing, 29 November 1982, HKRS934/8/68, HKPRO.

Notes

4. Landslide Dangers to Squatters in Hong Kong and Kowloon, Geotechnical Control Office of the Engineering Development Department, November 1982, attached in Memo from Director of Engineering Development to Secretary for Housing, 29 November 1982, HKRS934/8/68, HKPRO.
5. Letter from Principal Government Geotechnical Engineer E. W. Brand to Secretary for Housing, 20 November 1982, HKRS696/3/13, HKPRO.
6. Improvements to Squatter Areas, Memo for ExCo For discussion on 1 February 1983, HKRS696/3/13, HKPRO.
7. Slope safety in Hong Kong, Information Paper prepared by Principal Government Geotechnical Engineer E. W. Brand, April 1986 attached in Memo from Director of Engineering Development, 14 April 1986, HKRS934/2/91, HKPRO.
8. Guidance for District Officers on Slope Safety in Squatter Areas, Policy Paper prepared by Principal Government Geotechnical Engineer E. W. Brand, April 1986 attached in Memo from Director of Engineering Development, 14 April 1986, HKRS934/2/91, HKPRO.
9. The term was coined by Joseph Heller in his novel *Catch-22* (New York: Simon & Schuster, 1961) to describe the predicament of being trapped by contradictory rules.
10. Improvements to Squatter Areas, Memo for ExCo For discussion on 1 February 1983, HKRS696/3/13, HKPRO.
11. Memo from Registrar General (LO/Is. & S.K.) to District Lands Officers (Sai Kung), 24 September 1982, HKRS934/2/91, HKPRO.
12. *Leakey & Ors v National Trust* [1980] QB 485 Court of Appeal, available at http://www.e-lawresources.co.uk/cases/Leakey-v-National-Trust.php.
13. Memo from Secretary for Lands and Works to Attorney General's Chambers, 22 July 1983, HKRS934/2/91, HKPRO.
14. Minutes of Meeting of Working Group on Widespread Unlawful Activities, 3 October 1979, HKRS163/13/60, HKPRO.
15. Secretary for Housing to Attorney General, 8 December 1976, HKRS934/2/91, HKPRO.
16. Secretary for Housing to Attorney General, 8 December 1976, HKRS934/2/91, HKPRO.
17. Improvements to Squatter Areas, Memo for ExCo For discussion on 1 February 1983, HKRS696/3/13, HKPRO.
18. Extract from record of RS(HK&K)'s Meeting held on 7 December 1983, HKRS934/8/69, HKPRO.
19. Memo from Director of Housing to Secretary for Security, 8 July 1982, HKRS1874/1/4, HKPRO.
20. Memo from Lands and Works Branch to DED, 29 March 1983, HKRS934/8/69, HKPRO.
21. Minute from AS(D) 1 (HK&K), 28 September 1983, HKRS934/8/68, HKPRO.
22. Review of Public Housing Allocation Policies, Executive Council Draft Memo for discussion on 4 September 1984, attached in Memo from Secretary for Housing, 9 August 1984, HKRS696/3/4, HKPRO.
23. Clearance of Squatters Outside Development Zones, Memo for Housing Authority Operations Committee, 24 February 1984. HKRS696/3/125, HKPRO.

286 Notes

24. Squatter Control, Memo for the HA Operations Committee, 29 April 1983, HKRS696/3/124, HKPRO.
25. Memo from Crown Counsel David Fitzpatrick to Deputy Crown Prosecutor J. M. Duffy, 22 April 1982, HKRS927/1/13, HKPRO.
26. Enclosure of the Additional Staff for the Clearance Division Operations Branch, Memo for Housing Authority Operations Committee, 29 November 1984, HKRS696/3/125, HKPRO.
27. Squatter Control, Memorandum for the Operations Committee, 29 April 1983, HKRS696/3/124, HKPRO.
28. Survey of Occupants of Squatter Areas, Memorandum for the Operations Committee, 5 July 1984, HKRS696/3/125, HKPRO.
29. Survey of Occupants of Squatter Areas, Memorandum for the Operations Committee, 30 March 1984. HKRS696/3/125, HKPRO.
30. Minutes of the Hong Kong Housing Authority Operations Committee held on Thursday, 5 April 1984, HKRS696/3/125, HKPRO.
31. Survey of Occupants of Squatter Areas, Memorandum for the Operations Committee, 5 July 1984, HKRS696/3/125, HKPRO.
32. Minutes of the Hong Kong Housing Authority Operations Committee held on Thursday, 20 September 1984. HKRS696/3/125, HKPRO.
33. Survey of Occupants of Squatter Areas, Memorandum for the Operations Committee, 16 October 1985, HKRS696/3/126, HKPRO.
34. Survey of Occupants of Squatter Areas, Memorandum for the Operations Committee, 5 July 1984, HKRS696/3/125, HKPRO.
35. Survey of Occupants of Squatter Areas, Memorandum for the Operations Committee, 30 March 1984. HKRS696/3/125, HKPRO.
36. Minutes of the Hong Kong Housing Authority Operations Committee held on Thursday 5 April 1984, HKRS696/3/125, HKPRO. Trawling was the procedure of transferring long-term residents of THAs to permanent public housing to make space available in the THAs.
37. Proposed Additional Rehousing Criterion for Squatters Involved in Clearances, Fires and Natural Disasters, Memorandum for the Operations Committee, 16 July 1986, HKRS696/3/127, HKPRO.
38. Proposed Additional Rehousing Criterion for Squatters Involved in Clearances, Fires and Natural Disasters, Memorandum for the Operations Committee, 16 July 1986, HKRS696/3/127, HKPRO.
39. Another escape route for the squatter problem is raised in the deliberations of the Working Party on Widespread Unlawful Activities in 1977. They focused on illegal extensions of commercial and industrial activities onto streets and lanes. An Independent Commission Against Corruption report noted that "Control measures have been introduced on a rather ad hoc basis, with the result that several different agencies are responsible for enforcement" and that "many of the structures under consideration are also used for domestic purposes." Failure to control these structures, then, in a context where all other kinds of new squatting came under control, could result in an expansion of use of this niche for shelter. See, Unlawful Structures Occupying Public Roads, Pavements and Lanes in Urban Areas,

Corruption Prevention Department Report Assignment No. 15/76, 3 March 1977, HKRS163/13/60, HKPRO.
40. Proposed Additional Rehousing Criterion for Squatters Involved in Clearances, Fires and Natural Disasters, Memorandum for the Operations Committee, 16 July 1986, HKRS696/3/127, HKPRO.
41. Minutes of the Hong Kong Housing Authority Operations Committee held on Thursday, 10 April 1986, HKRS696/3/126, HKPRO.
42. Survey of Occupants of Squatter Areas, Memorandum for the Operations Committee, 16 October 1985, HKRS696/3/126, HKPRO.
43. Freezing Survey for Environmental Clearance, Memorandum for the Operations Committee, 1 April 1986, HKRS696/3/126, HKPRO.
44. Policy on Clearance of Squatter Areas and Temporary Housing Areas, Informational Paper for Legislative Council Panel on Housing by the Housing Branch, October 2000, available at https://www.legco.gov.hk/yr00-01/english/panels/hg/papers/a79e01.pdf.
45. Or loosen, but that is not relevant here.

Chapter 11

1. *The Straits Times*, 7 January 1964, quoted in Yuen (2007, 288).
2. Such anti-insurgency resettlements were common in other colonies. An early study of the program in Algeria was conducted by Pierre Bourdieu and Abdelmalek Sayad (2020, orig. in French, 1964).

Conclusions

1. Press Release of LCQ15: Development Plans for Three Squatter Areas in Kowloon East, a Written Reply of the Secretary for Development Michael Wong to Question from Hon Wu Chi-wai in the Legislative Council on 27 March 2019, https://www.info.gov.hk/gia/general/201903/27/P2019032700340.htm?fontSize=1.
2. World Monuments Fund, "Pokfulam Village," accessed 22 October 2022, https://www.wmf.org/project/pokfulam-village.
3. Enclosure of the Additional Staff for the Clearance Division Operations Branch, Memo for Housing Authority Operations Committee, 29 November 1984, HKRS 696/3/125, HKPRO.
4. Press Release of LCQ15: Repair and Rebuilding of Squatter Huts, Reply of Secretary for Development Carrie Lam to Question from Lau Kong-wah in LegCo Meeting on 7 July 2010, available at https://www.info.gov.hk/gia/general/201007/07/P201007070172.htm.
5. See Census and Statistics Department, 2016 Population By-Census: Main Results, Hong Kong: Population By-census Office of the Government of Hong Kong Special Administrative Region, accessed 5 August 2021, https://www.censtatd.gov.hk/en/data/stat_report/product/B1120098/att/B11200982016XXXXB0100.pdf.
6. See Chapter 3: Management of Squatter and Licensed Structures, Director of Audit's Report No. 68, Hong Kong: Audit Commission, accessed 3 April 2017, https://www.aud.gov.hk/pdf_e/e68ch03.pdf.

7. See Chapter 3: Management of Squatter and Licensed Structures, Director of Audit's Report No. 68, Hong Kong: Audit Commission, accessed 3 April 2021, https://www.aud.gov.hk/pdf_e/e68ch03.pdf.

8. "Former Official and Wealthy Businessmen 'Squatting' Gov't Land in Prized Tai Tam Area," Hong Kong Free Press, 9 June 2016, accessed 3 July 2021, shorturl.at/ CIRUY.

9. "Lands Dep't to Follow Up 'Seriously' on Gov't Land Occupation by Former Official and Businessmen," Hong Kong Free Press, 10 June 2016, accessed 3 July 2021, shorturl.at/lmox0.

10. "Luxury Squatters? Probe over 89,000 sq. ft. of Government Land Occupied by Former Hong Kong Civil Servant and Businessmen," *South China Morning Post*, 9 June 2016, accessed 3 July 2021, shorturl.at/cpSTW.

11. "Lands Department Announces the Findings of its Investigation and Follow-up Actions in Tung Ah Pui Village," Press Release of Government of the Hong Kong Special Administrative Region, 22 June 2016, accessed 3 July 2021, shorturl.at/ ikPRT.

12. Lands Department, Squatter Control Policy on Surveyed Squatter Structures, June 2021, p. 2, available at https://www.landsd.gov.hk/en/land-mgt-enforce/squatter-control.html.

13. Chapter 3: Management of Squatter and Licensed Structures, Director of Audit's Report No. 68, Hong Kong: Audit Commission, accessed 3 April 2017, https://www.aud.gov.hk/pdf_e/e68ch03.pdf; https://www.landsd.gov.hk/en/land-mgt-enforce/squatter-control.html%22.

14. Press Release of LCQ15: Repair and Rebuilding of Squatter Huts, Reply of Secretary for Development Mrs Carrie Lam to question from the Hon. Lau Kong-wah in LegCo Meeting on 7 July 2010, available at https://www.info.gov.hk/gia/general/201007/07/P201007070172.htm.

15. "Squatter Residents of Cha Kwo Ling Fire Incident Would Be Rehoused Before 27 January," *Apple Daily*, 24 January 2006, A16 (in Chinese); "Six Fire Victims Lived in Community Centre for 90 Days, Home Affairs Department Announced to Go by Next Wednesday," HK01, 4 April 2017, accessed 3 July 2021, shorturl.at/mPRW2 (in Chinese).

16. "When a Kowloon Squatter Village Goes: New Homes for Some, Anxiety for Others Uncertain of Right to Compensation," *South China Morning Post*, 17 November 2019, accessed 3 July 2022, shorturl.at/dilUZ.

17. See the Chief Executive's 2019 Policy Address, accessed 12 July 2022, https://www.policyaddress.gov.hk/2019/eng/pdf/PA2019.pdf.

18. See "Cha Kwo Ling Being Resettled Soon, Lands Department Rejects Helps to Squatter Residents to Enter Public Housing; District Councillor Criticised as Inhumane," InmediaHK, 7 July 2021, accessed 3 July 2022, shorturl.at/fimZ2 (in Chinese).

19. On-site observation on 19 March 2021.

20. Lands Department, Squatter Control Policy on Surveyed Squatter Structures, December 2021, p. 4, available at https://www.landsd.gov.hk/doc/en/publication/sqco/scpp_e.pdf; https://www.landsd.gov.hk/en/land-mgt-enforce/squatter-control.html%22.

Notes   289

21. Lands Department, Squatter Control Policy on Surveyed Squatter Structures, December 2021, p. 8, available at https://www.landsd.gov.hk/doc/en/publication/sqco/scpp_e.pdf; https://www.landsd.gov.hk/en/land-mgt-enforce/squatter-control.html%22.

22. Chapter 3: Management of Squatter and Licensed Structures, Director of Audit's Report No. 68, Hong Kong: Audit Commission, p. 6, accessed 3 April 2017, https://www.aud.gov.hk/pdf_e/e68ch03.pdf.

23. Lands Department, Squatter Control Policy on Surveyed Squatter Structures, June 2021, p. 2, available at https://www.landsd.gov.hk/en/land-mgt-enforce/squatter-control.html.

24. Press Releases of Squatter Occupants Voluntary Registration Scheme now open for applications from eligible occupants of squatter structures, Development Bureau, 1 November 2018, accessed 15 July 2022, https://www.devb.gov.hk/en/publications_and_press_releases/press/index_id_10156.html.

25. Press Release of LCQ8: Squatter Structures and Agricultural Structures, Reply of Secretary for Development Michael Wong to question from the Hon. Steven Ho in LegCo Meeting on 4 November 2020, available at https://www.info.gov.hk/gia/general/202011/04/P2020110400359.htm?fontSize=1.

26. "World's Most Expensive Cities, Global Property Guide," accessed 5 August 2021, https://www.globalpropertyguide.com/most-expensive-cities.

Bibliography

Abdul Aziz, Faziawati. "The Investigation of the Implications of Squatter Relocations in High-Risk Neighbourhoods in Malaysia." PhD diss., Newcastle University, 2012.

Abdullah, Yusfida Ayu, Julieven Nonoi Kuek, Hazlina Hamdan, and Farrah Lyana Mohd Zulkifli. "Combating Squatters in Malaysia: Do we Have Adequate Policies as Instrument?" *Planning Malaysia* 15, no. 2 (2017): 25–36.

Advisory Group on Forced Evictions. *Forced Evictions—Towards Solutions? Second Report of the Advisory Group on Forced Evictions to the Executive Director of UN-HABITAT*, Nairobi: UN-HABITAT, 2007. http://www.unhabitat.org/pmss/getPage.asp?page=bookView&book=2353.

Aguilera, Thomas, and Alan Smart. "Squatting, North, South and Turnabout: A Dialogue Comparing Illegal Housing Research." In *Public Goods versus Economic Interests: Global Perspectives on the History of Squatting*, edited by Freia Anders and Alexander Sedlmaier, 29–55. New York: Routledge, 2016.

Airriess, Christopher A. "Governmentality and Power in Politically Contested Space: Refugee Farming in Hong Kong's New Territories, 1945–1970." *Journal of Historical Geography* 31, no. 4 (2005): 763–783.

Airriess, Christopher A. "Spatial Liminality as Moral Hazard and Boat Squatter Toleration in Post-World War Two Hong Kong." *Habitat International* 44 (2014): 121–129.

Akers-Jones, David. *Feeling the Stones: Reminiscences by David Akers-Jones*. Hong Kong: Hong Kong University Press, 2004.

Aldrich, Brian C. "Winning Their Place in the City: Squatters in Southeast Asian Cities." *Habitat International* 53 (2016): 495–501.

Alvarez, Maria Khristine, and Kenneth Cardenas. "Evicting Slums, 'Building Back Better': Resiliency Revanchism and Disaster Risk Management in Manila." *International Journal of Urban and Regional Research* 43, no. 2 (2019): 227–249.

Ascensão, Eduardo. "Interfaces of Informality: When Experts meet Informal Settlers." *City* 20, no. 4 (2016): 563–580.

Ashton, S. R. "Keeping a Foot in the Door: Britain's China Policy, 1945–50." *Diplomacy & Statecraft* 15, no. 1 (2004): 79–94.

Baken, Robert-Jan. *Plotting, Squatting, Public Purpose and Politics: Land Market Development, Low Income Housing and Public Intervention in India*. London; New York: Routledge, 2003.

Bibliography

Ball, Michael. *Housing Policy and Economic Power: The Political Economy of Owner Occupation.* London: Methuen, 1983.

Bauman, Zygmunt. *Liquid Modernity.* Cambridge: Polity Press, 2000.

Bayly, Christopher A. *Empire and Information: Intelligence Gathering and Social Communication in India, 1780–1870.* Cambridge: Cambridge University Press, 2000.

BBC News. "Hong Kong's Mong Kok Clashes: More than Fishballs," February 9, 2016. https://www.bbc.com/news/world-asia-china-35529785.

Beckert, Jens, and Matías Dewey, eds. *The Architecture of Illegal Markets: Towards an Economic Sociology of Illegality in the Economy.* Oxford: Oxford University Press, 2017.

Benjamin, Solomon. "Occupancy Urbanism: Radicalizing Politics and Economy beyond Policy and Programs." *International Journal of Urban and Regional Research* 32, no. 3 (2008): 719–729.

Benjamin, Solomon, and Bhuvaneswari Raman. "Illegible Claims, Legal Titles, and the Worlding of Bangalore." *Revue Tiers Monde* 206, no. 2 (2011): 37–54.

Benjaminsen, Tor A., Stein Holden, Christian Lund, and Espen Sjaastad. "Formalisation of Land Rights: Some Empirical Evidence from Mali, Niger and South Africa." *Land Use Policy* 26, no. 1 (2009): 28–35.

Bennett, Colin J., and Michael Howlett. "The Lessons of Learning: Reconciling Theories of Policy Learning and Policy Change." *Policy Sciences* 25, no. 3 (1992): 275–294.

Berner, Erhard. "Legalizing Squatters, Excluding the Poorest: Urban Land Transfer Programs in the Philippines." (Working Paper / Universität Bielefeld, Fakultät für Soziologie, Forschungsschwerpunkt Entwicklungssoziologie, 257). (1996): 1–12.

Bhaskar, Roy. *A Realist Theory of Science.* London; New York: Routledge, 2008.

Bian, Yanjie. "Bringing Strong Ties Back in: Indirect Ties, Network Bridges, and Job Searches in China," *American Sociological Review* 62, no. 3 (1997): 366–385.

Bickers, Robert. "Loose Ties that Bound: British Empire, Colonial Authority and Hong Kong." In *Negotiating Autonomy in Greater China: Hong Kong and Its Sovereign before and after 1997,* edited by Ray Yep, 29–54. Copenhagen: NIAS Press, 2013.

Bissell, William Cunningham. *Urban Design, Chaos, and Colonial Power in Zanzibar.* Bloomington: Indiana University Press, 2010.

Bourdieu, Pierre. *On the State: Lectures at the Collège de France, 1989–1992.* Cambridge: Polity Press, 2014.

Bourdieu, Pierre, and Abdelmalek Sayad. *Uprooting: The Crisis of Traditional Agriculture in Algeria.* Translated by Susan Emanuel. Cambridge: Polity Press, 2020[1964].

Brand, Edward W., Jerasak Premchitt, and Hugh. B. Phillipson. "Relationship between Rainfall and Landslides in Hong Kong." In *Proceedings of the 4th International Symposium on Landslides.* Vol. 1. Toronto: Canadian Geotechnical Society, 1984.

Bray, Denis. *Hong Kong Metamorphosis.* Hong Kong: Hong Kong University Press, 2001.

Bremner, G. Alex, ed. *Architecture and Urbanism in the British Empire.* Oxford: Oxford University Press, 2016.

Brewer, Curtis, John W. Gasko, and Derek Miller. "Have we been here before? Lessons learned from a microhistory of the policy development of universal kindergarten." *Educational Policy* 25, no. 1 (2011): 9–35.

Bromley, Ray. "Power, Property and Poverty: Why De Soto's 'Mystery of Capital' cannot be Solved." In *Urban informality: Transnational Perspectives from the Middle East, Latin*

America, and South Asia, edited by Ananya Roy and Nezar AlSayyad, 271–288. Lanham, MD: Lexington Books, 2004.

Brown, E. H. Phelps. "The Hong Kong Economy: Achievements and Prospects." In *Hong Kong: The Industrial Colony,* edited by Keith Hopkins, 1–20. Hong Kong: Oxford University Press, 1971.

Browne, Katherine E. *Creole Economics: Caribbean Cunning under the French Flag.* Austin: University of Texas Press, 2004.

Bruce, John W. "Simple Solutions to Complex Problems: Land Formalization as a 'Silver Bullet'." In *Fair Land Governance: How to Legalise Land Rights for Rural Development,* edited by Jan M. Otto and Andre Hoekema, 31–55. Amsterdam: Leiden University Press, 2012.

Bruhn, Miriam, and David McKenzie. "Entry Regulation and the Formalization of Microenterprises in Developing Countries." *The World Bank Research Observer* 29, no. 2 (2014): 186–201.

Bunnell, Tim. "Kampung Rules: Landscape and the Contested Government of Urban(e) Malayness." *Urban Studies* 39, no. 9 (2002): 1685–1701.

Bunnell, Tim. "Out of Place in the Global Cityscape: Moral Geographies of Squatting in Kuala Lumpur." In *Challenging Sustainability: Urban Development and Change in Southeast Asia,* edited by Wong Tai-Chee, Brian J. Shaw, and Goh Kim-Chuah, 323–339. Singapore: Marshall Cavendish Academic, 2006.

Bunnell, Tim, and Alice M. Nah. "Counter-global Cases for Place: Contesting Displacement in Globalising Kuala Lumpur Metropolitan Area." *Urban Studies* 41, no. 12 (2004): 2447–2467.

Calor, Inês, and Rachelle Alterman. "When Enforcement Fails: Comparative Analysis of the Legal and Planning Responses to Non-Compliant Development in Two Advanced-Economy Countries." *International Journal of Law in the Built Environment* 9, no. 3 (2017): 207–239.

Carroll, John M. *Edge of Empires: Chinese Elites and British Colonials in Hong Kong.* Hong Kong: Hong Kong University Press, 2005.

Castells, Manuel. *The Shek Kip Mei Syndrome: Public Housing and Economic Development in Hong Kong.* Hong Kong: Centre of Asian Studies, University of Hong Kong, 1986.

Castells, Manuel, Goh Lee, and Kwok R. Yin-Wang. *The Shek Kip Mei Syndrome: Economic Development and Public Housing in Hong Kong and Singapore.* London: Pion Limited, 1990.

Census and Statistics Department. *Hong Kong 1981 Census: Main Report, Vol. 2.* Hong Kong: Government Printer, 1981.

Census and Statistics Department. *Hong Kong 1996 Population By-Census: Main Tables.* Hong Kong: Government Printer, 1996.

Chalana, Manish, and Jeffrey Hou, eds. *Messy Urbanism: Understanding the "Other" Cities of Asia.* Hong Kong: Hong Kong University Press, 2016.

Chan, Chi Kit. "China as 'Other': Resistance to and Ambivalence towards National Identity in Hong Kong." *China Perspectives* 1 (2014): 25–34.

Chan, Elaine. "Defining Fellow Compatriots as 'Others' – National Identity in Hong Kong." *Government and Opposition* 35, no. 4 (2000): 499–519.

Chan, Johannes Man Mum, Hualing Fu, and Yash Ghai, eds. *Hong Kong's Constitutional Debate: Conflict over Interpretation.* Hong Kong: Hong Kong University Press, 2000.

Bibliography

Chan, Lau Kit-ching. "The Hong Kong Question during the Pacific War (1941–45)." *The Journal of Imperial and Commonwealth History* 2, no. 1 (1973): 56–78.

Cheek-Milby, Kathleen. "Recent Developments in the Hong Kong Government." *Hong Kong Journal of Public Administration* 4, no. 2 (1982): 219–245.

Cheung Bing-Leung, Anthony. "Political Participation." In *Fifty Years of Public Housing in Hong Kong: A Golden Jubilee Review and Appraisal*, edited by Yeung Yue-man and Timothy Kai-ying Wong, 207–233. Hong Kong: Hong Kong Housing Authority, 2003.

Cheung, Gary Ka-wai. *Hong Kong's Watershed: The 1967 Riots*. Hong Kong: Hong Kong University Press, 2009.

Cheung, Siu-Keung. "Speaking Out: Days in the Lives of Three Hong Kong Cage Dwellers." *Positions: East Asia Cultures Critique* 8, no. 1 (2000): 235–262.

Cheung, W. M., and Y. K. Shiu. "Evaluation of the Effectiveness of Squatter Clearance Actions in Reducing Landslide Risk." GEO Report No. 141, Hong Kong: Geotechnical Engineering Office, Civil Engineering Department, The Government of the Hong Kong Special Administrative Region, 2003. https://www.cedd.gov.hk/filemanager/eng/content_296/er141.pdf

Chen, Yun-chung, Mirana M. Szeto. "The Forgotten Road of Progressive Localism: New Preservation Movement in Hong Kong." *Inter-Asia Cultural Studies* 16, no. 3 (2015): 436–453.

Chiu, Stephen Wing-kai, Ho Kong Chong, and Lui Tai Lok. *City-States in the Global Economy: Industrial Restructuring in Hong Kong and Singapore*. Boulder: Westview, 1997.

Chiu, Catherine C. H. *Small Family Business in Hong Kong: Accumulation and Accommodation*. Hong Kong: Chinese University Press, 1998.

Chu, Wai Li. "We Had No Urge to Do Away an Ex-colony: The Changing Views of the British Government over Hong Kong's Future, 1967–1979." MPhil. thesis, Hong Kong Baptist University, 2017.

Chu, Yin Wah. "Informal Work in Hong Kong." *International Journal of Urban and Regional Research* 16, no. 3 (1992): 420–441.

Chua, Beng-Huat. "Public Housing Residents as Clients of the State." *Housing Studies* 15, no. 1 (2000): 45–60.

Chua, Beng-Huat. *Political Legitimacy and Housing: Singapore's Stakeholder Society*. London; New York: Routledge, 2002.

Chui, Ernest. "Housing and Welfare Services in Hong Kong for New Immigrants from China: Inclusion or Exclusion?" *Asian and Pacific Migration Journal* 11, no. 2 (2002): 221–245.

Chun, Allen. *Unstructuring Chinese Society: The Fictions of Colonial Practice and the Changing Realities of "Land" in the New Territories of Hong Kong*. London: Harwood, 2000.

Clark, Trevor. "The Dickinson Report: An Account of the Background to, and Preparation of, the 1966 'Working Group Report on Local Administration.'" *Journal of the Hong Kong Branch of the Royal Asiatic Society* 37 (1998): 1–17.

Clarke, John, Dave Bainton, Noémi Lendvai, and Paul Stubbs. *Making Policy Move: Towards a Politics of Translation and Assemblage*. Bristol: Policy Press, 2015.

Clayton, David. "Labour-Intensive Industrialization in Hong Kong, 1950–70: A Note on Sources and Methods." *Asia Pacific Business Review* 12, no. 3 (2006): 375–388.

Clayton, David. "From 'Free' to 'Fair' Trade: The Evolution of Labour Laws in Colonial Hong Kong, 1958–62." *The Journal of Imperial and Commonwealth History* 35, no. 2 (2007): 263–282.

Clayton, David. "The Riots and Labour Laws: The Struggle for an Eight-Hour Day for Women Factory Workers, 1962–1971." In *May Days in Hong Kong: Riot and Emergency in 1967*, edited by Robert Bickers and Ray Yep, 127–145. Hong Kong: Hong Kong University Press, 2009.

Cohen, Gerald Allan. *Karl Marx's Theory of History: A Defence.* Oxford: Clarendon Press, 2000.

Cobain, Ian. *The History Thieves: Secrets, Lies and the Shaping of a Modern Nation.* London: Portobello Books, 2016.

Comaroff, Jean, and John L. Comaroff. *Of Revelation and Revolution, Volume 1: Christianity, Colonialism, and Consciousness in South Africa.* Chicago: University of Chicago Press, 1991.

Commission of Inquiry. *Kowloon Disturbances 1966: Report of Commission of Inquiry.* Hong Kong: Government Printer, 1967.

Cooper, Eugene. *The Wood-Carvers of Hong Kong: Craft Production in the World Capitalist Periphery.* Cambridge: Cambridge University Press, 1980.

Coppoolse, Anneke. "Hong Kong on Display: Things, Time and Urban Space." *Journal of Urban Cultural Studies* 8, no. 1 (2021): 121–133.

Cross, John C. *Informal Politics: Street Vendors and the State in Mexico City.* Stanford: Stanford University Press, 1998.

Cross, John C., and Alfonso Morales, eds. *Street Entrepreneurs: People, Place, & Politics in Local and Global Perspective.* London; New York: Routledge, 2007.

Curran, Dean, and Alan Smart. "Data-Driven Governance, Smart Urbanism and Risk-Class Inequalities: Security and Social Credit in China." *Urban Studies* 58, no. 3 (2021): 487–506.

Darnton, Robert. *The Great Cat Massacre and Other Episodes in French Cultural History.* New York: Vintage Books, 1985.

Datta, Ayona. *The Illegal City: Space, Law and Gender in a Delhi Squatter Settlement.* London: Routledge, 2016.

De, Indranil. "Slum Improvement in India: Determinants and Approaches." *Housing Studies* 32, no. 7 (2017): 990–1013.

De Biasi, Alaina. "Squatting and Adverse Possession: Countering Neighborhood Blight and Disinvestment." *City* 23, no. 1 (2019): 66–82.

De Herdt, Tom, and Jean-Pierre Olivier de Sardan, eds. *Real Governance and Practical Norms in Sub-Saharan Africa: The Game of the Rules.* London: Routledge, 2015.

de Soto, Hernando. *The Other Path: The Economic Answer to Terrorism.* New York: Basic Books, 1989.

de Soto, Hernando. *The Mystery of Capital: Why Capitalism Triumphs in the West and Fails Everywhere Else.* New York: Basic Books, 2000.

Dikötter, Frank. *Mao's Great Famine: The History of China's Most Devastating Catastrophe, 1958–62.* New York: Bloomsbury Publishing, 2010.

Drakakis-Smith, David W. *High Society: Housing Provision in Metropolitan Hong Kong, 1954 to 1979, a Jubilee Critique.* Hong Kong: University of Hong Kong, Centre of Asian Studies, 1979.

Bibliography

Du, Juan, and Stefan Greiving. "Reclaiming On-Site Upgrading as a Viable Resilience Strategy-Viabilities and Scenarios through the Lens of Disaster-Prone Informal Settlements in Metro Manila." *Sustainability* 12, no. 24 (2020): 10600.

Dupré, Jean-François. "Making Hong Kong Chinese: State Nationalism and its Blowbacks in a Recalcitrant City." *Nationalism and Ethnic Politics* 26, no. 1 (2020): 8–26.

Durand-Lasserve, Alain. "Informal Settlements and the Millennium Development Goals: Global Policy Debates on Property Ownership and Security of Tenure." *Global Urban Development* 2, no. 1 (2006): 1–15.

Dwyer, Denis J. "The Problem of In-migration and Squatter Settlement in Asian Cities: Two Case Studies, Manila and Victoria-Kowloon." *Asian Studies* 2, no. 2 (1965): 145–169.

Elias, Norbert. *The Civilizing Process*. Oxford: Blackwell, 1996.

Elkins, Caroline. *Imperial Reckoning: The Untold Story of Britain's Gulag in Kenya*. New York: Henry Holt and Co., 2005.

England, Joe. *Hong Kong: Britain's Responsibility*. London: Fabian Society, 1976.

England, Joe, and John Rear. *Chinese Labour under British Rule: A Critical Study of Labour Relations and Law in Hong Kong*. Hong Kong: Oxford University Press, 1975.

Enright, Michael J., Edith E. Scott, and David Dodwell. *The Hong Kong Advantage*. Oxford: Oxford University Press, 1997.

Erni, John Nguyet. "Citizenship Management: On the Politics of Being Included-Out." *International Journal of Cultural Studies* 19, no. 3 (2016): 323–340.

Evans, Peter B. *Embedded Autonomy: States and Industrial Transformation*. Princeton: Princeton University Press, 1995.

Fairbanks, Robert P. *How It Works: Recovering Citizens in Post-Welfare Philadelphia*. Chicago: University of Chicago Press, 2009.

Fall, Robin, and Cedric Sam. "Closing Time: How Hong Kong's Street Hawkers Struggle to Survive," *South China Morning Post*, November 23, 2014. https://multimedia. scmp.com/hawkers/.

FASE Rio de Janeiro. "Covid-19 and the Injustice of Life in the Favelas and Urban Peripheries in Rio de Janeiro." April 24, 2020. https://www.opendemocracy.net/ en/democraciaabierta/covid-19-y-la-injusticia-de-la-vida-en-las-favelas-y-periferias-urbanas-de-río-de-janeiro-en/.

Faure, David, ed. *Society: A Documentary History of Hong Kong*. Hong Kong: Hong Kong University Press, 1997.

Faure, David. "In Britain's footsteps: The Colonial Heritage." In *Hong Kong: A Reader in Social History*, edited by David Faure, 658–678. Hong Kong: Oxford University Press, 2003a.

Faure, David. *Colonialism and the Hong Kong Mentality*. Hong Kong: Hong Kong University Press, Centre of Asian Studies, 2003b.

Feige, Edgar L., ed. *The Underground Economies: Tax Evasion and Information Distortion*. Cambridge: Cambridge University Press, 2007.

Fernandes, Edésio, and Ann Varley, eds. *Illegal Cities: Law and Urban Change in Developing Countries*. New York: Zed Books, 1998.

Fong, Brian Chi-hang. "One Country, Two Nationalisms: Center-Periphery Relations between Mainland China and Hong Kong, 1997–2016." *Modern China* 43, no. 5 (2017): 523–556.

Foucault, Michel. "Governmentality." In *The Foucault Effect: Studies in Governmentality*, edited by Graham Burchell, Colin Gordon, and Peter Miller, 87–104. Chicago: University of Chicago Press, 1991.

Foucault, Michel. *The Birth of Biopolitics: Lectures at the Collège de France, 1978–1979*. Houndmills: Palgrave MacMillan, 2008.

Fung, Anthony Ying Him. "Postcolonial Hong Kong Identity: Hybridising the Local and the National." *Social Identities* 10, no. 3 (2004): 399–414.

Fung, Anthony Ying Him, and Chan Chi Kit. "Post-handover Identity: Contested Cultural Bonding between China and Hong Kong." *Chinese Journal of Communication* 10, no. 4 (2017): 395–412.

Fung, Bosco C. K. "Squatter Relocation and the Problem of Home-Work Separation." In *Housing in Hong Kong*, edited by Wong Luke Sui-kwong, 233–264. Hong Kong: Heinnemann Educational Books, 1968.

Fung, Chi Keung Charles. "Colonial Governance and State Incorporation of Chinese Language: the Case of the First Chinese Language Movement in Hong Kong." *Social Transformations in Chinese Societies* 18, no. 1 (2022): 59–74.

Fung, Chi Keung Charles, and Fong Chi Shun. "Going out under the Shadow of Red China: The Geopolitical Origin of Hong Kong's International Status." *Asian Education and Development Studies* 8, no. 2 (2019): 173–185.

Fung, Chi Keung Charles, and Fong Chi Shun. "The 1967 Riots and Hong Kong's Tortuous Internationalization." *East Asia* 37, no. 2 (2020): 89–105.

Fung, Edmund S. K. *The Diplomacy of Imperial Retreat: Britain's South China Policy, 1924–1931*. Hong Kong: Oxford University Press, 1991.

Gandolfo, Daniella. "Formless: A Day at Lima's Office of Formalization." *Cultural Anthropology* 28, no. 2 (2013): 278–298.

Garfinkel, Harold. *Studies in Ethnomethodology*. New Jersey: Prentice-Hall, 1967.

Garrido, Marco Z. *The Patchwork City: Class, Space, and Politics in Metro Manila*. Chicago: University of Chicago Press, 2019.

Ghertner, D. Asher. "Calculating Without Numbers: Aesthetic Governmentality in Delhi's Slums." *Economy and Society* 39, no. 2 (2010): 185–217.

Ghertner, D. Asher. *Rule by Aesthetics: World-Class City Making in Delhi*. New York: Oxford University Press, 2015.

Giddens, Anthony. *The Constitution of Society: Outline of the Theory of Structuration*. Cambridge: Polity Press, 1984.

Gilbert, Alan. "On the Mystery of Capital and the Myths of Hernando de Soto: What Difference does Legal Title Make?" *International Development Planning Review* 24, no. 1 (2002): 1–19.

Ginzburg, Carlo, John Tedeschi, and Anne C. Tedeschi. "Microhistory: Two or Three Things that I Know about It." *Critical Inquiry* 20, no. 1 (1993): 10–35.

Golger, Otto J. "Hong Kong: A Problem of Housing the Masses." *Ekistics* 33, no. 196 (1972): 173–177.

Goodstadt, Leo F. *Uneasy Partners: The Conflict between Public Interest and Private Profit in Hong Kong*. Hong Kong: Hong Kong University Press, 2005.

Bibliography

Goodstadt, Leo F. "Government without Statistics: Policy-Making in Hong Kong 1925–85, with Special Reference to Economic and Financial Management." *HKIMR Working Paper No.6/2006.* Hong Kong: Hong Kong Institute for Monetary Research, 2006.

Goodstadt, Leo F. *Reluctant Regulators: How the West Created and How China Survived the Global Financial Crisis.* Hong Kong: Hong Kong University Press, 2011.

Goodstadt, Leo F. "Fiscal Freedom and the Making of Hong Kong's Capitalist Society." In *Negotiating Autonomy in Greater China: Hong Kong and Its Sovereign before and after 1997*, edited by Ray Yep, 81–109. Copenhagen: NIAS Press, 2013.

Granovetter, Mark S. "The Strength of Weak Ties." *American Journal of Sociology* 78, no. 6 (1973): 1360–1380.

Grantham, Alexander. *Via Ports: From Hong Kong to Hong Kong.* Hong Kong: Hong Kong University Press, 1965.

Grashoff, Udo, and Yang Fengzhuo. "Towards Critique and Differentiation: Comparative Research on Informal Housing." In *Comparative Approaches to Informal Housing around the Globe*, edited by Udo Grashoff, 1–26. London: UCL Press, 2020.

Guha-Khasnobis, Basudeb, Ravi Kanbur, and Elinor Ostrom. "Beyond Formality and Informality." In *Linking the Formal and Informal Economy: Concepts and Policies*, edited by Basudeb Guha-Khasnobis, Ravi Kanbur, and Elinor Ostrom, 1–20. Oxford: Oxford University Press, 2006.

Guo, Youliang, Zhang Chengguo, Wang Ya Ping, and Li Xun. "(De-)Activating the Growth Machine for Redevelopment: The Case of Liede Urban Village in Guangzhou." *Urban Studies* 55, no. 7 (2018): 1420–1438.

Gupta, Akhil. *Red Tape: Bureaucracy, Structural Violence, and Poverty in India.* Durham: Duke University Press, 2012.

Haig, Brian D. "Précis of 'An Abductive Theory of Scientific Method.'" *Journal of Clinical Psychology* 64, no. 9 (2008): 1019–1022.

Hamilton, Gary G., ed. *Cosmopolitan Capitalists: Hong Kong and the Chinese Diaspora at the End of the Twentieth Century.* University of Washington Press, 1999.

Hamilton, Peter E. *Made in Hong Kong: Transpacific Networks and a New History of Globalization.* New York: Columbia University Press, 2021.

Hampton, Mark. *Hong Kong and British Culture, 1945–97.* Manchester: Manchester University Press, 2015.

Hampton, Mark. "British Legal Culture and Colonial Governance: The Attack on Corruption in Hong Kong, 1968–1974." *Britain and the World* 5, no. 2 (2012): 223–239.

Hansen, Karen Tranberg, Walter E. Little and B. Lynne Milgram. "Introduction." In *Street Economies in the Urban Global South*, edited by Karen Tranberg Hansen, Walter E. Little, and B. Lynne Milgram, 3–16. Santa Fe: School for Advanced Research Press, 2013.

Harris, Peter B. "The Frozen Politics of Hong Kong." *The World Today* 30, no. 6 (1974): 259–267.

Harris, Peter B. *Hong Kong: A Study in Bureaucracy and Politics.* Hong Kong: Macmillan, 1988.

Harris, Richard. "The Silence of the Experts: 'Aided Self-Help Housing,' 1939–1954." *Habitat International* 22, no. 2 (1998): 165–189.

Harris, Richard. "Modes of Informal Urban Development: A Global Phenomenon." *Journal of Planning Literature* 33, no. 3 (2018): 267–286.

Hart, Keith. "Informal Income Opportunities and Urban Employment in Ghana." *The Journal of Modern African Studies* 11, no. 1 (1973): 61–89.

Hart, Keith. "The Informal Economy." In *The Human Economy*, edited by Keith Hart, Jean-Louis Laville, and Antonio David Cattani, 142–153. Cambridge: Polity Press, 2010.

Harvey, Penny, and Hannah Knox. *Roads: An Anthropology of Infrastructure and Expertise.* Ithaca: Cornell University Press, 2015.

Hase, Patrick. "Review: Hong Kong Metamorphosis by D. C. Bray." *Journal of the Hong Kong Branch of the Royal Asiatic Society* 41 (2001a): 427–429.

Hase, Patrick. "The District Office." In *Hong Kong, British Crown Colony, Revisited*, edited by Elizabeth Sinn, 123–146. Hong Kong: Centre of Asian Studies, University of Hong Kong, 2001b.

Hayes, James. *Friends and Teachers: Hong Kong and its People 1953–87.* Hong Kong: Hong Kong University Press, 1996.

Hayes, James. *The Great Difference: Hong Kong's New Territories and Its People, 1898–2004.* Hong Kong: Hong Kong University Press, 2012.

Herzfeld, Michael. "Methodological Legalism." In *Norms and Illegality: Intimate Ethnographies and Politics*, edited by Cristiana Panella and Walter E. Little, 37–58. Lanham: Lexington, 2021.

Heyman, Josiah M., ed. *States and Illegal Practices.* London: Berg, 1999.

Heyman, Josiah M., and Alan Smart. "States and Illegal Practices: An Overview." In *States and Illegal Practices*, edited by Josiah M. Heyman, 1–24. London: Berg, 1999.

Ho, Chi-yeung. "Housing, Planning and Political Will in Colonial Hong Kong, 1946–1983." MPhil. thesis, University of Hong Kong, 2011.

Ho, Denny Kwok Leung. "The Rise and Fall of Community Mobilization: The Housing Movement in Hong Kong." In *The Dynamics of Social Movement in Hong Kong*, edited by Chiu Stephen Wing Kai and Lui Tai Lok, 185–208. Hong Kong: Hong Kong University Press, 2000.

Ho, Denny Kwok Leung. "Citizenship as a Form of Governance: A Historical Overview." In *Remaking Citizenship in Hong Kong: Community, Nation and the Global City*, edited by Ku Agnes S. and Pun Ngai, 18–33. Abingdon, Oxon: Routledge, 2004.

Home, Robert. *Of Planting and Planning: The Making of British Colonial Cities.* New York: Routledge, 2013.

Hong Kong Government. *Hong Kong Annual Report 1984.* Hong Kong: Government Printer, 1985.

Hong Kong Housing Authority. *Annual Report 1978–79.* Hong Kong: Government Printer, 1979.

Hong Kong Housing Authority. *Annual Report 1983–84.* Hong Kong: Government Printer, 1984.

Hong Kong Housing Authority. *Annual Report 1984–85.* Hong Kong: Government Printer, 1985.

Hong Kong Housing Authority. *Annual Report 1985–86.* Hong Kong: Government Printer, 1986.

Bibliography

Hopkins, Keith. "Housing the Poor." In *Hong Kong: The Industrial Colony*, edited by Keith Hopkins, 271–335. Hong Kong: Oxford University Press, 1971.

Hopkins, Keith. "Public and Private Housing in Hong Kong." In *The City as a Centre of Change in Asia*, edited by Denis J. Dwyer, 200–215. Hong Kong: Hong Kong University Press, 1972.

Howell, Philip. "Race, Space and the Regulation of Prostitution in Colonial Hong Kong." *Urban History* 31, no. 2 (2004): 229–248.

Hsia, Ronald, and Laurence Chau. *Industrialisation, Employment and Income Distribution: A Case Study of Hong Kong*. London: Croom Helm, 1978.

Hsu, Madeline Yuan-yin. *Dreaming of Gold, Dreaming of Home: Transnationalism and Migration between the United States and South China, 1882–1943*. Stanford: Stanford University Press, 2000.

Hu, Fox Zhiyong, George C. S. Lin, Anthony Gar-On Yeh, He Shenjing, and Liu Xingjian. "Reluctant Policy Innovation through Profit Concession and Informality Tolerance: A Strategic Relational View of Policy Entrepreneurship in China's Urban Redevelopment." *Public Administration and Development* 40, no. 1 (2020): 65–75.

Huchzermeyer, Marie. *Cities with 'Slums': From Informal Settlement Eradication to a Right to the City in Africa*. Claremont: UCT Press, 2011.

Ip, Iam-chong. "Welfare Good or Colonial Citizenship? A Case Study of Early Resettlement Housing." In *Remaking Citizenship in Hong Kong: Community, Nation and the Global City*, edited by Agnes S. Ku and Pun Ngai, 34–48. London: RoutledgeCurzon, 2004.

Ip, Iam-Chong. "Politics of Belonging: A Study of the Campaign against Mainland Visitors in Hong Kong." *Inter-Asia Cultural Studies* 16, no. 3 (2015): 410–421.

Ingold, Tim. "Bindings against Boundaries: Entanglements of Life in an Open World." *Environment and Planning A* 40, no. 8 (2008): 1796–1810.

Jansen, Stef. "Hope For/Against the State: Gridding in a Besieged Sarajevo Suburb." *Ethnos* 79, no. 2 (2014): 238–260.

Jensen, Steffen, Karl Hapal, and Salome Quijano. "Reconfiguring Manila: Displacement, Resettlement, and the Productivity of Urban Divides." *Urban Forum* 31, no. 3 (2020): 389–407.

Jones, Carol, and Jon Vagg. *Criminal Justice in Hong Kong*. London: Taylor and Francis, 2017.

Jones, Catherine. *Promoting Prosperity: The Hong Kong Way of Social Policy*. Hong Kong: Chinese University Press, 1990.

Jones, Margaret. "Tuberculosis, Housing and the Colonial State: Hong Kong, 1900–1950." *Modern Asian Studies* 37, no. 3 (2003): 653–682.

Jütting, Johannes, and Juan R. de Laiglesia, eds. *Is Informal Normal? Towards More and Better Jobs in Developing Countries*. Paris: Organization for Economic Co-operation and Development, 2009. Available at: https://www.oecd-ilibrary.org/development/is-informal-normal_9789264059245-en.

Kehl, Frank. "Hong Kong Shantytowns: The Demography and Household Economy of Intra-urban Migration and Housing." PhD diss., Columbia University, 1981.

King, Ambrose Yeo-chi. "The Administrative Absorption of Politics in Hong Kong: With Special Emphasis on the City District Officer Scheme." Hong Kong: Social Research Centre, Chinese University of Hong Kong, 1973.

King, Ambrose Yeo-chi. "Administrative Absorption of Politics in Hong Kong: Emphasis on the Grass Roots Level." *Asian Survey* 15, no. 5 (1975): 422–439.

Kornatowski, Geerhardt. "The Reconceptualization of Homelessness Policy and the Social Welfare Response of Non-governmental Organizations in Hong Kong." *Japanese Journal of Human Geography* 60, no. 6 (2008): 53–76.

Koselleck, Reinhart. *The Practice of Conceptual History: Timing History, Spacing Concepts.* Stanford: Stanford University Press, 2002.

Koselleck, Reinhart, and Michaela W. Richter. "Crisis." *Journal of the History of Ideas* 67, no. 2 (2006): 357–400.

Koster, Martijn, and Alan Smart. "Performing In/formality beyond the Dichotomy: An Introduction." *Anthropologica* 61, no. 1 (2019): 20–24.

Krasner, Stephen D. "Problematic Sovereignty." In *Problematic Sovereignty: Contested Rules and Political Possibilities*, edited by Stephen D. Krasner, 1–23. New York: Columbia University Press, 2001.

Krul, Kees, and Peter Ho. "Beyond 'Empty' Forms of Formalization: The Credibility of a Renewed Attempt at Forest Titling in Southwest China." *Geoforum* 110 (2020): 46–57.

Ku, Agnes S. "Immigration Policies, Discourses, and the Politics of Local Belonging in Hong Kong (1950–1980)." *Modern China* 30, no. 3 (2004): 326–360.

Ku, Anges S., and Pun Ngai. "Introduction: Remaking Citizenship in Hong Kong." In *Remaking Citizenship in Hong Kong: Community, Nation and the Global City.* Edited by Ku Agnes S. and Pun Ngai, 1–17. Abingdon, Oxon: RoutledgeCurzon, 2004.

Kuan Hsin-chi. "Power Dependence and Democratic Transition: The Case of Hong Kong." *The China Quarterly* 128 (1991): 774–793.

Kwok, Brian Sze Hang. "Spatial Tactics of Hong Kong Street Hawkers: A Case study of Fa Yuen Street." *Visual Ethnography* 8, no. 1 (2019): 44–61.

Kwong, Chi Man, and Tsoi Yiu Lun. *Eastern Fortress: A Military History of Hong Kong, 1840–1970.* Hong Kong, Hong Kong University Press, 2014.

Kwun Tong City District Office. Survey of Squatter Areas, Unpublished document in possession of Alan Smart collected during the fieldwork in 1983–1985, 1983.

Lacorne, Denis. *The Limits of Tolerance: Enlightenment Values and Religious Fanaticism.* Translated by C. Jon Delogu and Robin Emlein. New York: Columbia University Press, 2019.

Lai, Lawrence Wai-Chung. "Reflections on the Abercrombie Report 1948: A Strategic Plan for Colonial Hong Kong." *The Town Planning Review* 70, no. 1 (1999): 61–87.

Lai, Lawrence Wai-Chung. "Un-forgetting Walls by Lines on Maps: A Case Study on Property Rights, Cadastral Mapping, and the Landscape of the Kowloon Walled City." *Land Use Policy* 57 (2016): 94–102.

Lam, Kit Chun, and Liu, Pak Wai. *Immigration and the Economy of Hong Kong.* Hong Kong: City University of Hong Kong Press, 1998.

Lam, Wai-man. *Understanding the Political Culture of Hong Kong: The Paradox of Activism and Depoliticization.* Armonk: M. E. Sharpe, 2004.

Bibliography

Lam, Yuet-choi, Lam Ka-chung, Ng Chi-kang, Tse Hoi-yin, and Tsung Pui-sum Francis. "Challenges of Regulatory Theory and Practice: A Study of Hawker Control in Hong Kong." Master of Public Administration thesis, University of Hong Kong, 2015.

Lane, Kevin P. *Sovereignty and the Status Quo: The Historical Roots of China's Hong Kong Policy.* Boulder: Westview Press, 1990.

Lanamäki, Arto, and Tauri Tuvikene. "Framing Digital Future: Selective Formalization and Legitimation of Ridehailing Platforms in Estonia." *Geoforum* (2021). https://doi.org/10.1016/j.geoforum.2021.01.016.

Lau, Kwok-yu. "Targeting the Needy in Public Rental Housing." In *Fifty Years of Public Housing in Hong Kong: A Golden Jubilee Review and Appraisal.* Edited by Yeung Yue-man and Timothy Ka-ying Wong, 179–206. Hong Kong: Chinese University Press for the Hong Kong Housing Authority, Hong Kong Institute of Asia-Pacific Studies, 2003.

Lau, Siu-kai. *Society and Politics in Hong Kong.* Hong Kong: The Chinese University of Hong Kong Press, 1984.

Lau, Siu-kai. *Decolonization without Independence: The Unfinished Political Reforms of the Hong Kong Government.* Hong Kong: Centre for Hong Kong Studies, Institute of Social Studies, the Chinese University of Hong Kong, 1987.

Lau, Siu-kai, and Kuan Hsin-chi. *The Ethos of the Hong Kong Chinese.* Hong Kong: The Chinese University of Hong Kong Press, 1988.

Law, Kam-yee, and Lee Kim-ming. "Citizenship, Economy and Social Exclusion of Mainland Chinese Immigrants in Hong Kong." *Journal of Contemporary Asia* 36, no. 2 (2006): 217–242.

Law, Wing Sang. *Collaborative Colonial Power: The Making of the Hong Kong Chinese.* Hong Kong: Hong Kong University Press, 2009.

Leach, Edmund Ronald. *Political Systems of Highland Burma: A Study of Kachin Social Structure.* London: Athlone Press 1964.

Lee, Chin-Chuan, and Chan Joseph Man. "Government Management of the Press in Hong Kong." *International Communication Gazette* 46, no. 2 (1990): 125–139.

Lee, Kah-Wee. "Transforming Macau: Planning as Institutionalized Informality and the Spatial Dynamics of Hypercompetition." *Environment and Planning A* 46, no. 11 (2014): 2622–2637.

Lee, Nelson K., and Choi Sam C. W. "Geopolitics, Territorial Governance and the Making of Water Supply System: The Case of Cold War Hong Kong, 1949–1979." In *Advances in Environmental Research* (Volume 73), edited by Justin A. Daniels, 141–175. New York: Nova Science Publishers, 2020.

Lee, Ming Kwan. "Hong Kong Identity: Past and Present." In *Hong Kong Economy and Society: Challenges in the New Era*, edited by Wong Siu-lun and Toyojiro Maruya, 153–175. Hong Kong: Centre of Asian Studies, The University of Hong Kong, 1998.

Leeming, Frank. *Street Studies in Hong Kong: Localities in a Chinese City.* Hong Kong: Oxford University Press, 1977.

Leung, Hon-Chu. "Politics of Incorporation and Exclusion: Immigration and Citizenship Issues." In *Remaking Citizenship in Hong Kong: Community, Nation and the Global City*, edited by Agnes S. Ku and Pun Ngai, 87–102. London: RoutledgeCurzon, 2004.

Leung, Ka Man, Chung Yim Yiu, and Kin-kwok Lai. "Responsiveness of Sub-divided Unit Tenants' Housing Consumption to Income: A Study of Hong Kong Informal Housing." *Housing Studies* 37 no. 1 (2020): 1–23. https://doi.org/10.1080/02673 037.2020.1803799.

Leung, Wai-Tung. 1983. Squatter Improvement in Hong Kong: A Preliminary Assessment. *Annals of G.G.A.S., University of Hong Kong.* No. 11.

Li, Tania Murray. *The Will to Improve: Governmentality, Development, and the Practice of Politics.* Durham: Duke University Press, 2007.

Li, Ziming, Abhinav Alakshendra, and Suzanna Smith. "A People-Centered Perspective on Slum Formalization Policy." *Housing Policy Debate* (2021): 1–20. https://doi.org /10.1080/10511482.2021.1905025.

Lim, Tai Wei. "'Fishball Revolution' and Hong Kong's Identity." In *Politics, Culture and Identities in East Asia: Integration and Division*, edited by Lam Peng Er and Lim Tai Wei, 35–41. Singapore: World Scientific, 2017.

Lin, George C. S., and Pauline H. M. Tse. "Flexible Sojourning in the Era of Globalization: Cross-Border Population Mobility in the Hong Kong–Guangdong Border Region." *International Journal of Urban and Regional Research* 29, no. 4 (2005): 867–894.

Lin, George C. S., Alan Smart, Li X., and Hu Fox Zhiyong. "Financializing Chinese Cities: State-Capital Nexus and the Uneven Geography of Housing Speculation." *Area Development and Policy* 4, no. 4 (2019): 435–453.

Lin, Tzong-Biau, Ho Yin-ping, and Victor Mok. *Manufactured Exports and Employment in Hong Kong.* Hong Kong: Chinese University Press, 1980.

Lindberg, Kari Soo. "China Says Next Hong Kong Leader Must Tackle Housing Crisis," *Bloomberg News*, July 16, 2021. https://www.bloomberg.com/news/ articles/2021-07-16/china-says-hong-kong-s-next-leader-must-tackle-housing-crisis.

Ling, Minhua. "Container Housing: Formal Informality and Deterritorialised Home-Making amid Bulldozer Urbanism in Shanghai." *Urban Studies* 58, no. 6 (2020): 1141–1157.

Lipsky, Michael. *Street-Level Bureaucracy: Dilemmas of the Individual in Public Services.* New York: Russell Sage Foundation, 2010.

Littlewood, Michael. *Taxation Without Representation: The History of Hong Kong's Troublingly Successful Tax System.* Hong Kong: Hong Kong University Press, 2010.

Liu, Kerry. "Hong Kong: Inevitably Irrelevant to China?" *Economic Affairs* 40, no. 1 (2020): 2–23.

Liu, Ran, and Wong Tai-Chee. "Urban Village Redevelopment in Beijing: The State-Dominated Formalization of Informal Housing." *Cities* 72 (2018): 160–172.

Lo, Shiu Hing. "The Politics of Localisation of the Civil Service in Hong Kong and Macau." *The Journal of Commonwealth & Comparative Politics* 33, no. 1 (1995): 103–136.

Lo, Shiu Hing. *The Politics of Democratization in Hong Kong.* Basingstoke: Macmillan Press, 1997.

Loh, Kah Seng. "Conflict and Change at the Margins: Emergency Kampong Clearance and the Making of Modern Singapore." *Asian Studies Review* 33, no. 2 (2009a): 139–159.

Loh, Kah Seng. "Kampong, Fire, Nation: Towards a Social History of Postwar Singapore." *Journal of Southeast Asian Studies* 40, no. 3 (2009b): 613–643.

Lomnitz, Larissa Adler. "Informal Exchange Networks in Formal Systems: A Theoretical Model." *American Anthropologist* 90, no. 1 (1988): 42–55.

Low, Setha M. "The Anthropology of Cities: Imagining and Theorizing the City." *Annual Review of Anthropology* 25, no. 1 (1996): 383–409.

Lui, Tai-lok. "Urban Process in Hong Kong: A Sociological Study of Housing Conflicts." MPhil. thesis, University of Hong Kong, 1984.

Lui, Tai-lok. *Waged Work at Home: The Social Organization of Industrial Outwork in Hong Kong.* Aldershot; Hong Kong: Avebury, 1994.

Lui, Tai-lok. "'Flying MPs' and Political Changes in a Colonial Setting: Political Reform under MacLehose's Governorship of Hong Kong." In *Civil Unrest and Governance in Hong Kong: Law and Order from Historical and Cultural Perspectives*, edited by Michael H. K. Ng and John D. Wong, 76–96. Abingdon, Oxon; New York: Routledge, 2017.

Lui, Tai-lok. "Flexible and Plastic National Identification in Hong Kong: Its Historical Configuration and Changes since 1997." *Journal of Asian Sociology* 48, no. 1 (2019): 71–90.

Lui, Tai-lok., Kuan Hsin-chi, Chan Kin-man, and Chan Sunny Cheuk-wah. "Friends and Critics of the State: The Case of Hong Kong." In *Civil Life, Globalization and Political Change in Asia: Organizing Between Family and State*, edited by Robert P. Weller, 58–75. Abingdon, Oxon; New York: Routledge, 2005.

Lumb, Peter. "Slope Failures in Hong Kong." *Quarterly Journal of Engineering Geology and Hydrogeology* 8, no. 1 (1975): 31–65.

Ma, Eric Kit-wai. *Culture, Politics and Television in Hong Kong.* London; New York: Routledge, 1999.

Ma, Eric Kit-wai, and Fung Anthony Ying Him. "Negotiating Local and National Identifications: Hong Kong Identity Surveys 1996–2006." *Asian Journal of Communication* 17, no. 2 (2007): 172–185.

MacKay, Christopher John. "Housing Management and the Comprehensive Housing Model in Hong Kong: A Case Study of Colonial Influence." *Journal of Contemporary China* 9, no. 25 (2000): 449–466.

Madokoro, Laura. "Borders Transformed: Sovereign Concerns, Population Movements and the Making of Territorial Frontiers in Hong Kong, 1949–1967." *Journal of Refugee Studies* 25, no. 3 (2012): 407–427.

Madokoro, Laura. *Elusive Refuge: Chinese Migrants in the Cold War.* Cambridge: Harvard University Press, 2016.

Magnússon, Sigurður Gylfi. "'The Singularization of History': Social History and Microhistory within the Postmodern State of Knowledge." *Journal of Social History* 36, no. 3 (2003): 701–735.

Magnússon, Sigurður Gylfi, and István M. Szijártó. *What is Microhistory? Theory and Practice.* Abingdon, Oxon: Routledge, 2013.

Majumdar, Shruti. "In 'Juridical Limbo': Urban Governance and Subaltern Legalities among Squatters in Calcutta, India" *Hague Journal on the Rule of Law* 9, no. 1 (2017): 83–108.

Malone, Andrew W. "Risk Management and Slope Safety in Hong Kong." *Hong Kong Institution of Engineers Transactions* 4, no. 2/3 (1997): 12–21.

Malone, Andrew, and Ken Ho. "Learning from Landslip Disasters in Hong Kong." *Built Environment* 21, no. 2/3 (1995): 126–144.

Manion, Melanie. *Corruption by Design: Building Clean Government in Mainland China and Hong Kong.* Cambridge, MA: Harvard University Press, 2004.

Mark, Chi-Kwan. *Hong Kong and the Cold War: Anglo-American Relations 1949–1957.* Oxford: Clarendon Press, 2004.

Mark, Chi-Kwan. "Defence or decolonisation? Britain, the United States, and the Hong Kong question in 1957." *The Journal of Imperial and Commonwealth History* 33, no. 1 (2005): 51–72.

Mark, Chi-Kwan. "The 'Problem of People': British Colonials, Cold War Powers, and the Chinese Refugees in Hong Kong, 1949–62." *Modern Asian Studies* 41, no. 6 (2007): 1145–1181.

Mark, Chi-Kwan. "Crisis or Opportunity? Britain, China, and the Decolonization of Hong Kong in the Long 1970s." In *China, Hong Kong, and the Long 1970s: Global Perspectives*, edited by Priscilla Roberts and Odd Arne Westad, 257–277. Cham: Palgrave Macmillan, 2017.

Mathews, Gordon. "Hèunggóngyàhn: On the Past, Present, and Future of Hong Kong Identity." *Bulletin of Concerned Asian Scholars* 29, no. 3 (1997): 3–13.

Mathews, Gordon. "Asylum Seekers in Hong Kong: The Paradoxes of Lives Lived on Hold." In *Migration in China and Asia: Experience and Policy*, edited by Zhang Jijiao and Howard Duncan, 73–85. Dordrecht: Springer, 2014.

Mathews, Gordon, Ma Eric, and Lui Tai-lok. *Hong Kong, China: Learning to Belong to a Nation.* London: Routledge, 2008.

Mathews, Gordon, and Yang Yang. "How Africans Pursue Low-End Globalization in Hong Kong and Mainland China." *Journal of Current Chinese Affairs* 41, no. 2 (2012): 95–120.

McAdam, Doug, Sidney Tarrow, and Charles Tilly. *Dynamics of Contention.* Cambridge: Cambridge University Press, 2001.

McGee, Terence Gary. *Hawkers in Hong Kong: A Study of Planning and Policy in a Third World City.* Hong Kong: Centre of Asian Studies, University of Hong Kong, 1973.

McGee, Terence Gary, and Yeung Yue-man. *Hawkers in Southeast Asian Cities: Planning for the Bazaar Economy.* Ottawa: International Development Research Centre, 1977.

Merry, Malcolm. *The Unruly New Territories: Small Houses, Ancestral Estates, Illegal Structures, and Other Customary Land Practices of Rural Hong Kong.* Hong Kong: Hong Kong University Press, 2020.

Merry, Sally Engle. *Colonizing Hawai'i: The Cultural Power of Law.* Princeton: Princeton University Press, 2000.

Milgram, Stanley. "The Experience of Living in Cities." *Science* 167, no. 3924 (1970): 1461–1468.

Mill, John Stuart. *On Liberty, Utilitarianism and Other Essays.* Oxford: Oxford University Press, 2015[1859].

Miller, Peter N. *Peiresc's Mediterranean World.* Cambridge, MA: Harvard University Press, 2015.

Misztal, Barbara. *Informality: Social Theory and Contemporary Practice.* London: Routledge, 2000.

Mitchell, Timothy. *Colonising Egypt.* Cambridge: Cambridge University Press, 1988.

Bibliography

Mok, Florence. "Public Opinion Polls and Covert Colonialism in British Hong Kong." *China Information* 33, no. 1 (2019a): 66–87.

Mok, Florence. "Political Culture and Policy Making in British Hong Kong, c. 1970–80." PhD Diss., University of York, 2019b.

Mok, Florence. "Chinese Illicit Immigration into Colonial Hong Kong, c. 1970–1980." *The Journal of Imperial and Commonwealth History* 49, no. 2 (2021): 339–367.

Mok, Florence. "Town Talk: Enhancing the 'Eyes and Ears' of the Colonial State in British Hong Kong, 1950s–1975." *Historical Research* 95, no. 268 (2022): 287–308.

Moore, Sally Falk. *Law as Process: An Anthropological Approach.* London: Routledge and Kegan Paul, 1978.

Morris, Jeremy, and Abel Polese, eds. *Informal Economies in Post-Socialist Spaces: Practices, Institutions and Networks.* London: Palgrave Macmillan, 2015.

Mott, Hay and Anderson. *Diamond Hill Development Study: Consultant's Report.* Unpublished document in possession of Alan Smart collected during the fieldwork in 1983–1985, 1983.

Mukhija, Vinit. *Squatters as Developers?: Slum Redevelopment in Mumbai.* Burlington: Ashgate Publishing, 2003.

Nagata, Judith A. *Malaysian Mosaic Perspectives from a Polyethnic Society.* Vancouver: University of British Columbia Press, 1979.

Neuwirth, Robert. *Shadow Cities: A Billion Squatters, A New Urban World.* New York: Routledge, 2005.

Neuwirth, Robert. *Stealth of Nations: The Global Rise of the Informal Economy.* New York: Pantheon Books, 2011.

Newman, Simeon J. "The Emergence of de facto Bureaucratic Priorities: Extending Urban Citizenship in fin-de-millénaire Lima, Peru." *The Sociological Quarterly* 63, no. 1(2020): 1–30. https://doi.org/10.1080/00380253.2020.1816863.

Ng, Chun-hung. "In Search of Local Consciousness in Hong Kong." In *Reading Hong Kong Popular Culture, 1970–2000,* edited by Ng Chun-hung and Cheng Chi-wai, 86–98. Hong Kong: Oxford University Press, 2001. (in Chinese)

Ng, Kenny K. K. "Screening without China: Transregional Cinematic Smuggling between Cold War Taiwan and Colonial Hong Kong." *Journal of the European Association for Chinese Studies* 1 (2020): 161–188.

Ngo, Tak-Wing. "Industrial History and the Artifice of Laissez-Faire Colonialism." In *Hong Kong's History: State and Society under Colonial Rule,* edited by Ngo Tak-Wing, 119–140. London: Routledge, 1999.

Ngo, Tak-Wing. "Changing Government-Business Relations and the Governance of Hong Kong." In *Hong Kong in Transition: The Handover Years,* edited by Robert Ash, Peter Ferdinand, Brian Hook, and Robin Porter, 26–41. London: Palgrave Macmillan, 2000.

Niiniluoto, Ilkka. "Defending Abduction." *Philosophy of Science* 66 (1999): S436–S451.

Nthenda, Louis. "Recent Trends in Government and Industry Relationship in Hong Kong." In *Hong Kong: Economic, Social, and Political Studies in Development, with a Comprehensive Bibliography,* edited by Lin Tzong-Biau, Lee Lily Xiao Hong, and Udo Ernst Simonis, 167–180. London: Routledge, 2017.

Obeng-Odoom, Franklin. "The Mystery of Capital or the Mystification of Capital?" *Review of Social Economy* 71, no. 4 (2013): 427–442.

Obeng-Odoom, Franklin, and Frank Stilwell. "Security of Tenure in International Development Discourse." *International Development Planning Review* 35, no. 4 (2013): 315–333.

Ortega, Arnisson Andre C. "Manila's Metropolitan Landscape of Gentrification: Global Urban Development, Accumulation by Dispossession and Neoliberal Warfare against Informality." *Geoforum* 70 (2016): 35–50.

Ortmann, Stephan. "The Development of Hong Kong Identity: From Local to National Identity." In *Citizenship, Identity and Social Movements in the New Hong Kong: Localism after the Umbrella Movement*, edited by Lam Wai-man and Luke Cooper, 114–131. London: Routledge, 2017.

Otto, Jan Michiel, and André Hoekema. "Legalising land rights, yes but how? An introduction." In *Fair Land Governance: How to Legalise Land Rights for Rural Development*, edited by Jan M. Otto and André Hoekema, 7–30. Amsterdam: Leiden University Press, 2012.

Oviedo, Ana Maria, Mark R. Thomas, and Kamer Karakurum-Ozdemir. *Economic Informality: Causes, Costs, and Policies — A Literature Survey*. Washington: The World Bank, 2009.

Padhi, Balakrushna, Udaya S. Mishra, and Triveni Tutika. "Assessment of Living Condition of Urban Slum Dwellers in India in the New Millennium." *Urban Research & Practice* 15, no. 4 (2022): 604–626. https://doi.org/10.1080/17535069.2021.1887923.

Panman, Alexandra, and Nancy Lozano Gracia. "Titling and Beyond: Evidence from Dar es Salaam, Tanzania." World Bank Policy Research Working Paper 9580, Urban, Disaster Risk Management, Resilience and Land Global Practice, World Bank Group, 2021. https://openknowledge.worldbank.org/bitstream/handle/10986/35288/Titling-and-Beyond-Evidence-from-Dar-es-Salaam-Tanzania.pdf?sequence=1.

Pasquetti, Silvia, and Giovanni Picker. "Urban Informality and Confinement: Toward a Relational Framework." *International Sociology* 32, no. 4 (2017): 532–544.

Pante, Michael D. "Settlements and the Heritage Dilemma in Manila." *City & Society* 32, no. 2 (2020): 408–420.

Patel, Amit, Phoram Shah, and Brian E. Beauregard. "Measuring Multiple Housing Deprivations in Urban India using Slum Severity Index." *Habitat International* 101 (2020): 102190.

Peck, Jamie. "Milton's Paradise: Situating Hong Kong in Neoliberal Lore." *Journal of Law and Political Economy* 1, no. 2 (2021): 189–211.

Peterson, Glen. "To Be or Not to Be a Refugee: The International Politics of the Hong Kong Refugee Crisis, 1949–55." *The Journal of Imperial and Commonwealth History* 36, no. 2 (2008) 171–195.

Pickering, Andrew. *The Mangle of Practice: Time, Agency, and Science*. Chicago: University of Chicago Press, 1995.

Podmore, David. 1971. "The Population of Hong Kong." In *Hong Kong: The Industrial Colony*, edited by Keith Hopkins, 21–54. Hong Kong: Oxford University Press, 1971.

Bibliography

Portes, Alejandro, Manuel Castells, and Lauren A. Benton, eds. *The Informal Economy: Studies in Advanced and Less Developed Countries.* Baltimore: John Hopkins University Press, 1989.

Power, Michael. *The Audit Society: Rituals of Verification.* Oxford: Oxford University Press, 1997.

Pryor, Edward G. *Housing in Hong Kong,* First Edition. Hong Kong: Oxford University Press, 1973

Pryor, Edward G. *Housing in Hong Kong,* Second Edition. Hong Kong: Oxford University Press, 1983.

Putnam, Robert D. *Bowling Alone: The Collapse and Revival of American Community.* New York: Simon & Schuster, 2000.

Rabinow, Paul. *French Modern: Norms and Forms of the Social Environment.* Chicago: University of Chicago Press, 1989.

Rao, Ursula. "Tolerated Encroachment: Resettlement Policies and the Negotiation of the Licit/Illicit Divide in an Indian Metropolis." *Cultural Anthropology* 28, no. 4 (2013): 760–779.

Roberts, Priscilla. "Cold War Hong Kong: The Foundations." In *Hong Kong in the Cold War,* edited by Priscilla Roberts and John M. Carroll, 15–25. Hong Kong: Hong Kong University Press, 2016.

Roberts, Priscilla, and John M. Carroll, eds. *Hong Kong in the Cold War.* Hong Kong: Hong Kong University Press, 2016.

Roy, Ananya. *City Requiem, Calcutta: Gender and the Politics of Poverty.* Minneapolis: University of Minnesota Press, 2002.

Roy, Ananya. "Urban Informality: Toward an Epistemology of Planning." *Journal of the American Planning Association* 71, no. 2 (2005): 147–158.

Roy, Ananya. *Poverty Capital: Microfinance and the Making of Development.* London: Routledge, 2010.

Royal Observatory Hong Kong. *Meteorological Results 1972.* Hong Kong: Hong Kong Government Printer, 1973.

Sahlins, Marshall. *Islands of History.* London and New York: Tavistock Publications, 1985.

Sahlins, Marshall. *Apologies to Thucydides: Understanding History as Culture and Vice Versa.* Chicago: University of Chicago Press, 2004.

Salaff, Janet W. *Working Daughters of Hong Kong: Filial Piety or Power in the Family?* Morningside Edition, New York: Columbia University Press, 1995.

Sandhu, Kernial Singh. "The Saga of the 'Squatter' in Malaya: A Preliminary Survey of the Causes, Characteristics and Consequences of the Resettlement of Rural Dwellers during the Emergency between 1948 and 1960." *Journal of Southeast Asian History* 5, no. 1 (1964): 143–177.

Sautman, Barry. "Hong Kong as a Semi-ethnocracy: Race, Migration, and Citizenship in a Globalized Region." In *Remaking Citizenship in Hong Kong: Community, Nation and the Global City,* edited by Ku Agnes S. and Pun Ngai, 103–124. Abingdon, Oxon: RoutledgeCurzon, 2004.

Sayer, Andrew. *Method in Social Science: A Realist Approach.* London; New York: Routledge, 1992.

Bibliography

Schiffer, Jonathan. "Urban Enterprise Zones: a Comment on the Hong Kong model." *International Journal of Urban and Regional Research* 7, no. 3 (1983): 429–438.

Schneider, Jane, and Peter Schneider. "Is Transparency Possible? The Political-Economic and Epistemological Implications of Cold War Conspiracies and Subterfuge in Italy." In *States and Illegal Practices*, edited by Josiah M. Heyman, 169–198. London: Berg, 1999.

Scott, Ian. *Political Change and the Crisis of Legitimacy in Hong Kong.* Honolulu: University of Hawaii Press, 1989.

Scott, Ian. *The Public Sector in Hong Kong.* Hong Kong: Hong Kong University Press, 2010.

Scott, Ian. "Institutional Design and Corruption Prevention in Hong Kong." *Journal of Contemporary China* 22 no. 79 (2013): 77–92.

Scott, Ian "Bridging the Gap: Hong Kong Senior Civil Servants and the 1966 Riots." *The Journal of Imperial and Commonwealth History* 45, no. 1 (2017): 131–148.

Scott, James C. *Weapons of the Weak: Everyday Forms of Peasant Resistance.* New Haven: Yale University Press, 1985.

Scott, James C. *Seeing Like a State: How Certain Schemes to Improve the Human Condition Have Failed.* New Haven: Yale University Press, 1998.

Scott, Janet Lee. *For Gods, Ghosts, and Ancestors: The Chinese Tradition of Paper Offerings.* Hong Kong: Hong Kong University Press, 2007.

Seng, Eunice Mei Feng. *Resistant City: Histories, Maps and the Architecture of Development.* Singapore: World Scientific, 2020.

Sewell, William H. Jr. *Logics of History: Social Theory and Social Transformation.* Chicago: University of Chicago Press, 2005.

Sharma, Aradhana. "New Brooms and Old: Sweeping up Corruption in India, One Law at a Time." *Current Anthropology* 59, no. S18 (2018): S72–S82.

Shelton, Barrie, Justyna Karakiewicz, and Thomas Kvan. *The Making of Hong Kong: From Vertical to Volumetric.* London: Routledge, 2011.

Sheng, Mingjie, Chaolin Gu, and Weiping Wu. "To Move or to Stay in a Migrant Enclave in Beijing: The Role of Neighborhood Social Bonds." *Journal of Urban Affairs* 41, no. 3 (2019): 338–353.

Sinn, Elizabeth. "Xin Xi Guxiang: A Study of Regional Associations as a Bonding Mechanism in the Chinese Diaspora. The Hong Kong Experience." *Modern Asian Studies* 31, no. 2 (1997): 375–397.

Sit, Victor Fung-shuen, Wong Siu-lun, and Kiang Tsin-sing. *Small Scale Industry in a Laissez-Faire Economy.* Hong Kong: Centre of Asian Studies, University of Hong Kong, 1979.

Siu, Helen F. "Immigrants and Social Ethos: Hong Kong in the Nineteen-Eighties." *Journal of the Royal Asiatic Society Hong Kong Branch* 26 (1986): 1–16.

Siu, Helen F. "Remade in Hong Kong: Weaving into the Chinese Cultural Tapestry." In *Unity and Diversity: Local Cultures and Identities in China*, edited by Liu TaoTao and David Faure, 177–197. Hong Kong: Hong Kong University Press, 1996.

Skully, Michael T., ed. *Financial Institutions and Markets in the Far East: A Study of China, Hong Kong, Japan, South Korea, and Taiwan.* London: Macmillan Press, 1982.

Smart, Alan. "The Squatter Property Market in Hong Kong: Informal Regulation and the State." *Critique of Anthropology* 5, no. 3 (1985): 23–40.

Bibliography

Smart, Alan. "Invisible Real Estate: Investigations into the Squatter Property Market." *International Journal of Urban and Regional Research* 10, no. 1 (1986): 29–45.

Smart, Alan. "Old Huts and New Regulations: Changes in the Hong Kong Squatter Property Market." *International Journal of Urban and Regional Research* 12, no. 2 (1988): 303–307.

Smart, Alan. "Extreme Case Comparison: Housing Provision and the State." *City and Society* 3, no. 1 (1989a): 165–179.

Smart, Alan. "Forgotten Obstacles, Neglected Forces: Explaining the Origins of Hong Kong Public Housing." *Environment and Planning D: Society and Space* 7, no. 2 (1989b): 179–196.

Smart, Alan. *Making Room: Squatter Clearance in Hong Kong.* Hong Kong: University of Hong Kong, Centre of Asian Studies, 1992.

Smart, Alan. "Gifts, Bribes and Guanxi: A reconsideration of Bourdieu's Social Capital." *Cultural Anthropology* 8, no. 3 (1993): 388–408.

Smart, Alan. "The Emergence of Local Capitalisms in China: Overseas Chinese Investment and Patterns of Development." In *China's Regions, Polity, & Economy: A Study of Spatial Transformation in the Post-Reform Era*, edited by Li Si-ming and Tang Wing-shing, 65–95. Hong Kong: Chinese University Press, 2000.

Smart, Alan. "Unruly Places: Urban Governance and the Persistence of Illegality in Hong Kong's Urban Squatter Areas." *American Anthropologist* 103, no. 1 (2001): 30–44.

Smart, Alan. "Agents of Eviction: The Squatter Control and Clearance Division of Hong Kong's Housing Department." *Singapore Journal of Tropical Geography* 23, no. 3 (2002): 333–347.

Smart, Alan. "Sharp Edges, Fuzzy Categories and Transborder Networks: Managing and Housing New Arrivals in Hong Kong." *Ethnic and Racial Studies* 26, no. 2 (2003a): 218–233.

Smart, Alan. "Impeded Self-Help: Toleration and the Proscription of Housing Consolidation in Hong Kong's Squatter Areas." *Habitat International* 27, no. 2 (2003b): 205–225.

Smart, Alan. *The Shek Kip Mei Myth: Squatters, Fires and Colonial Rule in Hong Kong, 1950–1963.* Hong Kong: Hong Kong University Press, 2006.

Smart, Alan. "Unreliable Chinese: Internal Security and the Devaluation and Expansion of Citizenship in Postwar Hong Kong." In *War, Citizenship, Territory*, edited by Deborah Cowen and Emily Gilbert, 219–240. New York: Routledge, 2008.

Smart, Alan. "Housing Support for the 'Undeserving': Moral Hazard, Fires, and Laissez-Faire in Hong Kong." In *Ethnographies of Social Support*, edited by Markus Schlecker and Friederike Fleischer, 17–37. New York: Palgrave Macmillan, 2013.

Smart, Alan. "The Unbearable Discretion of Street-Level Bureaucrats: Corruption and Collusion in Hong Kong." *Current Anthropology* 59, no. S18 (2018a): S37–S47.

Smart, Alan. "Structuration." In *The International Encyclopedia of Anthropology*, edited by Hilary Callan. Hoboken: John Wiley & Sons, 2018b. https://doi.org/10.1002/9781118924396.wbiea1564.

Smart, Alan. "Squatter Housing." In *Oxford Research Encyclopedia of Anthropology*. Oxford University Press, October 27, 2020. https://doi.org/10.1093/acrefore/9780190854584.013.222.

Smart, Alan. "Anthropological Shades of Gray: Informal Norms and Becoming (Il) legal." In *Norms and Illegality: Intimate Ethnographies and Politics,* edited by Cristiana Panella and Walter E. Little, 21–36. Lanham: Lexington, 2021a.

Smart, Alan. "Anthropology of Law." In *The Sage Handbook of Cultural Anthropology,* edited by Lene Pedersen and Lisa Cliggett, 348–363. London: SAGE, 2021b.

Smart, Alan. "Does Formalisation make a City Smarter? Towards Post-elitist Smart Cities." In *Digital (In)justice in the Smart City,* edited by Debra Mackinnon, Ryan Burns, and Victoria Fast. Toronto: University of Toronto, 2023.

Smart, Alan, and Dean Curran. "Prospects and Social Impact of Big Data-Driven Urban Governance in China: Provincializing Smart City Research." In *China Urbanizing: Impacts and Transitions,* edited by Weiping Wu and Qin Gao, 205–227. Philadelphia: University of Pennsylvania Press, 2023.

Smart, Alan, and Eliot Tretter. "Spillover Effects of Fire, Riot and Epidemic from Slums: Early Urban Planning and Hong Kong's Squatter Areas." In *The Oxford Handbook of the Modern Slum,* edited by Alan Mayne. Oxford: Oxford University Press, 2023.

Smart, Alan, and Ernest Chui. "Expansion and Exclusion in Hong Kong's Squatter Resettlement Program: The Ratchet of Exclusion into Temporary and Interim Housing." In *Homing Devices: The Poor as Targets of Public Housing Policy and Practice,* edited by Marilyn M. Thomas-Houston and Mark Schuller, 181–198. Lanham: Lexington Books, 2006.

Smart, Alan, and Filippo M. Zerilli. "Extralegality." In *A Companion to Urban Anthropology,* edited by Donald M. Nonini, 222–238. Malden, MA: John Wiley & Sons, 2014.

Smart, Alan, Godfrey Yeung, and Lui Tai-lok. "Gift to a Former Mentor: Hong Kong's Contribution to the Rise of China and the Consequences of That Rise for the Current Relationship." *Social Transformations in Chinese Societies* 11, no. 2 (2015): 81–113.

Smart, Alan, and James Lee. "Financialization and the Role of Real Estate in Hong Kong's Regime of Accumulation." *Economic Geography* 79, no. 2 (2003): 153–171.

Smart, Alan and Josephine Smart. "Introduction." In *Petty Capitalists and Globalization: Flexibility, Entrepreneurship, and Economic Development,* edited by Alan Smart and Josephine Smart, 1–22. Albany: State University of New York, 2005.

Smart, Alan, and Josephine Smart. "Learning from Disaster? Mad Cows, Squatter Fires, and Temporality in Repeated Crises." In *The Political Economy of Hazards and Disasters,* edited by Eric C. Jones and Arthur D. Murphy, 267–293. Lanham: Altamira Press, 2009.

Smart, Alan, and Josephine Smart. "Hong Kong Petty Capitalists Investing in China: Risk Tolerance, Uncertain Investment Environments, Success and Failure." In *Globalization from Below: The World's Other Economy,* edited by Gordon Mathews, Gustavo Lins Ribeiro, and Carlos Alba Vega, 103–119. London; New York: Routledge, 2012.

Smart, Alan, and Josephine Smart. "Formalization as Confinement in Colonial Hong Kong." *International Sociology* 32, no. 4 (2017a): 437–453.

Smart, Alan, and Josephine Smart. "Judging Publics and Contested Exclusion: The Moral Economy of Citizenship in China." In *Popular Politics and the Quest for Justice in Contemporary China,* edited by Susanne Brandtstädter and Hans Steinmüller, 74–90. New York: Routledge, 2017b.

Bibliography

Smart, Alan, and Lam Kit. "Urban Conflicts and the Policy Learning Process in Hong Kong: Urban Conflict and Policy Change in the 1950s and after 1997." *Journal of Asian Public Policy* 2, no. 2 (2009): 190–208.

Smart, Alan, and Lui Tai-lok. "Learning from Civil Unrest: State/Society Relations in Hong Kong Before and After the 1967 Disturbances." In *May Days in Hong Kong: Riot and Emergency in 1967*, edited by Robert Bickers and Ray Yep, 145–159. Hong Kong: Hong Kong University Press, 2009.

Smart, Alan, and Tang Wing-Shing. "On the Threshold of Urban Hong Kong: Liminal Territoriality in New Kowloon." In *Negotiating Territoriality: Spatial Dialogues between State and Tradition*, edited by Allan Charles Dawson, Laura Zanotti, and Ismael Vaccaro, 230–248. New York: Routledge, 2014.

Smart, Alan, and Thomas Aguilera. "Towards a Political Economy of Toleration of Illegality: Comparing Tolerated Squatting in Hong Kong and Paris." In *Comparative Approaches to Informal Housing around the Globe*, edited by Udo Grashoff, 39–65. London: UCL Press, 2020.

Smart, Josephine. "Dog Kings, Triads and Hawkers: Spatial Monopoly among the Street Hawkers in Hong Kong." *Canadian Journal of Development Studies/Revue canadienne d'études du développement* 4, no. 1 (1983): 158–163.

Smart, Josephine. "The Impact of Government Policy on Hawkers: A Study of the Effects of Establishing a Hawker Permitted Place." *Asian Journal of Public Administration* 8, no. 2 (1986): 260–279.

Smart, Josephine. *The Political Economy of Street Hawkers in Hong Kong*. Hong Kong: Centre of Asian Studies, University of Hong Kong, 1989.

Snow, Philip. *The Fall of Hong Kong: Britain, China and the Japanese Occupation*. New Haven and London: Yale University Press, 2003.

So, Alvin Y. "The Economic Success of Hong Kong: Insights from a World-System Perspective." *Sociological Perspectives* 29, no. 2 (1986): 241–258.

So, Alvin Y. "Cross-Border Families in Hong Kong: The Role of Social Class and Politics." *Critical Asian Studies* 35, no. 4 (2003): 515–534.

So, Alvin Y., and Chiu Stephen Wing-kai. *East Asia and the World-Economy*. Thousand Oaks: SAGE Publications, 1995.

Soliman, Ahmed M. "Rethinking Urban Informality and the Planning Process in Egypt." *International Development Planning Review* 32, no. 2 (2010): 119–143.

Solimene, Marco. "The (In)formal, the (Il)legal and the (Il)licit: Roma Informal Settlements and Institutional Pragmatics of Compromise and Compassion in a Roman Periphery." *Cities* 95 (2019): 102369.

Special Committee on Housing. *Final Report*. Hong Kong: Government Printer, 1958.

Squatter Area Improvements Division. *Report of Squatter Area Improvements 1982*. Hong Kong: Hong Kong Housing Department, 1982.

Steenberg, Rune. "The Art of Not Seeing Like a State. On the Ideology of 'Informality.'" *Journal of Contemporary Central and Eastern Europe* 24, no. 3 (2016): 293–306.

Steiner, Zara S. *The Foreign Office and Foreign Policy, 1898–1914*. New York: Cambridge University Press, 1969.

Steinmetz, George. *The Devil's Handwriting: Precoloniality and the German Colonial State in Qingdao, Samoa, and Southwest Africa*. Chicago: University of Chicago Press, 2007.

Stoler, Ann Laura. *Duress: Imperial Durabilities in Our Times*. Durham: Duke University Press, 2016.

Stoler, Ann Laura, and Frederick Cooper. "Between Metropole and Colony: Rethinking a Research Agenda" In *Tensions of Empire: Colonial Cultures in a Bourgeois World*, edited by Frederick Cooper and Ann Laura Stoler, 1–56. Berkeley: University of California Press, 1997.

Strathern, Marilyn, ed. *Audit Cultures: Anthropological Studies in Accountability, Ethics and the Academy*. London; New York: Routledge, 2000.

Ta, Trang X. "A Space for Secondhand Goods: Trading the Remnants of Material Life in Hong Kong: A Space for Secondhand Goods in Hong Kong." *Economic Anthropology* 4, no. 1 (2017): 120–131.

Tanasescu, Alina, and Alan Smart. "The Limits of Social Capital: An Examination of Immigrants' Housing Challenges in Calgary." *Journal of Sociology & Social Welfare* 37, no. 4 (2010): 97–122.

Tanasescu, Alina, Ernest Chui, and Alan Smart. "Tops and Bottoms: State Tolerance of Illegal Housing in Hong Kong and Calgary." *Habitat International* 34, no. 4 (2010): 478–484.

Tang, James Tuck-hong, and Frank Ching. "The MacLehose-Youde Years: Balancing the 'Three-Legged Stool,' 1971–86." In *Precarious Balance: Hong Kong between China and Britain, 1842–1992*, edited by Chan Ming-Kuo, 131–148. Hong Kong: Hong Kong University Press, 1994.

Tang, Wing Shing, and Him Chung. "Rural-Urban Transition in China: Illegal Land Use and Construction." *Asia Pacific Viewpoint* 43, no. 1 (2002): 43–62.

The Economist. "Get Sick or Go Hungry." April 18, 2020a.

The Economist. "Covid Dries up a Cash Cow." April 18, 2020b.

Thomas, Martin. "Colonial States as Intelligence States: Security Policing and the Limits of Colonial Rule in France's Muslim Territories, 1920–40." *Journal of Strategic Studies* 28, no. 6 (2005): 1033–1060.

Tong, Clement Tsz Ming. "The Hong Kong Week of 1967 and the Emergence of Hong Kong Identity through Contradistinction." *Journal of the Royal Asiatic Society Hong Kong Branch* 56 (2016): 40–66.

Topley, Marjorie. "Capital, Saving and Credit among Indigenous Rice Farmers and Immigrant Vegetable Farmers in Hong Kong's New Territories." In *Capital, Saving and Credit in Peasant Societies: Studies from Asia, Oceania, the Caribbean and Middle America*, edited by Raymond Firth and Basil S. Yamey, 157–186. Chicago: Aldine Publishing Company, 1964.

Tsai, Jung-fang. *Hong Kong in Chinese History: Community and Social Unrest in the British Colony, 1842–1913*. New York: Columbia University Press, 1993.

Tsang, Shun-fai. "Border Control in Colonial Hong Kong, 1958–1962." MPhil. thesis, University of Hong Kong, 2010.

Tsang, Steve, ed. *Government and Politics: A Documentary History of Hong Kong*. Hong Kong: Hong Kong University Press, 1995.

Tsang, Steve. "Strategy for Survival: The Cold war and Hong Kong's Policy towards Kuomintang and Chinese Communist Activities in the 1950s." *The Journal of Imperial and Commonwealth History* 25, no. 2 (1997): 294–317.

Bibliography

Tsang, Steve. *A Modern History of Hong Kong.* Hong Kong: Hong Kong University Press, 2004.

Tsang, Steve. *Governing Hong Kong: Administrative Officers from the Nineteenth Century to the Handover to China, 1862–1997.* Hong Kong: Hong Kong University Press, 2007.

Tsz, Thomas Kwan-choi. "Civic Education and the Making of Deformed Citizenry: From British Colony to Chinese SAR." In *Remaking Citizenship in Hong Kong: Community, Nation and the Global City.* Edited by Ku Agnes S. and Pun Ngai, 49–66. Abingdon, Oxon: Routledge, 2004.

Turner, Frederick Jackson. *The Frontier in American History.* New York: Henry Holt & Co, 1920.

Turner, John F. C. *Housing by People: Towards Autonomy in Building Environments.* New York: Pantheon Books, 1976.

Turner, Matthew. "60s/90s: Dissolving the People." In *Hong Kong Sixties: Designing Identity*, edited by Matthew Turner and Irene Ngan, 13–34. Hong Kong: Hong Kong Arts Centre, 1995.

Ure, Gavin. *Governors, Politics and the Colonial Office: Public Policy in Hong Kong, 1918–58.* Hong Kong: Hong Kong University Press, 2012.

Vagg, Jon. "The Borders of Crime: Hong Kong-China Cross-Border Criminal Activity." *The British Journal of Criminology* 32, no. 3 (1992): 310–328.

Van Naerssen, Ton. "Squatter Access to Land in Metro Manila." *Philippine Studies* 41, no. 1 (1993): 3–20.

van Schendel, Willem, and Itty Abraham, eds. *Illicit Flows and Criminal Things: States, Borders, and the Other Side of Globalization.* Bloomington: Indiana University Press, 2005.

Varley, Ann. "Private or Public: Debating the Meaning of Tenure Legalization." *International Journal of Urban and Regional Research* 26, no. 3 (2002): 449–461.

Varley, Ann. "Gender and Property Formalization: Conventional and Alternative Approaches." *World Development* 35, no. 10 (2007): 1739–1753.

Veg, Sebastian. "The Rise of 'Localism' and Civic Identity in Post-Handover Hong Kong: Questioning the Chinese Nation-State." *The China Quarterly* 230 (2017): 323–347.

Vickers, Edward. "The Politics of History Education in Hong Kong: The Case of Local History." *International Journal of Educational Research* 37, no. 6/7 (2002): 587–602.

Vogel, Ezra F. *Canton under Communism: Programs and Politics in a Provincial Capital, 1949–1968.* Cambridge, MA: Harvard University Press, 1969.

Wagner-Pacifici, Robin. *The Art of Surrender: Decomposing Sovereignty at Conflict's End.* Chicago: University of Chicago Press, 2005.

Wagner-Pacifici, Robin. "Theorizing the Restlessness of Events." *American Journal of Sociology* 115, no. 5 (2010): 1351–1386.

Wagner-Pacifici, Robin. *What Is an Event?* Chicago: University of Chicago Press, 2017.

Watson, James L. *Emigration and the Chinese Lineage: The Mans in Hong Kong and London.* Berkeley: University of California Press, 1975.

Wedel, Janine R. "Rethinking Corruption in an Age of Ambiguity." *Annual Review of Law and Social Science* 8 (2012): 453–498.

Wesley-Smith, Peter. *Unequal Treaty, 1898–1997: China, Great Britain and Hong Kong's New Territories.* Hong Kong: Oxford University Press, 1980.

Wong, Hung, and Chan Siu-ming. "The Impacts of Housing Factors on Deprivation in a World City: The Case of Hong Kong." *Social Policy & Administration* 53, no. 6 (2019): 872–888.

Wong, Siu-Lun. *Emigrant Entrepreneurs: Shanghai Industrialists in Hong Kong*. Hong Kong: Oxford University Press, 1988.

Wong, Yue Chim Richard. *Hong Kong Land for Hong Kong People: Fixing the Failures of our Housing Policy*. Hong Kong: Hong Kong University Press, 2015.

Wong, Tim Ling. "Tiny Affordable Housing in Hong Kong." *Indoor and Built Environment* 27, no. 9 (2018): 1159–1161.

Wong, Ting-Hong. *Hegemonies Compared: State Formation and Chinese School Politics in Postwar Singapore and Hong Kong*. New York: RoutledgeFalmer, 2002.

"Wong Tai Sin District Board. Hsin-an hsieh-chih and Now Wong Tai Sin District." Unpublished document in possession of Alan Smart, collected during fieldwork, 1983–1985, n.d.

"Wong Tai Sin District Board. 1984. District Report." Unpublished document in possession of Alan Smart, collected during fieldwork, 1983–1985, 1984.

World Bank. *Philippines: Third Urban Development Project*. February 26, 1980. https://documents1.worldbank.org/curated/en/955891468332475468/text/multi-page.txt.

Wu, Venus. "Hong Kong's Vanishing Archives and the Battle to Preserve History," *Reuters*, September 6, 2017. https://www.reuters.com/article/us-hongkong-anniversary-archives-idUSKCN1BH0OY.

Wyrtzen, Jonathan. "Colonial Legitimization-Legibility Linkages and the Politics of Identity in Algeria and Morocco." *European Journal of Sociology* 58, no. 2 (2017): 205–235.

Xie, Qingshu, Ali. R. Ghanbari Parsa, and Barry Redding. "The Emergence of the Urban Land Market in China: Evolution, Structure, Constraints and Perspectives." *Urban Studies* 39, no. 8 (2002): 1375–1398.

Yan, Yunxiang. *The Flow of Gifts: Reciprocity and Social Networks in a Chinese Village*. Stanford: Stanford University Press, 1996.

Yang, Alfred Lei, and Eric Ying Ngai Hong. "Should the Doctrine of Adverse Possession Be Abolished in Hong Kong?" *King's Student Law Review* 8, no. 2 (2017): 66–78.

Yang, Mayfair Mei-hui. *Gifts, Favors, and Banquets: The Art of Social Relationships in China*. Cornell University Press, 1994.

Yang, T. L., S. Mackey, and E. Cumine. "Final Report of the Commission of Inquiry into the Rainstorm Disasters 1972." GEO Report No. 229, Hong Kong: Geotechnical Engineering Office, Civil Engineering Department, The Government of the Hong Kong Special Administrative Region, 2008[1972]. https://www.cedd.gov.hk/file-manager/eng/content_414/er229links.pdf

Yao, Alice. *The Ancient Highlands of Southwest China. From the Bronze Age to the Han Empire*. Oxford: Oxford University Press, 2016.

Yeh, Anthony Gar-On. "Unfair Housing Subsidy and Public Housing in Hong Kong." *Environment and Planning C: Government and Policy* 8, no. 4 (1990): 439–454.

Yeoh, Brenda S. A. *Contesting Space in Colonial Singapore: Power Relations and the Urban Built Environment*. Singapore: National University of Singapore Press, 2003.

Bibliography

Yep, Ray. "'Cultural Revolution in Hong Kong': Emergency Powers, Administration of Justice and the Turbulent Year of 1967." *Modern Asian Studies* 46, no. 4 (2012): 1007–1032.

Yep, Ray. "The Crusade Against Corruption in Hong Kong in the 1970s: Governor MacLehose as a Zealous Reformer or Reluctant Hero?" *China Information* 27, no. 2 (2013a): 197–221.

Yep, Ray. "Understanding the Autonomy of Hong Kong: Looking Beyond Formal Institutions." In *Negotiating Autonomy in Greater China: Hong Kong and Its Sovereign before and after 1997*, edited by Ray Yep, 1–28. Copenhagen: NIAS, 2013b.

Yep, Ray. "A Historical Perspective on Hong Kong Autonomy: Traditions of British Imperialism, Maritime Enclave and Contending Views of British Interest." In *Hong Kong 20 Years After the Handover: Emerging Social and Institutional Fractures After 1997*, edited by Fong Brian Chi-hang and Lui Tai-Lok, 231–254. Cham: Palgrave Macmillan, 2018.

Yep, Ray, and Lui Tai-Lok. "Revisiting the Golden Era of MacLehose and the Dynamics of Social Reforms." *China Information* 24, no. 3 (2010): 249–272.

Yep, Ray, and Robert Bickers. "Studying the 1967 Riots: An Overdue Project." In *May Days in Hong Kong: Riot and Emergency in 1967*, edited by Robert Bickers and Ray Yep, 1–18. Hong Kong: Hong Kong University Press, 2009.

Yeung, Henry Wai-chung. *Transnational Corporations and Business Networks: Hong Kong Firms in the ASEAN Region*. London: Routledge, 1998.

Yeung, Yue-man. "Milestones in Development." In *Fifty Years of Public Housing in Hong Kong: A Golden Jubilee Review and Appraisal*, edited by Yeung Yue-man and Timothy Kai-Ying Wong, 19–43. Hong Kong: Hong Kong Housing Authority, Hong Kong Institute of Asia-Pacific Studies, Chinese University Press, 2003.

Yeung, Yue-man, and David W. Drakakis-Smith. "Comparative Perspectives on Public Housing in Singapore and Hong Kong." *Asian Survey* 14, no. 8 (1974): 763–775.

Yew, Chiew Ping, and Kwong Kin-ming. "Hong Kong Identity on the Rise." *Asian Survey* 54, no. 6 (2014): 1088–1112.

Yiftachel, Oren. "Theoretical Notes On `Gray Cities': The Coming of Urban Apartheid?" *Planning Theory* 8, no. 1 (2009): 88–100.

Yip, Maurice. "New Town Planning as Diplomatic Planning: Scalar Politics, British-Chinese Relations, and Hong Kong." *Journal of Urban History* 48, no. 2 (2022): 361–380. https://doi.org/10.1177/0096144220948813.

Yip, Ngai-ming. "Managing and Serving the Estates." In *Fifty Years of Public Housing in Hong Kong: A Golden Jubilee Review and Appraisal*, edited by Yeung Yue-man and Timothy Kai-Ying Wong, 357–382. Hong Kong: Hong Kong Housing Authority, Hong Kong Institute of Asia-Pacific Studies, Chinese University Press, 2003.

Young, John D. "The Building Years: Maintaining a China-Hong Kong-Britain Equilibrium, 1950–71." In *Precarious Balance: Hong Kong between China and Britain, 1842–1992*, edited by Chan Ming-kuo, 131–149. Armonk, NY: M. E. Sharpe, 1994.

Yu, Andrew C. K. "Was Governor MacLehose a Great Architect of Modern Hong Kong?" *Asian Affairs* 51, no. 3 (2020): 485–509.

Yuen, Belinda. "Squatters No More: Singapore Social Housing." In *Land and Urban Policies for Poverty Reduction: Volume 1*, edited by Mila Freire, Ricardo Lima, Dean

Cira, Bruce Ferguson, Christine Kessides, José Aroudo Mota, Diana Motta, 269–294. Brasilia: Institute for Applied Economic Research, 2007.

Yung, Betty, and Fung-Ping Lee. "'Right to housing' in Hong Kong: Perspectives from the Hong Kong Community." *Housing, Theory and Society* 29, no. 4 (2012): 401–419.

Zaki, Pakhriazad Hassan, Mohd Zaki Hamzah, Mohd Hasmadi Ismail, Khairil Awang. "Malay Customary Tenure and Conflict on Implementation of Colonial Land Law in Peninsular Malaysia." *Journal of Law and Conflict Resolution* 2, no. 2 (2010): 33–45.

Zhang, Li. *Strangers in the City: Reconfigurations of Space, Power, and Social Networks within China's Floating Population.* Stanford: Stanford University Press, 2001.

Zhang, Shu Guang. *Economic Cold War. America's Embargo against China and the Sino-Soviet Alliance, 1949–1963.* Stanford: Stanford University Press, 2001.

Zhu, Jieming. "Urban Development under Ambiguous Property Rights: A Case of China's Transition Economy." *International Journal of Urban and Regional Research* 26, no. 1 (2002): 41–57.

Žižek, Slavoj. *Event: Philosophy in Transit.* London: Penguin Books, 2014.

Index

abduction, xii
autonomy, 5–6, 16, 20, 27, 51–52, 55, 89,
 101–102, 104–105

Beijing, 6, 53, 61–62, 64, 89–90, 217, 232,
 251, 261–262, 268
Bray, Denis, 97–98, 121–123, 273, 277
Building Ordinance, 48, 116, 148, 198,
 223–224; Office, 148, 198, 223–224

Chai Wan, 120, 138, 188–190, 282
Cha Kwo Ling, 251, 258, 288
China, 1, 4, 6, 16, 18–19, 22, 24, 28,
 37–38, 41–42, 44, 53–54, 59, 61, 66,
 70, 72–73, 75, 77, 90, 99–102, 104,
 119, 130–131, 134–135, 147, 149,
 167, 172, 174, 176–178, 181, 187,
 191–192, 230–233, 250–251, 261,
 263, 268–269, 277–278, 280–281,
 283, 288
Chinese immigrants, 153–154, 176,
 181; anti-immigrant, 173, 175–176,
 178–179, 181; new immigrants
 (*xinyimin*), 173; local/migrant
 distinction, 175
citizenship, 22, 34, 57, 99, 101, 130, 155,
 175, 232
City District Officer (CDO), 89, 97, 125,
 171, 176, 191–192, 280
Cobain, Ian, 9
Cold War, 6, 52, 54, 61, 99, 154
colonial, rule, 16, 20, 54, 91, 94–95, 155,
 234, 241, 259

Colonial Office (CO), 6, 51, 55, 57–58,
 60, 102–105, 269, 271
corruption, 19–20, 26–28, 34, 41, 45–46,
 48, 52, 82, 94–95, 118, 145, 191, 275,
 277, 286–287
COVID-19, 30, 40, 64, 109, 268
crises, 11–12, 16, 20, 92–93, 106
Cultural Revolution, 19, 66, 73, 90

dangerous slopes, 22, 147, 202–203,
 209–211, 215–218, 226, 257, 266
Defence Secretary, 95, 172, 271
de Soto, Hernando, 2, 27–28, 33, 36–38,
 122
development clearance, 23, 121, 125,
 129, 132–135, 140, 142–144, 149,
 161–162, 164, 168, 170–171, 177,
 186–187, 193, 197, 204, 208–209,
 215, 217, 219, 224–227, 252, 257,
 260
Development Loan Fund, 159
Diamond Hill, 18, 43, 66, 75–82, 84–85,
 114, 142, 193–195, 200–201
Drakakis-Smith, David, 56–58, 135,
 157–161, 233
duty of care, 210, 213–214, 266

electrification, 188, 190–192, 197,
 202–203, 207, 282–283
eligibility, 22, 63, 68–69, 75, 111, 117,
 130, 134–138, 140–143, 149–151,
 153, 157–158, 161, 168, 170, 175,
 177–180, 195, 203, 218, 222–225,

239, 246, 249, 252, 260, 274, 277, 279, 281–282
Elliott (Tu), Elsie, 79–82, 84, 164–165, 167, 206, 219
environmental clearances, 149, 223–224
ethnomethodology, 30
events, 8, 12–15, 30, 50, 80, 84, 88, 92–94, 106–107, 109, 128, 198, 205, 214, 264
exclusion, ratchet of, 10, 144, 150, 171, 177, 179, 225

fairness, 23, 128, 137, 143, 150, 152, 154, 179–180, 252–253
fire prevention, 85, 192–194, 202, 283
fires, 8, 40, 46, 56, 61, 86–87, 109, 111, 121, 135, 137–140, 161–164, 168, 177, 182, 185, 189, 192–197, 199, 201, 204–205, 208–209, 216, 252, 274–275, 286–287; Kowloon Bay fire, 172, 178
Fishball Revolution, 263
forced eviction, 38, 228–229, 231, 233
Foreign and Commonwealth Office (FCO), 91, 95, 100, 102–106, 111–112, 125–126, 130, 133
formalization, 1, 4–5, 7, 10–11, 14, 16, 18, 20–21, 23, 26–28, 30–31, 35–38, 40–41, 49–50, 65, 98, 108–109, 132, 182–183, 188, 207, 228, 232, 240, 246, 253, 264–265
Foucault, Michel, 15–16, 175, 209

geopolitics, 6, 10, 46, 49–53, 61–62, 89, 99, 105, 126, 154, 217, 226, 241, 251
geotechnical hazards, 199
Giddens, Anthony, 11–12
Goodstadt, Leo, 19, 43, 48, 89–90, 96–97, 99, 101–103, 159, 207
Government Information Services, 176, 280
Government Low-Cost Housing (GLCH), 157
Grantham, Alexander, 54–55, 60–61, 90, 101

gray spaces, 34
guanxi, 28

Hart, Keith, 2–3, 33, 35
hawkers, 45, 263–264
Herzfeld, Michael, 31–32, 265
Home Ownership Scheme, 144, 203
Hong Kong, identity, 22, 99, 153, 174–175, 181–182, 226; Hong Kong belonger, 173, 203; sense of belonging, 155; *Heunggong-yan*, 175
Hongkong Observers, 167, 278
Hong Kong Public Records Office, ix, xiv–xv, 75, 262, 267
House of Lords, 111–112, 126
Housing Authority, 9, 75, 98, 106, 116, 129–130, 133–134, 140, 145, 151, 157, 159–160, 176, 206, 209, 217, 224, 240, 259, 268, 274, 276–278, 280, 284–287
Housing Board, 106, 111–112, 116–117, 119–120, 123, 125–126, 129, 163, 185–188, 272–273, 278, 282
Housing Department, 9, 114, 130–131, 138–141, 145, 147, 149–150, 156, 170, 172, 190–191, 194–195, 199–202, 205–206, 210, 212, 215, 217, 224, 254, 257, 274, 281

India, 15, 24, 230, 243–249
informality, economic, 17, 26–27, 32–33, 35, 41, 268
infrastructural power, 171
intelligence, 39, 171, 274
Intensive Patrol Areas, 145, 147, 168, 193
interim housing, 68, 84, 86, 114, 136, 224–225, 258

King, Ambrose Yeo-chi, 88, 171
Kowloon City, 56, 149, 192
Kuala Lumpur, 24, 229, 235–237, 249
Kwun Tong, 17, 114, 132, 147, 198, 200

Index

Lam Tin, 200

landslides, 5, 8, 109, 118, 138, 161, 185, 197–199, 204, 207–212, 214–216, 252, 284

Lau, Siu-kai, 53, 88, 96, 98, 117, 171, 174, 180

legibility, 171

legitimacy, 62, 96, 100, 154–155, 171, 181, 237, 245, 248–249, 279

Lei Yue Mun, 177

Li, Tania, 37, 184–185

licensed areas, 46, 48, 68, 70–71, 84, 124, 130–131, 135, 138–139, 149, 157, 162, 170, 188, 233, 252, 268, 277

London, 6, 20–21, 23, 51–55, 58, 60, 62, 64, 66, 90, 95–96, 99, 101–107, 112, 115, 119–121, 125–126, 130, 155, 183–186, 207–208, 252–253, 260, 268

loyalty, 21, 99–101, 130, 151, 154–155, 164, 170–171, 175, 178–179, 181–182, 250

Ma Chai Hang, 177–178, 193

MacLehose, Murray, 7, 20–21, 49, 57, 65, 72, 90, 94–96, 98–101, 103–106, 117, 127, 130–131, 136, 154–156, 171, 176, 182, 216, 271, 276, 278

Malaysia, 24, 230, 233, 235–237, 239

mangle of practice, 7, 20, 108–111, 126–128, 185, 212, 252–253, 262, 264–265, 276

Manila, 24, 239–243, 249, 266

microhistory, 8, 267

Mok, Florence, 44, 89, 97, 100, 155, 171–173

nationalism, pan-Chinese, 156

New Left, 156

New Territories, 55, 68, 77, 79, 113–115, 118, 122, 137–138, 140, 149, 177–179, 181–182, 194, 210, 216, 222, 254, 277, 279, 283–284

New Towns, 130–131, 133, 140, 142, 173, 178, 197

Nga Choi Hang, 200

Ngau Chi Wan, 251, 255, 258

On Lok Tsuen, 177

path dependency, 11, 20

pavement squatting (street squatting), 47, 70, 162, 245

Pickering, Andrew, 7, 20, 108, 126

plausible explanations, 16, 18, 23–24, 50, 55, 59, 183, 215, 227, 252, 262

Pok Fu Lam, 251

political semiosis, 93–94

practical, 6, 16, 20, 23, 28, 34, 46, 71, 83, 90, 102, 107–108, 111, 113, 115, 120, 124–126, 138, 141, 143, 152, 154, 164, 172, 178–180, 185, 190, 192, 195, 197, 204–205, 211, 214–215, 219–220, 249, 252–253, 265

publicity, 66, 80, 84, 148, 150–151, 155, 176, 194, 218–219

public opinion, 95, 98, 100, 143, 155, 171–172, 177, 179, 212, 214; opinion polling, 100, 167, 173, 179; sentiment, 22, 61, 72, 156, 171, 173, 175–176, 178–179, 181

Public Works Department, 81, 119, 157, 198

queue jumping, 140, 218

racketeers, 7, 24, 80, 118, 138, 146, 149, 177, 179, 195–196, 204, 217–219

reach-base policy, 173

rehousing, 10, 18, 46, 62–63, 111, 113–115, 120, 125, 132, 134, 136–137, 139–141, 143–144, 148–151, 157–158, 161, 163–165, 167, 170, 177–181, 186, 194, 196, 198, 200, 204–205, 212, 215, 217–219, 222–223, 225, 234–235, 237, 239, 252, 257–260, 269, 275–276, 279, 281–284, 286–287

Resettlement Programme, 17, 21, 55, 79, 109, 114, 252, 270

320   Index

Resite Area, 80–85, 111, 138, 140–141,
   162, 178, 187
Review of Public Housing Allocation
   Policies, 22, 129, 273, 275–276,
   285
Revision of Squatter Clearance and
   Housing Allocation Policy, 177–178,
   281
rich tenants, 152, 180–181
riots, 11, 19–21, 27, 40, 57, 62, 65–66,
   87–91, 94, 96–99, 103, 105–107, 154,
   160, 174, 233, 265
rooftop structures, 148–149, 219, 224,
   276
Rose, Typhoon, 161

Sahlins, Marshall, 8, 12–14
Sau Mau Ping, 198–200, 202–203, 284
Scott, Ian, 6, 28, 45, 48–49, 87, 89–91,
   96–97, 171, 181, 308
Sewell, William, 12–14, 93
Sham Shui Po, 46, 192
Shek Kip Mei, 9, 19, 56–57, 60–61, 87,
   103, 177, 234
Singapore, 5, 10, 24, 183, 229–230,
   232–235, 243, 250
Sino-British Joint Declaration, 6, 18, 53,
   87, 279
smart cities, 39
smoking guns, 6, 18, 50
smuggling, 32, 42
Society for Community Organization,
   168
Special Branch, 82, 91, 114, 270
Squatter Area Improvement, 21, 23–24,
   116, 183–184, 190, 194–195,
   199–200, 204–205, 207, 209, 215,
   252, 257–258, 282–284
squatter balloon, 146, 150, 218, 223, 251,
   256, 260
squatter control, 4, 8, 22, 24, 48, 63, 66,
   70, 75, 79–85, 106, 114–116, 122,
   128, 134, 138, 140, 144–149, 157,
   168, 170, 172, 177, 182, 191, 193,
   202, 204, 217–218, 220, 225–226,

228, 251–252, 254, 256–257, 259,
   261, 269, 274–275, 278, 281, 286,
   288
Squatter Occupancy Survey (SOS), 128,
   209
Squatter Occupants Voluntary
   Registration Scheme, 260
squatter structure survey (a.k.a. Squatter
   Survey), 146, 168, 213, 222, 239,
   255–256
squatter titling, 10, 207, 249
Star Ferry, 19, 66, 88, 90
sterilization, of files, 64, 267
stigmatization, 23, 179, 243
structuration, 10–12, 16
sub-divided unit, 258, 261
supply/demand imbalance, 181–182

Tai Hang Tung, 178
Temporary Housing Areas (THA), 46,
   84, 114, 131–142, 162, 168–170, 177,
   179, 181–182, 197, 224–226, 258,
   274–275, 287
Ten-Year Housing Programme, 22, 98,
   117, 125, 127, 129, 131, 153–154,
   156, 160, 188, 226
transit centres, 139–140
Trench, David, 5, 7, 14–15, 21, 38, 65,
   90, 94–98, 101, 105, 110–115, 119,
   125–126, 129–130, 137, 185, 205,
   207, 226, 252, 272, 274
Tuen Mun, 136, 139, 141–142, 178, 204,
   274–275
Tung Tau Tsuen, 156

United Nations, 41, 66, 72, 82, 99,
   243–244

Waiting List, 22, 75, 117, 133–134, 137,
   142–144, 147, 153–154, 158–165,
   167–168, 170–171, 173, 177–181,
   218–219, 223–225, 252, 278–279
Weber, Max, 29–30
Wong Tai Sin, 77–78, 85, 195, 206,
   283

Index

Working Party on Housing, 66, 69,
269–270, 273

Yep, Ray, 20, 51–52, 60, 89–90, 94–95,
103–104, 130
Youde, Edward, 203, 216, 284

zero tolerance, 229